The Magical Training of Quareia

Volume I

The Tenth Anniversary Edition
Revised and Updated

Josephine McCarthy

Copyright 1993 – 2025 © Josephine McCarthy
All rights reserved

Without limiting the rights under copyright reserved above,
no part of this publication may be reproduced, stored in,
or introduced into a retrieval system, or transmitted,
in any form or by any means
(electronic, mechanical, photocopying, recording or otherwise)
without prior permission of the copyright owner
and the publisher of this book.

First edition published by Quareia Publishing UK 2016
Second edition published by Quareia Publishing UK 2025
Exeter UK

www.quareiapublishing.com

A catalogue record for this book is available from the British Library

Hardback ISBN: 9781911134749
Paperback ISBN: 9781911134756
Ebook ISBN: 9781911134763

Cover image by Stuart Littlejohn
Cover design by Stuart Littlejohn
Formatted and typeset by Quareia editor Liza Kalys

Acknowledgements

Thank you to the people who made this course possible
when it was first being written:
Stuart Littlejohn, Frater Acher, Michael Sheppard, Aaron Moshe,
Toni Paris, Christin C and SC.

And a big thank you to the Quareia volunteers
who tirelessly worked through these modules line by line
to bring the course up to date, tidy it up, re-edit, and to make it better:
Liza K, GF, Frank R Hartman, Christina E, Dave P.

And a special thank you to Zoë and Rebecca A
for not only working on the editing
but also organising the rest of the volunteer team and collating the work.
Without you two and the rest of the team,
this updated version of the course would not have been possible.

And a massive thank you to all donors to Quareia over the last ten years;
without you the course would not have happened nor would it have continued.

Contents

Introduction 13
Read before starting the course 14

Module I Core Skills 17

Lesson 1 Meditation Techniques   19
1. Practical Considerations 19
2. First meditation exercise 20
3. Second meditation exercise 21
4. Third meditation exercise 22
5. Magic and Meditation 23
6. Task: Daily meditation 24
7. Task: Keeping notes 24

Lesson 2 Tarot Basics   27
1. The Rider Waite deck 27
2. Major Arcana 28
3. Minor Arcana 29
4. Working with the cards 30
5. Four-directional layout using six positions 31
6. Task: Reading about the energy in your home 32
7. Task: Balancing a difficult space 34
8. Summary 36
9. Task: Keep a tarot journal 36
10. Task: Further readings 37
11. Task: Keeping notes and following up 37
12. Addendum:
    Cleaning and care of cards and yourself after reading ... 37

Lesson 3 Visionary Magic Basics   39
1. Exercise 1: Memory 40
2. Exercise 2: Navigating a space 41
3. Exercise 3: Going for a walk 42
4. Summary 42
5. Task: Work with this method of visualisation for ten sessions 43

Lesson 4 Ritual Techniques   45
1. How does a ritual work? 46
2. Ritual micro-actions 47
3. Task: Body stretching 49

	4.	Energy 49
	5.	Example of a directional ritual 50
	6.	Analysis of the ritual 52
	7.	Directional ritual 55
	8.	Practical directional work 57
	9.	Working the directions 58
	10.	Task: Practising the directional ritual 62
	11.	Task: Keeping notes 62

Lesson 5 Inner Senses   63

1. Inner Hearing 65
2. Inner sight 68
3. Inner touch and smell 69
4. Dreams 69
5. Precognition 70
6. Task: Inner touch 70
7. Task: Inner sense – feeling power patterns 71
8. Task: Inner and outer boundaries 73

Lesson 6 Sacred Language & Magical Scripts   77

1. Magical Scripts and the 16th Century 77
2. Creating Patterns 80
3. Magical Symbols 80
4. Sigils 81
5. Sacred language and utterance 82
6. Translations of sacred languages 83
7. Sound and symbol in magical action 85
8. Practical work 85
9. Working with magical symbols:
   Pentagram, Hexagram, Cruciform 86
10. Working the pentagram 87
11. Task: An experiment 88

Lesson 7 Magical Protection   89

1. Threats and Saviours 89
2. Getting clean and staying clean 91
3. The ritual cleansing of a person 93
4. The ritual cleansing of a space, room, or house ... 95
5. Other cleaning methods 97
6. Smells that clear 98
7. Sounds 100
8. Getting and staying balanced 103
9. Task: Pentagram research 107

	10. Breastplates	108
	11. Talismans	110
	12. Task: Making a Talisman	111
	13. Task: The experiment's results	113
	14. Working these talismans for protection: points to remember	114
	15. Maintenance	115

Lesson 8   Astrology — 117

1. The Basics — 118
2. Transits — 118
3. Astrological signs — 119
4. Houses — 119
5. The Planets — 121
6. Task: Investigating your own chart — 125
7. Task: Ritual exercise – the pentagram and the natal chart — 126
8. Task: Your personal pentagram — 127
9. Module One Summary — 128

Module II   Patterns and Maps in Magic — 131

Lesson 1   Directions — 133

1. Directional dynamics of power — 133
2. Task: The visionary ritual of the directions — 136
3. Task: Ritual of confirmation — 137
4. Task: Directional ritual of power, Part I — 139
5. Task: Directional ritual II (the full ritual) — 141
6. Task: Journal — 143
7. Task: An experiment — 144

Lesson 2   The Tree of Life Tarot — 145

1. The Tree of Life tarot layout — 146
2. Working with the Tree layout — 147
3. Interpreting the reading — 148
4. Example reading — 150
5. Task: Practising this spread — 154

Lesson 3   The Full Pentagram Ritual — 157

1. Task: Working with the Dynamics — 157
2. The Full Pentagram Ritual — 166
3. Experiment: Adjusting the ritual — 170
4. A note on letting go — 171
5. Task: Researching the Grindstone and the Threshing Floor — 171
6. When to use this ritual — 172

| Lesson 4 | The Full Hexagram Ritual | 173 |

1. Hexagram ritual, part one
   The Ritual of the Gates – the building of the Hexagram.......... 174
2. So what was happening?.. 178
3. Hexagram ritual, part two
   Born of the Void.. 180
4. Task: Learning and practising the ritual............................. 184
5. Task: Mapping the sigil of the ritual 185
6. Task: Research.. 186

| Lesson 5 | The Elemental Patterns and Maps | 189 |

1. The magical elements in nature 189
2. Regional elemental expression.. 191
3. Analysis of the findings 193
4. Practical work... 196
5. Task: Identifying elemental manifestations 196
6. Task: Mapping.. 197
7. Working: The ritual communication with the land 200

| Lesson 6 | The Metatron Cube and the Quarry Mark | 207 |

1. Task: Drawing and working with the Metatron Cube 210
2. Experiment: Energies.. 211
3. Task: Research.. 212
4. Experiment: Modelling the Cube 214

| Lesson 7 | Combinations | 215 |

1. The Cruciform and the Cup... 217
2. The Sword and the Stone 220
3. Task: Practical Work... 222
4. Task: Research.. 227

| Lesson 8 | Natural Patterns of the Land | 229 |

1. Task: Visiting the site in vision.. 231
2. Task: Visiting the site physically 234
3. Module Two Summary... 236

| Module III | The Power Dynamics of Creation | 239 |

| Lesson 1 | Introduction | 241 |

1. Creation and magic 241
2. The use of visionary technique 243
3. The garden.. 245
4. The inner threshold.. 247

	5. The polarities of creative power	248
	6. The Inner Beings	251
	7. Task: Researching *Ma'at*	251
	8. Task: Researching the Scales	251
	9. Summary	253

Lesson 2 — The Inner Garden and Outer Vessels — 255

1. Talking to vessels 256
2. Random inhabitation 257
3. Magical inhabitation 259
4. The Inner Landscape 260
5. Task: Connecting with the inner landscape 261
6. Task: Visionary ritual of mediation 264
7. What just happened? 267
8. Readings 269
9. The tools and symbols 269

Lesson 3 — The Grindstone — 271

1. The angelic power 271
2. The Role of the Grindstone in creation 273
3. The Grindstone in life 274
4. Examples of the Grindstone in action 275
5. Task: Grindstone tarot readings 280
6. Task: The Grindstone in your chart 280
7. Task: Grindstone ritual 281

Lesson 4 — The Unraveller — 283

1. The Unraveller in creation 284
2. The Unraveller and magic 285
3. Unravelling magic: effects 285
4. The Unraveller in action 286
5. The personal Unraveller 288
6. Task: Looking in the mirror 288
7. Task: Readings 290
8. Task: The Unraveller and your astrology chart 290
9. Task: Unraveller ritual 290
10. Study 291

Lesson 5 — The Inner Guardians — 293

1. The realm of the Inner Desert 293
2. The Weaver 295
3. The Three Fates 296
4. The Keeper of Justice 298

5.	The Keeper of the Threshold	299
6.	The Utterer and the Wheel	300
7.	The Noble Companions/the Noble Ones	301
8.	Task: The Vision of the Sandalphon	303
9.	Task: Visiting with the Sandalphon	304
10.	Task: Stravinsky's *Rite of Spring*	305
11.	Task: Research	305
12.	Task: Working with an image	306

Lesson 6   The Laws of Fate   307

1. Self 308
2. Fate web of the family 315
3. Fate and the wider world 316
4. Task: Fate recognition 317
5. Task: Looking at historical fate patterns using tarot 318
6. Task: Looking at your personal fate pattern with tarot 319

Lesson 7   Working with your Past   321

1. Crafting notes 321
2. On the rest of the module 322
3. Passing into the past 322
4. Practical Work 324
5. Task: The Egyptian Book of the Dead 328

Lesson 8   Working with your Future Fate Pattern   335

1. Hitting the blocks in the road 336
2. Task: Viewing the web ritual 340
3. Task: Painting the spider 343
4. Task: Research 344

Appendices The Quareia Apprentice Study Guide   347

Appendix A   How Quareia Works   349

1. The ethics and code of Quareia: *Ma'at* 350
2. The rule of absolutes 352
3. Repeat repeat! 354
4. From the outside in 355
5. The three stages 356
6. Circles within circles 359
7. The good and the bad 360
8. Learn the rules first 363
9. Conclusion 364

APPENDIX B	COMMON STUDY ISSUES	367
	1. Magic and modern life	367
	2. Distraction and commercialism	367
	3. Television	368
	4. Smartphones	369
	5. Sleep	370
	6. Time restraints	371
	7. Family	372
	8. Resources	373
	9. Ethics and culture	374
	10. Myths	375
	11. Fear	375
	12. Dead Ends	376
	13. Hitting a wall	377
	14. Cherry picking	379
	15. Broken links	380
APPENDIX C	APPROACHING MAGICAL STUDY	381
	1. Discipline	381
	2. Study approach	382
	3. Confirmation bias	383
	4. Messiah trap	384
	5. Narrowed attention	386
	6. Not everything is magical	386
	7. Loss aversion	387
	8. Mythic reading and psychologising	388
	9. Discernment	389
	10. Tides and timings	389
	11. Emotions in magic	390
	12. Reading and learning	392
	13. The horizon	393
APPENDIX D	MEDITATION ISSUES	397
	1. The stages of development	398
	2. Questions	401
	3. Summary	403
APPENDIX E	TAROT	405
	1. Issues, problems and approaches	405
	2. Working with a deck	405
	3. Uses of tarot	407
	4. The skill of interpretation	407

	5. Interpreting the cards	411
	6. Looking at the present and the issue of privacy	412
	7. Energetic hygiene	414
	8. Some student questions	415
Appendix F	**Visionary Work**	**419**
	1. Issues, techniques, and questions	419
	2. What is visionary magic?	420
	3. How do you know when it is real?	421
	4. The first step of visionary work	421
	5. What are boundaries?	423
	6. I cannot see anything	423
	7. Advice	427
Appendix G	**The Adversity Of Magical Training**	**429**
	1. The function of adversities	430
	2. Simple adversities	431
	3. Loneliness	432
	4. Cultural persecution	433
	5. Lack of money	434
	6. Complex adversities	434
	7. A challenge to preconceptions	438
	8. Crime and disease	440
	9. Gender and identity	442
	10. The Challenge of the Gods	444
Appendix H	**Religions**	**447**
	1. Why does a magician need to learn about religions?	448
	2. Understanding the evolution of religion	449
	3. Working with different religious patterns in Quareia	450
	4. Dogmas and dangers	451
	5. What if you are an adherent of a specific religion?	453
Summary		**456**

Introduction

2024 is the tenth year from when I started writing the Quareia course. Ten years on, I am far more aware about how some text can be timeless, and some cannot. When I was writing the first couple of modules, I was oblivious to the temporary nature of websites: I put hyperlinks into the text, only for the sites to vanish a couple of years later. Some of the books that I recommended have now also become very expensive and inaccessible. And my regional Yorkshire sayings often confused foreign students. Moreover, when our small publishing team (Stuart, Michael, and myself) published the course as books, it was the first time that we had ever done such a thing, and we made lots of spacing, editing, and layout mistakes.

The final difficulty that we didn't see coming was the size and weight of the three big books that cover the three sections of the course: the Apprentice, Initiate, and Adept books. We only make our books available online, and due to rising postage costs they now often make a loss. The large Quareia books, however, now make such a loss that they have stopped being stocked at all in many countries.

I talked with Stuart and Michael and we decided that it was time to overhaul the course, tidy it up, future-proof it, and break it down into smaller books. We also decided, wherever possible, to include the chapters from my other books that are recommended reading, along with the Quareia Course Study Guide, and any other reading material that is now public domain.

A valiant team of volunteer Quareia students stepped up, many of them writers, academics, teachers, etc., and they have gone through the course line by line to spot mistakes, dead internet links, spacing errors, and anything else that needed addressing. The result is this 2024 edition of Quareia, printed in a more accessible size and with additional material.

The book series also has a new name. This is simply because the online retailer algorithms easily mix up any books whose titles begin with 'Quareia'.

None of the magic in this course has changed, but I have occasionally adjusted rituals to make them more relevant to the age we now live in and for what is to come. (For instance, in Apprentice Module One Lesson Seven, the cleansing ritual has been expanded.) I have also provided some additional explanations. But no change is so big that students would need to re-study anything. We hope we have made the course fitter and more on-point for the times ahead around the world.

I wish you well on your magical path of adventure.

Josephine McCarthy

Read before starting the course

Pace yourself and be realistic

This is a long and sometimes difficult course which will take years, not months. It is a full magical training that will teach you everything you need to know to be a fully competent magician who can work in any system and also *know how it works, why it works, what doesn't work, and why.* As you start the course you will realise there are some lessons, like for example the meditation lessons, where you can move on to the next lesson while still practising your technique or skills. However, this course is not a race. It is not something where you can complete all three sections in a year, or even three. It is likely to be the hardest and longest training you have ever done. Just like in bodybuilding or professional athletics, the power you will gradually encounter and work with can be exhausting. Quareia training will strengthen you, push you to your limits, and open a vista of worlds to you that you never realised existed. So take your time and enjoy it, instead of racing to the finish line.

The course is also designed so that you can leave your studies at any point to take a long break, and simply pick up where you left off when you return. You do not need to go back to the beginning, even if you had a break for many years. If you leave the course and do not return, then what you will have learned from the practical work will stay within you, like magical muscle memory, and it will be useful in whatever magical or mundane path you have decided to follow.

Work alone

Quareia training is specifically designed to be studied and worked with alone. In the last hundred and fifty years in the west, magicians have become used to having teachers at hand all the time, with group workings, lodges, etc. This has facilitated weakness in magical students, as a true and powerful magical path is essentially walked alone with only occasional input from an adept whose path you cross. At present (2024) mentoring is offered free to Quareia students who have completed the Apprentice section successfully and *who have had their work and journals checked by an adept.* However, Quareia mentoring is not about teaching, but checking that you have done the work you claim to have done, so that you can be fully recognised as a Quareia Initiate or Adept, should you wish that. In the longer-term future such mentoring may not be available, so it is important that a student can work alone, though with the inner contacts, spirits, and other beings that a magician meets through their training, they will never be truly alone. Do not be tempted by study groups: in such groups there is always someone who emerges as the dominant force that everyone else defers to. The inner pattern of Quareia is magically constructed for an individual to develop self-reliance and autonomous decision making, as well as magical skills. To defer to the guidance of another will disengage a student from this pattern, as well as weaken them magically.

Keep records and journals

You are prompted repeatedly in this course to write down your experiences and findings. Some are specifically outlined as 'tasks', but there are many other 'tasks' embedded within the main texts for which you should also keep written records. Keeping detailed notes and journalling is not just about wanting to be mentored later on in your training; it is also about establishing and keeping up with an important aspect of magical training and work. Often your experiences may seem trivial, strange, or even nonsensical, but later on as you become more experienced you will realise just how important some of these 'trivial' experiences actually were.

It is good practice to keep a separate exercise book/journal for each module. At first it will mean lots of blank pages in each one. But over time you will find yourself going back to those journals and adding in more writing about subsequent realisations, additions, and flashback visions. Your journals will become your own personal magical library.

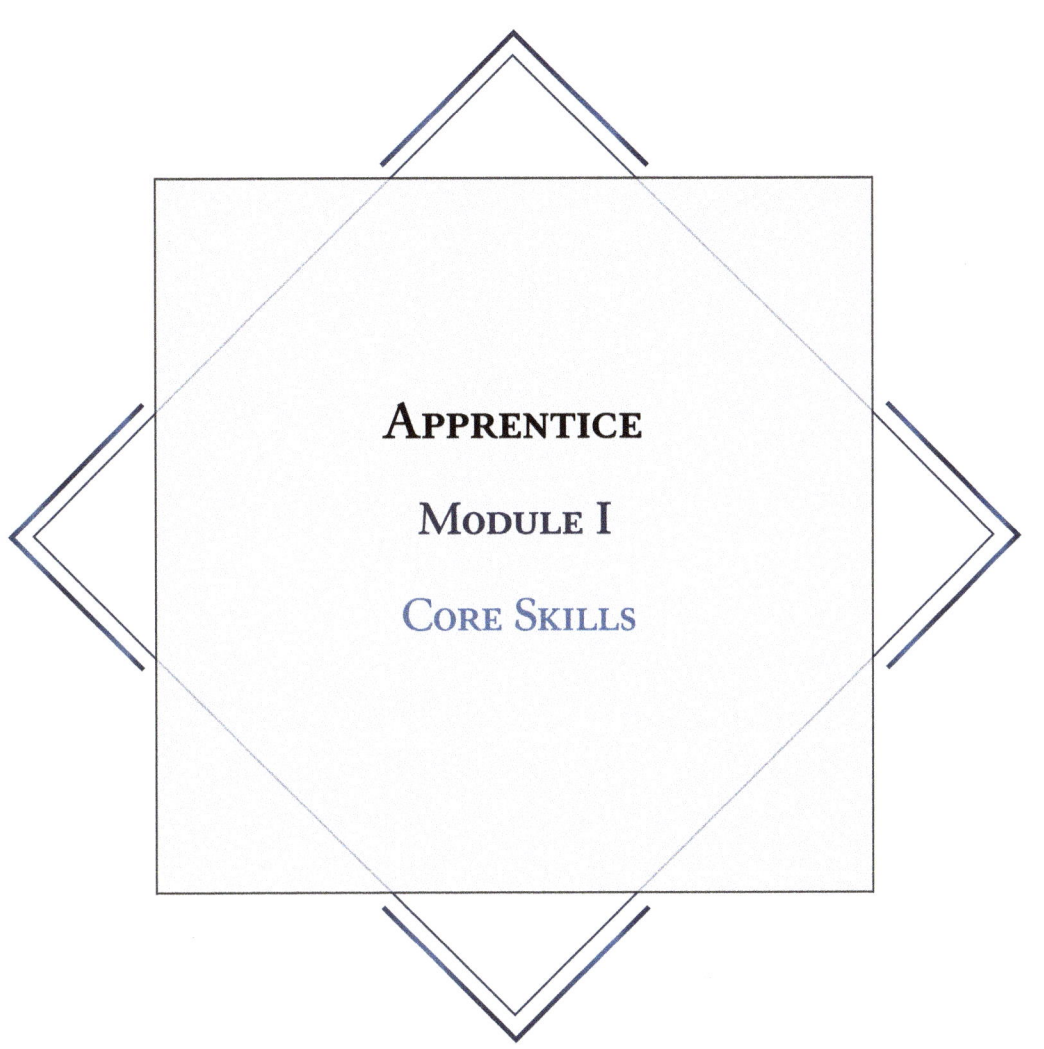

Apprentice

Module I

Core Skills

Lesson 1
Meditation Techniques

There is a very good reason why meditation is the very first skill that you learn in magic: without knowing how to use your mind properly, there *is* no magic. To be still, to clear your mind and to direct your thoughts are necessary skills for operating magically. To be able to do those things, one must meditate daily. When an aspirant first begins to meditate it can often be a struggle: the mind and body can be difficult beasts to tame, but with perseverance, meditation eventually becomes a normal part of your everyday life. Once you get to adept level, you should be able to close your eyes and immediately go into a very deep space where you can draw upon power and where your inner (psychic) senses are always ready and available. How you get there is through practice, practice, practice, but not fight, fight, fight. It is a skill that for most people takes a long time to master, and little without struggle is better than longer sessions that are a battle.

1. Practical Considerations

There are a few practical considerations that I would like you to pay attention to before you start your meditation practice. These considerations can have a bearing on how well your meditations go.

Meditation does not need to be done on the floor with your legs twisted like a pretzel. If you already sit that way, through practising yoga etc., then all is well and good. If you are not used to doing yoga and have not meditated before, then do not think you must struggle to sit in a position that is not easy for you. Sit in an upright chair, or on a mat on the floor – you meditate briefly on a train, or waiting in line for something; it is a condition of mind, not an action of body. The only thing I would advise against is lying down: you are not going to sleep, you are meditating. Lying down will encourage your mind to go into sleep mode, which is not what you want at all. So if you were considering lying down, stop being a wuss and sit in a chair.

Wear comfortable clothing. Have a silent clock or watch placed nearby so that you can see it if you open your eyes. During the first stages of magical training, you will be observing your timing. Have a window open if at all possible, even if it is noisy: the fresh air and the energy within the air is good for you. If possible, choose a room that is not near a road so that you can open the window and not breathe in fumes. Turn off phones etc. Have a candle, a plain white small candle or tea light. If you are in a place where you cannot have a candle lit, then just place the candle before you or near you as a focus with the intention that one day, you will light it. If you function best in the morning, then get up an hour earlier than normal and meditate first thing in the morning. It will be a struggle at first, but it will set up your mind for the day. If this is not possible (i.e. you already get up for work at 5am) then meditate late afternoon, or early evening. If you are a night owl, then meditate at night. But magically the best time to meditate is dawn, though few of us have the luxury of such in today's crazy work world.

If you already meditate and are able to still your mind, don't skip this lesson as there are a couple of techniques introduced here which are vital to this course. You will just find it much easier to do these exercises if you already meditate. Just learn the basic techniques and then move on. Students have often asked me how long they should spend on this lesson, and some poor souls have battled this lesson for a year without moving forward. Don't fall into the perfection trap; rather get the basics so that you can sit and be quiet for ten minutes, and then move on to the next lesson while continuing to meditate. Don't beat yourself up if you have bad days or even bad weeks with meditation – it can be like that and it is not a battle. Learn to flow with it. And you can enhance your practice with a simple technique; when you are bored and waiting for something, don't reach for your phone to entertain you. Put it on silent, and just daydream. Daydreaming out of boredom is a major component for a magical mind later on.

2. First meditation exercise

Light a candle, note the time, sit down and close your eyes. Turn your head to the right, take in a deep breath and then breathe out. Turn your head to the left, take a deep breath, and then breathe out. Face forward, take a deep breath and then breathe out.

With your right hand (regardless of whether you are right or left handed), place your thumb and fourth (ring) finger on either side of the root of your nose where your eyes and nose meet, and place your index finger on your forehead just above the nose/eyebrow line (third eye area).

Sit and breathe normally, being aware of your finger on your forehead. Focus on your finger. Every time your mind wanders and you begin to think about mundane things, bring your focus back to your finger.

Once your arm is tired, drop your arm and keep focusing on that spot on your forehead. See yourself breathing in white smoke and breathing out grey or black smoke. As you breathe in, imagine that the white fresh energetic smoke is filling your body and pushing out the stale black smoke.

Every time your mind wanders, pull it back to the spot on your forehead. Once you feel you cannot focus any more, open your eyes and check the clock. If you have not sat for at least ten minutes, close your eyes and continue. If you have sat for longer than ten minutes, close your eyes again for a few moments and tap on the third eye area with your right index finger while taking good deep breaths through your nose.

Get up. Stretch up with your arms and then, keeping your legs straight, stretch down to put your hands on the floor. Hold for a few seconds. Stand up, turn your body right while keeping your hips facing forward, arms outstretched to your sides, and hold.

Turn and repeat on the opposite side. Stand facing forward, arms outstretched to the side, and look at what is before you. As you look at what is before you, also think about what is behind you, what furniture, wall, door, etc. Stand and make sure your brain can process looking at one thing while thinking about something else.

Finally, turn to the east, bow, and finish. You are bowing in recognition of every adept who has gone before you, every student who has made real adept level and beyond. You are bowing in recognition of all the inner and outer teachers. And it is also practice for when you come to work in the inner worlds. This is a deep sign of respect in magic: do not just mindlessly bob your head or body in a meaningless gesture. Think about what you are doing. As you bow, be aware that you are entering a line of historic magicians, an ancient line, an ancient tradition that deserves your respect.

Remember, twenty minutes or even ten minutes a day of meditation is far better than one or more hours once or twice a week. Little and often is the key. If you cannot meditate every day, then do your best while being honest with yourself. This is lone practice and no one is supervising you or watching you – you are expected to have the maturity to know that all of this work is for your own magical development. If you get lazy and try to fool yourself, then think about the level of maturity needed to handle power magically. This is where power training starts, with self discipline. But if you are sick, then don't meditate, just sleep and heal. Short meditations can become your solace when needed, and that comes from regular meditation so that it becomes second nature.

3. Second meditation exercise

Once you have mastered the previous meditation exercise, keep practising it for ten minutes a day, and practise the following technique for a further ten minutes or more a day. End your session with the stretch and bow outlined in the first meditation exercise.

Once your system is settled and you are used to the basic meditation technique outlined in the first exercise, then it is time to work with colour. This is the foundation of learning how to move power in, around, and out of your body. The advanced technique begins here. First you learn how to move colour in and out of your body; then you learn how to trigger the regeneration and cleaning of your inner energies. You are going to work with three colours, red/left, blue/central, and white/right: action, fulcrum, silence, life developing, fulcrum, life harvested.

Starting with the right side, block your left nostril by pressing against it with your left index finger. Breathe in through your right nostril and as you breathe in, imagine the right side of your body filling with white smoke. Breathe out through your mouth and imagine that you are breathing out white smoke. Breathe in white, breathe out white. Repeat this whole sequence three times.

Now press on your right nostril with your right index finger and breathe in through your left nostril. Imagine you are breathing in red smoke that fills the left side of your body and breathing out red smoke through your mouth. Repeat this three times.

Place your hands on your lap and breathe in through both nostrils, imagining that you are breathing in blue smoke that fills the centre-line down your body from head to toe, and breathing out blue smoke from your mouth. Repeat this three times. **If you cannot visualise colour, then know that it is red or blue.** Using the mind by 'knowing' helps you to develop your own unique form of visualisation, which may not have any visuals at all, but a deep sense of knowing.

Once you have finished, sit quietly and imagine the blue channel flowing down through your centre, the white channel flowing down the right side of your body, and the red channel flowing down the left hand side of your body. Spend some time just sitting and being aware of the three colours flowing in your body.

Finally, spend a little time sitting quietly and allowing the mind to silence itself. If you find yourself remembering things or thinking about things, just gently stop thinking about them and return to silence. This is the hardest skill of all to learn in meditation, and it is best to build it up a few minutes at a time until eventually the bulk of your meditation time is spent being still. Be aware that this can take years for many people, as stillness is the hardest of all things to reach. Two minutes or even a minute of stillness is progress, and your mind will adapt in its own time.

4. Third meditation exercise

Once you are accustomed to visualising in meditation then it is time to learn the meditation of the inner flame. This is the start of a skill set that once you have mastered it, will be one of the many tools you can engage to help protect you, transport you, heal you and energise you. It is an ancient method of magical meditation and something you will use throughout your magical life. Again, like the other meditations, it takes time to develop the skill and it will not happen overnight for most people.

Essentially this meditation works with the image of a flame. This image will be slowly connected, through your training, to a state of mind and a state of power called the Void which is reached through stillness. This power is something that exists within all living beings, and all elements, substances and patterns: it is the nothing from which all things flow. To connect with that power you must first learn how to work with it in meditation, and for that we work with a flame. You must learn to visualise a flame in front of you and a flame within you in the place you consider your 'centre' or core. For most people that is the space in the abdomen below the ribs and above the pelvis. The flame is not a burning or heating fire, it is a pure energy of life that can eventually be tapped into to work with.

For now, you will learn the very basic meditation of the 'flame within.'

Close your eyes and do one of your simple breathing exercises until you are settled. Using your mind's eye, imagine a flame burning gently in the centre of your body, however that imagined or 'felt' visualisation works for you. It does not harm you, it does not burn you; it is a flame of vital force that energises you, and it is an aspect of your life force.

As you breathe in and out, be aware of the flame within, ever constant, ever present. Notice its colour. Notice how it moves gently as you breathe.

Every time your mind drifts away from the flame and thoughts start to crowd into your head, gently stop the flow of thoughts and remember the flame in your centre. Focus back on the flame, on the feeling of its warmth through your body. Notice how safe it feels and how beautiful it is. If you feel confident about it, in your mind, reach into the flame with your hands and wash your hands and arms in the flame. Cup some of the flame in your hands and see or 'know' yourself washing your face with its power.

Open your eyes and check your clock. If you have been sat for ten minutes or more, get up, stretch and do your bow. If you have only been sat for a few moments, close your eyes and focus your mind back on the flame in the centre of your body. Do your best, but don't ever turn meditation into a battle; learn to let it become your safe and peaceful place. If that means stopping early sometimes, so be it. Let it be your best, not the best of someone else.

5. Magic and Meditation

Meditation is a central and core skill for magic, as magic uses the mind in many different ways and learning how to operate the mind consciously is very important. A still mind allows the magician to focus power, and the ability to consciously use the imagination to build images in the mind's eye allows the magician to form patterns and doorways that allow their consciousness to expand beyond their body. It is a skill that is developed slowly over years, and in the life of a magician the form it takes varies as the magician develops their magical skills. Some magicians use lengthy meditations, some use very short but focused meditations, it all depends on what works best for you. But to get to that point, the basics are first developed and then practised.

In today's world of constant noise, media, and chatter, it can be very difficult for the aspiring magician to learn how to be quiet, how to listen, and how to be still. The way to overcome that difficulty is to work at it. For some of you, your mind or your body or both will rebel. Don't turn your meditation sessions into a battle of wills; rather turn them into a rhythm. Remember as a child not wanting to brush your teeth or wash your face, or to sit quietly until the adults had finished eating? It was hard as a child to do such disciplines, and yet as an adult you move through such things without even thinking about them. So it will become with meditation. And that stage is arrived at by doing it every day.

I used to practise meditation with a baby on my lap, or on the bus on longer journeys: I would keep my eyes open but focus on the flame within, or the colours, and then slip into stillness with all the noise around me. That put me in good stead for later years when I would find myself suddenly facing a powerful being or a dangerous situation – I could instantly become still and focused.

Magic flows from that still, focused place. Robes and tools and altars are a part of magic, but if they become a crutch then you are doomed to destruction or failure. A magical attack will not wait patiently for you to finish what you are doing, put on a robe and pick up a sword: it will catch you unawares in the midst of a busy day. As you will learn in your training, while you will use magical tools, your body is also all of those tools combined, and your mind is the most potentially powerful tool you can use. That power comes first from meditation, and then from the use of visionary magic.

6. *Task:* Daily meditation

Meditate each day for a minimum of twenty minutes. Initially, start with just the first meditation. Once you have understood and are able to do the first meditation, add the second meditation. Once you are comfortable with the first two meditations, then go on to work with the flame meditation. Once you have mastered all three forms, start a regular daily routine that incorporates all three in succession. Meditate for a minimum of twenty minutes each day, but do not meditate for more than an hour a day – you are training to be a magician, not a monk. You will find that after a few weeks of struggle and failures, you will start to fall into a habit that works for you.

Once you are comfortable with working with the three meditations, move on to the next lesson while still practising and improving your meditation skills. It will take you a few modules of training work before you find you can meditate more easily.

7. *Task:* Keeping notes

Keep short notes in your journal of your progress in your meditations: list how long you meditated (and be truthful!), whether you felt it was easy or hard, and how you felt afterwards. The meditation journal is just for you, and it can be used to track reactions to external influences. The journalling of early days training can be invaluable to you in the future, and today, ten years on from the birth of the course, students bemoan the fact that they failed to journal properly in the early part of their training.

Your early warning system

The reason for keeping a daily note of how you felt at the end of your meditation is that eventually it will show you how your early warning system is developing. As the weeks pass and you become more experienced in meditation, there will be times when you emerge from your meditations feeling slightly 'off' or 'jangled.' This can often be an early warning of trouble or illness. It is like a very, very quiet whisper at first, something you can barely feel.

But as you work more, and as you practise other core skills, slowly but surely you will start to recognise your 'good' energy feeling, your 'bad' or 'getting sick' energy feeling, and your early warning system of 'something is not quite right.'

Once you have recognised the distinctive feel of the early warning system, you can use other core skills to identify what is potentially going wrong, or if you are in some sort of danger.

The more you recognise these signals, the stronger they will become over time. Sometimes it is just your own consciousness playing tricks on you, but you need to learn to feel the difference when that happens. Because everyone senses things in slightly different ways, the only way to truly learn what your own feelings in stillness are telling you is by observing them through a daily journal.

If you get sick, look back a few days in your journal to see how you felt after meditation. Sometimes the body gets a little energy high twenty-four hours before sickness: this is your immune system gearing up for the attack. Others feel out of focus, and some people describe feeling like they are the 'wrong shape' just before they get sick. If something bad or difficult happens, again, look back over your journal. A couple of words each day are all that it takes. As you start to see a pattern develop through your descriptions, you will begin to recognise the quiet warnings that your inner energy or body tries to give you. So write them down each day without fail.

Note: If you find that during meditation you see beings or feel a presence, *turn your attention away from that contact* regardless of how shiny, angelic or special it may seem. You are training to focus, to not be interrupted, and you are also training to recognise parasitical beings that may try to take advantage of you while you are meditating as a beginner. This is very important, and a major first magical lesson – do not allow distraction, do not allow flights of fancy in the mind, and do not allow spirits to interrupt you. If it is a genuine being that means no harm, they will realise what you are doing, and that you are a beginner. They will return if necessary under better conditions and when you are able to fully converse with them. It is not unusual for a contact that first becomes aware of you while you meditate, to leave and then return sometimes years later when you are ready to work with them. But most intruders of meditation are beings or spirits that are parasitical by nature and want to suck on your vital force.

Meditation will become an aspect of your magical life for the rest of your life, so get used to it!

Lesson 2
Tarot Basics

If you already work with tarot, do not skip this lesson as there are certain points within it that are essential for future work in this course. Just read through the lesson and if you find any exercises, layouts, or other elements that you have not done before, focus on them and complete them.

Tarot is a core skill for magical training and it will become a major tool in your magical life. It is of the utmost importance that you master the skill of tarot if you wish to grow into an initiate and eventually into an adept. **So do not just do this lesson and then forget about tarot** – the tarot training in the early Apprentice years give you core skills that you can apply to check something out, find something, identify threat, and identify potential beings or spirit contacts. Without this skill, as magician you are essentially flying blind. Quareia uses tarot as a major magical tool, not as an exercise in philosophy or psychology, so if you are already familiar with tarot, you may find the tarot lessons and usage very different to what you are used to.

Some people learn the various tarot skills quicker than others, and if you find them difficult it is important to keep practising until you become proficient. Do not measure your level of accomplishment against the achievements of others: everyone who trains in magic is better at some things and weaker at others. It is rare that any magician becomes adept at all the magical skills in their lifetime. The key is to become proficient at all of them, and adept at some of them. The skill of tarot comes from practice, and plenty of it. Remember, to be a successful magician you must have at least proficiency in predictive card divination but preferably you should have good solid skills in the Arte.

1. The Rider Waite deck

Before you tackle actual readings, it is important to get to know the deck in basic terms. So let us have a look at the deck to see how it works. The Rider Waite tarot follows the classic tarot format, and it is the best deck for a beginner to use. It is not best because it is good, it most certainly isn't at all, but it has a divinatory and visual language that is well established in magic. Learning first with the Rider Waite tarot is akin to learning Latin first before you then go on to study European languages – Latin is a common denominator for a fair few European languages. Latin is also a language used in the sciences, which makes knowledge of it useful. As with Latin, so it is with the Rider Waite. Once you have gotten used to it and done the basic lessons, and then have developed to a point where you realise what limitations that deck has, then you can get rid of it and work with a better deck. But do not skip using the RW for the early Apprentice lessons – the struggles with it are more important than you would think.

2. Major Arcana

The classic tarot deck is divided into the Major Arcana and the Minor Arcana. The Major Arcana tells you about the powers and influences that are flowing through a person or a situation. The Minor Arcana shows you how these influences actually manifest in a situation.

Power in people, events, and nature

Separate out the Major Arcana from the Minor Arcana and put the minor cards to one side for now. Spread out the major cards and put them in numerical sequence. You will notice as you look at them that some of the cards represent types of powers that run through people (the Fool, the Magician, the High priestess, etc.), some depict forces that influence events (the Tower, Death, the Wheel, etc.) and some depict powers that affect every living thing (The Sun, the Moon, the Star, etc.).

The 'people' powers tell you about various stages of human development that we all go through in one form or another. As a magician, you will learn to interpret these people powers in relation to who the person is, and if they are a magician or not.

For example, the Hierophant can represent an adept who has learned how to bridge between the worlds. But it can also represent someone who holds power in a spiritual or religious form, but is not a magician. So for example, if you were doing a reading about a nation and the Hierophant showed up, it is very likely that the person who wields the most power in that nation is a religious leader. The Hierophant can also represent dogmatic adherence to a religion. Really, it is all about the question, the context and the people involved. Such skill of interpretation takes time and lots of practice, and that will not come overnight.

Without me giving you guidance, separate out the major cards into three groups: power in people, power of events, and power in nature. Write down which cards you have grouped into the three different groups. Later on, revisit these groups to see if you would change anything as your understanding has grown.

Finding your key words

Bearing in mind the three groups you have created, now look at the little booklet that came with the deck. Look up the major cards and read through their descriptions. If you have a tarot book, look up the meanings behind each card. There will be subtle differences between a book and the booklet depending upon who wrote the book.

Don't worry about that for now; everyone views each card slightly differently, but each card has a common theme. Spot the common theme, think of one word that encapsulates its meaning, and write it down beside the name of the card.

Ensure that the one word (two at a stretch) also reflects the group that you have placed that card in. So for example, staying with the Hierophant, the key word could be 'bridge', or 'priest' (male or female), both of which essentially mean the same thing, but which can be interpreted very differently in readings.

It is important that you settle on a word that works for you and that also reflects the card's description in the book.

3. Minor Arcana

Once you have a list of key words for each of the major cards, put them aside and get out the minor cards. Lay them out in front of you and you will notice that they are divided into four sets: Swords (air), Cups (water), Pentacles (earth) and Wands (fire). This is the first stage of learning about the four magical directions and elements.

The four magical directions

These four suits will teach you about the different expressions of influence that flow from the four magical directions, and they will also teach you about the four magical tools that belong in the four directions: the Sword, the Wand, the Cup and the Shield. They will teach you about how the elemental powers can manifest, how the magical tools can work, and what sort of power they bring through. That learning will come as a result of your work with tarot, and also through your ritual and visionary work as you go through each module.

Finding your key words

For now, look through all the minor cards, starting with the Sword/air cards, then the Wand/fire cards, the Cup/water cards, and finally the Pentacle/earth cards. Look at the pictures to see what they tell you. Then look at the booklet or book that you have on tarot and see what it tells you about each card, and when you have a reasonable idea of its meaning, choose a key word for the card.

Write your key words out in an easily readable list and when you do readings, use your key words for the major and minor cards to guide you in your interpretation. Don't worry about card reversals: we will not be working with those as it can just make life more complicated than it needs to be. The negative aspect of a card can be discerned from a combination of the card in relation to the question, and in relation to the position it lands in. Keep these word lists in your Quareia journal and revisit them periodically to see if your word choice has changed.

To get started with reading the tarot, we will first work with the four-directional layout. This layout will help you to develop your understanding of the magical directions when you come to work with them in the ritual magic lessons.

Note: The illustrated and lesson layout has the 'north' card at the top of the reading; the only reason for this is that most western maps have north at the top. When you work in ritual with the directions, your 'home' standing/working position will be in the centre facing south. And for many eastern cultures, south is 'up' on a map. So if you wish to work with the south at the top of the layout, that is fine. Just ensure you mark the top of each reading with S at the top for 'south'. If an adept needs to look at your journal, they will be able to make sense of the reading.

4. Working with the Cards

Shuffling

How you approach shuffling the cards can be just as important as any other aspect of working with tarot. Everyone develops their own shuffling technique, but there are some points to consider in order to help the shuffling be successful.

One key factor is to ensure that you are fully focused on the question in hand as you shuffle. Do not be distracted by talking or allow your mind to wander: keep the question foremost in your mind as you work the cards. Also keep in mind as you shuffle what layout you will use: you need to focus on the question and the layout.

One good method for doing this is to work with your eyes closed. As you shuffle, think about the question, the layout you are going to use, and imagine you are searching for something through a 'mist.' Use your inner vision and imagination to create the sensation of trying to 'pierce a veil.'

As you develop your own technique, you will find that after the initial shuffle, your hand action begins to slow down so that the cards are placed more precisely in their order. Once everything is in the right position you will sometimes feel them 'lock' in place. The accuracy of a reading relies on the focus of intention you hold as you work the cards.

Laying out

Once your deck is ready, then work from the top of the pile and place each card out. Once you have become accustomed to working with the cards, you may find that the answer you were looking for seeps into your mind even before you lay the cards out. It is as if you get a preview of what is coming. Not all readers have this experience, but for those with a strong natural ability, the flavour of the reading often emerges in the reader's mind before the cards are laid out.

Interpreting

Once you have laid out the cards, take a moment to look at them in their positions. Remember, the meaning of the card and the meaning of its position should be read together. Go through each card one by one until you get to the end, and then go back to the beginning. Often a card/position will not make any sense until you have looked at the whole reading; then the meaning starts to unfold. If there is still something you are not getting, sometimes it works to sit quietly and say to yourself, 'okay, tell me about this'.

Write down or photograph the reading so that you can go back to it after a few hours and look again. What I have always found is that when in doubt, the simplest interpretation is often the right one. Some students may find it helpful to regularly refer to my book *Tarot Skills for the Twenty First Century*.[1]

5. Four-directional layout using six positions

Figure 1: The four-directional tarot layout

---

[1] *Tarot Skills for the Twenty First Century* by Josephine McCarthy. TaDehent Books 2020 Exeter UK. Is also available for free as a PDF on Quareia's website on the 'free books' page.

The directional attributes

These are general magical attributes that can be used not only in magic, ritual and vision, but also in divination. Once you have a basic idea of the powers that flow from these magical directions, you can use that knowledge to work with the directions for tarot readings.

1. **Centre**
   Body/self/land/starting point.
   (Always start at ground zero – you are seeing from this perspective and this is what all of the directional powers are affecting.)
2. **East**
   Air, swords, words, intellect, training, teacher, mind, utterance, incoming, the beginning.
3. **South**
   Fire, wands, leadership, energy, the stars, reaching potential, the future, the path ahead.
4. **West**
   Water, cups, emotions, relationships, psychic ability, populace, outgoing, end of something.
5. **North**
   Earth, stones, pentacles, substance, ancestors, ancients, Underworld, the distant past.
6. **Relationships**
   This position is about how things directly affect you and your relationship with them. It can stand for people, animals, powers, spirits, toxins, basically anything that affects you directly.

There are many more directional attributes, and as you develop as a magician you will learn far more subtleties, interlinks and connections. But it is unwise to swamp yourself beneath a ton of lists: start simple and go from there. These are a very basic list of magical directional powers and how you use them in readings will depend largely on what you are reading about and what you need to know.

6. *Task:* Reading about the energy in your home

In your first reading, you will look at the energy in your home. This is an important tarot skill to develop, and over time you will learn many different ways to look at the energy of a place. Different reading layouts can be used depending on what you are looking for and what the situation is, but for now you will work with this simple layout. Today you are simply going to look at the overall energy of the space in which you live. If you live in a house with more than one storey, do a reading for each storey in turn. If your living space is just one room, then just read for that room.

Doing the reading

Mix up your deck properly and shuffle them using the shuffle method outlined above. Keep in mind your question, which is "*show me the energies present in my living space,*" and also keep in mind the directional pattern that works through the layout: 1 = centre, 2 = east, 3 = south and so forth. If you are opting to lay out the cards with south on top, bring the cards out in the same order, just put east to your left instead of to the right.

When you have finished shuffling, lay out your cards in the sequence pictured in the diagram above and then sit back and look at it. Look first at the centre of the reading. This shows you the core energy that is currently in your living space. Then look at what is in the east (position 2). Think of that card in relation to what is in the east section of your space: is it a bedroom? A kitchen? Look at each of the directions and think of the spaces that are in those directions. If the reading is for a one room living space, look in that direction of the room, what is there? What pictures, belongings, furniture etc.?

Once you have spent a little time looking at the cards, looking at the pictures and understanding what element it is (fire/Wands? air/Swords?) or what power it is (is it a person card like a King or Queen?), then write down the reading so that you have a record of it. You can take a picture of it, but also write it down in your journal.

The first thing to note in your interpretation is, where are the major cards? If any major cards have fallen in any of the directions, that will tell you that the power coming from that direction, be it good or bad, is stronger than the others. If you get a lot of major cards (and you had mixed up your cards properly and shuffled well), then it may be an indication that you are sat on top of a power spot, or that there is a lot of power around you as an individual, or the room is having a shift of power and is coming into focus. You will learn more about such things later in the course. For now, just take a note of that.

Identifying good and bad areas

If you get a very bad card in one (or more) of the directions, then you need to identify which room or area of a room it refers to and mark that down in your journal. Once you have finished this general look at your living space, you will focus on any really difficult areas.

In the general reading, note the very good directions and the very bad. Identify which area of the house or which room that refers to. The good ones will show you where the strong, healthy and regenerative areas of the house or room are, and the bad ones will show you where there are unhealthy areas of the house or room, or even an object that is a bad influence on the space.

Transient energies

If you get minor cards that are not looking so good, they may refer to transient energies, so you would need to repeat the exercise in a week's time to see if the difficult influence is still present. If it is, you will need to address it by doing a directional reading for the difficult room. Write down which areas show up as difficult (if you are unlucky, all directions will show problems). At this point, it might be an idea to get a basic but functional compass – it will come in very handy for rebalancing spaces, and is a tool I use all the time.

Figuring out why an area is difficult

Now go and look at those areas in the house. Are there statues, magical objects, mirrors, piles of clutter, or anything obvious that could potentially cause an issue? Is it an area of the house that is very busy and used a lot? There are a variety of basic things you can do for now to make your space a bit easier energetically until you learn how to tackle the problem properly.

7. *Task:* Balancing a difficult space

Once you have identified the difficult areas of the house, clean up any clutter, organise whatever is in that area or room, and make sure the room is clean. Use the four-directional reading to identify which direction in the room has the most problems (major bad card, or lots of Swords). In each very difficult direction place a good sized jar filled with three quarters salt and a quarter water, and do not put a lid on it – it needs to be able to absorb the bad energy into the water. Basic small grain cooking salt is all that is necessary, you do not need fancy salt. Be aware that as the water evaporates it can leave salt behind which can damage furniture, so place the salt water cure on a plastic or ceramic mat. Do not use metal as it will get discoloured or damaged from the salt. Carefully top it up with water when it dries out and don't fill it to the point that it spills over as it will also spill some of the bad energy held in it. It is good to change them after a few months. To dispose of them, get a bin bag or plastic bag. Carefully carry the saltwater and jar outside, place it in the plastic bag without spilling any on yourself, tie up the bag and carefully put it in the trash bin. If that is not possible for any reason, empty the jar down a drain **outside**, do not empty it in your home. Put the jar in the plastic bag and throw in the trash. Then go home and wash yourself with salt and liquid soap, and put your clothing in the wash.

If there are artworks or sacred pieces (demon masks, deities and so forth) in the direction, you need to discern if they are helping, hindering or causing the problem. If they are causing a problem, wrap them up and get them out of the space or put them in a cupboard. If that is not enough then you need to find a way to get rid of them or give them away to someone whom they will not affect badly.

The way to find that out is to do a four-directional reading for the room asking *"what would the energy of this room look like if I took out X?"* That way you will be able to figure out what is helping and what is not by the answers that you get.

If there is a serious problem, don't panic: you have lived there okay so far, but it is something that you will need to tackle in the long term. Follow the advice in this lesson, and as you progress through the first module, you will learn more and more techniques for dealing with problematic energies. You need to learn how to do those techniques properly for them to be effective, and that is going to take time.

For now, the salt water cure will lessen any issues. And keep the problem areas as quiet as possible. If there is a sound system there, move it. If there are lots of very 'busy' things like computers, toys etc., move them. What will also help is to identify the really good energy areas in the house/room and use them more than the bad energy area. It may mean having to change the whole room around, but if that is possible, then it is good energetically for the space as it stops long term 'clumping' of energies in corners.

Flying Star Feng Shui

If the balancing of house energies is something that really interests you, then look up the Flying Star Feng Shui system. I have found it very useful in difficult houses, but I have also found that it does not work exactly: maybe the land where it developed and the land where I lived were not quite the same in terms of relationships with the stars etc., but it was near enough to be very useful. I don't get into the deep complexities of the Flying Stars system, but I do pay careful attention to the basics such as the inherent directional stars and the visiting/flying stars, and the relationship between them. Again, use the tarot layout to track your progress, to see what would work and what would not.

Example: a difficult kitchen

Let's suppose we have done a reading for a house and in the south, the Tower card appears. We identify the south room on that floor of the house as being the kitchen. So we do a second reading for just that room, and once again a destructive card, the Ten of Swords (which is the lesser version of the Tower), appears in the south position. We look around the kitchen with a compass and note that the cooker is in the south.

Now, remember that often the simplest interpretation is the best. In a kitchen, we have a cooker in the south (which is a fire position). A cooker is also often a source of house fires (fryers bursting into flames etc.). So you need to find out if there is a fault with the cooker that is going unseen and will set the house on fire, or if there is just too much of the element of fire in that direction.

To identify the issue, I would use a Tree of Life layout[2] to first look at the cooker and ask, *"is this cooker safe to use for the next twelve months?"* The final card will let you know if there is a major danger. If it is not the cooker or cooking methods (also check that with a Tree of Life reading), then it is most likely too much fire energy is in that area. That can be countered by placing a vase or jar full of water near the cooker, or a small pan full of water left on the cooker. However, stale water attracts bad energies, so ensure that you pour it out each day and put in fresh water. If you need to jump ahead to Apprentice Module II Lesson 2 in order to learn the Tree of Life layout for identifying danger, then do so. Then come back and continue on with your step by step training.

Sometimes, particularly if you are on a fiery land (like desert or a volcanic outcrop etc.) having a cooker in the south in a south room might just be a bit too much. You may need to do a further reading which looks at the problem from a slightly different angle. This one would ask, *"what would the energy of this room look like if we fixed or replaced the cooker?"* (rather than asking if the cooker is ok.) If the reading looks fine, then there is a hidden fault in the cooker which is building up to become a house fire. Remember, energetically, a fire starting in the south of a room has a lot more energy behind it to take off. (This might be reversed if you live in the southern hemisphere, I honestly don't know.)

8. Summary

Learning good tarot skills is paramount to your success as a magician. Do not fall into the trap of learning tarot through psychology or heavily interpreting your tarot through psychology: it really does not work well that way as divinatory tarot. Learning tarot in the way I suggest above will give you a wide field of understanding that will grow and develop as you grow and develop into an initiate, and finally, an adept.

These first steps of learning how to read using the directions will provide you with a rock solid magical base of understanding that dovetails in with the early phases of your ritual and visionary training. Together, these will provide you with the most ancient magical keys that are necessary in order for you to move forward with your training. Like all magical skills, tarot is about practice.

9. *Task:* Keep a tarot journal

Have a separate journal that you keep (a physical one, not an online one) for all of your tarot readings. This is really important. Your tarot lessons and your tarot practice should be written down in such a way that you can look back in a year or two's time and still understand what you've written. Not only will you be able to gauge how much progress you have made, but you will also be able to track the events, powers and influences that are running through your life.

---

[2] Tree of Life layout Apprentice Module II, Lesson 2.

10. *Task:* Further readings

Do a four-directional reading for your home. And then do one for each room in the house. If you live in a single room dwelling, then read for your room, and also for the land the building stands on. Write down the results and any remedies you decided to use to balance troublesome areas of the house (salt/water etc.).

If you decide to look up Flying Stars Feng Shui, do a map of your house or room for the year as many of the influences are always moving year on year. Traditionally, the change over occurs in early February each year (Chinese new year), but I have found over the years that sometimes you can feel the shift starting to occur a month or more before February. So sometimes I do the change around of elements and colours in late December or January depending on how strongly I felt the shift. As you get more confident with your intuition, you can check that intuition with a Tree of Life reading.

Once you are used to the layout, do a four-directional reading for your neighbourhood, and then one for your city. Work with the directional layout to look at different things over a period of two weeks, until you feel that you are getting the hang of the layout and are able to interpret it adequately.

11. *Task:* Keeping notes and following up

Write each reading down, take note of the difficult areas it reveals in your neighbourhood and city, and then if you can, go visit them to see if you can feel the energy – or even identify where the bad energy is coming from. Also take notes on your observations and any actions that you take to change a room or space. When you have changed a space, do a followup reading to see if the change was a good remedy or if more action is needed. Write everything down.

12. Addendum:
Cleaning and care of cards and yourself after reading

Once you have finished reading, it is advisable to go and wash your hands with soap. If it has been a difficult reading, or if the reading was used to look at difficult, dangerous or unhealthy situations, or your hands just feel off or a bit grimy it is a good idea to put some salt in the cup of your hand before adding liquid soap and water. This will break any energetic ties, and it will also clean off the 'sticky' energetic residue that can sometimes accumulate on your hands during readings.

Cleaning the deck

Depending on how often you use the deck (and always after very difficult readings) it can be a good idea to clean the deck itself. This can be done by 'bathing' the deck in the smoke of frankincense resin burned on charcoal, or by putting the deck in a plastic bag, pouring in dry salt, and giving it a good shake. Another method I use is to pour some drops of pure frankincense into the cup of my hands, rub my hands together and then handle the cards by rubbing them lightly. I also put a few drops in the box they are stored in, and also on the cloth I lay out to do the readings on. I also regularly put the reading cloth in the washing machine with my washing.

Using salt or oil to cleanse a deck can limit the lifespan of a deck, but it is more important to stay clean than to have a grubby favourite deck for years. This is why, for most readings, it is wiser to use a common, simple deck that can be easily and affordably replaced on a regular basis. My deck usually lasts me about a year before I have to replace it, and I use my deck regularly. Sometimes I keep a deck for the long term and only use it for very special readings, and I get backup copies of the same deck to use regularly. Remember, a deck is a tool, not a keepsake.

Store your deck in a box, and keep it away from children, pets, etc. Wrapping the deck in a cloth and using a cloth for layouts also helps to limit any unhealthy energy residue from being left behind on the surface that you lay the cards on, and also it helps to stop the deck getting dirty. The cloth should be washed regularly.

Cleaning yourself

The first rule for keeping yourself clean after a reading is to wash your hands with salt and soap as soon as you have finished. Do not do or touch anything else until you have cleaned your hands. If the reading session was particularly hard or the subject matter was very unhealthy, then also rub some salt over your 'third eye' area, and then wash your face.

Lesson 3
Visionary Magic Basics

Visionary magic uses the imagination as an interface that allows the magician to access inner beings and inner realms. When I say inner, I do not mean inside you, but inside a dimension that is not of the physical realm (some call it the astral realm). This dimension is accessed through the use of the imagination, through the mind's eye, hence the term 'inner.' First you need to learn how to use your imagination in a controlled way. Then you need to learn how to trigger events with spirit beings and inner places by using your imagination.

Psychologists, artists and thinkers all use their imaginations as a tool in order to do their work. A magician also uses the imagination as a tool, but what makes it different for a magician is the use of the imagination as a doorway through which their mind steps in order to reach other places. In order to use your mind in such a way, you must first be able to meditate, which is why your very first lesson was in meditation techniques. Secondly, you must be able to interact with your mind in a focused way, to trigger your imagination, and to hold your focus. Learning how to imagine something, learning how to see the 'something' that you have imagined in your mind's eye, and learning how to build an image using your imagination are all of paramount importance in magic.

There are some people who cannot visualise things in their mind in terms of what the image looks like, what colour it is etc. and this is called *aphantasia* which is the inability to form a mental image in the mind of something. This is more common than a lot of people realise, and it is also something that can happen to people on occasion who are normally good visualisers. If you think you might have aphantasia, don't panic.

Mental imagining is just one form of 'seeing' in the mind. For some, the information is processed as 'knowing' – you 'know' there is something stood before you, and whether it is friendly or not. You could not describe what it looks like, but you gain the information by just knowing. Some people gain information by smelling, or hearing – the human brain can process spirit and inner energetic information in a variety of ways and by doing the following exercises you will learn how your individual brain works. Learn to trust your instincts and write down in your journal everything you pick up on these exercises, and how your processing of information develops through doing the repeated exercises. Skill in this area is achieved through a series of specific exercises which you will learn in this lesson. These exercises must be done and mastered before you go on to attempt visionary magic.

If you choose a bad memory to observe, remember to try and keep yourself emotionally separate from the event – that event no longer exists regardless of the long term effects it may have triggered. This can be a very good exercise to come back to later on in your training, to approach a traumatic event from years ago and observe it from two different perspectives. Also, observing your emotional reactions and logging them in writing for you to read later in life can be very useful. If you keep returning to the same trauma and observing, you may find that over time the emotional connection to the event lessens. If it does the reverse and affects you negatively, then do not do that observation again.

1. *Exercise 1:* MEMORY

This exercise is designed to tap into your memory and use the mechanism that your brain uses in remembering. Working with this exercise not only helps your memory; it also teaches you to use wider areas of your brain when engaging the imagination.

1. Sit quietly after you have meditated for a few minutes to silence yourself. Think of an event that happened five years ago, an event that is easy for you to remember, like a birthday, an accident, or a family celebration. See yourself in that event: observe yourself from a distance, as though you were stood in the corner of the room. Remember the people who were there, what the room looked like, any smells that were apparent. Then see the event from within yourself looking out at the other people, look around the room, watch any details you can remember.
2. Now remember something from five days ago. Remember waking up, making a drink, or going to work. Were you driving? Can you remember the road, the cars on the road, what the traffic was like, people you passed by? Or choose an event from that day and focus on it. See it from outside of yourself first, and then see it from inside yourself: you are watching yourself driving or working. Observe your moods, your actions of that day during a particular incident or event.
3. Repeat the whole exercise by remembering something from ten years ago and then ten days ago. Watch the memory from outside yourself and then from inside of yourself.

The object of this exercise is to train the imagination to focus while also engaging the long-term and short-term memory.

Engaging the long-term memory first (which is a filing system that is usually fairly efficient and accessible) also triggers the short-term memory files which are often harder to access and slightly more chaotic. This is why if you wish to try and remember something from a few days ago, first remember something from a few years ago. Opening your long-term memory helps you to remember short-term events. Linking the memory and the imagination together allows the visionary process to engage wider areas of the brain, which in turn helps the visionary process to become more solid.

2. *Exercise 2:* Navigating a space

This is the next step in training the imagination. Learning how to move around a space using your mind is a good exercise, and it is also the first step in learning how to step through the imagination into actually travelling using your mind. It is also a major training exercise for remote viewing, which is the term for using the imagination to travel about in the physical world and observe happenings. Use your own home, but if you live in a single room or apartment block, stay within your room or apartment, or travel down public access staircases. If your space for experimenting is very small, do your own space and then spend more time on exercise three that looks at public spaces.

To prepare for this exercise, do a round of meditation or breathing exercises or both. Once you are nice and still and your mind is calm, begin by imagining yourself stepping out of your body. Turn around and look at yourself sitting on the floor. Look at the room you are in, look at the window and work out what direction it is in relation to your body. Turn and look at the door, and then look around the room, noting the colours and textures of the room's furniture, and if there is a mirror, go and stand before it. Look at your reflection and note how you look in spirit: it is often different from how your body appears.

Next, go to the door and out into the next room or hallway. Walk around the room, noting the windows, doors and any fireplaces (entrances and exits), note the furniture, the textures and colours, and any creatures (cats etc.) in that room. If there are people in that room, observe them briefly, noting if they emit any particular colour. (Colour is a frequency of energy, a vibration. The colours that people give off can tell you a great deal about their health and state of mind.)

Repeat this action in each room of the house or building you are in, until you find that your imagination is starting to break up and you are losing focus. At that point, start walking back to your body, noting each room you pass through to get back to your body. Once you get to your body, step in, settle yourself down, and when you are ready, open your eyes.

Don't be tempted to 'jump' from place to place. Make sure you walk the space: it is really important for later magical skill that you learn to walk from place to place and are able to hold the focus necessary to do this. This discipline begins to work your visionary 'muscle,' and it can be quite hard and tiring at first. The more you practise each day, the longer you will be able to sustain the vision and the further you will be able to go without losing focus.

Another important reason for making sure you walk through the exercise is that when you use visionary methods to reach into the inner worlds, taking your time to get there by walking through the various stages in between helps your mind to transition from imagination to actually seeing what is happening in a particular space. It helps to loosen your mind and spirit, and it also works with a magical dynamic of tides and oppositions which you will learn about later in the course.

It is a particular feature of visionary magic that the time taken to get to a place helps the gathering of power, helps the body adjust to the changes in power, and also helps your body to cope with the impact. Once you have mastered that technique, it is easy to come back quickly and jump from one space to another, but the going to a location must always be unfolded slowly and never rushed, no matter how experienced you are.

3. *Exercise 3:* Going for a walk

Once you have managed to walk around a few rooms in a house, and can hold the vision so that you can observe the details of a room, then it is time to learn how to leave the building that you are in. Start the exercise in the same way: stillness – breathing – step out of body and observe the room in which you are seated. Pick a nearby public building, store, train station or place that has public access, and see yourself stepping out of the house and walking down the street. Note the cars, the people, and the animals that you pass.

Enter your chosen building through its door and go to one particular room that you have chosen. Walk into the room, look around, and note the entrances, windows, etc. Look at any people in the room. Go up to one of them and, using the breathing exercise of colour that you have practised, see yourself gently blowing white smoke towards the person. The white smoke brings peace, energy and cleansing. Note if there is any reaction and then draw away. If a person reacts, it is likely they are naturally psychic and maybe not aware of it.

See yourself walking back out of the building, back down the street and into your house. Go back to the room where you first started, sit down into your body, and when you are ready, open your eyes.

4. Summary

Work with these various exercises until you can do them with ease, and once you get to that stage, you can begin to tackle the next level of visionary exercises. Don't skip any of the stages, as they are designed to slowly build your inner skill for visionary work, and some people will gain the skill quicker than others. If you build a solid skill for moving about using your imagination, that skill will put you in good stead should you encounter difficulties when navigating the inner worlds. Hence it is important to become familiar with the sensation of using the mind to move about, and to be able to hold the vision if you encounter unexpected beings, powers or events.

Most injuries and shocks sustained while working in vision happen because the magician is not used to holding the vision in the face of the unexpected, so taking the time to build a solid working technique is well worth the effort.

Using visionary skills in this realm is also a handy tool to use to check your home when you are away, to ensure there is no one in the building who should not be there, and that the building is safe. This is a form of remote viewing.

5. *Task:* Work with this method of visualisation for ten sessions

Keep journal entries for each time you do each exercise, and write down everything you encounter, even if it may seem silly or unrelated at the time. These journal entries will become invaluable to you in the years to come, as you will learn so much from re reading them, and then adding to them.

If after ten sessions you are able to visualise yourself moving about with ease, are able to switch perspectives from looking out from within your body to looking from an outside point of observation, and are able to visualise going out of your house and going to a building down the street, then you are ready to move on. If you are still struggling with these exercises, don't rush yourself. Everyone is different; everyone develops at their own pace. Keep working with this phase of the work until you are happy that you have gained the skill. Don't try and skip this phase if you are struggling with it, as it is the core skill that enables visionary magic to work. It does not matter if it takes you a year to learn this skill: all that matters is that you learn how to do it. Keeping working with the exercises and also study the other lessons in the module, but don't attempt any more visionary magic lessons until you have mastered these basics.

In terms of remote viewing skills, working with these exercises every so often throughout your magical life will help to develop deeper ability in remote viewing techniques. These skills can be very helpful if you need to check on a family member from a distance, or check out the safety of a space before you go there.

Lesson 4
Ritual Techniques

Before we dive in to learning how to do a ritual and how to do ritual magic, let's first have a look at what ritual magic actually is. You would be surprised at the number of people involved in magic who have no real understanding as to what a ritual actually is and how it works. Many people think that the robes, tools, altars, speeches and officers are the ingredients that make a ritual work. That is a common incorrect assumption.

A ritual is a pattern of energy created by a certain action, utterance, substance and tools brought together in a certain way and then infused with inner power and contact to bring it to life. The latter part of that description is the part that is most often missed. Why? Because so much modern magical training only focuses on the outer aspect of the ritual, i.e., the recipe book.

The grimoire or ritual text is often mistaken for being the whole ritual, but it is not. It is only fifty percent of the actual ritual; the rest consists of magical skill applied through the use of inner vision, power mediation and inner contact. Throughout history magical texts leave that part out, not just to protect the magic from dabblers, but because there is no point in adding it in – you either know because you are a working magician, or you don't because you are not. Either the magician is properly trained and knows how to switch the ritual into life, or they do not. If they do not, they will achieve at best a fragment of what the ritual has the potential to trigger. This protects the dabbler from their own ignorance, protects the integrity of the magic, and also protects everyone around the dabbler.

If a ritual pattern has been used repeatedly in the same way over a long period of time, it can potentially work regardless of who operates it, provided it was originally constructed with inner contact, and it is conducted with the key elements present. But in general, the inner connection is the key to success. You can give someone a script for a ritual, a robe, a wand, a sword, an altar, officers, the whole works… and nothing will happen if they do not have the power and ability to make it all work.

On the other end of the spectrum, a properly trained adept can walk up to a candle, or go out into the sunshine or the wind, or can walk into a church or temple and just stand there. They can utter a single ritual call or intent with no dressing, no candles, no robes, scripts, or wands, and all the power will immediately switch on and start working. That is because the adept is plugged into the power properly and the simple action of intent with focus, uttering that intent or using a physical action to trigger exteriorisation of that intent, will bring the magic powerfully into action.

It is this need for both sides of the coin to be present to make the work successful that protects the ritual texts, grimoires, and ancient temples. You can recreate complex rituals from books and grimoires till the cows come home, but if you do not have the ritual plugged into power, or do not know how to access that power, then it just will not work; or if any beings are around you, it may raise a small puff of power – but nothing more.

That is why it is very important for any budding magician to ensure that they learn both ritual magic and visionary magic: ritual magic is the construction of outer patterns and also puts out the call, and visionary magic accesses the power and consciousness of inner worlds, and bridges the beings that bring the ritual magic to life. Ritual magic gives form to the inner power, and the inner power fuels the ritual. One without the other is a waste of time.

1. How does a ritual work?

The construction of a ritual has two main aspects: human and energetic. The actual style of magic used (the language, tools, robes, incantations etc.) largely depends on what type of magic you are doing and what you are trying to achieve. The elements of the style of magic are not the magic itself: they are the surface variables, the details of the 'dressing,' and they are not actually necessary for the foundational construction of a ritual; rather they give the ritual a particular 'accent' which in turn attracts the attention of specific spirits.

The foundation of the ritual itself consists of the combined platform of energy and humans. Let's have a look at the human aspect of ritual first. All humans have ritual in their lives whether they realise it or not. Rituals make things easier, more predictable and more efficient. They are the things we do the same way every day: how we brush our teeth, how we wake up, how we drink our coffee, how we dress. We all have our own ways of doing things, and as we get older our patterns become more settled and predictable.

A ritual begins to form when a person chooses to do something in a particular way. If they continue to repeat this action in the same way over a long period of time, the action becomes *engrammed* into their brain and consciousness until it becomes an unconscious action. Driving a car is the most commonly understood example of engramming, which means repeating a pattern of action in exactly the same way on a regular basis until it becomes second nature.

This method of pattern making, which is what both magic and engramming is, can often be observed in the training of gymnasts, acrobats, ballet dancers and silk weavers. Repeating a movement exactly the same way over a long period of time results in your being able to execute the action at far greater speed and power than an untrained person could. When you combine an engrammed action with the focused use of your mind, you have the foundation of a ritual. Making your coffee in a certain way each morning to help you get focused and ready for the day can become a ritual: it is the use of a repeated action to affect consciousness. It is not a magical ritual, but it is a ritual nonetheless.

So what does this have to do with ritual magic? Everything. It is very important to understand the different forms of ritual that exist in our lives, and it is very important to know all of the components that go into the construction of a successful magical ritual. How you physically do your magical ritual, particularly if it is one that you often repeat, is very important: your own physical pattern of behaviour builds a doorway in your consciousness and your body which enables your mind and body to then fully engage with the power the ritual can connect you to. That physical engagement with the ritual can take the form of processing around the directions, standing before an altar, using physical stances, mudras, body actions... all these physical patterns can be components of a ritual.

2. Ritual micro-actions

As the magician becomes more advanced in ritual, something happens that very few magicians are aware of, but which can ultimately undermine rituals that use high levels of power. That something is called a 'micro-action.' This is a pattern of behaviour that you need to be aware of from the very earliest stages of your training, so that you can spot it when it starts, and remove it from your body.

When a magician repeats the same ritual on a daily basis over a period of time, it becomes engrammed. Once the ritual action is engrammed into the brain, the brain starts to get 'bored' and will fight the engram by introducing a micro-action into the ritual. This is a phenomenon that is known in the various forms of classical dance that require the dancer to perform repetitive actions over a long period of time. A micro-action manifests in a way that is very subtle and can seem harmless, and it is often mistaken for 'personal style.'

Let's have a look of a practical example of micro-actions invading an engram so that you get a good idea of what I am talking about.

A magician is working a hexagram ritual each day to instil balance within herself and balance in the working space, as well as using the ritual as a moving meditation. The ritual involves her moving around the room, making certain arm actions and speaking certain words. After a few months of repeating this ritual, the magician can do it without thinking and often works through the ritual without remembering doing it: she is on autopilot, and the ritual is an active engram.

One day, without noticing what she's doing, when the magician uses her finger to trace shapes in the air she finishes the tracing with a small flourish of her finger or wrist; and when she walks from direction to direction, she turns in a small 'flourish' or adds in a particular small head movement. These little novelties immediately reward her brain with a small dose of 'feel-good' – and that is how you recognise when your brain is fighting an engram. Repeated engrammed movements do not reward the brain in the same way as change does: they are not as interesting. So the brain adds in new actions in order to generate rewards in those parts of the brain that like to receive performance feedback. The brain does not wish to work like a machine; it likes to perform with tiny variables that are quirky and interesting.

So what has this to do with magic? Well, quite a lot actually. That tiny micro movement of dissent can change the structure of the inner sigil or pattern that is being formed by the repeated ritual, which subsequently undermines its power. It is also a signal that the magician's focus is not as good as it should be. Magic is all about absolute focus, where your conscious intent is in total control, not the body itself. Micro-actions are the result of a subtle power struggle, and the sooner they are recognised and restrained, the better the magician will be. You are essentially teaching your body to work in a way that gives no immediate reward: each time the brain adds in a small flourish it gets a chemical treat and the magician feels 'important' or 'powerful.' But it is a fake feeling, as it comes purely from brain treats, not from real power itself.

When a magician's brain chemistry is out of balance, it can often be spotted in the over exaggerated use of flourish during rituals (and also during conversations, public speaking etc.). This is not the same as talking with one's hands, but is about quirks of eye, or shoulder, or leg or head movements. The person will have a series of body movements that are like 'catchy phrases': our own brains become interested when we see them and we latch on to them. This is how subtle advertising works at its best. The catchy phrase or action is hardwired to give a 'brain treat.'

In everyday life we are constantly exposed to these 'brain treats,' and if one's personality is young, underdeveloped or weak, it will immediately latch on to those brain treats in order to get the chemical boosts which generate feelings of pleasure and power. This is why such underhand advertising methods work best on teens and young adults: that is a prime time for feeling powerless, and also when the personality is still not yet fully developed. In everyday life, enjoying these brain treats does no real harm and we often grow out of them naturally.

In magic however, micro-actions can be the little grains of sand that slowly grind away until they have torn apart a chunk of the magician's power. Hence the need for this rather long section on the subject: knowing about micro-actions is fifty percent of the problem solved. The other fifty percent consists of being vigilant, spotting micro-actions as they occur and reining in your focus. Once you have learned a ritual by heart and you are working in an engrammed way or on autopilot, watch for these tiny flourishes trying to creep into your actions. As soon as you spot them, be aware of how they make you feel on a subtle level, recognise at which point of the ritual action they creep in, and stop the flourish from happening.

It can feel surprisingly intense to block such micro-actions, but it is the start of learning how to be completely and utterly focused, and in control of your mind and body. One way to get rid of a micro action that has crept into a ritual, is to do the ritual at a super slow speed, and observe carefully. Every time the micro action happens, stop and do the action again very slowly with focused intent. Don't worry about it messing up the flow of the ritual, as at this stage of training, getting such actions under control is far more important. By slowly training out any micro-actions, you are beginning the real training of absolute focus of action, and that in turn will blossom into a magical focus that is like a laser point.

In time you will learn how to create and dismantle magical patterns simply by looking at a flame, and the skill set required to perform such powerful actions comes first from being able to direct a focused action without any interference from your brain, body or wandering mind. In this way, the inner patterns and inner sigils you create will be exact, powerful and solid.

3. *Task:* Body stretching

The other important element of preparation for powerful ritual is the flexibility and stability of the musculoskeletal system. Traditionally this preparation for magical power was done through the practice of yoga. Yoga prepares the body slowly for the influx of power that advanced ritual brings, and ensures that the body's structure can process that power properly. It is not about building muscle, but flexibility: the more the body has the capability to properly stretch and flex, the more power it can cope with as it passes through and around the magician. Through learning physical flexibility, the inner body too becomes more pliant and able to bend and flex against impact: by training the outer body, you also train the inner body.

When you begin any serious practical study of magic, such as this course, it is important also to take up a physical discipline like yoga, martial arts, classical dance, or anything that pushes the body in terms of stretching and long muscle strength and stability. Body building, circuit training or other heavy impact or aerobic exercises do not have the same benefit: you do not want to 'bulk up' against power so much as learn to 'bend' and flex with it.

To this day I still do a daily stretch and muscle stabilising routine. Just ten minutes a day is all that is needed to maintain my flexibility and core strength. Find something that works for you and do it daily. If you cannot do it daily, then a minimum of three times a week will suffice. When I walk into a room of magicians, I can spot immediately which magicians have such a routine discipline and which do not: the way their body holds itself energetically is directly linked to how it is maintained and cared for.

4. Energy

The second component of a ritual is energy. Energy is needed to construct an inner pattern that will focus and channel power in the intended direction. And I do not mean physical energy. In the energetic component of a ritual, energy from the elements are lined up and woven into a particular inner shape which in turn creates a pathway for power to be conducted along. Think of it like a circuit board: the energetic pattern of the ritual is the lines and channels that power flows down that in turn triggers a successful outcome.

That energetic pattern is built from the directional elements. When someone looks at a ritual that has been properly constructed, a successful one will have ingredients of energetic directional patterns, and these will include a properly enlivened tool (i.e. sword, wand, or finger), the use of speech to call a being, spirit/beings, an altar or multiple altars, and the use of elements themselves (flame, water, rock, speech/air/incense).

Often when people are taking part in a ritual, they do not realise this is how these objects, words, beings and substances work. They think the objects, words and flames 'represent' something, but they do not – they *are* something. Let's put this into a practical context to make it easier to understand.

5. Example of a directional ritual

Let us look at a ritual designed to protect a space from a specific threat (as opposed to giving general protection).

The magician places an altar in the east. She puts a plain white altar cloth upon the altar and also a plain white candle. She takes a magical consecrated sword out of its scabbard and places the sword on the altar. She then goes to prepare by taking a ritual bath.

The magician returns to the ritual space in clean clothing, closes the door behind her and sits down in the centre of the space. She meditates for a short while and works with visionary meditation to go into the Void, into a visionary state of nothingness. (That is the first step of the ritual – cleansing, clearing.)

The magician then stands up, staying within the state of nothingness, and faces east towards the altar. Instead of walking straight to the eastern altar, she simply bows, and then turns and walks a full clockwise circle around the room before arriving at the south. The magician stands before the south wall, is aware of the power in the south, the solar deities, angelic beings, spirits and inner contacts. She bows to them and utters an acknowledgement of them. She repeats that action in the west and north before turning back to the east.

As she approaches the altar in the east, the magician takes a deep breath and, within her stillness, remembers the feeling of the power of air in its purest, most magical form; and she breathes that power through her into the direction of east. She is still holding the sense of nothingness and thinking about nothing except the simple ritual actions she is undertaking. Then it is time to light the candle.

The magician stands before the altar and deepens the sense of the Void within her. She becomes aware of herself as a shell that encases a spark of Divinity. She sees that spark of Divinity as a flame. The magician stands, aware of the flame within her, aware of the power of the south to her right, and the power of the north to her left. She is aware of the west behind her and of the east before her. With that pattern of awareness building, the magician then lights the candle flame. That is the construction of the energetic pattern from the elemental directions.

To do that construction successfully, the magician must have absolute single focus, and be able to connect at an inner level with the magical and elemental power of a direction just by thinking about it.

The magician positions the sword on the altar so that it lies across the altar like a barrier. The magician, using her mind, builds up the image of the gates of the east opening, and feels the wind of the east blow over her as the gates open wide. She becomes aware in her mind of the contacts and spirit beings that work regularly with her, and she acknowledges their presence and thanks them for helping.

The magician then places her hands upon the blade and, using her voice, calls into the east for the particular power that she wishes to come and help her. This could be a deity power, an angelic power, a demonic power, or a land/wind consciousness power. How she calls upon them depends on what type of being it is. For example, deities often have specific prayers and appeals that trigger them, whereas angelic or planetary beings have specific words that trigger them but tend not to need or want appeals – they prefer simple, direct instructions.

As the magician is reciting the request, she has full physical contact with the consecrated sword, thus bringing it into her energetic sphere. She has been maintaining the Void meditation throughout this ritual, but at this point she becomes still more deeply aware of the Void and its potential. All things flow from the Void, and the opening and holding open of the Void creates a threshold for beings and power to pass through.

Then the magician, as she is reciting, picks up the sword and turns around to face the room. The sword is held up, blade pointing down (guarding/defence) and at the end of her recitation the magician takes a deep breath, holds the awareness of the open east gates behind her, and blows the power of air over the sword while uttering the name of the being she wishes to help her. The magician closes her eyes and becomes aware of the power streaming out of the east, through the sword and into the room.

The use of the sword focuses and directs the beings/power into a defensive or guarding stance: it is a filter that says, 'defend.' Still holding the sword, the magician walks to the centre of the room and then conducts a ritual action to specifically direct the beings and the sword to defend the east, south, west, north, centre, above, and below. The magician then places the sword on the floor in the centre of the room and goes to the east altar.

She bows and thanks the spirits for their help. The magician will then either blow out the candle but 'see' in vision the inner candle still burning and working, or the magician will leave the candle burning indefinitely.

This is just one of many different ritual forms that can be done to protect a space, building or town. The size of the area protected depends on the mental projection of the magician during the part of the ritual when she defines to the beings what area she wants defending. The use of the four directions when working in the centre defines the shape of the space: if the magician wishes to protect a large area, she projects the sense of 'south', for example, as being as far south of her as necessary to hit a city boundary. The magician should already know where those boundaries are, so that she can project that mental image to the beings working with her.

6. Analysis of the ritual

So let us have a closer look at what was going on in that simple ritual, and what ingredients were used to make it work.

The first thing to notice is that the ritual did not rely on grimoire-type magic or prescribed recipe book magic – this is not a type of ritual that anyone can do if they have the book/script and description. This ritual depends almost exclusively on the skill and knowledge of the magician: it is an adept ritual, but one that clearly and simply demonstrates the use of basic, simple elements and ingredients in creating a successful ritual.

You will also notice is that there was no use of banishing or protection before the ritual started. The need to banish and protect is drilled into almost all beginner students these days and they are told it is the corner stone of adept magic. No, it is not. Those actions were originally introduced into ritual magic as a beginner exercise, and while there are different versions of banishing and protecting rituals that you will learn on this course, it is very important that, as a student, you understand that they are not a major part of adept-level magic – and let me show you why.

The first action of the magician was to take a ritual bath. This purifies her of all energetic dirt, minor magical attacks, any hangers-on, etc. It cleans, purifies and helps the magician to think clearly and cleanly. She then puts on clean clothing. It is important that her body, mind and clothing are clean with nothing that can potentially interfere with the magic. She did not use ritual robes.

Ritual robes have two real magical functions: the first is that the robe is ritually clean, and the other use of a robe is where the robe has been consecrated and worked with magically to shield the magician. A robe can act in some circumstances like a bulletproof vest to deflect attacks when needed. But it is very rare that such use in ritual is actually necessary if you are properly trained. How many times do you wear a bulletproof vest in your everyday life? And how many times, when you have been in sudden danger, have you had time to put on a protective body shield? It is important to learn how to work without such robes, so that you can learn to be ever-ready, using simply your own skills and knowledge.

Once she is clean, the magician returns to the ritual room. The first thing she does is meditate, and then she goes into the deep nothingness of the Void.

That is the inner bulletproof vest needed for inner work: absolute stillness in the 'nothing.' Should a being try to attack her, then because she is holding the nothingness, not only is she more or less unseen in the inner worlds, there is no discernible form for that being to grab onto – she appears shapeless.

This skill takes a long time and a lot of practice to acquire, but it is with you at all times and instantly accessible. If you are used to hiding behind robes, amulets and banishing rituals, you will get caught out one day. You cannot spend your whole magical life hidden behind armour: there comes a time when you need to learn inner social skills, true magical martial skills, and safety awareness.

From that stillness the magician introduces a pure element that she will work with as the primary threshold – the flame. She also works with the element of air, and uses her knowledge of the inner power of air to bring that inner power and outer breath together.

From there, she can use that empowered breath to call upon the beings that she needs to help her. The empowered breath ensures that her call is heard by the beings it is directed to, a bit like a personal telephone. That empowered breath comes from long-term training in the use of the magical elements as tools, something you will learn during the Apprentice section of the course.

The intent and the names used direct the call, and the empowered breath fuels the call; it also ensures that it reaches the right frequency of beings. The use of breath and name informs the beings that they are being called to work with a human who is plugged into the inner Divine manifestation of life: the use of sacred breath is the most powerful magic of all. Sometimes the magician will not call upon beings, but will use the empowered breath to utter a sacred combination of letters or sounds that express a particular aspect of Divinity. That action triggers a specific type of inner pattern that can then power a ritual, and it is also an inner pattern that automatically protects the working space along with the magician.

From there, the magician then used a ritually consecrated tool to direct the being/power into action. The use of a magical sword says defend, guard or attack, and when the beings see the use of this ritual tool and feel its frequency, they know what is being asked and expected of them. They can work through the sword, using its substance, its consecrated power and its shape to do their job. The magician used the four directions to map out the area that needs defending, and the breath across the sword ensured that the deep inner power of air was awakened within the sword. That awakening creates another layer of automatic protection: an awakened sword in action blocks out interference.

The sword will then be kept out of its scabbard, with the scabbard kept close to it, and it will work for however long it has been directed to work. The beings that were called upon to help will have empowered the ritual pattern and they will uphold that pattern for the required length of time and will also protect it. Each day the magician will tune briefly into the pattern, and she may also light a candle in the east each day, just to keep things ticking over.

So the ingredients are: fire, air, sword, inner contact, utterance, meditation, void, and movement around the directions to establish a pattern. The use of speech, breath, use of mind/vision, movement, a candle, a sword and an altar is all very simple, and also very effective.

The pattern, elements and actions create a frequency in the space which automatically excludes interference by beings, powers or other magicians.

Let's have a look at how that ritual will operate in and protect a space. If you went into that protected room to look at it from an inner point of view, there would be a few things you would see.

The first would be open gates in the east: notice she did not close the directional gate down; she simply blew out the outer candle while letting the inner candle still burn, and she left the gates open. The second thing you would see from an inner point of view is the pattern of the four directions and a clockwise walking pattern. That creates an inner pattern that looks a bit like a spinning circle. It is a turning circular movement that, once set going, will continue to turn until it is closed down.

The third thing that you would see is the inner pattern of the sword. Every outer object has an inner version. Every outer consecrated sword is merged with the one, big, original, archetypal consecrated sword, and if you looked into that space in vision, what you would see is a very large, very impressive-looking sword with a lot of power emanating from it. This sword will create an environment whereby nothing gets into the space except the being that was called upon to help and any others who are compatible with the work being done: the space becomes tuned to a very specific frequency. And that will be the fourth thing that you would see: the being that was called upon. If the being called was a deity, then the deity itself would not be stood in the room, but the power signature of the deity would be there, and that power signature works in the same way that the deity does. Anything that tries to interfere with that space will bump up against that deity power, and if that deity power is aggressive then the intruder will most likely get attacked.

If the being that is working with the ritual is angelic, it will appear as a pattern or shape in the room that nothing can penetrate. No matter what any intruder tries to do to magically invade the space, they will just bounce off as though there is an invisible barrier (which there is). If the magician called upon a land being or spirit, or a demonic being to guard the space, then the being will appear to anyone who is trying to invade the space: they would see a terrifying face with lots of eyes, teeth and weapons threatening them.

The cleanliness of the magician ensures that the being sees only the magician and does not mistake them for anything else, so clean equals safe. The specific use of directions and elements ensures that the frequency of the ritual is such that it excludes low-level beings, invaders, ghosts, parasites, etc. (hence no need for banishing), and the use of the sword, inner contact, empowered breath, utterance and being ensures that no aggressive spirit or magician can interfere. It also ensures that energetic filters are in place to stop any sort of power surge.

A power surge is where the gates are opened, power is called upon, but there is no proper filter to step down the power to make it safe. The inner contacts in the directions, the gate, and the constant working with the circular pattern in vision which then triggers during ritual, and the consecrated sword across the threshold of the altar all ensure that power filters are in place.

So you can see how there are many different skills that are brought into work with a ritual, and that it is not just a matter of having certain robes, speeches, actions, etc. Effective ritual cannot be copied out of a book; it is a coming-together of a varied amount of well-practised skills.

The first step towards acquiring that skill level is learning how to open and close gates in ritual, how to move around a space in ritual, how to use tools, how to use your voice, and how to pull all of those things together, along with using your mind in vision while also doing the ritual. We will start that process by looking at the use of the elements, tools and directions in ritual, and then we will go on to practical exercises.

7. Directional ritual

Many ritual foundations, regardless of style, work with specific magical directions that allow the magician to access certain streams of consciousness and power. Not all ritual uses directional application, but once you have learned it and know how to work with it, you will begin to recognise it in many different forms, and not just in magic – the use of the directional powers is also evident in many ancient and more modern religions.

Some styles use directional ritual in a very obvious way, whereas other styles use a pattern that is not obvious in its directional use. Once you have learned the skill and have worked with it for a while, you will recognise its use in the most obscure ways. The knowledge of how to operate with magical directions allows you also to access the inner and more mystical aspects of religions, as well as magical forms.

The first thing that is important in a ritual is to know the physical directions of the space you are working in, and to be clear about which direction/directions you are working in and why. The reason for this is that each direction has a certain quality of power that flows through it, and that flow of power will affect your work. If you have a working space that is not aligned straight to the directions, then you choose the magical direction by working with the walls/altars that are the nearest to a direction. So for example if a wall in a working space is north-northeast, then it becomes magical north.

The definitions of directional powers vary according to which tradition or magical method is being used, but in the northern hemisphere it is generally expressed as follows:

- Air, utterance, sword, sacred writing, new patterns, rising sun, in the East
- Fire, creativity, future, creative destruction, in the South
- Water, cups or vessels, harvest, threshold of death, mortality, in the West
- Earth, land, shield, ancestors, the Underworld, in the North

The use of directional magical patterns can also be apparent in many religions that use ritual, if you know how and where to look. For example, if you were to walk into a Norman church, you would immediately recognise the magical use of directional powers in the layout of the church. The altar is in the east and this is where the priest works. East is the power of air, utterance and the 'Word.' The priest works in that direction, uttering the sacred words to the people and offering the ritual to the deity (Jesus) who is in the east. When you read parts of the New Testament, you will find many references to the 'Word', and also to the 'Sword'. It is also a religion of the 'book.'

If you look west in the church, you will find the doors that open out to humanity (God in the east, humans in the west). And the baptismal font, the vessel of water, is in the west. The priest stands in the east and mediates the Word of God from the east to the people in the west. To the south, usually depicted as a south transept, you often find images of St. Michael the Archangel, who is the power of fire. In the north transept you will find the Lady Chapel or side chapel to Mary, the female divine power and the female expression of the Divine Container (Earth). Also in the north, particularly in very old churches, you will find the Lyke door: a door that opens out to the graveyard which is traditionally in the north: North – earth – ancestors – female.

In many churches after the reformation, the north transept was ritually blocked off and you will find that area of the church is often walled off, curtained off and filled with trash, old furniture, or the organ. This is a deliberate attempt to block both the power and the worship of the female Divine or Miriam powers. This layout is not used throughout the Christian world, but it was a feature of the Norman conquest of northern France and Britain, and the magical mysteries they brought with them. The blocking off of the north transept is most commonly found in Britain and was a direct result of the protestant influence.

Churches in other countries that were not part of the Norman territory have different ritual layouts and it can be very interesting indeed to go around these sacred places in different countries to see how various magical ritual patterns were used. Most churches built after the 1600s do not have ritual layouts, as by then that knowledge had been lost. The idea of the ritual layout in a church was that it enabled directional powers to be brought into the space and gather at the centre where all the directions came together. Some churches had their altar there, a stone altar known as the *Corpus Christi* (Body of Christ), and all the powers were funnelled into that substance which then became the centre of the ritual. All of the powers, the utterance and the magician/priest worked with the stone/substance of the altar to bring Divinity into physical manifestation, which was then taken in by the people (transubstantiation ritual).

You can see examples of this sort of ritual patterning and use of power in European churches, and once you know the techniques for opening the gates, you can sit in a church, open the gates and feel the power flow into the space.

One word of warning though: if you do such an action, do it with respect for the religion. If you open the gates, do it with the intent that the power flows through the Christian pattern and nourishes the congregation. It serves no purpose to be hostile to any ritual expression of Divinity, no matter how humans have corrupted it. The other reason for being respectful is that such churches often have guardians, and you can get your ass slapped if you do not operate with integrity.

8. Practical directional work

So now that you have an idea of how the directional powers can work in ritual, it is time to learn the basics in a practical way. For this you will need a compass. It does not need to be an expensive or fancy one, just one that works.

The first step is to choose a working space. This can either be a room set aside for ritual, an actual temple space (lucky you!), or it can be a regular room in a house used for normal life. Or you can work outdoors. Indoor work is usually best for ceremonial/ritual magicians, and outdoors for earth magicians/witches, etc. In reality, for training purposes, it is wise to work in both ways, to learn how the different spaces operate and how different the magic can become. A good magician can work anywhere, at any time and with any style. And if you are being trained by me, then you will learn all ways: I expect my students to be adaptable and able to work in any magical form from shamanistic styles of magic to high ceremonial ritual magic.

We will start with indoors. Pick a room and stand in it with your compass. Take a note of the directions and if your room is not directly lined up with the directions, assign the magical directions to the nearest four walls (a south east wall can become 'south' if it is more south than east). Take a note of where the windows, doors and any fireplace are (potential portholes), and take a note of potential altar surfaces. This can be cabinets, chests of drawers, tables, chairs, bookcase tops, etc.; I have even worked on top of the cooker in the kitchen when needed. Piles of books can make great altars, as can basic wood or bamboo breadboards. I live in a tiny house with small rooms and no ritual space. I use the furniture, a chair with a bread board on it, a box, basically whatever is to hand, it really doesn't matter what it is.

You also need five plain white cloths to use as altar cloths. A good cheap way to do that is to get a plain bed sheet and cut it up. Mark each cloth with the initial of the direction, so that you can identify it and continue to use it in the same direction. Get five white candles and also mark the candles and holders so that you continue to use the same candle/holder in each direction. Why? Energetic build-up. But it is not absolutely necessary to use the same candles. In some spaces pillar candles are not allowed, but tea lights are. Because my space is so small and I am so clumsy, I use tea lights in small glass holders and I put small hard mats underneath them so that they do not heat damage any surface they are on.

When something is repeatedly used in the same magical direction, it slowly builds up a harmony with the energetic frequency of the direction. So a skilled magician will potentially be able to pick up a directional candle holder or tool, and will be able to sense which direction it has been working in. The repeated use of the same things in the same place is the very beginning of energetic engramming: we looked earlier at physical engramming, but it also works in terms of ritual energy.

Altars

Set up your altars in the four directions and one in the centre. Each altar should only have a cloth and possibly the same candle at this phase. It is very important to learn how to operate altars properly. An altar is a work-space and a threshold. All that should be on it are the specific tools you are going to work with. A magical altar is very different from a spiritual or religious altar, and all of them are different from a New Age 'feel-good' altar. A religious altar will have a deity image, offerings, and the preferred tools of that deity on it.

A new age 'feel-good' altar will have various deities, images, gifts, trinkets, oils, incense, and lots of other trash. Such an altar does nothing spiritually or magically, it just makes the owner feel good (in the same way a toy train collection does) and it becomes a status symbol splashed about on social media. All it actually does is advertise how little a person knows.

For now you will work with no tools until you learn how to open the gates. Before you learn how to open the gates you need to learn how to create the energy pattern in the room. This is done by 'working the directions.' Once you have set up your altars, have all five candles ready and a box of matches. Then it is time to prepare yourself. Go and take a bath or shower, or at least wash your hands and face, brush your teeth, and put on clean clothing.

9. Working the directions

Start in the east. Whenever you work directional magic, always start in the east. This is where the power opens, and it also helps you to tap into a ritual pattern that has been used for millennia. The pattern you create will resonate with the ancient pattern and will be fuelled, stabilised and brought to life through this resonance.

When you walk into the room, walk a full circle around the central altar, walking clockwise, and then approach the altar in the east. Always walk clockwise to build up that flow of power, and never approach the east altar directly; always walk a full circle before you start any initial ritual action.

Approach the east altar and stand before it. Take a few moments to close your eyes and still yourself before you begin to work. When you are ready, open your eyes and light the candle. Stand for a moment before the candle and try to empty your mind. After a few minutes, take a step or two back, turn and walk to the south altar and repeat the same action: stillness, light the flame, be silent for a few moments. Repeat this in the west and the north.

When you have finished in the north, step back, turn, and go to the central altar. Repeat the same action. Once all the candles are lit, walk a full circle around the central altar and approach the east altar.

Stand before the altar and close your eyes. Imagine that you see two large gates beyond the altar. Take your time. Build up the image slowly, and don't try to project what you think it should look like. It doesn't matter if you don't get a strong visual sense at this stage, just a 'knowing' is enough. Sometimes at this stage of training you can sort of imagine a double door gateway or doorway but no details, and that is fine. When you feel you have a nice strong image of an east gate, take a step back from the altar, turn and go to the south. Repeat the same action in each direction. You may find that each gate in each direction is different; each direction will have its own unique feel.

Once you have finished in the north, turn to the central altar, stand before it (facing south) and close your eyes. Imagine a large column of fire that reaches up beyond the ceiling and stretches into the stars, and it also plunges down into the Underworld: a column of fire that is like an axis that goes through all the worlds.

Open your eyes and walk a full circle around the centre altar and approach the east. Place your hands upon the altar at either side of the candle flame and look beyond the flame. If you are using a low altar, kneel down and hold your hands in the air just above and to each side of the altar if it is too small to touch. With your eyes open, use your mind's eye to imagine the east gates.

Using your voice, utter the following words:

> "I acknowledge the gates of the east,
> I acknowledge the angelic threshold of the east
> and I acknowledge the wind of the east."

Step back from the altar, bow, turn and walk to the south.

Repeat the same exercise, using the words:

> "I acknowledge the gates of the south,
> I acknowledge the angelic threshold of the south
> and I acknowledge the fire of the south."

In the west, do the same and repeat the words:

> "I acknowledge the gates of the west,
> I acknowledge the angelic threshold of the west
> and I acknowledge the water of the west."

And in the north:

> "I acknowledge the gates of the north,
> I acknowledge the angelic threshold of the north
> and I acknowledge the stone of the north."

When you have finished in the north, take a step back, turn and stand before the central altar. Remember the visual of the column of fire and utter the words:

> "I acknowledge the central fire
> that flows through all worlds, all times and all substance,
> I acknowledge the angelic threshold of the Void,
> the threshold of Divinity as it flows through all things,
> and the light of all living beings
> as it flows from the stars to the Underworld."

Close your eyes and imagine the stars in the sky above you. Imagine the earth below you, the east wind to your left, the western water to your right. Be aware of the power of fire in the south before you, and of the power of the earth in the north behind you. Imagine a spark or flame deep within your centre, a light that stretches up to the stars and down to the earth – it meets in your centre in the form of a small flame within you. This is the spark of Divinity within all things and it embeds the pattern of the central axis not only in the centre of the ritual room, but also in the centre of your own body.

The use of the word Divinity does not denote a deity; rather it recognises the creative and destructive power of the universe. Build up that sense of the elemental powers in the directions around you. Open your eyes and look at the central flame.

Hold out your arms and declare:

> "The Sword in my left hand,
> the Cup in my right hand,
> the Fire of inspiration before me,
> and the Rock of my ancestors behind me."

Drop your arms and walk a full circle around the flame and once you have done a full circle, go to the east and turn to face the central flame.

Hold out your arms and declare:

> "The Wand of creative fire and the future in my left hand,
> the Shield of the ancestors and the past in my right hand,
> the Cup of humanity before me,
> and the Breath of God behind me."

Eventually you will learn to do this magical positioning with the powers and tools for all the directions, but two directions is enough to get you started. Eventually you will be able to use this directional and elemental tuning within seconds by simply thinking about it, but that skill is built through repeated use of this ritual in the early stages of training.

When you have finished, walk a full circle around the central altar and go to the east. See in your mind's eye the gates of the east. Blow out the candle and see the gates vanish. Step back, bow to acknowledge the powers, and repeat that action in the south, west and north.

Step back from the north, bow and turn to face the central flame. Stand before the central flame and see in your mind's eye the column of fire that reaches through all of the worlds.

Notice that in the centre of the column, where the candle flame is, there seems to be a small void, a nothing in the centre of the light.

Utter:

> "I acknowledge the Void in the centre of the light,
> the nothing from which all comes."

Blow out the candle flame and bow.

Sit down and close your eyes. Meditate for a few moments to still yourself and be aware of the directions around you, the east to your left, the west to your right, and remember the elements in each direction, air, fire, water, earth, the light in the centre, and remember the magical tools in each direction: the sword, wand, cup and shield. Remember the Void in the centre of the flame.

Allow those images to rise and then fall away from your mind until you are simply seated in the room. Remember what the room looks like, see the door in your mind's eye, see the walls, the room's contents, and see yourself seated before the central altar. When you are ready, open your eyes. Starting in the east, collect up the cloths, fold them up, and wrap them around the candles or put them carefully in a box or drawer. They must not be used for anything else. Put the room back into its normal state.

This exercise is akin to learning how to sing scales. It builds up the magical directions, the elements and tools in your mind, it starts the building of the gates that you will learn how to open and close, and it starts to form the circular motion of power in the space. This should be done weekly for at least a couple of months until it has built strongly in your mind and until you body has become used to walking the room in a certain way (clockwise starting in the east).

At this stage of your early training, it is likely you will feel nothing happening in terms of power, unless you are a natural magician. Don't worry about that. At this stage you are simply learning the scales: once that pattern is built up strongly within you by memory, then the power will slowly start to flow: at that point you will start to feel the power that the simple tuning ritual can trigger.

Do not skip this exercise; it is probably the most important foundational exercise you will ever learn. Do it again and again until you can do it automatically, from memory, without needing to refer to notes. It also instils within you the power connections between your body and the directional magical tools. The repetitive element of this exercise instils these dynamics deep into your psyche, like learning something rote fashion. When you come to wield the magical tools in the depths of power, this rote learning will trigger deep reservoirs of power within you, and will allow you to plug directly into the inner magical powers that flow through the tools.

Once the full extent of the directional powers are embedded within you, when you come to work different forms of magic, it will automatically trigger this deep pattern just by the action of thinking about it, and it will open out the deeper hidden aspects of many magical rituals. You will be in the midst of a ritual and suddenly become aware of all the inner powers around you, the directional gates opening, and the enlivened tools plugging into their directional 'batteries.'

10. *Task:* Practising the directional ritual

Do the directional ritual once a week, on the same day if possible, each week for two months. You will be doing other tasks through each week that are assigned in the other lessons of this module, so ensure that you have enough time set aside to do this discipline.

Once you are coming to the end of the two month exercise, experiment to see how well it has engrammed into your mind: stand in a room, any room, or outside, and face east. Close your eyes and imagine you are standing in front of the east altar, imagine the south altar to your right and the north altar to your left. Once you have a feel of that, now take three steps backwards, turn and face south.

Imagine the central flame before you, that sense of the column of fire that reaches from stars to Underworld, and imagine the south altar in front of you beyond the central flame. Hold out your arms. Imagine the sword in your left hand and the cup in your right hand. Do you get a sense of the ritual? Can you imagine all of the altars around you, their directions and their flames? Can you imagine the four gates in each direction and the flame before you? If you can, then you have established the pattern within you.

If you are still struggling to retrieve that sense of the ritual, or to imagine the four directional powers, gates and altars, then you need to work with the ritual for another month, or two to three times a week until it is embedded in your mind. At the end of the month, try this testing exercise again. It does not matter how many months it takes you; there is no competition or deadline, it will take as long as it takes. The important thing is that you do get it.

This is the foundation stone for learning how to switch on a ritual at speed, how to switch on a sacred space, and how to bring power around you at a moment's notice, wherever you are and whatever you are doing. Eventually you should be able to retrieve this pattern in your mind and senses within seconds, in the midst of a busy city street, or in a room full of people. By doing so, you will be immediately surrounded by inner power that will guide and protect you.

11. *Task:* Keeping notes

Keep notes in your journal of when you do this ritual, what dates you work on, what it felt like, if it was easier or harder than usual, and anything else that crops up. When you look back over the journal, you will be able to track your progress and see if your ability to work is enhanced or withheld by astrological or physical variables. Is it harder or easier at a full or new moon? Is it harder or easier during a period if you are a woman? Or is it constant? Write down everything you observe and reflect back on your notes from time to time.

Lesson 5
Inner Senses

Everyone has some sort of inner sense to a greater or lesser degree, but most Western child-rearing and education tends to teach a small child how to filter it out, to ignore it, and to suppress it. This can be a major stumbling block for many budding magicians, and trying to recover lost senses is a slow and sometimes frustrating process.

Think of it in terms of everyday senses. If a very young child is taught that eyes do not see anything, if they are actively discouraged from using their eyes, and all interaction cues come from hearing and touch, eventually the quickly developing brain of the child will adapt, rewire, and rely less and less on the sense of sight. So it is with inner senses.

What exactly are inner senses? There are a wide variety of inner senses that are hardwired into the human body and most are suppressed very early on. Some senses can be stronger in some and weaker in others, and most vanish as the child grows up and they are ignored or squished into a dark corner of the brain, only to pop out at inopportune moments. The full array of inner senses would include things like inner hearing, inner sight, inner touch, inner smell, inner emotive triggers, inner immune triggers, precognition and time jumping. This all sounds very exciting, but in reality it is pretty mundane. Because of the influence of Hollywood, and the human penchant for drama and excitement, any understanding of the subtlety of inner senses gets drowned out in a chorus of overhyped fantasy. People who have been raised on Hollywood ideals have an unnatural view of inner senses and with that, unnatural expectations.

Inner abilities were most likely a part of our survival mechanism that has been slowly cast aside in modern life, a sort of inner 'fight or flight' adrenal mechanism, and just like natural physical mechanisms, inner senses are often tied to actual organs and seem to function through the central & peripheral nervous system, and brain. Some people tend to keep these senses despite their upbringing, and others manage to retain them because of their upbringing; so social/cultural aspects are only one part of the story. There are some people who appear to have no inner senses whatsoever: these people are like sensory bricks, and that can be a curse or a blessing, just as with someone who has highly developed inner senses: either extreme can cause great distress or can be a wonderful gift. It all depends on how the person lives with them.

Whatever your natural level of inner senses, and whatever type of inner senses you have that are dominant over the others, you can develop your natural facility through working with them. What cannot be done is to force the development of an inner sense that you just don't have. Very few people have all the inner senses; like everything else in life, some get more than others, and everyone has very different combinations. The first step is to identify which inner senses you are most likely to have, and then work at developing them. It is not something where you do a few exercises and *ping!* you have it. It is a lifetime of development that you start in your early training and the senses grow as you grow, mature and develop.

For some the inner senses can be overwhelming, and upbringing is not quite enough to shut them down. In such instances it is not about developing latent skills, it is about learning how to manage uncontrollable skills and bring them to a level where you can learn to live with them. Too much inner sense is as much of a curse as no inner sense at all.

There are instances where an inner sense can be suddenly switched on, but such forcing of a sense is pointless. For example, when a middle-aged person who has been blind from birth has surgery to give them sight, they do not immediately have wonderful sight that can process everything meaningfully: the brain has to learn how to process the signals from the eyes and make sense out of what they are actually seeing. After a person has the surgery they can see the doctor, the nurses, the room, the equipment, the bleeping lights, the cleaner pushing a vacuum past them, etc.

But the signals from their eyes to their brain are unfiltered, unsorted, and have no established vocabulary. So the newly seeing person finds it hard to figure out what part of the jumble of images they are seeing are the humans and which parts are the furniture; nor will they be able to process the moving cleaner and his vacuum, as their brain will have no vocabulary for processing visual movement.

Over time the brain will learn the language of images and will take cues from the senses of hearing and touch which are well-established with the patient. If the patient was deaf and blind from birth and they are given sight and hearing, the chances are that they will never, as an adult, be able to use those senses in any real meaningful way: their brain will have no reference points besides touch and smell. And so it is with inner senses that are being awoken. If they were used in childhood and then faded off (which is common), there is at least a baseline pattern in the brain that can relearn how to process the incoming information. Over time the skill becomes normalised and becomes a part of everyday life like smell, sight, and so forth.

If someone was shut down from birth or had blocked senses from birth, and the inner senses are forcibly triggered, then they will not be of any use: there will be no processing pattern. Such total shut-down is actually quite rare, and most people have fragments of inner senses that they are just not aware of. They can be so subtle as to be easily missed – and this is where Hollywood has done so much damage: our expectations are unrealistic, so the actual reality gets ignored, as it is too subtle in the face of full-on drama.

So first, let's briefly go through the various inner senses, and see how they can manifest quietly in a life, often unnoticed. This will help you to spot which (if any) of these senses you actually have and didn't realise. Then we will look at exercises to strengthen them and bring them right out over time.

1. **INNER HEARING**

This description is longer than the others, simply because it contains many different dynamics that also apply to the other skills. So remember, what applies in this description also applies in the others.

Inner hearing can manifest, like most inner senses, on two different levels, one being much rarer than the other. Inner hearing can either be a literal hearing with the ear, which is very rare, or hearing within the mind. Often the two types of inner hearing are combined, with the former being a rare occurrence and the latter being its more normal everyday manifestation.

Inner hearing that manifests by the subject hearing sounds or voices outside of themselves usually only happens in extreme potential danger. It can occasionally be objective (i.e. someone else also hears it), but it is most often subjective.

Before we get into the reality of inner hearing, it is important to discount other hearing anomalies that can manifest and be mistaken for inner hearing, but are in actual fact biological processes. Some of the rarer manifestations of tinnitus can lead someone to believe that they have inner hearing, when in fact their auditory nerve or their brain is playing up. This often manifests as the subject hearing music or sounds that do not in fact exist. This is known as musical hallucination, and it is a rare form of tinnitus. It can be triggered by brain tumours, epilepsy, migraines, and it is an occasional occurrence with OCD sufferers. The musical hallucination is often marked by the music being something the person remembers from childhood, and it tends not to be music that the subject is familiar with.

The other biological event that can be mistaken for inner hearing is symptoms of paranoid schizophrenia. In such cases there is often a whole array of mental health symptoms that help to rule out inner hearing. As with musical hallucinations, there are often underlying medical conditions that are already known about, and the 'hearing' is just one of a number of symptoms.

When however a subject is mentally stable, healthy, and most important of all, the event in question is a manifestation of an experience that the subject has always had, then it is likely that the subject does indeed have inner hearing abilities. Inner hearing with the ear can manifest as the person hearing their name shouted in an empty room, or a sudden warning whispered or shouted into the person's ear. I am in my fifties and it has happened to me three times that I can remember, and each time it was a warning of impending immediate disaster.

For example, once I heard 'slow down' shouted loudly close to my ear. I was alone in my car, with the music blaring, and the voice was clear and loud enough for me to hear over the music. I immediately slowed right down and narrowly missed being hit head-on by an oncoming truck on a blind corner. Slowing down gave me enough time to safely pull my car over into a lay-by as a truck, coming at me at high speed and overtaking on a corner, was coming straight at me on a single lane highway.

If I had been going at my regular speed, I would not have been able to process events fast enough to get out of the way, and most likely I would also have lost control of the car.

Those types of spectacular hearing events are rare in most people, except for a very small selection of people who have very defined auditory inner skills. The most common type of inner sense, and one that most people tune out or discount, is the small inner voice that can talk to you in your mind. The inner hearing happens within your mind's hearing, but it has a subtle difference to your own mind rambling along. Sometimes it is your deeper subconscious 'self' talking to you, and other times it is beings around you talking to you, and you process that communication as a voice within your mind.

As you develop that sense, it will eventually become clear to you what an 'outside' voice is and what your own deeper voice is. Sometimes it is impossible to distinguish between the two, and sometimes it really doesn't matter, so long as you learn to listen and act, and what is said is reasonable.

One of the things that magicians come to realise, if they are truly immersed in magic, is that everything communicates in one way or another. The skill is to learn what to tune out and what not to tune out – just like normal hearing. So for example, say you are walking through a city, and your mind is rambling along in its usual way, and suddenly the dialogue changes. Your mind's voice says something like, 'when you walk around that corner you will meet someone who is going to offer you a job, take it.' You walk around the corner and someone you know from years ago crosses your path. You get talking and they offer you a job. Maybe they are looking for a worker in an area of work you would not normally consider. The fact that the voice gave you a heads-up is a signal that the job is something you need to accept, because it is going to lead to something important.

It does not matter whether the voice is your own subconscious or an outside being; what is important is that you act upon the message, particularly when it presents in such a way that you could not possibly have known what was coming. Accepting and acting upon such communication helps to widen the channel so to speak, so eventually you will learn to distinguish between the feel of the voice that is your deeper self, and the voice of a being communicating with you through your mind.

As with all inner senses, you can immediately see the dangers of confusing inner senses with mental obsessions and illnesses, and as with all things magical, you must approach such things intelligently, carefully and with common sense. If you hear voices telling you to kill people, you have a problem. Clean yourself up magically, and if you are still hearing them, go see a doctor.

But if you are hearing things that tend to come true, or are valid warnings that save your ass, then it is your inner hearing kicking in. I have had stones talk to me, trees, beings, houses, deities… hell, everything talks. I also hear snatches of people's thoughts on rare occasions, which can be very distressing, and I have learned over the years to tune a lot of that out, as it is useless, intrusive and stressful.

Inner senses are very strong in some of the women in my family, and I was lucky enough to have a mother and older sister who did not seek to shut it down or to dramatise it, as either are destructive. Sometimes inner hearing is extremely helpful, and other times it is trivial and baffling. For example, "your sister is about to call you," and then the phone rings a few seconds later and my sister is on the other end. So what??

Some manifestations can appear trivial to us, but in fact it is guardian beings just doing their job. A voice says, "there is a man going to knock on the door," and a couple of minutes later there is a knock at the door and a rather overworked delivery man is standing there with a package. The guardians are just doing their job of warning you that a potential intruder or unexpected person is coming into your space.

Another manifestation of inner hearing is a call for help. One particularly stunning one that happened to me still makes me smile to this day. I was walking in the woods near my house, which is an ancient burial area and full of springs, standing stones etc. I was wandering about enjoying the rare spring sun, when I heard a distinct voice in my head saying "help me!" It was very insistent, and I presumed an animal was in distress, as they are pretty good at sending out signals.

I could not see anything that would be in potential distress, but the voice kept going. As I got to a pile of wood from trees that had been logged and harvested, the voice got stronger. Still I could not see anything. But I did notice a large piece of wood that felt really interesting. I like to work with such bits of wood for art etc., so I picked it up and as I picked it up the voice stopped. Because I am dumb, I did not equate the cessation of the voice with the large lump of wood in my arms. It was a slice of a very large tree, not a branch, but a slice of the trunk. I figured I could strip the bark off of it and use it to carve designs on.

I got the wood home and the moment I walked through the door, all of the spirits that live with me got very excited and started chattering. That should have alerted me, but it didn't: like I said, dumb. The day after, I started to strip the bark off the wood and a very clear "thank you" echoed around my head. Now I was really confused. I looked closer at the wood that was now debarked and my heart stopped.

In the natural shape of the wood was a young woman, with small breasts, a cloak, and a black face of very fine features. Wow! A tree spirit! I began to oil her to feed the wood, and to massage her body. "Turn me around" rang through my head. So I turned her around and did one of those cartoon gulps. On the other side of the young woman was a shape made up of wood scar regrowth, and the shape was very clear, very defined and very detailed. In the wood was an old woman, her sagging stomach, her old face, her long thing legs that ended in hooves instead of feet.

I then finally realised what I had brought home. She was a natural image manifestation of the most important ancient goddess of this ancient land of Britain. This was the Cailleach, the ancient goddess of the land who shows herself in spring and summer as a strong young woman, and in autumn and winter as an old hag.

This naturally-formed image would allow that consciousness to interface with me, and I could work with her to help bring balance to this localised area. Since that time she has become very vocal, very protective and is teaching me a great deal. So the first step is to learn to listen and act. At first you will not be able to distinguish what is going on, but you must learn not to dismiss, but rather to listen, regardless of whether you think it is your mind or an outside being. First just learn to listen; discernment comes later.

2. Inner sight

Inner sight, like inner hearing, can manifest in a number of ways.

The most common manifestation is looking at something solid, like a human, but seeing things that are not apparent to the normal human. So for example, looking at someone who looks beautiful and healthy, but seeing them as ugly or sick: you cannot understand why people think they look great. What is often happening here is that the inner and outer sight are overlaying each other and the brain processes both lots of information as coming from one source (i.e. your optic nerve).

The other way that inner sight can manifest is seeing something supposedly solid that is not there, or is not seen by others. A common example is someone seeing a building in the distance, looking away, looking back, and finding that the building has vanished. Sometimes the person is seeing the 'inner building' or ghost of a building that was once there, or they are seeing a building that exists only on the inner planes. This has been described in detail by people around the world.

A striking example is a group of people out on a hike in Iceland. They paused at the top of a hill and all pointed at an unusual-looking strange coloured house that seemed to be in the middle of nowhere. The group began to walk towards it, and as the path took them out of view of the house, and then back in to view from behind trees, the house vanished. The men presumed it was some sort of 'snow mirage' until later they found that many people had indeed seen this house over the years, and it was considered locally as a house of the Huddle Folk (faery beings).

Sometimes people with inner sight will look at something and it just doesn't look right; that is usually because there is in fact something wrong with what they are looking at. Deeper skills with inner sight allow people to 'see' beyond barriers, blocks, or walls. This is a stranger form of inner sight and it takes some time to develop.

Personally I think it is a form of passive remote viewing as opposed to actual plain inner sight, as though the spirit or consciousness of a person can move ahead of the body and perceive what is behind something. Sometimes it is a deeper skill, less of a 'sight' and more of a 'feeling.' It doesn't mean that someone can stare at a building and see everything inside it – life is not a sci-fi movie! But it does mean that someone with inner sight who is searching for say, a missing child, will be able to look at a building and ascertain whether that child is in the building or not. They will 'see' the light of the life force of the child in the building.

As the magician works with various experiments and exercises, they will find their own unique expression of the inner sight. Mine seems to work almost exclusively in tandem with my actual eyes, so sometimes I can have great difficulty in separating out what I am seeing with my outer eyes and what I am seeing with my inner sight.

3. Inner touch and smell

These are the most common inner senses and tend to be something that almost everybody has to some degree. Something will just not feel right when it is touched, or something or some place will smell bad (and there are no drain issues, farting dogs, etc.). This can develop into learning how to recognise certain beings by their signature smell, or to know when something is energetically unhealthy by the horrible feel of it.

Sometimes the sense of inner touch doesn't work through the hands, but the hands trigger it. So for example a person picks up an object that has really bad energy attached to it, maybe a knife used to kill someone (extreme example!). Upon touching the object, the person feels horrible, panicked, dirty, or has flashes of images appearing in their imagination of people being hurt. The touch triggers deeper senses. These two senses are not only the most common, but are the easiest to train into usable skills for magic.

4. Dreams

The issue of dreams spans different avenues of magic, and they manifest as different types of dreams. Dreams that come from our inner senses kicking into action tell us what is happening to or threatening our bodies, if something magical is threatening us, or if an inner contact, dead person or being is trying to communicate with us.

Threat dreams are the most common, and the key is in the interpretation. Inner senses working through our dreams are usually the purest form in which our inner senses manifest: when we dream, our conscious minds are in a passive state, so deeper senses can rise to the surface. Bear in mind that our dreams also process everyday things and are involved in brain filing and reorganising, so not every vivid dream is an inner senses dream.

Threats to the body such as infection, physical or psychic intruders, or impending accidents trigger vivid dreams that can often be confounding if one does not know how to read them. If the body is infected with a virus or bacteria that also has a consciousness (not all do, but some do), we can dream of struggling with a person who is being aggressive. These dreams often rise to the surface once we have begun chemical treatment for the illness, or when our immune systems are getting the upper hand.

When we are not doing well in the infection battle, the consciousness of the infection stays hidden from us and we just feel very sick. But once the infection is weakened, its 'cloaking mechanism' fails and we start to 'see' it: this often appears in dreams as battling with a person or an animal or even a strange being (viruses often appear as bizarre looking beings). It is important to take note of what you see, as it can give you clues as to how to speed up the recovery and prevent reinfection. Using magic to take the inner power out of an outer infection is a skill you will learn later in the course.

If you are under threat from an intruder, particularly if you have spirit guardians working with you, you will be alerted in your dreams by being shown the intruder, and often you will find that you are awoken suddenly in order to deal with the threat. If this happens repeatedly, you need to ascertain if it is a physical intruder stalking around the outside of your home, or if it is a magical or spirit intruder that has been sent magically. To differentiate, you can use tarot to pinpoint what type of intruder it is, and also what their intentions are. Again, these are skills you will learn later in the course, once you have acquired the necessary interpretation skills.

5. Precognition

Most of us are already familiar with the idea of precognition, so there is no need to go into depth, and this lesson is already long enough. Precognition can range from full flashes of dangerous future events which are either processed by inner sight (you see a scene unfolding), or in dreams (the same thing basically, just triggering in sleep), to a strong but indefinable sense that something will happen. Sometimes it is combinations of these, if the risk is great.

One weird aspect of precognition is that not only do precogs get warnings of dangers, they also get warnings of completely trivial events. The precognition itself can be quite strong and spectacular, but the event that is predicted is often as silly as "a green car will drive past at exactly 10.31am with an old woman driving." Really…? Sure enough, at 10.31am precisely, a green car driven by an old lady lumbers past. What the hell was that all about?

Okay, that is enough background information for you on all the different types of inner senses; now it is time to roll your sleeves up and get to work.

6. *Task:* Inner touch

Do this during the daytime when you are not tired and have time to be able to not rush this exercise. You are going to go to different stores that sell used goods. Different types of stores will give you different experiences. Before you go out of the door, wash your hands really well with liquid soap[1] and a spoonful of plain cooking salt. When your hands are dry, how do they feel? Do they feel very clean and smooth?

When you go out, take with you a bag of salt, a small bottle of liquid soap, a small clean towel or teatowel to dry your hands, a coursework notebook[2] and pen, and a large bottle of water with you. Plan to visit a charity/thrift store, and then an antique store,

---

[1] Use one that is not heavily perfumed and that is not antibacterial, or use a plain, unperfumed soap bar.
[2] Keep a set of notebooks for your course notes.

the more upmarket the better. Before you go into each store, pour some liquid soap, some salt and then water into your hands and wash them so that they are clean.

Go to the thrift/charity store first. If you can, pick one in a poor area. Walk around the whole store: look at the various shelves, racks, etc. and see if anything really jumps out at you. If it does, pick it up and handle it. As you handle it, still yourself and then feel into your emotions: how do your feelings change, if at all? If they do change, it may be very subtle, so learn to listen carefully.

Then put the object down. Move away and feel your hands: how do they feel? Pick up random objects (not clothing, that is coming) and do the same thing again. How do your emotions feel? How do your hands feel when you have put them down? Do they feel sticky, or rough, or wrong in any way? Now it is time to go through the clothing. Feel through the clothing, hold the clothing out: what do you feel? How do your hands feel? How does your body feel? Does anything give you a headache or make you slightly nauseous? Test different selections of clothing of different sizes, and feel the difference between young/teen clothing and clothing that is obviously for elderly people.

Remember the various feelings and when you leave the store, clean your hands again with the soap, salt, and water, and then notice the difference. Now write down your findings. What were the differences between objects and clothing? What were the differences between various age groups of clothing? If you got nothing at all, then simply write that down in your notebook. If anything gave you a headache or made you feel strange, a cup of coffee with some sugar will usually stop it.

Now it is time to go to an antique store. Go to a nice one that is not cluttered and is more on the pricey side. Do exactly the same exercise: pick up things, see how they make you feel physically and emotionally, and see how they make your hands feel. See if there is a difference between non-personal items and things that people would have kept close to them. Write down your findings after cleaning your hands.

The third part of the exercise is to go to a decent clothing store that sells new clothing. Run your hands through the clothing and see if they make your hands feel different, or if they remain the same. Remember how new clothing feels. Finally, go back to the thrift/charity store or go to a different one and run your hands through the clothing again and handle various types of clothing. Remember how it makes your hands feel. Wash your hands and then write down your findings.

7. *Task:* Inner sense – feeling power patterns

We are often confronted by inner power patterns that are magically or psychologically constructed on purpose to achieve an aim. It is important to be able to spot these patterns using your inner senses. Most people would be shocked to know the amount of large companies and corporations that use psychology, chemistry or even magic to manipulate the customer. (More than you would think... I know, I have worked for a few in my more stupid past.)

Again this is an exercise of shopping. Have a day set aside when you can do this without having to rush around. Choose a small independent café, a corporate food chain, a large chain clothing store that has a niche market, a small indie clothing store, a high end health food supermarket, and then an ordinary supermarket. What you are looking for is a lot more subtle than your thrift store experience, so pay attention. Take with you a notebook and pen.

First go to a small independent café and have a drink and a snack so that you have something in your stomach (this bit is important). Sit very calmly with no screen in front of you, just your notebook, and watch people come and go. What is the base atmosphere of the café? Do you feel any particular urge to eat more? Do you feel any stress reactions? Or do you feel calm, relaxed, and happy with what you have? As you watch the people come and go, what is your first impression of them emotively? Write down your findings.

When you are ready to leave, go straight to a corporate food chain outlet, buy only a drink, and go sit down. Still yourself and place your notebook before you. How do you feel? Do you feel the urge to get something to eat even though you have just eaten something? Or are you fine? Do you feel relaxed or do you feel alert and watchful? Is there any shift in your emotions?

Look at the people (without looking like a crazy person), and then look down at your notebook but 'feel into' the person. How do they feel? Do they feel stressed or relaxed, do they feel strange? Do they look strange? Write down your findings and anything else you observe that catches your interest. The key is to be still: recover that stillness feeling from your meditations, remember what it feels like so that you become still: the inner senses work much better in stillness.

Now it is time to go around the shops. Feel the subtle differences between the high energy corporate niche stores, and the small independent stores. How do the high end places make you feel? Do you want to spend money even though you do not need something? Is there a difference in those feelings when you visit a small store? How does your subtle energy react to the big stores as opposed to the little ones? Do the mega health stores make you want to buy lots of things, whereas a small one does not have the same effect? Write down your findings.

Remember, there are no right or wrong answers, and there is nothing to prove. This is about learning how places make you feel in a subtle way that you might not have noticed in the past. You are training yourself to pay attention, and to spot the feel of different patterns used in marketing and sales. Some major companies use psychology and chemistry (smells) to entice people to buy or to want. Such use often opens up patterns that inner power can flow into, which in turn makes it stronger. Sometimes this is accidental, and sometimes this is intentional. Some mega health stores use a small group who meditate and project a pattern onto a store to encourage people to want to stay longer and buy more. It is a subtle form of magical manipulation. I have come across some major companies that use all out magic to influence their customers. Naughty.

Through these exercises, you will learn to feel that subtle manipulation, be it magical or psychological, or even working by triggering your brain chemistry (smells). Being aware is usually enough to obviate its effects upon you, or at least allow you to override the effects and ignore them.

Keep all your notes in your journal so that you can look back over them in the future. Looking back over old journals, adding in comments or updates on observations or things you have since learned, are all valuable to your path as a magician.

8. *Task:* Inner and outer boundaries

Learning how to recognise and establish inner and outer boundaries is very important for a magician's overall safety. Just as in life we have our own personal space and house space, so too does the spirit. Learning to work with your own boundaries is a sideways method for triggering inner senses that relate to 'early warning systems.' Such warnings can work through a variety of the inner senses, and through this work you will learn to distinguish communications with the land and inner beings around you, along with learning how to recognise your own inner radar system.

Go out of your house. Take your journal or notebook with you and a compass. Walk around the boundary of the property where you live, and then go stand before your front door. If you live in an apartment building, walk around the building and then stand before your own front door. If you live in the country and a patch of land is part of your property, walk first around the boundary of the property, and the around the house itself.

As you walk around the boundary, look closely at what is naturally occurring around the boundary: look at what trees are there, how old they are, what plants are growing naturally, even between cracks in the pavement (nettles, wild garlic, etc.), any rock outcrops, wells, springs, watercourses like rivers or ponds, or drains, and if there are any hills or mountains nearby. Also look at what man-made things are around your boundary like electrical transformers or substations, churches, temples, factories, schools, etc. Write all of them down in your journal. Also look to see if any of the buildings have carved faces or images, gargoyles (they appear in the weirdest places) and statues.

Now it is time to go and look at your front door. Stand in front of it and look closely. Are any spiders living around your door? Do you have a face on a door knocker? Do any animals like dogs or cats regularly sleep by your front door? Write down everything you observe.

If your front door is not inside a building, turn around and look at what is directly opposite your front door. Is it someone else's front door? Is it a building, a tree, a fast-moving river or a gentle stream? Write everything down and then draw a map in your journal of the boundary. Mark down the directions, which direction your front door faces, where spiders, trees, water, rocks, key buildings are, etc.

Now walk the boundary again with the map and stop at every key natural feature. Stand before them and quieten yourself. What does that feature 'feel' like? Listen to your own inner senses, emotions and thoughts. Do any of the natural features cause a subtle shift in how you feel? Write down on your map a key word that would describe that shift. Take your time with this. It may take a few times of walking the boundary and visiting these natural features before you begin to sense them.

Once you have visited the natural features, go around again and talk to each one in turn. Talk in your mind and also with your voice (unless there is a real risk of being dragged off for being a nutter), say hello, introduce yourself, ask if they need anything, tell them where you live. Treat everything as if it had a consciousness, even the rocks, the rivers, the spiders: talk to everything.

Do the same for any outstanding man-made structures like churches, carvings, statues, fences: talk to everything. What you are doing is opening lines of communication to the beings that live around you, alerting them to the fact that you are willing to acknowledge them, listen to them and work with them. If you find rocks that appear to have faces in them, ask one if you can place it by your front door as a guardian.

Everything has the potential to talk back to you, but opening those lines of communications in a human that has been shut down can take practice. For others it triggers quickly and easily. For example stones themselves do not talk, but beings that live within or around them do. By talking to the stone, you are opening a doorway for communication. And the act of talking to everything and anything begins to loosen your ability to hear inner sounds: you learn to blur your own boundaries so that other consciousnesses can communicate with you.

Spend five minutes each night sitting quietly or lying in bed, and in your mind, go around the boundary, check each feature that you have been talking to, any door spiders (they are wonderful early warning systems for magicians), rocks, trees. In your mind, go to each one and say goodnight and ask them to alert you if an intruder crosses into your territory. If you live in an apartment block, focus the boundary checks on two levels: the first being the outer boundary of the building. Just ask them to alert you to any human or being with violent intent. And talk to any features on your front door and ask to be alerted if anyone approaches it. Having a door knocker with a face, creature or lion on it makes it easier. You can talk to the face and ask it to watch over the door. When you talk to man-made images like that, you are creating a subtle link with the image and your own consciousness: it is the first stage of creating a thought form. You slowly learn how to use the face as an extension of your own consciousness.

Walk the boundaries and say hello to all the features at least three times a week. The rest of the week, use your mind to check in with the features at night before you go to sleep. This slowly builds up a pattern of consciousness so that when something is coming that is a potential threat, the features will communicate back to you.

This can come in the form of a sudden 'feeling' that something is not right, or a voice in your mind saying, 'intruder,' or you will get a sudden flash out of the blue in your mind of a specific feature.

You may suddenly see the tree you talk to at the back of your house: it may appear in your mind suddenly for no apparent reason. What is happening is that the tree is communicating with you to tell you that something is coming that is a potential threat. It may be an intruder, but trees also warn about earthquakes, dangerous storms or magical attacks. If your communication is from an old tree, and the warning is about an impending earthquake, just remember that their measure of time is very different from ours. 'Immediate' to them could mean in the next couple of weeks.

If you get such a warning about an impending natural disaster, just make sure your house is ready for an earthquake and that you have a supply box ready, or make sure you have an emergency water/food/flash-light supply ready and up-to-date. If you get an intruder warning out of the blue and it is night time, switch all of the lights on immediately and make sure you have a phone to hand: that is often enough to deter someone or something intending to intrude.

The other extension of this boundary-keeping which triggers your inner senses is to have a night-time routine that you do (regardless of what anyone else in the household does) of checking locked doors and windows. As you check them, have an image in your mind of you sealing that window or door with a line of dark blue light. Again, this builds up an inner boundary and wards off physical or spirit intruders.

Ensure that the natural features you work with have what they need. If it is a tree, hang a bird feeder in it (trees and birds have a wonderful symbiotic relationship). Water a plant or bush or weed, touch a stone: learn to tend them as well as talk to them. So if they need something in return, they will let you know. Learn to listen and see with your mind as well as your ears and eyes. Write down occurrences, events and feelings that trigger into your journal.

Lesson 6
Sacred Language & Magical Scripts

There is a great deal of misunderstanding in the modern magical world when it comes to magical scripts and sacred languages, and it is crucial that magicians have a basic understanding of the origins, history and early use of these scripts as well as learning what works, what doesn't, what should not be worked with and why.

Basically this topic divides into two categories: magical script and sacred sound (the root of sacred language). Let's have a brief look at the magical scripts first. Before you read any further, go to a search engine on the web and look up the following scripts.

Look up examples of the following alphabets (Wikipedia is a good source for public domain images): *Malachim*, *Celestial*, *Passing the River*, and *Enochian*. Once you have downloaded them or pulled them up on screen, look at each script individually so that you get an idea of their styles, forms, similarities, and differences.

Now do a search and look up the alphabet for *Tifinagh*, which is a North African Berber script. Have a good look at it. And then finally, look up the *Hebrew* alphabet and also *Paleo Hebrew*. Once more, sit and have a good look at them.

Now you should have a basic idea of what magical scripts look like, and also what Hebrew and Paleo Hebrew looks like, so that when you read about the evolution of these scripts, you can see some of the history of these scripts seeping through the images. Most magical scripts in use by magicians today date back to the early to mid-16th century, with a smattering emerging in the 15th century. The following lesson will highlight to you just how important it is for the magician to have a solid background knowledge of history, which in turn allows for more discernment.

1. Magical Scripts and the 16th Century

From the late 15th century to the end of the 16th century in Europe was a peak time for magical texts, scripts and early books. But to understand those scripts and books, it is important to understand the culture of the period that these things emerged from. It was also a time when magical scripts, ciphers, and codes were the height of fashion.

It was a time of major change in Europe on lots of fronts, but some of the key ingredients that led to the emergence of these scripts and books was the expulsion of Jews from Spain and Portugal in the 15th century, and the fall of Constantinople in AD 1453. The Fall of Constantinople, the centre of the Byzantine empire, triggered an exodus of Greek Scholars to the Italian city states. They brought with them their extensive knowledge, books and documents.

The Jews that were expelled took with them their own cultural and religious knowledge. Some fled to Turkey, some fled to North Africa, and some moved to various regions in Europe including, most crucially, the Italian city states. Many Jews passed through northern Africa before moving into northern Italy, and these migrations resulted in various cross-fertilisation between languages and culture.

It was during this fertile time that early books on Kabbalah and on magic began to emerge. The Kabbalists in the Italian city states were rubbing shoulders with astrologers and alchemists, and the rise in interest in mystical magical texts was becoming very fashionable in the major European cities, and in particular the Italian city states and London. It would have been fascinating for the European Christian-based magicians, who drew heavily upon Greco-Roman texts some of which were brought to Europe by the fleeing Greek scholars, to come across Kabbalist magicians who used a mystical written language that would have looked completely alien to them. These Jewish Kabbalists would also have been familiar with Tifinagh from North Africa.

So our first ingredients are European magicians working from fragments of Greek, Alexandrian and Roman texts within a Christianised cultural format, and Jewish Kabbalists who used a sacred script magically, and who also knew a very alien-looking script they learned in North Africa.

Our second ingredient is a wish for power. Many of the Jewish communities in northern Italy and northern Europe lived under the constant threat of expulsion. In Venice, for example, they lived with heavy trade restrictions and were forced to live in a particular area of the city known as the Venetian Ghetto.

It was also a time of the emergence of the *Sculo*, or confraternities in Venice for the lower and middle classes, based upon their trade skills. These confraternities were highly ritualised and ceremonial, giving the merchant classes a sense of importance, identity and involvement. This was very necessary in order to maintain peace and control in the city: many cities were well aware of the peasant revolts that had happened in England in the previous century.

It is important to really understand these ingredients, as they cast a light on the shadowy world of 'special magicians' from that time. It was a time when being seen to belong to an order or fraternity that used secrecy, ritual, and special signs was a sign of someone who was doing well, a person to be respected and looked up to. In a time when not having status or money meant that you were condemned to a brutal life of extreme poverty and hardship, there was a massive incentive to be seen to be doing well, to being knowledgeable and in control of one's life.

The ritual element of the confraternities would have triggered an overall interest in ritual, which in turn would have encouraged these middle class merchants to seek out magicians to get an 'edge' on their business success. As we all know, demand creates a scramble to supply, and these cities soon had a few notable magicians that people would consult.

And do not forget that at this time people (particularly the merchant class and nobility) were travelling quite a lot from place to place, picking up bits, passing bits on, gossiping; doing what humans do. Soon it would have been a struggle to stand out as the best, and magicians would have taken advantage of the cross-pollination that was happening between themselves and the Kabbalists in order to gain magical knowledge and skills that others did not have.

The magicians watched the Kabbalists use a sacred language that the magicians could not penetrate: the Kabbalists used their magic seemingly for protection, money, status and health. And they always seemed to do well. So the magicians needed their own sacred secret magical language. Just as now, in those days there were honourable people and not so honourable people, there were drama queens, pedestal-standers, snake oil salesmen, the clueless, the clever con artists, and the few genuine folks. People were discovering 'secret ancient texts' all over the place, and were being channelled magical scripts from 'angels' (Enochian, Malachim, etc.).

Soon we had a mix emerging that consisted of fragmented Greco-Roman magic, Christian overlays, astrology, Kabbalah, Hebrew, Tifinagh, early mystical texts, and god knows what else thrown into the pot... pots which ended up presented as ancient texts such as *The Keys of Solomon*. People needed a recipe book that could be shown to be the font of all magical knowledge: a magician could walk into a royal or noble court, quietly infer that they had the magical secrets of wealth, power and happiness, secrets which those who were totally fascinated by such subject matter would have paid a truly princely sum to get their hands on. Those recipe books also had great street cred for any magician known to have one – and also to be able to read it.

Now this is where we step back a bit, and we have to tread cautiously. These books and scripts are still in use today and they are very fashionable indeed. (History always repeats itself, which is why it is good to learn history... you spot the same patterns.) Can you make these books work? To a lesser degree yes, and to a greater degree no. Some were written very cleverly with a layer of genuine and powerful magic hidden beneath an overlay of nonsense. Yet within the nonsense, clues were hidden for the true magician to find and open up the true magic within the book.

As a magical student, you need to be very aware as to why these scripts work a little bit and not a lot; you need to learn the mechanics of how these scripts operate. Later as an adept, you will learn how to spot the clues that are hidden within some of the grimoires, that reveal a hidden depth of true magic. Now that you know the historical background of why and how they emerged, you can put to one side the glamorous idea that they are indeed scripts from angels, and we can look at how scripts that were created this way can be triggered in magic.

2. Creating Patterns

When a script is created and then put to use, if it is done without an inner construction it will not work at first. But if it is repeatedly used over a period of time, and used in exactly the same way, a pattern is created that power can flow through. If the pattern is not magically constructed, the 'gateway' for power and communication builds slowly over time in a natural way and is similar to the idea of engramming that you were introduced to in an early lesson.

Actions repeated in exactly the same way, with intent, over a period of time, create a doorway that power can flow into. Most magical scripts, though not all, were haphazardly created and often for more economic and political reasons than magical ones – Enochian being a prime example. But their repeated use over long period of time triggered a doorway to emerge.

This haphazard construction is not without problems: when a doorway is created in this way, the magician has no control over what passes through that doorway. The idea that a name of a being will force that being to pass through or communicate through that script is a fallacy; more often that not what passes through these doorways are opportunistic low-level beings that are parasitical in nature. These beings will cooperate with the magician, but often at high long-term cost: the parasite's only reason for cooperation is a meal of energy, usually the energy of the magician.

If the magician has a good idea of what they are doing, and uses symbols that are already engrammed to actions connected to specific powers or deities, then the script can work, albeit in a haphazard way. Sometimes this can result in brilliant breakthroughs, though they are often unpredictable. Why is this? Often problems and instabilities in scripts occur because the magician is not aware of the difference between a functional sigil or symbol, and a letter that is magically tied into sound (which is sacred language, and we will look at that in a moment).

3. Magical Symbols

Let's have a look at an ancient symbol that appears in a 16th century magical script called Malachim that was created by Heinrich Cornelius Agrippa and appeared in his writings '*Book III Occult Philosophy*' (1510). The ancient symbol is used for the letter Samech and is a symbol that is an X with a line going down the middle of the X. In the Malachim script this represents the letter S and it is used in the script as an alphabet letter. The letter S in Malachim derives from the Hebrew letter Samech, and as you look at the Malachim script you can spot the use of Hebrew and Greek letter shapes as a basis for the created letters or sigils.

A lot of magicians who use Malachim use it as an alphabet, but in truth, it has fragments of functional sigils within it. Samach is a power of foundation, support, and upholding something. The shape stripped down is a foundational shape that was sometimes used as a mason mark in ancient Egypt, and is also the skeleton of the Flower of Life pattern. The Flower of Life pattern has appeared in a variety of cultures around the world, including on the wall of the Osirion at the sacred compound of Abydos in Egypt.

This symbol is very ancient indeed, and is a root pattern that is deeply connected to the more modern Metatron Cube, a Kabbalistic pattern that is about creation. When used magically, it is an anchor or foundation stone in magical construction. But what it is not is a sound in magical terms. When used in written script in order to construct a magical sentence, the use of this image acts a block of stone which will stop the flow of power. So it is counterproductive to use it in magical script that is meant for forming words.

When used properly, this symbol has such a strong magical effect simply because it is like a 'prime' symbol that has been used for thousands of years in a very tuned and knowledgeable way. Using it as an anchor or foundation stone in magical construction would ensure that the base of the construction is very solid and connected into true magical patterns that in turn would filter out parasite infestation.

So you can see how using these symbols properly can be powerful indeed, but using them without knowledge can be very counterproductive. By looking closely at so called 'powerful grimoires' you will be able to recognise which ones are indeed working with true magical knowledge and which ones are not. As an aside, in true magical grimoires, the incantations and spells are usually not actually a part of the magic; rather they are blind alleys put in to protect the magic. A true magician will know how to operate the grimoire, whereas an interloper will blindly follow the incantations, usually to limited success.

4. SIGILS

Sigils are essentially signs that a magician makes to connect with a very specific power. To work the most powerfully with sigils, the magician connects with the power using inner vision and visionary ritual, and then forms a sigil that becomes a 'signature' mark that allows the power to flow through it into a text or object. When you come to do *Module II Lesson 1*, you will do a directional ritual pattern. When you have finished that lesson, draw out the shape of your movements around the directions. That pattern will show you a sigil: that is the sigil of that specific ritual. I will not mention it in the lesson, so take note now and remember. It is the sigil for that specific power action. Whenever you see that sigil in ancient text (not 16th century), you will know that a similar power dynamic is at play.

Copying sigils created by other magicians only works if you are connecting from an inner magical perspective to the same power with the same level of communication. A properly crafted sigil is like a vessel that power can flow into, and over time it becomes a container for a specific power, activating action and communication. These days the use of sigils in some areas of magic has devolved down to fashion and glamour. But there are some magicians who work very powerfully with sigils to weave lines of connection and power into the sign.

5. Sacred language and utterance

True sacred magical language is rare indeed, simply because it takes so much to fully construct one, often taking generations, and requires a magician of a high skill level and deep mystical knowledge.

An example of a true sacred magical language is Hebrew, and another survivor is Egyptian Hieroglyphs. They work on a surface level in very different ways, but their underlying structural construction and use is the same. Both work with magical sound and vibration, and the use of image as a doorway.

Hebrew

In Hebrew, each letter is a root sound and has a connected utterance. These root sounds and the use of them in utterance is compatible with the frequencies of angelic thresholds (something you will learn about in another module). Angelic beings are triggered by, and operate with specific sounds or frequencies of sound that activate them to a specific action. That action is usually holding a door open for Divinity to flow through in one filtered form (Names) or another. The sounds themselves are learned and acquired through deep visionary work, and the symbols connected to them are then created by the consciousness of man in order to convey the sound.

The actual symbols of the Hebrew letters are magically constructed to be interfaces for those sounds, so combining the letters in a script will trigger a magical action in the same way that combining the sounds would. However, the use of the script is like a computer program that runs automatically, whereas the actual utterance of the sounds in the right way, in the right combination, and with the right inner resonance will open a doorway far wider and deeper than the simple use of the script would.

The ingredient that creates that depth of action is the living breath of a human being. But someone who does not have deep inner connection will not be able to reproduce the same level of power from the use of the sounds that a properly trained Jewish Kabbalist would. And that again protects the magic, and protects the outsider or dabbler from their own stupidity. The use of magical recitation with Hebrew is very much the domain of a specific mystical element of a religion: it is not a plaything to experiment with.

When these sacred languages, or Divine sounds, are used repeatedly in a consecrated space, it creates and upholds a constant flow of Divine power into a space: the fabric of the building absorbs the vibration which in turn keeps the space sacred and powerful. The Jewish Kabbalist would use Hebrew in complex patterns, the magician would use Divine sounds that are not connected to languages.

Hieroglyphs

Egyptian hieroglyphs work in a very similar way, but also have included within them specific deity images and symbols that help to filter and tune the use of sacred sound. The utterances along with the deity symbols would ensure a constant presence of the deities in a temple or tomb space, and not only would they instruct the priests, but they would also create a powerful inner construct that vast powers can flow through.

Walking around some of these temples still embedded with the sounds and images is a truly remarkable magical experience. Even after thousands of years, these spaces still work powerfully and will trigger if a magician who has inner connection walks into the space.

6. Translations of sacred languages

This is where magicians frequently trip up. You cannot translate and then use a magical sacred language in your own tongue. It would be akin to buying a diesel car and putting petrol in it. It just does not work, and more than that, it triggers a blind loop to trap magicians in a dead end. This is a defence mechanism in magic and is also a part of a magician's development: if magicians do not stay focused, they are often led down blind alleys that lead to dead ends.

Let's have a look at an example. A common one is whereby a Western magician attempts to access the powers that flow through Jewish Kabbalah in order to do 'results magic' or 'psychology magic.' Jewish Kabbalah in its real form is a deep, powerful, and mystical interface with Divinity, designed and used by a specific people; it does not find parking spaces for you. The magician translates the Hebrew words into English and then uses them in ritual and magical scripts. The first thing that happens is that when you take a sacred name in Hebrew and translate it into English, all you get is the outer meaning of the word. It will have no power, no inner connection, and will not create an interface.

So for example, the magician focuses upon the word *Netzach*, which is the name of a Sefirot on the Tree of Life. The use of the word Netzach in Jewish Kabbalah roughly equates to victory or endurance (victory through endurance). The use of the Hebrew letters that make up the word Netzach, when used magically by a Jewish Kabbalist, will trigger a flow of power into the life of the person that will teach him or her the wisdom that strength comes from endurance. It will literally trigger situations around the person that gives the opportunity to grow strong through constant struggle: not something that most magicians would choose to do.

The letters can also be used magically when life is throwing buckets full of shit at the Kabbalist in a seemingly endless fashion. It does not stop the buckets being thrown, but it helps the Kabbalist engage the power of Netzach to learn how to endure, be victorious, and consequently become strong and knowledgeable by overcoming adversity.

But the ability to use the words in such a way comes from the Kabbalist's deep understanding and knowledge of the Torah, of the sacred language, and how to work with it mystically.

If a Western magician converts the word into English and uses Tree of Life patterns with the English translations, then all that happens is that you learn the outer names and qualities of the Sefirot, but any engagement directly with that power is simply a psychological engagement with the self. That is something very different and is not a magical use *per se*. The deeper powers and angelic beings that flow through that Sefirot are not engaged and are not working with intent through and with the magician.

This in turn triggers a pattern of behaviour whereby the Tree and the Sefirot (through the use of translated names) become puzzles that the magician tries to unlock, and the magician can spend years going around in circles trying to intellectualise the use of these powers. They are not puzzles to be deciphered, nor are they psychological pointers; they are living breathing powers in their own right and must be respected.

This course will have no Kabbalah in it at face value or in terms of Jewish Kabbalistic language, as it is not necessary nor do I think it is appropriate. It has been very fashionable since the nineteenth century to have aspects of Hebrew and Kabbalah in magic, and I for one also ran with that for the longest time. It took me a while to learn that it is not necessary for a full magical education, as you will eventually find out – Kabbalah is religious mystical language that is used to engage with Divine powers in order to understand, to commune, to learn and to perfect oneself. There other languages for the same thing.

You will learn how to work with the powers and dynamics that underpin these sacred patterns and languages: it is important for magic to move forward in development, not constantly be stepping backwards and co-opting religious structures you are not connected to. It is important, however, for the magician to understand these sacred languages, where they come from, how they are used, and how they are misused. You cannot change them, co-opt them, or dabble with them.

To develop as a true mystical magician you must learn about sacred sound in a Divine but non-religious way. It is important to understand the dynamic behind sacred languages and how mystical sounds, directed utterance, etc. works, and learn about them in a way that forges forward into the future.

There are sounds that trigger actions, and the magician creates images that vibrate with the sounds. Those sounds are angelic calls and true angelic 'language.' Be very clear about this before you begin to step into magical work using sacred sound: know the difference between sacred language, magical symbols, and language that conveys meanings. They are all completely different things in terms of magical work and use.

7. Sound and symbol in magical action

Briefly, the combinations would be used like this. The magician is constructing a ritual patterned image to trigger a magical action or response. The magician uses sacred sound (the root principle of a sacred language) to connect the work to specific angelic beings who will be the triggers and doorways for the power. That sound will have a sigil or letter that the sound is magically connected to. A magical symbol or sigil (such as the one we looked at earlier) is placed strategically to be an anchor or foundation stone for the ritual action.

The magician then includes magical symbols that are doorways for specific beings, be they deities, Underworld beings, or guardians. Then the magician adds in words that denote specific actions (the intent of the ritual). These letters and symbols are then encased in an overarching symbol that is a vessel, the hexagram is the most often used container as the image is literally a container that allows power to flow in and out in a balanced way.

Once it is completed, the magician then uses the calls for the angelic thresholds using the sacred utterance, and while calling, the magician is also working in inner vision to bridge the connection between the inner beings and the outer pattern. The magician then uses their own everyday language to communicate with the beings triggered by the ritual action: this ensures that everyone involved knows what is happening, what is being asked for, and why. The everyday language by the magician is only used to communicate individual requests, interactions, and intentions.

So you begin to see how these grimoires were originally constructed, and why it is so easy to spot a fake one. The ones that have come down to us from the 16th century are more often than not fake and are people's attempts at that time to mimic what they perceived as being powerful magic. The fakes were also often peddled simply to make money by selling them to rich but clueless nobles. So now that you are aware of the differences, it is time to learn the beginnings of how to work with them.

8. Practical work

Coherence and foundation are important when you first start to learn how to work with sigils, symbols, and sound. As an apprentice in magic, you are not yet at the stage where you can fill these symbols or sigils with power, or use any sacred sound, but learning the foundation actions of using them will give you a platform of experiential learning that will prepare you and give you the necessary skills for later work.

When you are ready, you will learn how to fill these images with power, and how to work with the roots of magical utterance that is the foundation of all sacred language. Take plenty of notes during your exercises and experiments, as you will need to refer back to this lesson in the future in order to remember how you worked: you will learn half of the skill set now, and the rest later in the course.

9. Working with magical symbols: Pentagram, Hexagram, Cruciform

In relation to the use of your birth name in this exercise
Some people do not know their original birth name, in which case use the name that you were given. If you are transgender, it can cause a lot of soul searching and bring up unpleasant memories to use your birth name. However, this is not about your identity as an adult, it is about the fate pattern that formed around you at birth and for your first few months of life. It is a magically important part of you, regardless of gender, regardless of early trauma, and is something that should not be magically cast away. It becomes like a scar on your body that you survived. If you really struggle with this exercise, then write your birth name and underneath it write your current name. But for people who simply wish to forget their childhood and use a different name, or wish to use their magical name, do not do that. Later when you are magically more experienced you will realise why, and that the process you go through as a result of confronting that birth name is magically invaluable.

Draw out a pentagram. Have your notes from your ritual magic lesson that worked with the four directions and the powers that flow through those directions. The ritual exercises that you did in that lesson will now transfer onto paper so that you can see another way of working with the same technique and power.

Mark the head of the pentagram with the word 'South.' Now draw a line from the top of the pentagram to the bottom so that the line passes between the two legs and finishes below them. Mark the bottom of that line 'North.' Now draw a line from one arm of the pentagram to the other. Mark the left arm of the pentagram 'East' and the right arm 'West.'

Draw a small hexagram over the head of the pentagram. Draw a small cruciform (a cruciform is the same shape as a long sword with a horizontal cross hilt) in the 'hand' of the left arm of the pentagram, and a cup shape (half circle) in the right 'hand' of the pentagram. Draw an earth symbol at the bottom of the line, opposite the hexagram (circle with an equal-armed cross in it). Finally, draw a small circle in the centre of the pentagram.

Now write the words 'I will be' over the top of the head of the pentagram. Placing the words 'I will be' over the pentagram is the start of learning how to create a seal for the future. If English is not your first language, then use your first language expression for 'I will be.'

Underneath the earth sign at the bottom of the pentagram, write your family name (surname) that you were born with. On the left side of the pentagram, over the cruciform, write 'I give.' On the right side, over the cup, write, 'I receive.'

These words should be in your own first language (don't use English if it is your second language).

In the centre, write your own first name, the name that your mother called you. (so if you now use a middle name, but your mother used your first name, use your first name). Draw a circle around the whole thing to enclose it.

This is your seal in primary terms. The pentagram, which is badly misunderstood, is about Man, or the individual human that you are. The hexagram is Divinity; the pentagram is humanity. When you work with the seal of a human, it becomes the magical container that various magical acts can be connected to. Put this seal in a frame and place it somewhere where you can see it, but other people, like house visitors, would not. Make sure it is behind glass to protect it: you will be working with it.

In the future you will learn different applications for this seal: you will learn how to use sigils, hieroglyphs, and symbols in its construction, and how to use sound and inner vision to enliven it. But for now you are going to learn how it is you, and how to work with it as an expression of you. It can work as a stabiliser for you, and as a minor shield.

10. Working the pentagram

Stand in front of the image of your seal (hang it on the wall or prop it up on something). Look at it and fix the symbols in your mind. Hold your arms out to your sides so that you make a cruciform. Look at the hexagram at the head. This is the sign of Divinity that breathes down into your life. Say the words "I will be."

Now look at the earth sign, and say your surname (family birth name) and "I came from." Look at the cruciform in the left hand and say "I give," and then look at the cup in the right hand and say "I receive." Look at the centre of the pentacle and say "I am," and then your first name that is written in the centre.

Now close your eyes. See in your mind's eye the hexagram above you, and be aware that this is Divinity flowing down into creation, into you. See in your mind's eye the earth sign, your roots, and be aware that this is where you come from. See a sword in your left hand (holding the blade so it makes a cruciform shape) and a cup in your right hand. Imagine a small flame or spark in your centre, your vital force.

Hold those images, and imagine the sense of power flowing down into you from the stars above you, and power flowing into you from the earth beneath you. Imagine the sword and the cup, and your spark in the centre, and that your centre spark is the fulcrum between two scales, the sword on one side and the cup on the other: through actions that give and take in equal energy, you retain magical, energetic, and spiritual balance.

Do this exercise every day for a week. Should something happen to you in life that throws you, drains you, or stresses you, repeat this exercise. It is a basic shield and anchor for you. It will not protect you in the face of danger, but it will stabilise you and allow you to draw on your own inner power and the powers around you in a balanced way. This in turn helps you to act magically in a more efficient way when you are under threat.

The more you do this exercise, the more you will begin to make connections and gain awareness of certain symbols and their usage. Write those revelations down as they come to you, and take note of other things that rise into your mind in connection with this seal. Later you will learn how to work with it in more advanced ritual ways.

This exercise has taught you the beginning foundation of the combined use of everyday language, magical symbols, and magical patterns. In the second module of the Apprentice series, you will learn how to do some of these patterns in full rituals, most importantly the complete pentagram ritual and the complete hexagram ritual.

11. *Task:* An experiment

Get a large sheet of paper or a canvas, some acrylic paints, and a charcoal pencil. Paint a picture of yourself face on,[1] full length, with arms outstretched in the stance you used in the pentagram exercise. It does not need to be a major work of art: no one is going to see it.

Paint in a sword in your left hand and a bowl in your right hand. Now lightly draw the hexagram over your head and the earth sign between your feet, and a small spark of light in your centre. Trace the pentagram over your image with the charcoal.

Around your head, limbs and centre, and inside the pentagram, think about what colours would emanate around each limb/body part. There is no right or wrong answer, this is purely personal to you. Work instinctively, not intellectually, just put colour where you feel it should be. Paint it in and then sit back and look at it. What colours have been placed around you?

Now think about the health of your body and those limbs/body parts (arms, legs, head, centre). What do the colours tell you about what is going on in your own body? Do they seem to match? Is there any connection or not? Again, no right answers… You are learning to explore your own body's inner energies and their fluctuations. Think also about whether you are right handed or left handed. What magical tool (sword or cup) is in your dominant hand?

Think of the base energy movement attributes (give or receive) and how you are in your personality. Is there an imbalance? Giving and taking can be positive or negative in many different ways. Having a receiving quality as a dominant feature can mean either taking a lot, or putting up with a lot, like the saying, "I will take a lot of shit before I react and take action." Meditate upon this and see if there is any balance you need to restore in your life. Later you will learn how to use these different hands and qualities in specific magical actions.

---

[1] It will be a mirror image: the left arm in the image is your left arm as you face the image.

Lesson 7
Magical Protection

In this lesson we will look at the beginnings of basic magical protection: how it is used, when it should be used, and when it should not. We will also look at the wider issues pertinent to magical protection, to give you as a student a much deeper understanding of magical protection than is normally taught this early on in your training.

How to protect yourself magically is a major part of any magical training, but for the most part this sort of training tends to consist of 'recipe' magic (spells, rituals, talismans, etc.) to address specific situations, for example how to protect against another magician hurting you, how to protect yourself and your home from invasive spirits, etc. This approach to magical protection is commonplace and very few magicians actually stop to think past the recipe and look at the deeper and more long-term consequences. Throughout your magical life, there will of course be times when you need to protect yourself, your family, and your home by using magic, and throughout this course you will learn a variety of approaches and techniques so that you will have a wide range of skills to draw on for specific situations.

But before you learn how to protect yourself, you need to learn to distinguish between what are true dangers and what are not, and – most importantly – when not to protect yourself and why. The latter is complex, as complex as creation itself, but with some insight you will hopefully be able to make more informed choices. For the first part of this lesson we will look at the rarely considered or discussed peripheral issues that have a direct influence on magical protection. Then we will work practically with basic early-level protections that you can easily handle and not do yourself any harm with.

1. Threats and Saviours

Because of modern media, film, and TV, a lot of the Western world in general lives in a constant state of fear. We are told that there are threats around every corner, that our children must never go outside without supervision or an all-over body suit, and that if we go out at night the zombies will eat us.

The second lump of proverbial concrete around a person's neck is being raised in a religious country. Most American and English folks would not say they had a religious upbringing or that religion had affected their lives, but the subtle conditioning of a person's mind from birth within such a culture leaves its mark. It defines how we view the inner worlds, how we view magic, and it also defines what we fear.

We Westerners live in a heavily dualist society, with the angels, faeries, and good folks on one side, and the demons, spirits, devils, and evil people on the other.

However much a person may have risen above that childish view, some of it still sticks. And what sticks affects the magical training of a potential magician. So we need to look at that a bit closely, so that you fully understand exactly what really is a threat and what is not.

The first tripping point for people is our culture's lack of understanding of the difference between Divinity and deity. In Christian societies, 'God' is approached and thought of in a way that is actually deity worship, and not a direct connection with Divinity. So God is appealed to as you would appeal to a father, as though you were communicating with a human being, and when such an appeal is not answered, or something very bad happens, God is blamed or the person feels abandoned.

In a later module we will look in depth at the difference between deity and Divinity, and also at the many different types of beings that surround us. But for now, just keep an awareness that the way you think of religion is heavily coloured by your culture. Jesus is a deity. Divinity is Divinity: it has no religion, but flows through all of them. And this takes me to my second point, which it is important that I make before we go any further. And that is the validity of religions. Many pagans and non-Christian magicians are very hostile to Christianity, without really understanding what it is they are hostile to.

Religion is a pattern constructed by man in order to talk to Divinity. As a human construction all religions have great failings, but they also have sparks of Divine wonder within them, along with magical patterning. Various religions can become very useful to the magician, not in terms of worship, but in terms of operating systems. The true communion between Divinity and humanity is an individual relationship between a human and non-human Divinity.

But religions have within them various 'programs' that can be worked with in order to achieve something, usually protection. Think of religions as computer programs within an operating system, whose worshippers are often akin to the viruses, cookies, bugs, and god knows what else that slow that system down and make it inefficient: just think of the way people throughout history have used religion as an excuse, a prop, or a tool of status. But a magician can dodge past most of that and tap into the program itself to get a job done.

So do not discount using certain religious patterns for protection because of your dislike for religions. Through your training you will learn how to navigate such work without falling into traps or using obsolete techniques that leave you defenceless. The threats that most training magicians think about are ghosts, demons, and devils, with the odd evil magician thrown in for good measure. During the early part of your training, some of these (well, the ones that actually exist, not the fantasy versions) will generally not be a threat to you as you will still be very much 'below their radar' in magical terms.

The three most common threats to a budding magician are parasites (low-level beings that feed off people's emotions and energies), land beings that you happen to trigger and/or otherwise piss off by mistake, and predatory humans. Apart from these threats there is also something that is rarely thought of and addressed, but is very simple, and that is psychic dirt. This is decaying energy that is composting, and you can get covered in it if you are not careful. Some cities are full of it, as are some people. Think of psychic dirt in terms of excrement. If you don't have good personal hygiene; if you wallow in sewers and wash your hands in a toilet full of faeces, you will get sick.

The majority of magical protection, particularly at the early stages of magical training, consists of three things: stay clean, stay balanced, and stay alert. Those three things alone will keep you out of trouble. A fourth protection technique is an actual shield that you raise when there is real threat.

Later in training, you will learn many different methods of protection, as no one size fits all situations and you need to be ready to deal with anything that can potentially come along. But if you learn powerful shielding too early on in your training, you will not develop any magical muscle-power at all. You do not walk around in a bullet-proof all-over body suit in your everyday life, and you certainly don't need to do that in your magical life. So let's first have a look at staying clean. You have already started this process in your lesson on inner senses. Now you get the next step.

2. Getting clean and staying clean

You must never overuse any form of magical cleaning or protection, as this would begin to make you more vulnerable. Being exposed to some low-level threats helps to slowly build up your inner immune system, which is vital for every magician who wants to stay strong and healthy (just as a child needs to be exposed to certain types of viruses and bacteria).

Ritual cleaning can be used more often than protection, and use your common sense when it comes to how often you use it. If you have been into a city or a place that is particularly psychically grimy, you will feel it. You will feel 'dirty' and tired. Then it is time to have a ritual bath. Once you have felt what it is like to be clean, and you get used to that feeling, you will be able to better recognise when you suddenly become energetically dirty.

Note: When this was first written in 2014, there was no need for regular magical cleaning. However now ten years later, we are in the midst of a long destructive phase that ebbs and flows like a tide. It is part of the slow but massive change in power dynamics around the nations of the world, and these tides bring in a great deal of psychic dirt, parasites and predatory beings. For this reason I would advise that you discount the next paragraph for your own practice. There will come a time in the future that is not destructive, and the following paragraph will once again be relevant, hence I have not edited it out. But I don't think I will see that time in my lifetime. During this current time and over the next few decades I would suggest that ritual baths and ritual cleaning of the home are done twice a month, at full and new moon. Between those times, if you feel that you or your space has become energetically dirty, then clean up ritually. Just do not use the techniques daily.

This type of magical cleaning should not be used routinely, but only when it is needed. Think of it in terms of real life… if you are ever stuck for a reference point in magic, always convert it to a real life equivalent and go from there. You do not scrub your hands excessively every hour of the day: some bacteria on your skin and in your system is very necessary for your health, which is why antibacterial soaps are so damaging to us. It is the same with magic. A bit of psychic dirt helps us to gain immunity, too much makes us ill, and too little makes us vulnerable.

But it is vital that a magician knows when they need to get clean, because it can save you from all sorts of problems. If you go a magical gathering which is unbalanced, and you come home feeling odd, dirty, or drained – then get a ritual bath. You need to learn the ritual by heart so that you can do it on the spot without papers should you need to. Take the time to learn and practise it.

The following are two versions of the same ritual. One is to cleanse the body and the other is to cleanse the home. If there are serious energetic problems in your home, then you will obviously need to ritually clean it on a regular basis. If your house suddenly starts to feel 'wrong,' or still feels grimy even after you have physically cleaned it, then it is time to ritually cleanse it.

To get the ritual into your head and get used to it, do it for your home and your body once a week for six weeks. This will also peel off any deep layers of muck on you and your home, which in turn will help you to recognise what 'clean' actually feels like. After that, only use these rituals twice a month or when really needed.

Bear in mind that, as with most magic, ritual cleansing is not a cure-all, but it is a useful and powerful tool. It handles most magical and energetic problems very well; but if you are on the receiving end of an attack from a serious magician or a major land or Underworld power (very unlikely early on in your magical career), ritual cleansing will be one of a range of tools you will need to use, not the only one. And get out of the mindset that magic has one banishing ritual or one protection ritual that can save you – that is not only incorrect, but potentially very dangerous. If you are under serious attack that threatens your life, you have to use a combination of methods that are specific to the problem: real magic is truly an art form.

These rituals, because they are so important and useful, have been placed on all of my websites and in most of my books. If you have already used them, then make sure you know them by heart and do not need notes/scripts to perform them. It is very important that you know both versions of this ritual inside out. If you already know the ritual by heart and have used it on yourself and your home, then move on to the next part of this lesson, but first read through this section of the lesson in case there is something here that you have missed.

When it comes to the list of the clearing (where it lists all the things to be removed) if there is a specific dangerous thing that is not listed, something that you need to be rid of, then add that thing to the list.

But if that thing is a nature being (like a faery being), then do not cast it out or use the ritual cleansing: simply talk to the space, tell it that it needs to go, open the doors so it can get out, or put a stone down in the room for half an hour and tell it to get into the stone. Once it is in the stone, take it out and put it on the earth. The ritual bath is used for magic directed at you, hostile or dangerous beings, and energetic dirt.

3. The ritual cleansing of a person

Teaching Note: when you exorcise by the 'gods,' you are calling upon the deities, the 'substations' of Divinity to act, and are calling upon the substance you are exorcising to 'stand to attention.' Then a specific name of Divinity is used that bridges between the substations and Divinity. That name focuses a particular quality of Divinity that is relevant to the substance in question. And then finally the element or object is consecrated into the service of Divinity unnamed (not deity) so that it will work regardless of area, religions, styles, etc.

Have a bath full of water and a large bowl of salt. Light a candle in the bathroom. Use the first two fingers of the right hand to point at what you are working on. If you do not have access to a bath, then use a bucket of water in the shower, just do not shower off the salt water when you have finished. Ensure that you wash every part of your body with the mix.

Where you see + it means make the sign of an equal-armed cross over whatever you are working on (so the cross lays over the substance). This is nothing to do with Christianity; it is about the sign of earth, of Malkuth: the action of the equal-armed cross is used whenever you are tuning or consecrating something that is substance: a body, a stone, salt, water; anything of physical substance. It is the reiteration of the four directions.

All signs traced in the air should be done so that they lay horizontally 'over' the target substance, not hovering vertically above them.

Elohim Savaoth is pronounced 'Savoth'.

Recite over a bowl of salt while pointing first two fingers:

"I exorcise thee, creature of the earth,
by the living gods + the holy gods + the omnipotent gods + ,
that thou mayst be purified of all evil influence
in the name of Adonai, lord of all angels and men."

Hold the flat of the hand over the salt:

"Creature of the earth, adore thy creator.
In the name of God the Father + and God the Mother + ,
I bless thee and consecrate thee to the service of Divinity."

Recite over the bath while pointing first two fingers:

> "I exorcise thee, creature of the water,
> by the living gods + , the holy gods + , the omnipotent gods + ,
> that thou mayst be purified of all evil influence
> in the name of Elohim Savaoth, lord of all angels and men."

Flat of the hand:

> "Creature of the water, adore thy creator.
> In the name of God the Father + and God the Mother + ,
> I consecrate thee to the service of Divinity."

Recitation of pouring – recite the following as you pour the salt into the bath:

> "Lord God, Father of the heavens above;
> great Goddess, Mother of the earth,
> grant that this salt will make for health of the body,
> and this water for health of the soul."

Pour the salt into the water.

> "Grant that they may be banished
> from whence they are used all powers of adversity;
> every artifice of evil shall be banished into the outer darkness,
> in thy holy names,
> Amen."

Now that the salt and water are consecrated and primed, you need to instruct the mixture in what needs cleaning off whoever is going into the bath.

With the two first fingers of the right hand trace a triangle in the air over the bath while reciting:

> "In the Names which are above every other Name,
> and in the power of the Almighty..."

(point to the top of the triangle horizontally over the bath)

> "...and of the Mother..."

(to the bottom right hand corner of the triangle)

> "...and of the Holy Spirits..."

(bottom left hand of the triangle)

Complete the triangle and then point at the water through the middle of the triangle:

> "I exorcise all influences and seeds of evil
> from the person who will bathe in this bath:
> I exorcise all demons, parasites, thought-forms, golems, all ghosts,
> all beings that bring disease, all beings that bring death,
> all marks of destruction, all marks of death,
> and all spiritual dirt.
> And I exorcise from them all magical attacks
> that have been cast against them:
> all magical spells, curses and bindings,
> rituals, visions, beings, and utterances.
> I cast upon them all the spell chains
> and I cast them into the outer darkness
> where they shall trouble not this Servant of God.
> Amen, Amen Selah."

Now get into the bath and make sure that you go under the water at some point, so that every inch of your body has been submerged. When you get out, put on clean clothing. If you are using a bucket, wash every part of your body you can get to, and then pour the remains over your head and down your back.

4. The ritual cleansing of a space, room, or house

Have a bowl of water and a bowl of salt. Light a candle and put the two bowls in front of the candle. Use the first two fingers of the right hand to point at what you are working on.

Where you see + it means make the sign of an equal armed cross horizontally over whatever you are working on.

Recite over a bowl of salt while pointing first two fingers:

> "I exorcise thee, creature of the earth,
> by the living gods + , the holy gods + , the omnipotent gods + ,
> that thou mayst be purified of all evil influence
> in the name of Adonai, lord of all angels and men."

Hold the flat of the hand over the salt:

> "Creature of the earth, adore thy creator.
> In the name of God the Father + and God the Mother + ,
> I bless thee and consecrate thee to the service of Divinity."

Recite over a bowl of water while pointing first two fingers:

> "I exorcise thee, creature of the water,
> by the living gods + , the holy gods + , the omnipotent gods + ,
> that thou mayst be purified of all evil influence
> in the name of Elohim Savaoth, lord of all angels and men."

Flat of the hand:

> "Creature of the water, adore thy creator.
> In the name of God the Father + and God the Mother + ,
> I consecrate thee to the service of Divinity."

Recitation of pouring – recite the following as you pour the salt into the water:

> "Lord God, Father of the heavens above;
> great Goddess, Mother of the earth,
> grant that this salt will make for health of the body,
> and this water for health of the soul."

Pour the salt into the water.

> "Grant that they may be banished
> from whence they are used all powers of adversity;
> every artifice of evil shall be banished into the outer darkness,
> in thy holy names,
> Amen."

Once the salt and water are poured together, the mix is ready to cleanse and purify anything it touches.

Cleansing a space

Once you have consecrated the salt and water and poured them together, then it is time to use that mix to cleanse a space. If you are doing a house, make sure you do each room individually. If a room has been changed from two rooms to one room, do the original two rooms.

The triangle used is traced vertically in the air as it is working on a larger area. If you were working on a specific object, you would do it horizontally over the object.

Stand in the centre of each room, and with the two first fingers of the right hand trace a triangle vertically in the air and then point through the centre of the triangle while reciting the recitation of clearing:

> "In the Names which are above every other Name,
> and in the power of the Almighty..."

(point to the top of the triangle)

> "...and of the Mother..."

(to the bottom right hand corner of the triangle)

"...and of the Holy Spirits..."

(bottom left hand of the triangle)

Complete the triangle and then point in the middle of the triangle:

"I exorcise all influences and seeds of evil from this room."

Now begin to sprinkle the mix around the room as you recite.

Sprinkle above, below and around the directions.

"I exorcise all demons, parasites, thought-forms, golems, ghosts,
all beings that bring disease, all beings that bring death,
all marks of destruction, all marks of death and all spiritual dirt.
And I exorcise from this space all magic that has been cast against it,
all magical spells, curses, bindings, rituals, visions, beings, seals, sigils,
and utterances from this space.
I cast upon them the spell chains
and I cast them into the outer darkness
where they shall trouble not these Servants of God.
Amen, Amen Selah."

5. Other cleaning methods

There are other things you can do to keep your living/working space clean, and also to keep yourself clean. These techniques use sound and smell, which both affect inner beings quite strongly.

Different beings react in different ways to smells and sounds, and this can be useful when it comes to staying clear. Versions of the use of sound and smell can be found in most older religions and magical systems, and they can range from super-efficient to sort of okay depending on what you use and what you use it for. Smells come in handy for discouraging certain types of beings from wandering into your home, or to stop them from invading your body-space.

The same goes for sounds. These are methods of 'passive cleansing,' which means they will not work alone when a banishing is needed, but they are a tool that can be used along with banishing methods. The use of sounds and smells really comes into its own when you have ritually cleared a space and want to keep it clear. The right sounds and smells discourage parasites, land beings, faeries etc. from trying to invade your space or from taking up residence with you. But if you go into a space that is already heavily infested, you need to clear first, and then use sounds and smells. You can also use them before an exorcism (which you will learn in the adept phase of training) to loosen the grip of powerful beings in a space before you remove them.

So let's have a look at smells.

6. Smells that clear

Each country around the world has aromatic plants or tree resins that affect intrusive or aggressive beings by discouraging them from entering a space. There is great wisdom in nature, and when nature has a poison, the cure is usually found very close by: the two are always presented together. This is a dynamic that is crucial for a magician to understand, as it helps them to navigate through some of the more difficult sides of dealing with energies and spirits. And just as a poisonous plant often grows near its curing counterpart, so a difficult or badly-haunted patch of land often has its cure nearby.

If you have a garden or a patch of land, it is very helpful (and it also earns massive magical brownie points) if you take the time to research what should be growing there naturally (bear in mind it can be different just a few miles down the road). If you can find out, then get those plants growing in your garden: they will come in very useful at some point.

Back to smells. An example of a natural solution in nature is one that we will easily recognise, and that is wild garlic. Wild garlic grows in abundance where there is natural death energy in the land. These areas are like portals into the Underworld and they are often heavily haunted, energetically disruptive, and generally difficult to learn to live with. If you live in such an area, grow lots of wild garlic around your boundaries, and always have some hanging and drying in your house – this is where Bram Stoker got his vampire/garlic shtick from: it is a local folk cure.

When it comes to oils and incense, it depends upon the strength of the problem and also what area you are in. For example, in Montana, white sage and sweet grass (used seasonally) is a good cleanser for the home, but it doesn't work in Britain. So don't follow the plethora of recreated spiritual paths that are now so abundant: think about where you are and what you need. There are some smells that work universally, and they were often used in ancient and classical temples because of their wide ranging action.

Frankincense resin is a good all-over cleanser for a space, and it seems to work everywhere. Smudging a home with frankincense resin on charcoal (not incense sticks), or making your own mix of frankincense, oppoponax, cloves and benzoin will clear most spaces anywhere from low to mid-level issues. Similarly, pure frankincense oil either worn or on a diffuser in the home will deter low-level beings from coming into the house. This is why it is used so extensively in Orthodox and Catholic churches, and why it was so precious to the Egyptians.

Experiment with smells. But use pure resins and essential oils, not other people's mixes, or incense sticks etc. as they often have a lot of chemicals in them which don't work in clearing and can sometimes make the problem worse by attracting parasites. Parasites gather where there is a place or a person they can feed from. When a person uses a lot of chemical perfume on their body or in their home, it slowly affects their outer and inner immune systems, making them more vulnerable to being fed off.

This is why it is rare to find a proper magical adept who wears chemical perfumes or uses them a lot around the house.

These days, getting Frankincense that has not been over harvested is becoming harder to find. What I have found useful is searching out Somalian or Ethiopian traders in immigrant communities. Many times they are part of a family of Frankincense farmers or wild Frankincense harvesters, and many are aware of the issues and so collect sustainably. I have found them on the internet, through searching eBay, and through searching for traders as opposed to companies that sell essential oils. I now buy from one family who only sell during harvest season. Look for immigrant communities that would use Frankincense, and see if there are any traders.

If you build up a range of essential oils and resins, you can begin to experiment with smells. Use one at a time for a week or so and just observe any subtle shifts in how they make you feel or how the house feels. Write your results down in your journal. The smells that work well are the ones for you to focus on using in your magical practice. This can be very individual to the human and the space: there are only a few 'one size fits all' smells. If you have a very aromatic plant growing naturally around your home or in the area where you live, harvest some and bring it into your home.

Again, see if there is any subtle shift in the space. If you have sleep issues, try putting some of the local aromatic plants in your bedroom in small bunches and see if your sleep changes. If it does, then your sleep disturbance is not physical; it is psychic. If it is a plant that an essential oil is made from, then you have found an oil that can be an ingredient for your own personal magical oil mix.

If there does not seem to be an oil made from a local aromatic plant that works for you, get some frankincense oil and use it as a base. Put a few chopped and bruised leaves from the aromatic plant into the frankincense oil, and that becomes the 'starter' of your own magical oil mix. It can take a while for you to hit upon the series of smells that works very well for you, but once you have found the right combination, use it regularly on yourself and in your home. If you are going out to a difficult or crowded place, put your oil on and observe the reactions of the people around you. Some will gravitate into your space and will subconsciously feel safe around you; others, usually people who are heavily parasited, will react strongly to the scent of your oil and will back away from you.

Here is a short list of what I call 'priestly oils,' which are smells that seem to be universal in their actions; and then a list of nature oils that tend to be more localised in their action to where these plants live. It will give you some ideas that you can then build upon and experiment with. This is the beginning of the alchemical side of your magical training.

Priestly oils

Frankincense, Myrrh, Oppoponax, Vetiver, Benzoin.

Nature oils

Cloves, Garlic, Pine, Mint, Cedar, Sage, Sandalwood, Wormwood, Rose, Jasmine, Patchouli.

7. Sounds

Sounds are also very important for affecting change in your space and in your own body. The deeper you go into magic, the more you will learn about how different sounds, voices, and music can subtly affect you at a deep level. Some types of sound and music 'call in' parasites, Underworld beings, and loads of psychic dirt, whereas other types of music can dispel such forces. There are also types of sound and music that cannot clear dirt and problems, but once the space is clear, they will keep it clear.

The same is true for your body and spirit: once you are clean, certain types of music can keep you clean and help to keep you balanced.

So let's have a look at some different types of sounds that can cause a change around and within you. And bear in mind this is not about finding music that is to your personal taste for entertainment; this is about music that will work as a specific magical tool. If your personal taste in music includes music that can attract parasites, just bear that in mind, and put clearing music on afterwards. As you become very clean, you will find that some of the music you used to enjoy listening to starts to make you feel drained: that is caused by the parasites that come with the music, and your clean state is allowing you to feel the difference.

Chant

Chant, particularly very old chants without modern mixing or instruments, can be very powerful in rebalancing a space and quietening it down. A fashion evolved in the 1980s for mixing chants with drums, electronic music, or flutes, etc., and while these versions are all very nice and relaxing to listen to, they do not work in the same way or with the same level of power.

The sounds and vibrations of the human voice can have quite a strong effect upon a space, and when this is coupled with particular uses of language, the result can become quite powerful, magically speaking. Bear in mind though that just as there are powerful peaceful chants, there are also types of chant that are designed to destroy, or to wake up the more dangerous side of humanity. These types of chant were used to prepare for battle, so choose your sounds wisely!

The most common forms of chant that are available to us on modern media (CDs etc.) and that are effective to work with magically are plainchant, Sufi chants, and Tibetan chants. I am sure there are many more, I am just either not aware of them or have not worked with them. I tend not to recommend something if I haven't worked with it myself.

It is best to work with CDs which were made before recordings began to be shortened and messed with, or had sound effects or modern instrumentation added.

If you don't have a CD player and use MP3's, then look for high quality ones that have kept as much frequency as possible in the sound.

Each type of chant works in a slightly different way. Plainchant for the most part stills a room, and tunes it to a specific 'priestly' connection. This is why chants were used in the churches: to keep that inner priestly connection going. Eventually the music devolved down into hymns and chants that were 'showy' and were more about showing off, gaining funds, and being 'pious.' But we are lucky in this day and age that we can buy CDs of very early Christian chant, where the early notations have been revived and adhered to.

Look for chants from the Syriac church, and also the Armenian Church. (Though many of these have been affected by the Soviet era style of music, there are still some Armenian chants available that are the very old traditional ones, and these are one of the oldest forms of chants still being used today.) Look also for Orthodox chant and early chants of the Catholic Church.

True Sufi chant is harder to find, but there are some out there. Sadly Sufism has been hijacked by Western New Age fashions in Europe, so if you wish to work with Sufi chant, look for ones produced in the Near East, like ones from Turkey and Egypt. The Egyptian Sufi chants are a lot stronger than the Turkish ones, and are less likely to be the product of pseudo-Sufism.

The same is true of Tibetan chants. Most modern recordings are whimsical and specifically designed for a New Age Western market. But there were solid, powerful chants recorded in the seventies and early eighties, and these tend to be a lot more effective and work magically. Tibetan chant works in a different way to plainchant: they tend to push out parasites and low-level beings, and pull in powers that are protective and cleansing. They are best used after doing a ritual clean of the house. They can also be put on to still the house during volatile times: just set them going and leave them going while you are out of the house.

Drums

Certain drum sounds can also quieten a house down, depending upon what they are. Most African drums wake things up, get things ready for war or for creative power, for harvest or to raise spirits, and the sounds are aimed to be used by a collection of villagers or an extended family. Traditional African drum sounds should be used with caution, as they can be powerful and they tend to be specific calls to land beings in the region that the music comes from. If you have African ancestral roots, then they may be interesting for you to experiment with.

In fact, most indigenous drum sounds from around the world are designed to stir things up, to wake things up, and to pull in energy… sometimes energy that is a bit too adrenal for cleansing a home. But when you come across a single drum with a slow beat, it can act like a heartbeat for the land and calm the room down.

Nocturnes

Classical music by visionary composers, particularly nocturnes, can really still a house in a very natural way. The power that can come through them is not ritualised or sacred, however it is often the voice of nature that flows through the composer. Playing gentle, meditative compositions with the windows open so that the trees, plants, and birds can hear them can bring a settled energy to a house and a person.

Not all classical music works this way: it seems to depend on the visionary quality of the composer. If you are not familiar with classical music, learn to experiment. Nocturnes and adagios have layer upon layer of emotive frequencies within them, and those intricate frequencies weave a solid 'airspace' in the house.

Modern music

Modern music has no inner quality by nature of its composition and use of electronic instrumentation and mixing. The sounds that a real, physical instrument makes have a very different effect on a space compared to the sounds that a computer or electronic instrument makes. Use modern music for your own pleasure and entertainment, and more ancient music for your magical work, and learn to feel the difference.

If you are not used to listening to classical, sacred or indigenous music, your ear will not be tuned to their sounds and it may take a little while for your ear and mind to get used to them. Modern music wires the brain one way, and ancient music wires it a different way. As a magician, you need the capacity to understand both. Experiment, and you will find your own repertoire of music that fits with you and that you can work with. To get your ear and brain used to music that is strange to you, put it on while you are doing mundane jobs like cleaning, tidying, etc. Let your brain listen to it while it is doing something else. Like all strange music, you probably will not really like it at first, as we are beings that like familiarity with sounds and smells: it is part of our makeup. But once you have heard some new styles of music enough times, you will learn to differentiate between which work for you and which don't.

Here is a short list of suggestions for music and sounds which can be bought on CD.

The sacred music is particularly effective at stilling a space. But you will notice that on all of these CDs, some of the tracks work while others do not: this will make for a good lesson in learning how to feel what different pieces of music do magically. When you feel the difference, note that difference down in your journal. This list of sacred music will get you started, give you some ideas, and lead you to finding your own sacred music.

The short list of classical music will give you somewhere to start in that genre, too, and when you start hunting for your own taste in classical music, look for adagios, nocturnes, and meditative pieces. Some of these will make you feel still, but would not necessarily still a room. A lot depends on the composer in question, and whether they were tuned into inner powers or not.

Once you have listened to some of the sacred music, you will learn what 'still' feels like, and then you will have a reference point when it comes to discovering other types of music. Essentially, any music that is the voice chanting and nothing else will have an effect on a space: it is up to you to discover exactly what effect each piece has and whether or not it was the effect you were looking for.

Sacred music

- Any chants without instrumentation by Hildegard von Bingen
- Shvedov: *Liturgy of St John Chrysostom*
- *Ancient Voices/Vox Sacra* by the Anonymous 4 and Soeur Marie Keyrouz
- The Music of Armenia *Volume 1 Sacred Choral Music*[1]
- Any Gregorian chant without instrumentation
- Arvo Pärt *Triodion* Polyphony Stephen Layton
- *Tibetan Sacred Temple Music* by Eight Lamas from Drepung
- *The Gyuto Monks: Tibetan Tantric Choir -Guhyasamaja Tantra Chapter II & Melody for Mahakala*

Classical music

Chopin's Complete Nocturnes, J. S. Bach's Cello Suites, Debussy, Grieg, Prokofiev, and Arvo Pärt's sacred music. This is a tiny selection but will get you started in a journey of discovery. Some classical mixes on CD are very cheap and would introduce you to different composers. There are some both on CD and MP3 that are classical collections for meditation that would be interesting for you to experiment with. And while it is not classical music, I have also found the house reacting favourably to Tibetan singing bowls. There are lots of singing bowl music collections and most of them are terrible, and have been filled with new age background sounds. However one I bought cheaply was very good at stilling the house and had interesting sounds to paint to. It is called Seven Metals; Singing Bowls of Tibet by Benjamin Iobst. It is worth experimenting with such sounds to see which ones affect you, which ones affect the space, and which ones do nothing.

8. Getting and staying balanced

In the previous lesson, you learned about using the Pentagram as a tuning mechanism for your life force. That was the first step of learning how to actively and consciously engage your humanity rather than just riding through life unawares. The action of mentally tuning yourself to the Pentagram, with the other magical symbols, the sacred language, and the shape of the pattern brings you into a 'wholeness' and tunes you properly to a consciously magical state: this is the magical equivalent of

---

[1] Label Celestial Harmonies 1995.

learning a martial arts fighting stance. The martial artist learns how to form a stance that is ready for action and that puts their body in an easily defended position. It is very hard to knock a martial artist off-balance once they adopt their fighting stance.

In the early stages of magical training, the first line of protection is learning how to adopt a 'prepare for action' stance, whereby you can easily defend yourself and cannot be easily knocked off balance. The most an apprentice magician can expect to have to cope with are parasites, curious ghosts, curious land beings, infantile magicians trying to harass you magically, and unhealthy objects inadvertently brought into your space.

Many students over the last few years have emailed me in terror, thinking they are being attacked by 'demons' because it has made them feel so bad and affected their life so much. However on looking, it was inevitably a parasite. Students do not realise how bad these beings can affect you, nor do they believe that the simple act of cleaning oneself and ones home up magically, and cutting off the food source of the parasite which is usually an emotion, is all that is needed. They ignore their beginner training and any advice. The actions and rituals in this lesson are all a student needs, and is the same work an adept would use in similar circumstances.

Serious all-out magical attacks or super-aggressive beings are in general a rarity in the Western world, but when they do make an appearance, it tends to be more of an issue for adepts or the occasional initiate who has either crossed a line somewhere in their behaviour, or become very visible to hostile humans or beings.

Before you can learn anything about defensive magic, you have to learn how to balance, be still, be solid, and be strong. Then the more intricate defensive techniques can sit on that solid base, which in turn makes them very efficient. Most low-level issues, attacks, etc. can be dealt with in two steps: anchor and then shield. To anchor means to create a state whereby you are hard to knock over, hard to grab, and not easily manipulated emotionally (many beings try to scare humans).

One of the best anchors is the pentagram pattern. The pentagram was used by the original nineteenth century Golden Dawn magical group as a method for teaching beginners ritual patterning using sound, shape, and movement. However, it somehow morphed into a mishmash of fragmented understanding, immature use of deity patterns and Divine names, and a good sprinkling of drama. That became known as the Lesser Banishing Ritual of the Pentagram: the only thing it really banishes is the magician's common sense.

However, the pentagram pattern itself can be a very powerful anchor, as the pentagram is about being a human. It is a magical pattern that consciously declares, tunes, and roots a human life: it takes you to conscious awareness of the powers that flow through your space, the powers that open your future, and the powers that support you through your blood, and it is a pattern that reiterates the directions around you. It also establishes in your sphere the patterns of the two foundational magical tools: the sword and the cup. Eventually you will learn how this pattern operates through Kabbalah, but for now it is your solid anchor: it is your fighting stance.

If you have practised your pentagram seal exercise from your previous lesson, you should by now be able to stand, close your eyes, and 'see' with your mind's eye the pattern of the pentagram all around you, with the magical signs, root declarations in your own language and the root magical tools. The pentagram is never projected outside of yourself (the big mistake of the LBRP), rather you are 'in' it: it is the pattern of your humanity that you stand within.

If you feel yourself to be at magical risk in a situation, you can make mental use of the pentagram. If you have practised, you will be able to stand with your eyes open and visualise the pentagram as your body, the hexagram over your head, your ancestors/family name/the earth (Mother) below you, the magical implements in your hands, and your spark of life in your centre with your first name. Once you are able to do that, then you can declare what is known as the breastplate. (I will talk about its origins and actions in a moment.)

The breastplate as used with the pentagram is a ritual declaration which can be spoken out loud or said in the mind when you need to be verbally silent. The skeleton action of the breastplate has many different styles and usages, but to use the breastplate with the pentagram, you would declare this recitation once you have the image of the pentagram around you:

> "The Father is above me,
> The Mother is below me,
> the Sword to my left,
> the Cup to my right,
> the Guardian Angel behind me,
> the Sandalphon, (also known as the Noble Companions) before me,
> within me is life,
> within me is the Breath of God:
> I Will Be."

Before we move on, let's just take a little time to see how that recitation works, why it is constructed that way, and when you would use it. As I said earlier, this is a 'passive' form of protection: it is an anchor or fighting stance. The shape of the pentagram is the shape of humanity. That is the first layer of its anchoring strength: in our modern day of trying to be everything that we are not, we also subtly loosen our understanding of what and who we are. Impressing the shape of the pentagram upon ourselves reiterates the magical pattern of creation in terms of the human body: the human body is the body of clay that is ready to be filled with the Breath of Divinity.

The second layer is the conscious awareness of Divinity 'above' us in the form of the hexagram, which in turn is a shape of Divine completion. In magic, 'up' is the future, the forming of creation, and the Breath of Divinity. This breath flows down into creation. In the pentagram, you and the pentagram are 'creation,' with Divine consciousness above you. You will learn more about this later on in the course. This pattern is where the 'god is up' concept in religion comes from, though it is badly misunderstood and has become a degenerate concept.

In balance to Divine consciousness (which has no material form) above, you have earth/your ancestors below. This is also 'creation' which is the whole world, and is the receiving feminine aspect of Divinity: you are reiterating where you come from. By doing this, you anchor yourself deeply in the earth which is the female Divinity, and acknowledge that you are the sum total of your ancestors. This roots you in the strength of consciousness that flows through your blood: literally, your family upholds you.

In the left hand you hold the sword. You have not yet learned how a magical sword works, but by 'seeing' it in your mind's eye, in its correct position, you begin to establish the timeless line of magic that flows through your life. You hold it now in innocence, but eventually, as an adept, you will hold it in gnosis. By holding the sword in innocence now, you connect to your magic in the future.

It is difficult to explain to a beginner, but there is no 'time' in magic. By holding the magical tools, not only do you step into the pattern of the magician, but you connect yourself to the work you will do in the future: this creates a loop of power that flows out of time.

The sword in the magician's left hand is not a defence; rather it is an establishing of the power of utterance: it is the magician consciously engaging with that power that flows from Divinity. In a three-dimensional pattern, the sword in the east and the hexagram above are two sides of the same power – The Divine power flows down from above and when it reaches the threshold of Creation, our world, it ceases to be a simple downward flow and instead is perceived by us as flowing into creation via the directions. The Breath of Divinity flows to us from the east, and when we initiate a magical act, we also start in the east and we 'give.' Thus the sword/east is 'I give.'

The cup in the right hand is the receiver of power: it is a vessel waiting to be filled. It connects deeply to Creation, which is the vessel that receives Divine Breath in order to exist.

So you begin to see that the pentagram is a magical pattern of the creation of Humanity, and also the creation of magic by the magician. By including the two foundational magical tools, and working consciously with the pattern, you step from being a human who is buffeted helplessly by fate to being a human who consciously engages all the powers of creation around them.

This is one of the layers of meaning in the ancient and mystical maxim:

"Man, know thyself."

Which these days we would quote as

"Human, know thyself."

Then the ritual pattern establishes and acknowledges the angelic powers that work with humanity, and specifically with that portion of humanity that has consciously engaged at a deep inner level with the Mysteries.

A person's individual angelic being, who acts as their guardian, their threshold for life, is behind a person. They do not protect you from your own ignorance and stupidity; rather they quietly nudge you in the right direction.

Before you is the Sandalphon, the angelic power that guides humans into the Mysteries and shows them the way if they are willing to listen carefully. The Sandalphon is an angelic 'companion' to the magician, a passive teacher that points the way; hence they are 'before' you: "the Guardian Angel behind me, the Sandalphon before me." You are sandwiched between the two.

Finally comes the declaration of creation, "within me is life, within me is the Breath of God: I Will Be." You declare that you are finally aware of the flow of creation: the Breath of Divinity flowing into the vessel (in this case a human body), and you declare I will be. This is both a declaration of your constant evolution as a magical being, and an acknowledgement that you exist and will continue to exist only through the action of Divinity.

Now, hopefully, you understand how the pentagram can act as quite a powerful shield for your early days in magic, and why it functions as a fighting stance that someone would have a great deal of trouble knocking you over from: you become so rooted in what you are, and so aware of the Divine Breath flowing within you, that most low level beings, attacks, etc. would not be able to stick. It would take a focused and specific attack to knock you out of this 'stance.'

Also, now that you know a bit more of the secrets behind the pentagram, if you do some historical research, particularly in terms of ancient cultures, wall paintings, religious patterns, and wherever else the pentagram turns up in history, you will now have a deeper understanding at what the artist, religion or priest was hinting at.

The pentagram is badly misunderstood in modern magic, and many of the rituals of modern magical schools project the pentagram outside of themselves (they form it in the air), and add Hebrew letters (usually badly pronounced), different deities, etc., all of which create antagonistic patterns that fight the human form in its balance.

9. *Task:* Pentagram research

Now that you know how the pentagram works, do some research and look at the use of the shape through history (not modern usage) and in what context it was used. If you are using the internet, consider using 'Google Scholar' for your search as it will filter out a lot of new age nonsense. If you are using a library, look for ancient, classical and religious architecture books, or a book on the history of symbols.

From there, list the various cultures that used the pentagram, in what situation/context they used it, and then, rather than reading the modern interpretation of what archaeologists or historians thought, look at the symbol for yourself and see what understanding slowly rises to the surface of your mind.

This is the beginning of the process of learning how to extract ancient information through simply looking and meditating on an image. Don't worry about whether it is your interpretation that is coming to mind, or whether you have managed to tap into the mystery behind an image; just let the ideas flow and write them down.

Copy and draw or paste the images along with their surrounding images: for example where it appears in Egyptian texts, copy all the hieroglyphs, deities, and images that the pentagram appears alongside.

Write an essay from your notes and the images. Use the statement: "In the history of this culture, the historians say the use of the pentagram in this context meant X, but after studying it, from what I now know of the pentagram, I feel it was used for Y." If you agree with the history books, that is fine: say so, and why. If you do not agree with the history books, say so and why.

In the future you should revisit this essay, once you have worked deeply with magical patterns, and it will give you insight into how far you have progressed, and how your understanding has deepened and matured.

10. Breastplates

Various incantations known as 'breastplates' can be in modern magical texts, and often they are touted as being the 'Breastplate of Solomon.' It is assumed to be an ancient incantation and there are many variants around these days. A breastplate incantation is very similar to the pentagram ritual above, in that it defines a power above and below you, to your right and to your left, before you, behind you, and within you. There are also similar incantations found in the Pyramid texts that suggest the use of a breastplate incantation for the Pharaoh as he traversed through death.

The first written description in the West of a breastplate incantation is a part of the Faeth Fiada, which in old Irish means 'Magical Mist'. It is called the breastplate of St Patrick, and it is an old Irish prayer which was first written down in the 8th century. It is most likely a remnant of a pre-Christian Celtic magical incantation, which is apparent through the use of the elements and weather as a part of the breastplate.

> PATRICK MADE THIS HYMN.
> IT WAS MADE IN THE TIME OF LOEGAIRE SON OF NIALL.

The first section of the Breastplate is the calling of the elements and earth powers, and it establishes the speaker as a part of the natural elements.

> "I arise today
> Through the strength of heaven;
> Light of the sun,
> Splendour of fire,
> Speed of lightning,
> Swiftness of the wind,
> Depth of the sea,
> Stability of the earth,
> Firmness of the rock."

The later Christian version of the Breastplate, which magicians do not use, adds in:

> "Christ with me,
> Christ before me,
> Christ behind me,
>
> Christ in me,
> Christ beneath me,
> Christ above me,
>
> Christ on my right,
> Christ on my left,
>
> Christ when I lie down,
> Christ when I sit down,
>
> Christ in the heart of every man who thinks of me,
> Christ in the mouth of every man who speaks of me,
>
> Christ in the eye that sees me,
> Christ in the ear that hears me."

Now we begin to see the co-opting of Christ as overall protector as opposed to the gods/goddesses or local land powers. But the underlying structure is still there: there is power and presence all around and within you: you are truly not alone. Reciting a breastplate when you are stressed or going into a dangerous situation brings the lens of existence into sharp focus, and alerts the spirit beings around you that you are in need of protection.

To work a breastplate magically and successfully, it must have male and female Divinity, angelic presence, ancestral presence, and magical tools. That is topped by the utterance of conscious existence.

To use the pentagram breastplate as an immediate call for protection, you would use the incantation once you have quickly visualised the powers, symbols, tools, and beings around you:

"The Father is above me,
The Mother is below me,
the Sword to my left,
the Cup to my right,
the Guardian Angel behind me,
the Sandalphon before me,
within me is life,
within me is the Breath of God:
I Will Be."

Learn this incantation off by heart, and learn how to visualise the images and shapes quickly.

I have reiterated and talked quite a lot about the Pentagram for good reason (I am sure you are now sick to death of it): each section of the lessons that talk about the pentagram go deeper and deeper, inch by inch, into its mysteries. In the next module you will learn the full Pentagram ritual, how it works, and why. There will come a day when you will be glad that you know it inside out.

11. Talismans

For a beginner there are two basic ways to create and use a talisman. From these two foundations, you will eventually learn all sorts of different methods and techniques, but for now you will learn two distinct, old-fashioned and very useful ways to protect yourself.

One basic talisman method is passive, and the other is active. As a magician, you will come to realise that all magical protection falls into one or the other of those two categories. Whereas passive protection ticks quietly away in the background, active protection targets a specific threat such as a magical attack, or looks after you when you have to go into a very dangerous situation. You should only use active protection when it is truly needed. If you use active protection all the time, particularly as a developing magician, it will become seriously counterproductive. This is something we will look into in more depth in a future lesson.

Passive protection can take the form of an image (usually an Underworld deity) or a sacred text. Remember your lesson on sacred language: there is a major difference between language with magical meaning, and sacred language where the letters themselves have their own power.

The two most active and powerful sacred languages are old (Biblical) Hebrew, and Egyptian Hieroglyphs.

Using Hebrew letters in text combinations from the Torah, for example, puts the sacred language into a context: one of the unique things about the sacred use of

Hebrew is that a section of text has many layers to it. The first layer tells you a story. The second layer has names hidden within the letters of the text. The third layer has numerical harmonics woven within the text that create a specific magical pattern. The fourth layer is the vibration of the combined sounds that affect a space and change the power operating within it. Because the pattern of letters is intoned around the world on a daily basis, simply having that text on the wall is enough to trigger passive protection.

For active protection, talismans with specific actions are needed. So to bring this lesson to a close, let's look at one of the very basic ways to create and use an active talisman for protection. This method draws upon the visionary learning you did in the earlier lessons. Most people would think that a method that uses vision is quite advanced, but in fact it is much harder to make a talisman without using vision if you want it to actually work well. It is also important that you learn all the different layers of vision use in the earliest part of your training.

12. *Task:* Making a Talisman

You will need a plain metal or stone pendant. Choose something you can keep on your body for a week and that you are willing to throw away afterwards. You will also need a bowl of salt and five candles.

This is a silent, simple ritual that also uses visionary technique to pull power from the inner worlds into substance in order to get a job done. You act as a focal point, director, and bridge as you ask for a specific quality from each direction to be placed in the talisman. Later in your training, when you become more skilled at magic, you will learn how to combine these simple skills with outer ritual skills to create a full talisman using vision, ritual, sigils, magical symbols, and sacred sound. It is pointless being able to do all of the flashy stuff if you cannot make the inner connection – so that is what you learn first.

You can use the following method to make a talisman when you (or your children) need protecting from danger. When you work this simple ritual for real (not for an experiment) you have to be very careful how you phrase what you are asking for. We will go into that after we have gone over the experiment. For this experiment, the exercise is point-specific: you are going to ask for a specific thing to be put into the talisman. That is so that you can feel it working, feel it doing a specific thing. Once you have felt it and understood the feeling, then you can take it off.

An added bonus of this experiment is that it will teach you how it feels to have your energies shifted by magic, so that if someone later tries to bind you magically you will recognise the effects immediately.

Setting up

Get a cheap, plain pendant necklace, ring, or bracelet (a neck pendant is best) made from metal, with no magical quality, i.e. a silver chain with a small stone on it or a metal shape. Don't use a pendant with any magical, religious or New Age images: the plainer the better (a clean slate to work on). Put it in a bowl of dry salt and leave it there for at least 24 hours.

You will need five plain white candles and one long ordinary candle to use as a taper, or an ordinary purpose made taper – for this ritual the light is lit from the magical Inner Light, which means all other candles are lit from the fire of the previous one. When you light the first candle, it becomes the light from which all other light comes from. So matches for each candle will not work. Each candle must be lit from a lit candle.

You will also need five altars or small work surfaces located in the four directions and one in the centre. (Note how you are continuing to work with a directional pattern, which in turn will help to deepen your understanding of how many different ways you can use the directional powers.)

Place the candles in the four directions and one in the centre. Use altars if you can, but have nothing on the altars except the candles. If this is not possible, use small plain surfaces in the four directions (I have used large hardback books with white cloths over them) or place the candles in the directions directly on a clear floor. This is called creating a neutral space. Do not have images, ritual objects etc. on the altars, as these will influence or block the powers that you will need to work with. Ensure doors are locked, phones are switched off, and that nothing can disturb you as you work.

Creating the talisman

Take the pendant out of the salt and place it on the central altar. Light the candle that sits upon the central altar. Close your eyes and still your mind: spend a few minutes in stillness/void meditation before focusing upon the central flame using your inner vision. Perform the directional ritual you learned in Lesson 4 – ritual magic lesson but with one change. The candle in the east is lit from the central flame using the taper. The south candle is lit from the east flame using the taper. As you go around the directions, light the directional candle from the previous altar candle flame. Go around the directions starting in the east. Do the spoken acknowledgements of the directions, and the declaration of the sword and the cup.

When you have finished, stand in front of the central flame, facing the south altar on the opposite side of the central altar, and remember the pentagram shield. Place your arms out and be aware of the magical symbols around you, seeing them in your mind's eye. Make the spoken declaration of the pentagram finishing with the words "I Will Be." Those two ritual actions open the directions, establish your power and presence within humanity, and get you ready to work.

Walk a full circle around the central flame and go to the east altar. Imagine with your mind's eye that beyond the flame you can see gates. See the gates opening and a shadowy figure standing in the gateway, waiting. Hold the pendant over the flame (without setting fire to yourself) and say:

"Powers of the east,
I ask that you place into this pendant the power of invisibility,
so that no being, spirit, thought form, or parasite can see me.
I wish to learn the skills of the Quarry.
I am a student of the Quarry,
and I wish to learn the feeling of silence and invisibility.
I will honour the power of the lesson,
and remove the pendant once the lesson is learned."

See in your mind's eye the figure reaching out to touch the pendant. Hold the pendant there for however long the figure touches it. Once the figure withdraws their hand, take the pendant from the flame and hold it to yourself. Take a step back, bow to acknowledge the contact, turn and go to the south altar. Repeat the whole process again in the south, west, north, and finally also the central flame (you should be facing south with the flame before you).

Once you have finished, put the pendant back on the central altar. Walk a full circle around the flame and go to the east. Bow and say thank you. In your mind's eye, see the gates close. Once they are closed, blow out the candle, take a step back, turn and repeat in the south, west and north.

When the directional candles are out, take the pendant and hold it in your hands. Sit down on the floor facing south with the central flame before you. Cup the pendant in your hands and close your eyes. Your intention with putting on this pendant is to be fully cloaked so that beings cannot see you and you cannot see them. With your eyes closed, put the pendant on and imagine a black heavy shroud descending upon you, a shroud that totally envelops you, shuts out all light, all sounds, all images. Sit for a moment in that darkness and when you are ready, open your eyes and blow out the central flame.

13. *Task:* The experiment's results

This experiment has two lessons: one is what it feels like to be shrouded, and the other is the experience when you take it off. If you are very sensitive or psychic, this can be a tough lesson, as the silence can be shocking: you do not realise quite how much you hear on a day-to-day basis – your mind tends to tune it out and you do not realise how much spirit chatter there is until it goes.

If you are not psychic or sensitive, the lesson will not be so shocking and you will have to learn to pay attention to subtle shifts in your energy. You will most likely feel the difference more when you take it off.

Keep the pendant on for a week. The sensitive people may want to throw it after twenty-four hours: do not do that. You must learn this lesson for a variety of reasons: first, you need to know how these talismans work. You also need to know what everyday life is like for those who are not sensitive. You cannot serve or help as an adept in the future if you have no understanding of the silence that many people are trapped in, and the subsequent dangers that this silence can put them in.

If you discover through this experiment that you are a non-sensitive person, then you must learn to optimise what senses you do have. All of your senses work on an inner level as well as an outer level. Once the talisman is on, pay close attention to whether you find yourself doing things slightly differently. Are you driving differently? Are you talking with people differently? Are you finding it harder to weigh people up? Are you sleeping better or worse? Are you hungrier or not hungry at all?

All of these shifts, however subtle, will tell you where you had an inner sense or connection that has suddenly been shut down. Once you know what has changed (sense of smell, hearing, sight, mood, dreams, sleep, taste, energy) then you know how your body was actually operating at a psychic level, just very quietly. From there, you know what senses you can work on to strengthen them.

Keep a daily journal or notes that outline any shifts, and any incidental occurrences, (people not seeing you on the street and walking straight into you etc.). Note down your sleep and appetites, whether you get more or less tired, etc. At the end of the week, take off the talisman and throw it in a river or lake, or bury it if you are not around water. When you take it off, pause for a moment, be aware of the directions around you (see the altars in your mind and recover the feel of the working space), say thank you for the lesson, and then dispose of the pendant safely. Now go take a ritual cleansing bath. For the first twenty-four hours, note down any shift again: is everything louder and brighter? How long did it take for the chatter to come back? Is there no difference? There are no right or wrong answers with these experiments: it is all about learning your own individual level of sensitivity.

Note: do not try to do any magical work or exercises during your talisman lesson week – while you have it on you will not be able to do any magic, it just won't work. Also do no meditation and no tarot readings. Be totally mundane and simply observe and pay attention to how you feel.

14. Working these talismans for protection: points to remember

Don't try and 'fix' intent into these talismans when you are looking for protection. Simply ask the contact in each direction to put in whatever is needed for you to stay safe at that time (and give a time span, like 2 months or a week). That will ensure you are truly covered in terms of safety without blocking any learning experiences you need to go through.

So for example if you said, "protect me from my violent neighbour," and you then get hit by a bus, you were not well protected from danger. Let the contacts see from their perspective what you need to stay safe during a dangerous time. And don't get into wearing these sorts of talismans all the time: you will regret it. The only time it is a good idea to wear a talisman all the time is if you are very ill and therefore vulnerable, or if you are old and your strength is fading, but you are still active magically.

Use protection when it is needed, and only when it is needed. There may come a time in your later years, or during a long-term illness where you will need to wear a talisman for a prolonged period of time, but that is an unusual situation if you are young. In general, constant use will only weaken you.

15. Maintenance

Don't take the talisman off, even for a shower. A talisman has a limited lifespan and you will know when it has finished its job as you will either feel the shift or it will break and fall off. Talismans are meant to be for short-term protection, so don't overuse them or you will not gain your own inner protection. If the talisman takes a hit (breaks, explodes, refuses to stay on) then it is time to take it off and bury it or drop it in a river. Do not be tempted to keep it and reuse it.

Lesson 8
Astrology

Astrology is one of the many tools a magician can employ in order to look at a situation, a tide of power, or themselves. Astrology – real astrology, not the newspaper entertainment variety – is like a weather report for magicians: you can look at your transits and see what powers are currently in action in your life and work.

To learn astrology in its depths requires a long-term commitment to an art form, and some magicians take on that herculean task, whereas others do not: it all depends where your focus of work lies. But for most magicians, a simple, rudimentary understanding of astrology can be very helpful when they need to peer into the depths to get an overview of what forces are currently in action around them.

A magician can use their natal chart to tell where certain qualities lie, and it can help the magician focus on their strengths, while understanding and working on their weaknesses. The chart of a place or event can also shed a beam of light in understanding what underlying forces are at work at a given time.

I am no adept at astrology by any stretch of the imagination, and my understanding of the art form is basic but it is enough for me to be able to draw out information offered in a chart which in turn helps me understand certain events, tides, and powers that run through my life, my work, and the events that happen around me. Such snippets of information can be of great use when it is imperative for a magician to have as much information as possible on a given issue. It can also help bring to light the current forces that are affecting a defined area of land, or a nation.

It helps greatly to have an understanding of the powers that flow from the planets and affect everything of substance, particularly when it comes to planetary magic, fate, and ritual that works with planetary influence... all of which you will look into later in the course. The basic understanding of each planet, and how the planets relate to each other depending on their positions at any given time, can really open out your understanding over time of magical ritual work, and working with patterns, talismans and construction.

This lesson will give you a basic background of the astrological chart and enable you to look at your own chart, or the chart of an event, from a magician's perspective. It also lays the foundations for later learning in the course when you will come to work with planetary magic in depth. There are a variety of free programs on the internet where you can generate your natal/birth chart, and also then add current transits in to begin to gain understanding. Currently (2024) https://www.astro.com is the best one I have found. You can generate your natal chart, and if you click the option of 'Extended Chart Selection' you can put in a date and then look at the transits of that date in relation to the natal chart. There are also books that can be bought or borrowed from a library that should help you construct a natal chart.

You don't need to become an astrologer, you don't even need to be very good at charts – a magician just needs to be able to look at a chart, look at transits, and look at what is happening in the houses. If you already have a background in astrology, still have a look through the lesson, as the angle of this lesson looks at the planets and forces specifically from a magician's perspective. If you already understand that, simply look at the section of the lesson that deals with the astrological natal chart and the pentagram: it shows how the individual natal chart and the pattern of the personal pentagram can be brought together to gain insight into your own magical potential.

1. THE BASICS

A natal chart looks at the position of the planets at the moment you were born in relation to where you were born. The *ascendant*, or first house, shows you the horizon when you were born, and what was 'to the east' of you at the moment of your birth. In a natal chart, you are in the centre, and everything revolves around you.

Your natal chart shows you what tools and potentials you were born with. What you do with those tools and potentials is purely up to you: you can make the most of them and work with them, or you can ignore them and be enslaved, buffeted, and driven by them. The magician slowly learns to recognise what tools and gifts were given to them at the moment of their birth, and then learns how to optimise those gifts in their training and practice.

It also shows you where your weaknesses and vulnerabilities are: by knowing your weaknesses, you learn how to strengthen them, and also how to protect that vulnerable part of you. Your natal chart shows you the raw materials; it is up to you as a magician to take those raw materials and turn them into something beautiful, productive, and useful.

You can also draw up a natal chart for a specific event. This will show you where all the powers are, how they are presenting, and what the tides of power are doing at a particular moment in time. It is unwise to plan magical actions or events to coincide with specific astrological events; rather it is better to let the natural flow of fate do its job. You can look at the chart of an event once its details have been set, and it will give you an idea of the deeper powers that are flowing into that area at that particular point in time.

2. TRANSITS

Transits are the current (or future if you look forward in time with a chart) positions of the planets in relation to the natal chart. Usually the positions of the planets in your natal chart are drawn inside the chart, and the transits are shown moving around the outside of the chart. The natal positions and transit positions are viewed in relation to each other, and in respect of which house the transit falls in.

When a transiting planet works its way back to the position it was in when you were born, it deeply triggers that planet's action in your life (this is called a *return*).

When the planets fall at specific angles to each other, they produce a tension of power that strengthens, weakens, or otherwise alters the influence of both planets upon you. The meetings of planets can be volatile or productive and helpful, depending on the angles at which they connect with each other. They can be face to face, or at certain degree angles to each other, or they can wave at each other from across the chart. The complexities of these meetings can be enormous, hence to really understand a chart in depth takes years of study and practice.

If you do not have the time or resources to do that, then there are many online programs and books that can work for you as a reference point. So long as you understand the basics, you will be able to make sense of the information in front of you.

3. Astrological signs

We all know about the astrological signs (Cancer, Aries, Scorpio etc.), or we should. You can simply look them up on the internet if you are not sure about them. Look at their element (water, earth, etc.), look up how they work (mutable, fixed, etc.), and look up their qualities and personalities.

When you look at a chart, and you look at the houses, you will see that each house has a dominant astrological sign. That sign is like a background weather report for that house.

4. Houses

The 1st house: the Ascendant

This is the core of who you are, how you appear to others, how your personality functions, and any physical traits. It is located on the left hand side of the natal chart and is the threshold of the horizon in the east when you were born.

The 2nd house: Finance and belongings

This shows how you earn money, how you process money, and your material belongings.

The 3rd house: Communication, family

How you communicate with your immediate family and community, and how you operate generally with communications. It is also a house that shows learning in terms of apprenticeships and studies.

The 4th house: the Imum Coeli

Home life, family, roots. This is where you come from in blood terms, and also shows your home/family through your life. This is your foundation. It can also indicate influences from the mother.

The 5th house: Creation and true love

This is the house of children, of true and deep love, and also the house of your art form: whatever you create, be it a child, a book, a painting, an invention, this is the house of what you bring into this world, creations that you love unconditionally.

The 6th house: The house of Service, and also the house of health/illness

This house shows you if you are going into a life of serving through whatever it is that you do, and it also can show any long-term illnesses that must be endured. Service illustrated by this house can be anything, and not obviously service, for example a scientist, a doctor, a teacher etc., whatever your passion flows through that affects the lives of others.

The 7th house: the Descendant

Unions, marriage. How you deal with relationship or contract partners, open enemies. This house is about how you relate to other individuals that you are in a direct energy connection with. It is opposite the ascendant and is positioned on the right hand side of the natal chart: it is where the sun sets.

The 8th house: transformation, death, sex, magic, and other people's money

This house tells you about how deep hidden powers work through your life and how you connect with them. It is about power from outside of you coming to you and interacting with you: the power of magic, the power of transformation, the power of resources that come to you from outside of your own action (other people's money). This is an important house for magicians to understand: through the power of transformation and your ability to operate in a balanced way with energy (good or bad) coming to you, you will learn how to wield power maturely and successfully.

The 9th house

This house works in reflection to the third house and tells you about higher learning, religious or mystical patterns, other cultures, travel to other cultures, and is another house that is very important for magicians to understand. It will show what astrological tools are at your disposal or present difficulties for you plugging into ancient mystical patterns, religions, and cultures. Whereas the third house shows apprenticeships, this house shows advanced learning.

The 10th house: the Midheaven (top of the chart)

This is the house of government, of professional standing and achievement, and of social structure. It also has connotations towards what influence your father had upon you (it sits opposite the 4th house/mother).

The 11th house

This house tells us about our friends, our community, and how we are perceived by our chosen community. It represents group activities, your place within your community, and how your friends and community interact with you. It is a very humanitarian house.

The 12th house

This house shows hidden ordeals, hidden enemies, secrets, struggles, and solitude. It is a house of isolation, be it a hospital, prison, or the isolation of an inner crisis. This house shows us how we deal with our hidden enemies, what fate patterns of hidden ordeals are in our life, and how we deal with meltdown, isolation, and crisis. It can also be a house of the hidden mysteries, a path that is trodden in secret and alone.

5. The Planets

Starting with the slow-moving planets that have a deep effect upon a chart, and often show generational tendencies, we will look at the individual planets briefly, and view them from the point of view of a magician.

Pluto

Pluto is necessary destruction before regeneration. Pluto strips away all unnecessary baggage: he confronts your weaknesses and brings transformation. It is an Underworld planet in that it also governs the powers of sex, magic and the mediation of power. Pluto is the cleaner: Pluto shows you what is no longer viable in your life and teaches you to let go of things. If you work with Pluto, you learn how to become efficient, you learn to know yourself, your limitations, and your strengths. Through Pluto you also learn the true meaning of magical power. If you resist Pluto, he will destroy you mercilessly.

Saturn

Saturn is the universal taskmaster. Saturn slows you down, makes you focus on the boring details, the discipline, and accuracy of your true work. Saturn gives you burdens to carry in order to strengthen you, he teaches you about boundaries and discipline, and most of all, particularly for magicians, shows you how to be of use, how to be of service, and how to gain fortitude in the face of difficulty.

Uranus

Uranus is a dynamic and sometimes vicious energy. Uranus brings unforeseen elements to a situation: a sudden change of power, a revolution, independence and inventiveness. Uranus is eccentric, he thinks sideways, he does not run with the pack but forges a unique path that is unpredictable and flexible. For a magician, the impact of Uranus can be good or bad depending on the magician's ability to think and operate outside the box.

If you are a 'glass half empty' type of person, Uranus can bring untold suffering as he pushes you to think independently and forces you to come up with your own unique solutions. Uranus hits like a lightening bolt out of the blue, shaking you out of complacency and confronting you with situations that are unexpected and unknown.

If you are a 'glass half full' kind of person and are adaptable, Uranus sprinkles your life with unexpected opportunities that often come out of disaster. For every destructive experience that Pluto can bring, Uranus can turn up the unexpected jewel twinkling in the ruins.

For magicians, Uranus is the unexpected solution, the sudden inspiration, the unforeseen lightning strike. Uranus is the power that keeps you alert, on your toes, lean, and ready for action.

Neptune

Neptune is the planet of hidden qualities, of the inner sight. He is inspiration, he is mystery, and he is water. He is the power that can flow at great depths, the power that cleans, the element that cannot be easily grasped. In the chart of the magician, depending on which house this planet falls in the birth chart (natal chart) he hints at inner abilities, hidden depths, and parts of yourself that are a mystery to you and everyone around you.

When he is transiting your chart, he can show where something is being hidden, or where the power of water is flowing, or where your deep inner qualities are in action. In a natal chart if he is very close to the IC, he can point to a person who has inner visionary sight and powerfully so if Neptune is conjunct Venus close to or on the IC. He can also indicate where you can have 'blind spots,' fake paradise, or psychological difficulties. He can also indicate a deep inner awakening.

Jupiter

This is the power of expansion, of good fortune, of teaching, benevolence, and good luck. If his power flows in a chart that is self-centred, he can indicate a tendency towards pretentiousness and exaggeration. But overall, his influence is about success with responsibility, honours that are earned, stability and joy.

He is a power that governs teachers and lawyers: Jupiter is full of charisma, he wishes to share and educate, and most importantly, he is the power of Justice and fair play. All of these qualities can come together with Jupiter to fashion a leader who cares for his or her people and will work hard for them.

Mars

The power that flows from Mars is action, power, courage, virility, and combat. Mars puts power and energy behind things: he plugs you into your ability to forge forward, to fight, to produce, and to win. He is also sexual power, the testosterone that flows through both men and women, and when his power is balanced in your life, you can achieve great things. If you are not careful, Mars can turn you into a bully. Mars is also the power of the magical sword, the power of 'I give' in terms of action.

Venus

Venus is sensuality and beauty, and acts as a buffer for the raw power of Mars. Venus is the brightness, the oestrogen in both men and women, the ability to seduce, to charm, to light up a room, and is the magical power of receiving/the cup.

Venus can also indicate a love or talent in art, music, poetry, and dance. For magicians, Venus is the bright light of artistic expression within magic, the ability to hold power (the cup) and transform it into something beautiful and creative.

Mercury

Mercury is the messenger of the gods. He is the power of communication, of sacred language, of communion with inner beings, and governs all exchanges between minds. He points to the intellectual capacity, the ability to work magically with the utterance, and to study in depth the mysteries hidden within texts. He is also the guide upon the magical path; Mercury points the way forward and is the Keeper of the Way. Mercury governs the tongue: he enables the magician to utter the sacred sounds, to express the communications of the inner worlds, and to work with knowledge in the form of text.

Sun

The Sun shines a light on the individual personality, and is the truth of a person, as opposed to the Ascendant which is the public persona of a person. The Sun is noble, gives life and strength, and can give power to other prominent planets in your chart. The Sun can also shine too brightly if it is not worked with and balanced, bringing pride and self-aggrandising qualities.

The Sun shows where you shine, and warns you not to bask too much in the sunlight of your own personality.

Moon

The moon is a fast-moving body and casts a shadowed light at best. The moon is creative in visionary depth and reflects in the natal chart, for magicians, where their creative visionary ability will have its most profound impact on those around you and within yourself. It can also show you where you are veiled, hidden, where you can fly under the radar and work magically to bring subtle influence. The Moon also governs dreams, and where it falls in transit around your chart can indicate where your dream-self is working magically as you sleep.

Chiron

Chiron is a comet that operates between Saturn and the outermost planets. It is also influenced by Uranus and brings a healing quality to the life challenges that Saturn and Uranus can present.

Chiron is the governor of deep inner wounds and outer sickness, and the situations that Saturn presents in life in the form of restrictions can indicate where deep healing, courtesy of Chiron, can bubble up to the surface in the midst of that restriction. Chiron is often thought in astrology to be the wound that cannot heal, but that is a surface misunderstanding of this power. Chiron is the healer who cannot heal himself but can heal others – the wound that Chiron carries is the magical wound, the wound/sickness that never heals but through that wound of sickness, the magician learns to help and heal others, or it limits the magician's path enough that fate can operate through them. I have found, through tracking Chiron's actions over the years in my own chart and the chart of others, that the influence of Chiron is very much about learning or gaining the resources to flourish despite a wound or sickness. An old saying, 'When the door closes, a window opens' – Chiron is the window. You focus on the alternative solution and stride off to flourish on your path despite sickness or wounds, rather than sitting in front of the closed door and being defeated.

When Chiron is placed close to another slow-moving planet in the natal chart, it can indicate the possibility of deep healing through the influence of the other planet. So for example it if is placed close to Jupiter in the natal chart, it can indicate that a positive attitude and humour in the depths of crisis can facilitate healing within yourself and those around you. When Chiron in transit activates a part of your natal chart, it can indicate the chance for deep healing within that section of your life.

Chiron is a mediator, one who filters the power of a large planet as it flows into your life, and offers the chance for you to heal deep and lasting wounds through the action of the large planet it is activating.

6. *Task:* Investigating your own chart

On the internet, go to `astro.com` and sign up as a member (it is free). Then go to: *horoscope drawings … chart ascendant*. Fill in your details and it will draw up a chart for you. You can run many charts for free on this site, and once you get to know your way around, you will find all sorts of resources that you can use.

Look at your natal chart. Notice the pattern the chart makes, look at where most of the planets are, look at the houses and what planets are in them. Take notes, and don't worry if it doesn't make sense to you at first: interpreting a chart takes time, as it is like learning a new language. Whatever jumps out at you, simply write it down.

When you have looked as much as you can at your natal chart, now go on the `astro.com` website and click on *personal daily horoscope*. Scroll down to the bottom and click on the link to natal chart with transits. Now look at your chart with the transits.

Look and take note of which transiting planets are triggering planets in your natal chart. You will be able to tell which ones are activating natal planets by their angle, or by the relationship between the transiting planet and a natal planet. Note what house that is happening in.

`astro.com` also has short reports on your transits, so you can look up what some of your current transits are, read how they may affect you, and then look back at the chart again to see if you can spot the transit and understand its action.

Sit and think about what is going on in your life at this present time. Does the description of the transit bear any resemblance to your current situation? If so, look more deeply into the descriptions of the transit to see if there is advice in there for you about how to engage the transit consciously.

Like any form of divination, astrology takes time to learn, so don't expect to 'have it' straight away. Once you are comfortable with navigating the `astro.com` website, explore different charts by putting in different people's dates or the dates and times of events. Curiosity and playfulness is the best way to learn these skills in a basic form. Just don't overstep people's personal boundaries. I practised on charts of my children and family members.

It took a while for me to be able to look at a chart and get a rough idea of what it was saying. These days I find it very useful to look at charts for energetic 'weather' reports, and to look at my transits to see how I can best engage positively with current tides in my life.

Write down all of your findings in your journal, write down your current transits (the website will have a list of them), and print out your natal chart with transits so that you can work with it. Keep it in your journal so that you can look back at it.

7. *Task:* Ritual exercise – the pentagram and the natal chart

Draw a pentagram on a sheet of paper: this represents you standing in the centre of your chart. The arms of the pentagram are the horizon on the natal chart with the Ascendant (first house) on the left/east: the left arm of the pentagram is your left arm if you were stood facing south.

Now look at your natal planets on your chart. Remember that the horizon is your arms in this exercise. Put the pentagram and the chart side by side. Now look for where Pluto is in your natal chart. If you put the pentagram over the chart, where on the page of the pentagram would Pluto sit?

Is he by your right hand? Or your left leg? Or near your head? Look at the astrological sigil for Pluto (the sigils are on your chart) and place it in the relevant position around your pentagram.

Now do the same for all of the other planets. When you have finished, you should have a pentagram that represents you, with the sigils of your planets marked around it in a two-dimensional pattern. Look at their positions in relation to your body, and in relation to the two-dimensional aspect of the pentagram ritual. (Hexagram above you, earth below you, sword to your left/east, cup to your right/west.)

Look carefully at the position of each sigil. See which planets jump out at you the most, and choose one, two, or three planets to focus on. Alternatively you can start practising this technique with only one planet, and add in more as your confidence increases. So for example you may have Mercury in the upper right quadrant near your head, Saturn by your left foot in the lower left quadrant, and Jupiter on your eastern horizon (left arm).

Look up the qualities of those planets, then remember the qualities of the pentagram directions. If you use the planets I have just mentioned, you would read it something like this:

Mercury upper right quadrant, positioned between the hexagram and the cup – Divinity and the quality of receiving – Mercury is the messenger of the gods: this planet in this position in your pentagram indicates deep inner communication potential.

For a magician, this could be used for learning, teaching, or communicating with inner contacts. So when the magician does the ritual of the pentagram and uses her mind to see the sword/cup/hexagram etc., she would also add in the sigil of Mercury which she would see hanging in the air to her right, maybe slightly forward of her face to give it more of a three-dimensional aspect.

So you start to see how you can engage with the gifts that the natal planets give you by locating them on your own personal pentagram and working with them, first through visualising them in your pattern, and later through the use of seals, rituals and visions. This is one more baby step towards planetary magic.

If you wish to experiment further with this technique, work with a specific planet of your natal chart and find its location on your own pentagram. Now find out where it is currently transiting with regard to your personal pentagram, and be aware of the two positions as you work the pentagram ritual. If you choose a slow-moving planet like Saturn and work with it in its natal and transit positions in your pentagram (see the Saturn sigil in each of the two positions), you can build up the work over weeks or months as the transit position will hardly change.

This in turn will really strengthen your relationship with that planet's powers and influence upon you, which in turn will help you to engage actively with its energy. This will help you to activate the positive aspect of the planet fully, which will also help you to learn, grow and strengthen. If you are ambitious, once you are able to visualise a natal and transiting planet's sigils in your pentagram, start to build an awareness of where the various houses would be placed in your pentagram. If you can do that, it will give you a great deal of insight into your body, your energy sphere, and why certain things are happening around you.

The permutations of this pattern are endless, and with a bit of imagination, curiosity and a sense of experimentation, you can take this pentagram/chart exercise in many different directions.

Journal

Write down all the experimental work you do with your chart and the pentagram. Write down any inspirations that bubble up to the surface, any 'ah-ha!'s and write down any correlations about transits and body health that may emerge from this work.

8. *Task:* Your personal pentagram

Draw out your personal pentagram and put all of your natal planets around it. Choose two of the natal planets and look at their relation to the pentagram/your body. Now go back in your notes/journal to lesson six, and your experiment with drawing out the pentagram and adding in colours.

Look at your pentagram and the colours, and now look at your pentagram with the planets. What does the combination of the colours and the planets tell you about your body? Locate its strong points, weak points, sick points, etc.

Here is an example of how to read the two pentagrams side by side. A pentagram of a person that has Saturn in the sixth house in their chart. (Service, also long-term illness.) Saturn is currently transiting in the pentagram in the right hand arm of the pentagram (arm/hand). The colour on the pentagram for that arm is red. Does the person have joint pains in the right arm or hand? Or do they work hard with their right hand but it is currently restricted? (Saturn can indicate restriction.)

This is a very loose way of working and sometimes just brings up nonsense, but other times it can give quite startling insights. Play around with the chart/pentagram, and take notes of anything that seems to be important.

By this point in your first module, you should be sick to death of doing pentagram work. But this repeated looking at the pentagram from all different angles ensures that you gain a deep and very useful magical understanding of this shape that will embed itself in your consciousness.

That embedding and deep understanding is how the pentagram can become a powerful tool and shield in your magical work. By now you should have a good understanding of what it is and how it works, and you should be able to do the simple pentagram shield with ease and fluency. This will put you in good stead when it comes to doing deep ritual work with the planetary powers and angelic interfaces (for example the Arbatel).

9. Module One Summary

At this point of your early training, you should have a solid basic grounding in a few key magical techniques: meditation, vision, ritual, and pattern-making. You should also have by now settled into a good personal method of record-keeping, observation, and experimentation.

Establish for yourself a rhythm of meditation, practising skills already learned, and learning new skills. Develop a schedule of work that functions best for you and your everyday life, so that you do not become overwhelmed in your studies or shut out partners, family, or everyday life activities: magic should dovetail into your life, not take it over and isolate you from others.

Important – please read:

Each time you start a new module, start a new journal so that each module has its own journal, notes, experiments, etc. It will leave you with journals that are only half full, but in ten years time they will be very full. As you walk down the path of magical training, you will keep coming back to many of the lessons such as a vision you did in the early days of your training suddenly making sense, or something you saw in a vision finally actually happens. You will gain many deeper insights about your work as you go through your training, and going back to the early lesson and adding a page about the new insights, slowly builds these journals up into a library of magical development. You do not need fancy leather bound journals, school exercise books or plain note books are sufficient. I have a cupboard full of old notebooks that I go back to and add in something I have just remembered from years ago and now understand.

Use a mix of computer files and paper journals, and make sure that your online notes, essays etc. are backed up in a folder that is kept only for your magical study and work. If you choose to submit your work for mentoring at the end of the Apprentice section, it will need to be submitted as computer files, not journals.

We found we could not read the writing of people who submitted paper journals! But doing the handwriting in journals is a very important habit to get into magically. It prepares you for contacted writing, and there are huge differences magically and also in terms of brain use when you hand write something. I suggest you handwrite as you go along, and then type it up on computer.

Well done for getting this far. You have made your first major step in magical education!

Apprentice

Module II

Patterns and Maps in Magic

Study Guide for Module II

A lot of the lessons in this module are about learning to execute certain ritual patterns (and you have two easy lessons with not much action). It is important that you learn each ritual in turn, learning the recitations by heart, and learning the coordinated movements. If you are not good at memorising rituals or visions, then it might be a good idea to record them in your own voice and then listen repeatedly until you get it. I know, no one likes listening to their own voice, but that is also a magical lesson in itself – confronting who you are.

Read all of the text in each lesson – some students skip through the text to get to the good bits, but to do so is folly. Lots of important bits of information are tucked away in the text, as are tasks that are not listed under the tasks heading. Once you have learned a ritual and are able to do it properly, and have absorbed the lesson, you will have been instructed to repeat that ritual for a certain period of time. As you practise, you are also ready to continue on to the next lesson.

Your rhythm of study should be: read the lesson – practise the ritual movements and learn the recitations – do the ritual 'proper' – set up a timetable to repeat it – start the next lesson. Each week you should be doing meditations, tarot reading practice, practising rituals from previous lessons, learning new ritual/lessons, doing research or writing. If you have a heavy work schedule and cannot commit to that type of a time frame, work at your own pace: the main thing is that there are things you do regularly, and that you are practising the previous lesson while learning the new one, so that they overlap a little. There is no race and no value in cramming or pushing yourself too much.

Above all, make sure that you stay in the sequence of lessons and do not hop forward a few lessons.

Lesson 1
Directions

The second module of the apprentice training is all about magical patterns.

Patterns are the skeletons and nervous systems of magic, and without the use of patterns, magic falls apart. If the magician does not understand the patterns they are using, they will severely limit their work, learning, and power. This is why it is very important to learn some of the key patterns in the early stages of your training, so that all of your magical learning has a foundation to sit upon.

The first lesson of this module is about the directional pattern. In the first module, you learned the very basics of how to acknowledge the powers of the four directions and the power in the centre. That is the base template for rituals and visions that work around the directions. From that template, you now need to learn how to operate with the directions in visionary ritual in order to prepare for making inner contacts and working with them.

The four-directional pattern is probably the oldest pattern we are aware of in magic, and it is also the most versatile. It is used for making inner contact, for moving power around, for magical construction, for sending and receiving magic, for tuning, for protection... The applications of the four-directional pattern are wide-ranging because it is a template for the physical world. It is the map of the earth in terms of creation as viewed through the lens of Western magic.

Throughout your magical training you will revisit this pattern many times in very different ways, so that you slowly build up a strong understanding of the breadth and depth of this simple system. The four-directional pattern, along with certain other patterns inherent within magic, is a major key to working magic successfully. For this reason it is important to learn all these patterns' different levels, applications, methods of operation, and the magical interactions that flow through them.

Before we step into the practical work of visionary ritual, we need to shine a light on some of the work you have already done to give you a deeper understanding of what you have been working on. Let's open out the deeper mysteries of the magical directions a little bit, and give you a peek of how the powers work, what they are, and how you work with them as a magician.

1. Directional dynamics of power

East – West

When you work ritually around the directions and in vision, the power of humanity flows through the east–west axis. The two root tools flow from these directions, and out of these directions the full magical power of humanity can be drawn. Whenever a magician does a magical action, it will flow out of one or both of these directions.

So far in your basic ritual training, you have visualised a sword held in your left hand. This means you are facing south in your ritual work (facing south directs the magic into the future). The power of the east is the power of utterance, learning, and the sacred Breath of life; and it is embodied within the sword – which is held as a magical being, not as a magical weapon.

The key word of the east is *I Give*. This ritual positioning enables you to take action actively, to instigate a magical act that adds something to the universe. The key word *I Give* means you are initiating an action: you are creating. This puts the magic into the flow of creation, a flow that is constant, powerful, and Divine: *"In the beginning was the Word."* The first act of creation is the Breath of Divine Consciousness uttering from the Void.

This is why a lot of magic starts in the east, with a word or a breath, and why the sword (Air) lives in the east. This is also why religions based around the utterance turn east to pray. The east is male, not in a gender sense, but in the sense that when it acts creatively its power outputs or 'gives' like semen. The prayer that is physically uttered is powerful, and magic that is physically uttered is also the most powerful. Here is an example from a religion.

"Adonai s'fatai tiftach, ufi yagid t'hilatecha."

(Transliterated Hebrew. Translated:

"Adonai open my lips, that my mouth may declare your praise.")

That Hebrew prayer holds a great many magical keys of understanding hidden within it. East is the beginning of a magical action for us as humans. But it is not the actual first step. Before us, everything has to flow from a Divine or Universal Power source. The first step of a true magical action is the impulse leaving the Void and beginning its journey to express itself in the human world. The magician taps into that expression and mediates it through them in an act of release.

The sword as a magical object guards the Word, the magical utterance, and keeps its action limited, restrained, and focused. Remember the sword's powers when we later discuss the subject of using ritual action to connect with inner contacts, as the contacts are filtered by its attributes.

The west is the female direction in that it receives in the creative act like a womb does: the vessel. This is not about being watery and feminine; rather it is about the capacity to contain power and form it. The vessel receives the utterance or Word and incubates it, contains it, and forms it into something tangible. So you see that either human-based direction cannot work in isolation: the giving power needs to be received, and the vessel can only receive if something is actually placed within it.

Just as the east is dawn, the beginning, the west is sunset. By the time the vessel fully transforms the power it has received, it is already marching towards destruction. All creation is either rising to a peak or falling into destruction – there is never a plateau. Just as every human life grows, reaches a peak, and then immediately begins its slow decline to death, so too does all magical power instigated by humanity.

The key is to map out the future fate path of the magic so that it achieves its purpose while cycling through its rhythm of creation and destruction. That is done by balancing the creation (east) and destruction (west) with time: past and future. The magician stands in the present and draws power from the east to create a magical cycle, but that magical cycle must connect into the flow of time and substance in order to work. And this is where the other two directions come in.

North – South

North is the past, the ancestral realm, the ancient Mother, the rock beneath you. North is both behind you and beneath you: the shield that has your back is also the rock upon which you stand. You hold the sum total of your ancestral wisdom in your blood, and that blood wisdom is something a magician draws upon heavily. As a magician in a contacted line, you are also the sum total of every magician who has gone before you: that line buffers you and strengthens you.

So when the magician stands with her arms out, sword in her left hand (east) and cup in her right hand (west), her back is to the north: the shield guards her back and the rock/ancestors beneath her give her a huge reservoir of wisdom, stability, and strength to draw from: beneath and behind work together and are essentially the same directional power.

South is the future. South is the angelic threshold of the future; it is also the direction of potential as that potential is still being formed. This path of future potential is fuelled by angelic beings that create an interface for the future to flow through. This interface is perceived in magic as 'above.'[1] This is why on your pentagram shield the hexagram (Divinity in balance) is above you. The hexagram pattern flows down into manifestation and into the earth – which is why you have the symbol for earth below the genitals (generations) of the pentagram. Are you confused yet?

Hopefully by this stage you will begin to realise that the four-directional pattern is not four-directional at all: that is a hugely simplified reduction of a complex and beautiful pattern. And it should also be dawning on you that not only is the four-directional pattern multidimensional, but it is roughly divided in two: creation and destruction.

So, place yourself in the centre of the directions. The east and above work together to create the utterance, which is then sent on its path into the future via the south: which is why magicians point wands (or fingers) – wands/fire/south. The wand directs the magic into the future, into action, by way of the inspirational fire that brings formation. The west, the north, and below all work together to receive that magical action, to ground it, root it, contain it, and form it into a solid pattern.

Through the tension and polarity of the south/future/potential and the north/past/substance – with the magician in the centre to act as the fulcrum – a power builds up that is contained, formed, energised, and ready to burst into the future. And when I say future, remember that in magic "future" can mean in a hundred years' time,

---

[1] Why this is so will become very apparent in your adept studies.

in a year's time or in three seconds' time. All magic must be created for the future, otherwise it just will not work. If you make the mistake of creating magic for 'now' it will fail as there is no such thing as 'now' – time is constantly flowing.

If you are confused at this point, go back and reread this section and maybe draw out the pattern described, or stand and imagine it around you until you start to get a feel of its multidimensional aspect. Take your time understanding this: it can be a massive leap, but it is a necessary and important one if you are to be successful in your magical actions.

Now it is time, if you have basically grasped this multidimensional pattern, to begin to work it ritually and in vision. In the first module you learned how to use your mind to move about a space. This next practical exercise will build upon the directional ritual pattern you learned in module one, and will step your visionary process forward an inch in preparation for you stepping into the inner worlds.

You learned to move about your living space in your mind; now you need to learn how to move about a magical space both physically and in vision. At the same time you need to begin to learn how to move power around using your mind. This will prepare you for working with inner contacts and also for working with magical tools.

2. TASK: THE VISIONARY RITUAL OF THE DIRECTIONS

Working in your ritual space with the five altars, go around the directions lighting the lights and visualising the gates in the method that you learned in previous lessons.

Go and stand before the central flame, facing south. Be aware of the four directions around you, and of the fifth direction which is the centre. The centre direction is also above and below: it is the column of power that is the central fulcrum for all substance, and it is the highway of time (above = future, centre = present, below = past) just as the flow of time also expresses from past from the north to the future in the south.

Remember the breastplate from Module I, Lesson 7. Standing before the flame, hold out your arms and close your eyes. See the sword in your left hand and the cup in your right hand. Imagine, using your mind's eye, a road opening up before you that vanishes off into the south, and behind you a line of people that seems to vanish off into the depths of the north.

Between you and the line of people (the ancestral line) is your Guardian Angel, who has a hand upon your shoulder. Before you, on the path that goes off to the southern horizon, stands a group of angelic beings. These can appear in your mind as humans with very long hair that trails on the ground behind them or they may present themselves as simply beings that are so bright you cannot see any of their shape or features. They are holding out an arm as if to show you the way ahead. Holding those images in your mind, recite the breastplate:

> "The Father is above me,
> The Mother is below me,
> the Sword to my left,
> the Cup to my right,
> the Guardian Angel behind me,
> the Sandalphon before me,
> within me is life,
> within me is the Breath of God:
> I Will Be."

That ritual action and utterance has now tuned the space and tuned you to a frequency where you can work properly and safely.

3. *Task:* Ritual of confirmation

Only do this ritual once – it is a declaration that triggers the magical process of receiving the magical tools in the future.

Walk a full circle around the central altar, bow to the east altar, and walk a full circle a second time, finishing standing before the eastern altar. In your mind's eye, while also keeping your eyes open, 'see' the gates which are open. Now close your eyes. Imagine you extend your left arm across the altar and hold out your hand to the gates. Keeping your eyes closed, and using your physical voice, ask:

> "I, [*say your name*], as an apprentice of the Quareia,
> ask that I may begin the journey of the Sword."

Now extend your physical left arm out over the altar (be careful of the flame). With your eyes closed, using your mind's eye, see a shadowy figure emerge from between the open gates. The figure looks at your hand and then touches it as if feeling for something. Keep that image for however long the figure holds your hand. Once the figure lets your hand go, with eyes remained closed and holding the vision, physically bow and withdraw your hand. Take a step back, turn and walk a full circle around the central altar, and stop at the southern altar.

Place both your hands on or to the side the altar and close your eyes. See in your mind's eye the open gates. Look beyond the open gates and see a road going off into the horizon. On the road you will see some figures. One of them has a hand held up in a 'stop and wait' position. The being is showing you the way ahead but warning you that it is not yet time to step into and onto that path: first you must gain the skills needed to walk that path. But they are waiting patiently for you and will be there when you are ready.

Open your eyes and using your right hand, index finger pointed, draw a line straight down from 'above to below.' Now draw a diagonal line from upper left to lower right, and then a diagonal line from upper right to lower left (drawing an X through the line).

This is the *quarry mark*: you are defining your path ahead with the magic of the quarry.

Take a step back, bow and turn. Walk a full circle around the central flame and then end at the western altar. In your mind's eye, while also keeping your eyes open, 'see' the gates which are open. Close your eyes. Imagine you extend your right arm across the altar and hold out your hand to the gates. Keeping your eyes closed, and using your physical voice, say:

> "I, [*say your name*], as an apprentice of the Quareia,
> ask that I begin the journey of the Cup."

Now extend your physical right arm out over the altar (be careful of the flame). With your eyes closed, using your mind's eye, see a shadowy figure emerge from between the open gates. The figure looks at your hand and then touches it as if feeling for something. Keep that image for however long the figure holds your hand. Once the figure lets your hand go, with eyes remained closed and holding the vision, physically bow and withdraw your hand.

Take a step back, turn, and walk a full circle around the central altar, ending at the northern altar. In your mind's eye, while also keeping your eyes open, 'see' the gates which are open. Place your hands upon or to the side the altar and close your eyes. Using your mind's eye, using your imagination, look at the open gates and see many people gathering at the threshold of the gates: these are people you are connected to in time, be they blood ancestors, companions from other lives, etc. None of them cross the threshold to join you; they stay on the threshold, just showing you that they are there, that they 'have your back.'

One of them shines a lot brighter than the others, and when you look closely, you see the eyes of this person are like stars: it is then that you realise this is not another human, but your Guardian Angel. Do not try to make any verbal contact: it is too early in magical terms to make full contact – it is enough that you see, recognise, and acknowledge. Bow to the gathered people and the angel, and say out loud:

> "Thank you."

Open your eyes and take a step back.

Turn and walk a full circle around the central flame, and then stand in the north, facing south, with the central altar before you. Sit down and close your eyes. Meditate for a few minutes and think about the images and people in each direction that you have just visualised. When you are ready, either stand up and go around the directions to close the gates down, or continue on to your next ritual exercise.

Notes on this ritual

The ritual of confirmation is a very simple and yet deep-acting ritual that introduces you as a magical apprentice to the inner contacts. The apprentice asks to begin a journey that will lead to the magical tools, and also begins to see and acknowledge the contacts in the directions.

Regarding the inner contact touching the inner hand of the apprentice: through this visionary touch, the inner contacts can 'see' the best way to align your path to the path of the specific magical tools that you will work with in the future. It is a magical way of saying hello and handing over your resume.

This ritual does not tie you in any way to Quareia, rather it introduces you to powers and inner beings, and declares your intent to walk a magical path, any magical path. That path may veer away from Quareia to another path that is more suited to you, and that really does not matter. The ritual you have just done is about you and magic, regardless of how, where, when and with whom you do that magic. It is the moment you are presented to the inner worlds as one who wishes to walk a magical path.

4. *Task:* Directional ritual of power, Part I

If you are continuing on from your confirmation ritual, do a stillness meditation for a few minutes and then see the room and the altars with the flames in the directions in your mind's eye.

If you are starting this ritual afresh, light the directional lights and visualise the opening of the gates using the method you learned in Module One. Once the gates are open, sit down before the central altar, facing south, and do a stillness meditation for a few minutes.

Once you are still, you are ready to work.

The next part of the ritual is done seated before the central flame, with you facing east. You are going to work with visualisation with your eyes closed, using your imagination.

Turn your attention to the central flame. See a column of light coming down into the room, passing through the central flame and then plunging down into the ground.

See a thread of light coming out of the east and joining the central flame. From there it shoots out into the south, passing through the southern flame and through the open gates.

See the thread of light returning from the southern gate, passing through the central flame and going into the west. It hits the western flame and passes through the western gates.

The thread of light then flows back from the west to the central flame before passing into the north. It passes through the northern flame and vanishes through the northern gates.

So the flow of light processes as follows: From the east, centre, south. From the south, centre, west. From the west, centre, north.

See this flow of light/power pass around the directions from east to north three times until you can imagine the flow with ease. After the third time of imagining this power flow, open your eyes and stand up. Pick up a taper or long candle.

Process a full circle around the central altar and stop before the eastern altar.

Light the taper from the eastern flame and say:

"I give."

Turn to the central flame and join the flame of the taper with the flame of the central flame. Say:

"I create."

Now turn and walk to the southern altar. Join the taper flame with the southern flame and say:

"I give to the future."

Now blow out the taper flame and walk a full circle around the central flame, returning back to the southern altar.

Light the taper from the southern flame and say:

"I receive for the past."

Walk with the taper straight to the western altar – bypass the central flame for this particular part of the ritual. Join the flame of the taper to the flame on the western altar and say:

"I receive."

Turn and walk to the central altar and join the flame of the taper to the flame of the central altar and say:

"I destroy."

Turn and walk to the northern altar and join the taper flame with the northern flame and say:

"It is done and I release the fragments into the past."

Blow out the taper and put it on the northern altar. Turn and walk a full circle and finish before the eastern altar. Pause for a moment, say thank you, see in your mind's eye the gates closing, then blow out the eastern flame. Step back, bow, say thank you. Repeat in the south, west and north. Turn to the central altar, bow, say thank you, and blow out the central flame. Stand for a moment in the silence before leaving the room.

Do this action seven times (no more than once a day), until you have a strong sense of how it works and you can do it with ease. This is simply a template for the ritual. Once you are comfortable with the ritual so far, then it is time to step it up by introducing contact and power. The way to do this is as follows.

5. *Task:* Directional Ritual II (The Full Ritual)

> *This ritual uses a lot of visualisation. The best way to work is if you can use your mind's eye to imagine images while your eyes are still open. If you cannot yet do that, don't worry, just close your eyes for the visionary aspects of the ritual and then open them when you have to move around or do an action.*

Start first with a stillness meditation. Light all of the directional flames, starting in the east, and see the gates opening. Go back to the central altar, stand facing south with the altar before you, and stand for a few moments in silence to prepare yourself. Utter the breastplate. Now you are ready to work. Pick up a taper and start by approaching the eastern altar.

When you approach the east with the taper, see in your mind's eye a shadowy figure standing at the threshold of the gates. As you approach the eastern altar, the figure holds out their hand, and you see that a flame is nestling in its palm. They hold their hand out over the eastern flame so that the flame in their palm and the flame on the altar become one. As you light the taper from this flame, be aware that you are lighting it from the inner flame and the outer flame.

This time when you say

"I give,"

you direct that utterance to the flame of the taper.

As you step back, see a thread of light attached to the taper's flame, so that as you walk around the room, the taper leaves a trail of light where it has been. Go to the central flame. As you hold the taper's flame to the central flame, you see in your mind's eye a large burst of light in the central flame. That light starts to form a shape. You say,

"I create."

That shape passes into the taper's flame and, using your mind's eye, you see the shape held in the taper flame as you process to the south. (Do not try to force a shape with your imagination, just let whatever shape it is form itself.)

When you go to the south, see in your mind's eye the path through the gates and the beings stood on the path. Touch the taper's flame to the southern candle's flame. You say,

"I give to the future."

A being holds out his hand and accepts the shape of light in the flame from you. He walks off down the path into the future with the shape of light glowing brightly.

Blow out the taper's flame and walk a full circle around the central altar, and finish at the southern altar once more. Close your eyes and see the gates, the path ahead, and a figure walking down the path towards you holding something that looks like it is breaking down, or dark.

Light the taper with the southern flame and hold the taper's flame in the southern flame. See with your mind's eye the figure place the shape into the taper's flame. Say,

"I receive for the past."

Bow, step back, and turn to the western altar.

Stand before the western altar. Join the taper flame to the western flame and see a shadowy person standing at the threshold of the western gate. They take the shape and roll it in their hands until it is condensed and contained. Then they place the condensed shape into the taper flame. Say,

"I receive."

(Now comes the critical learning curve.) See the condensed shape pass from the western flame and from your taper into your body's centre, where your own flame of life resides. The shape is held within you, and the taper's light upholds you as you hold the shape. A thread of light connects the shape you are holding within you to the taper's flame: you are simply holding the shape briefly within you, but it is still connected to the taper's flame.

Turn to the central flame. Join the taper's flame to the central flame and say

"I destroy."

See the shape passing from your centre, through the taper's flame and into the central flame. As it passes from you, it is torn up into small pieces. See the pieces hanging in the central flame.

Turn and face the northern altar. As you walk to the northern altar, see a thread of light running from the central flame to the taper that follows you as you walk. In that thread of light, see the fragments as they travel into the north flame. Touch the taper flame to the flame in the north and see all the fragments pass into the northern flame. Say

"It is done and I release the fragments into the past."

See in your mind's eye the northern gate with the people standing on the threshold. They take the fragments and kneel down to the earth. They place the fragments into the earth and then stand back up. Bow to them and say

"Thank you."

Step back, bow once more, and walk a full circle around the room and finish before the eastern altar. Say

"Thank you."

Bow, and blow out the eastern flame. Repeat in the south, west, north and then centre (stand facing south).

Stand for a moment in the silence before leaving the room.

Notes on this ritual

This ritual is something you can practise once a week for a few weeks. It is a key foundation of all ritual that moves power around through time, and in and out of the material world. For now, the ritual teaches you how to take a simple fragment of energy, bridge it into the future, take it from the future, and place it in the past. It is about creating and destroying, power in and power out. It also teaches you how the directions work with power, which directions 'output' power, which directions 'input' power, and which directions do both.

This ritual also begins the process of learning how to establish inner contacts that you can work with in ritual. For now, you are learning how to bring these contacts to the threshold of your space. Later on you will learn how to bring them fully into your space safely, and also how to pass into their realms to work with them in their own worlds. This is also a good exercise to learn how power moves around, and how you can either hold power in a flame, and/or hold it within yourself safely. This foundation ritual can be used regularly (once a month, for example) to build up your inner muscle and to adjust your spirit and body to moving power around: it is a foundational action and an exercise. The longer you work with this ritual, the more powerful it will slowly become. As you get stronger and more solid in your work, the power handed to you will be greater.

Never ever be tempted to keep the power that is handed to you: the power that comes out of the east is not for you, it is for the future; you are merely the bridge for it. If you try to take it into yourself and hold onto it, it will destroy you. And that is not an idle or drama-ridden warning: although this is a beginner exercise, once you learn how to do this ritual, you will in fact be given power to move around and practise with, and there is always a temptation to hold onto that power once you start to feel it.

The reason the power would destroy you is that it is generally not compatible with the human body for more than a few seconds. You are a vessel, and as a human vessel, you are designed to carry power as a bridge. If you hang on to that power, the vessel comes under too much pressure and cracks. Further into your training you will learn how to reach for power that you can safely keep and work with. But this directional exercise is specifically tuned to connect you into directional power that is about the forming of the future, fate paths, and learning. Hanging on to it would be akin to placing a paving stone within you.

6. *Task:* Journal

Write down your observations and experiences with these directional rituals.

Go back to your lessons and notes from the first module, particularly the tarot module, and remember the qualities and attributes of the directions that you used in your tarot layouts. Look at those attributes and then think about the directional flow of power you have just worked with and meditate/ponder over the connections. Write down any inspired thoughts that come from that observation.

7. *Task:* An experiment

Choose a day and do the full directional ritual (II) with the intent that whatever power you move around will be for the benefit of the land you live on.

Before you start the ritual, be aware of what landmarks and landscapes are around your area and think carefully about the boundary of the area you are going to work with (your garden, your block, your neighbourhood, your town, etc.). Don't choose too big an area as it will exhaust you. Your garden or your block/immediate area is enough.

Stand in the room or the outside space you are going to work in, and in your mind's eye see the boundaries and landmarks in each direction. As you light the first candle to start the ritual, declare:

> "I do this for the good of the land upon which I stand.
> I do this in the spirit of service and of learning."

As you do the ritual, take a mental note of the shape the energy forms in the central flame. Note how it feels. When the degrading shape is taken to the west, take note of how it feels. When it is placed within you, note how it feels, and any image or thought that flashes into your mind.

When you release the fragments into the north, remember how that feels, and also remember what the people of the threshold look like in terms of age, culture, or time. When you do this work specifically in service for the land, the contacts that appear on the northern threshold might not be your own ancestors; they could be the ancestors or land spirits of that place.

When you have finished, write everything that you noticed into your computer log or journal, and draw a map of the area that you worked on. Over the coming months, take note of any unusual things that happen within that boundary, particularly things that create permanent change or bring something to a conclusion.

Lesson 2
The Tree of Life Tarot

| *Note:* For this lesson, you will need your tarot deck.

The Tree of Life is a foundational pattern found in various forms throughout western magic, not just in Kabbalah. It is a map of how power flows and it is useful for all magicians to learn this pattern. This lesson is about the Tree of Life pattern in terms of divination and as you progress through the course, you will begin to recognise the patterns in many different aspects of magic, cultures, and mystical expressions.

So let's have a look at the Tree of Life shape. It is essentially a map of creation. Note the use of the word *map*: many make the mistake of thinking that the shape or pattern is the magical 'truth' – it is not. The Tree of Life is simply a map for an inner dynamic that you can interact with. Learning the shape, pattern, and flow of the map before you come to actually learn about its expression in magical dynamics will help you enormously. Figure 2 shows an image of the Tree without any words, shapes, symbols, or attributes.

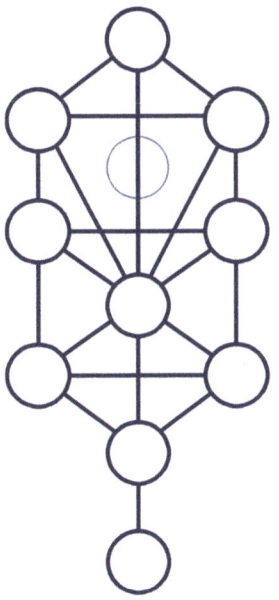

Note that there are ten spheres with a 'hidden' sphere marked in shadow. That is not actually a sphere, but it is a point on the map of great importance, something you will learn about later.

The top sphere is the beginning and the bottom sphere is the outcome.

Note the line running down the middle: the middle pillar.

This is the highway of creation and is the map for the column of light in the centre of your directional ritual work. It flows from above, from the beginning, down into the earth. Everything revolves around that middle pillar.

Now let's look at this map in terms of tarot.

Figure 2: The Tree of Life

1. The Tree of Life tarot layout

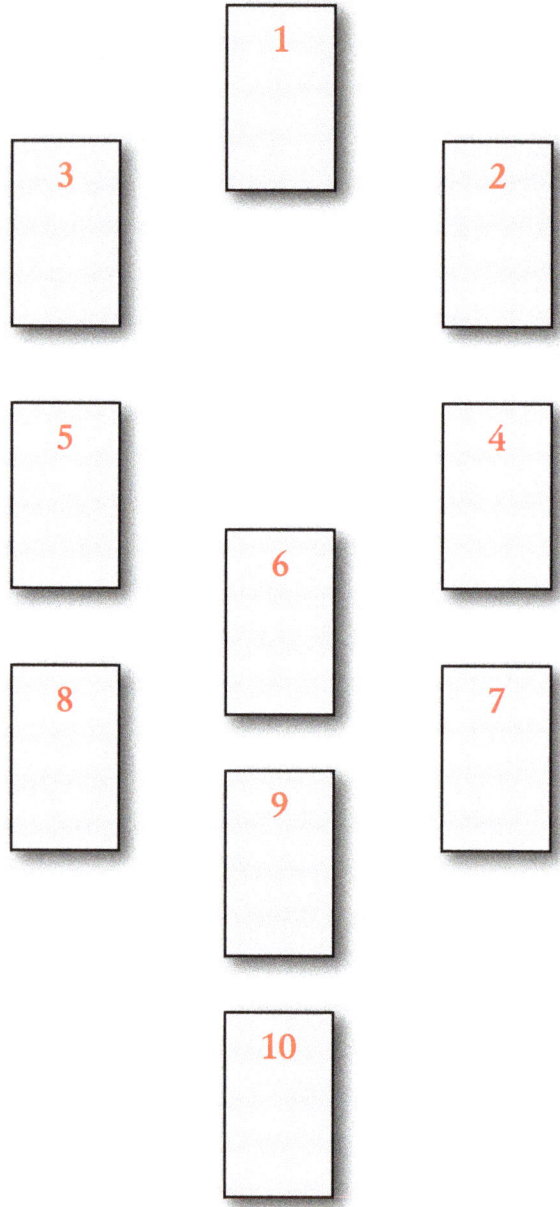

Figure 3: The Tree of Life tarot layout

The meanings of the positions on the tarot map are simplistic in order to gain a clear meaning from the cards that land in that position. If you study the tarot map, you will notice that one side of the Tree is about power coming into something: it is a *giving* side. The other side of the Tree *unravels* and *takes away*.

The centre is about how the story begins, what it revolves around, how it affects our family/home, and finally the outcome. Just as an aside, when people work magically with the Tree, they often equate the right side of the Tree (looking at it on paper) with the right side of their body. This is an incorrect assumption that has snowballed into a 'truth.' You do not look at the Tree as a reflection; you *are* in the Tree. So see it as if you are backed into it: what appears on paper as the right hand side is in fact your left hand side – you and tree on paper are looking at each other face to face.

2. Working with the Tree layout

So let's get straight to work. Get your cards, and remember your lesson about shuffling and laying them out. To start with, we are going to concentrate on learning how to work with the layout, so do not be concerned at this stage about the accuracy of the reading.

Pick a public figure, think about that person, and then think of a specific question relating to them: this layout is good for specific questions, but weaker at overall pictures. The reason for picking a public figure is that you can track their life's progress through the media if you wish to keep an eye on the reading's outcome. It is also better, when first learning to work with layouts, to do readings for things that are not too close to home. If you see something destructive in a reading, and are not yet feeling fully confident in your reading ability, you can end up terrifying yourself unnecessarily.

As you shuffle, keep thinking of the name of the person, and when you feel the shuffle is done, lay out the cards using the layout above. Before you get into interpreting each individual card, just take a moment to look at the general feel of the reading. Are there any predominant elements, like a lot of Swords (air) or a lot of Pentacles (earth)? Is it mainly minor cards with no – or just one or two – major cards? Or are there a lot of major cards?

Now look at the middle pillar. What is the general 'flavour' of the cards running down the middle? Have your card interpretation book or notes nearby (and your journal) but also just look at the pictures and see what they tell you. Once you have a feel of the general energy running down the centre of the reading, write down a key word that for that general feeling.

Look to the right hand side of the reading. Remember this is an 'inflow' into the person's life. What is flowing into their picture? Look at the images on the right hand side of the reading: what powers are they? Are they minor cards, people cards or major cards? Write down your overall impression of what is flowing into the person's life.

Look to the left hand side of the reading. This is the 'outflow' current. What is flowing away from the person's life? Again, look at the types of cards, their strength, and think of an overall term or feeling-word for that outflow.

By doing this, you gain a vague idea of what is going on at a deeper level in this person's life before you start interpreting individual cards. By looking at these power currents flowing through the reading, you tap into the deeper patterns that are operating through a person's life; the individual cards in their positions tell you how that power manifests for them.

Let's get to the individual card interpretation. I do not use reversals, as I use the positions of the cards to tell me whether a card has a negative or positive meaning.

3. Interpreting the reading

Position one, two and three

Are read together. This tells you what the story is about. The first card is the root of the question, the second card is what is coming into the situation, and the third card is what has gone from the situation. Neutral, positive, negative.

Position four

Is what is been given that will ultimately help, even if it is a bad card. Position four is the expansion of the card that falls in position two: what is coming into the situation is now taking a form where it can express itself.

Position five

Is what is being currently withheld so that it can be taken permanently out of a situation: the card in this position tells of the power, person, or event that is being prepared for composting/full removal.

Position six

Is the fulcrum of the situation. It is the position that balances the positive/giving position four, and the negative/withholding position five. It is also the full potential, should that full potential be realised.

Now we are getting to the part of the pattern that tells a more complex story. In the Tree pattern, positions seven, eight, and nine are the spheres that directly pass into our minds, actions, bodies, and situations. Up to this point, the positions are about dynamics, potentials, and powers. Now we start to see how those dynamics play out in our lives.

Position seven

Is the part of us that is being 'worked': it is a position of a Grindstone and it is also a position of emotion.

Our emotions trigger us to act and react. Through our emotions we carry burdens, process through restrictions, and we either learn to self-restrict through the adversity of our emotions or we are consumed by them.

The card that appears in position seven tells us how we cope with a situation, what our emotions are, and what boundaries can help or hinder us depending on how we view and approach them.

As we get closer to the outcome (position ten), you can see how the possibilities of interpretation become more complex, just as life becomes more complex as it matures. Interpret these lower positions in relation to the question and the subject matter.

Position eight

Is that part of us that can free things up or can unravel us. It is also the position of the mind and magic: the creativity of the mind and magic comes into full flow when we step away from conformity. But without a balance with restrictions and boundaries we easily unravel: hence position seven and eight work together to create a balance through polarity and tension. Each of these positions have cause and effect, problem and solution within them.

Interpreting positions seven and eight

Here is a simple key to help you interpret the cards that fall in these positions:

- **Position seven:** Emotions, look for what needs limiting, or look at what is being limited and see that the key to that is emotions.
- **Position eight:** Look for what needs loosening up, and see the mind or magic as the key, or see what in the mind or magic is being unravelled.

Sometimes these positions can be read really simply as seven = emotions,

eight = mind.

Position nine

Is the position of the moon: this is dreams, imagination, family, ancestors or the home. Read it in relation to the question.

Position ten

Is the outcome or full manifestation of the picture.

Module II – Patterns and Maps in Magic

Key words

Write down in your journal the reading you did for the public figure.

Go through the individual positions and think of a key word for each card and write it down. Alongside that key word, write down a second key word for the position: you read them together. Now look back over the reading and see if you can get an inkling of what it is telling you. Bear in mind that this is a very simple pattern that does not give you much detail; it simply highlights the key dynamics of an event.

Later on you will learn much more complex patterns that give you far more detail, but first you need to learn to walk before you begin flying and jumping off of buildings!

4. Example reading

Let's have a look at an example reading for a public figure. I have chosen General Sisi, the new president of Egypt.

My question is:

"Does President Sisi have the interests of the Egyptian people at heart, or is he grabbing power for himself?"

Get your deck, find the following cards, and lay them out in the Tree of Life layout so that you can look at the reading with me.

The cards came out as:

1. Magician
2. Three of Swords
3. Knight of Swords
4. Knight of Pentacles
5. Tower
6. Seven of Swords
7. Five of Cups
8. Four of Wands
9. Nine of Wands
10. Hermit

This is an interesting reading in that it shows an evolution of intention and understanding as the reading progresses.

Figure 4: The Tree of Life tarot layout – example reading

Analysis

We start with the Magician: this is the man Sisi, using his power to manoeuvre, control, and make something happen to his own agenda. He makes that happen by bringing in a power of separation (Three of Swords) which got rid of the Muslim Brotherhood, and what is withheld is the Knight of Swords, which is the dissent/aggression that attempted to stop that separation.

In the forth position is the Knight of Pentacles. In the context of this question, this earth card refers to the people whom he sees as being young and needing to be protected. Earth/Pentacles is interpreted in the magical earth context of ancestors tribe, etc.

In the fifth position we see the Tower. The Tower is withheld and shows that by doing what he did, he averted a major disaster for the people.

In the centre in position six is the Seven of Swords. My key word for the Seven of Swords is 'sneaking.' This suggests he used underhand methods in order to avert the disaster.

Now we are getting to the last four positions that show how the dynamics of the first six cards play out.

In position seven we have the Five of Cups. My key words for the Five of Cups are 'disappointment' and 'guilt.' The man cries over the three spilt cups but does not see the two full cups still standing.

In an emotive position like position seven, this tells me that Sisi has feelings of regret and guilt, and is in danger of being overwhelmed by negative emotion when there is still positive hope just out of sight.

Remember the dualistic nature of this position. It is about necessary restriction/boundaries and emotion. Through his sense of disappointment and guilt, he has the potential to self-restrict in order to fully partake of the two remaining cups.

In position eight we have the Four of Wands – celebration. Again remember the dualistic nature of this position and although intellectually he is celebrating his victory, that celebration, if not checked by more sober emotions, can unravel him. In that position, the Four of Wands has the potential to manifest as arrogance in victory, but because of the emotive quality we see in his position seven, the guilt and disappointment balances and limits the sense of relief and celebration in position eight.

In position nine we see the Nine of Wands. My key word for this card is 'survival.' He has survived the change in government and his election. It also shows, being the position of the tribe/ancestors, that it was – and still is – a difficult battle for him on all fronts, and like the surviving of all major battles, it leaves you changed. It takes your innocence and shapes how you view the world. He has survived, but at great cost.

His outcome is the Hermit. This is a very interesting outcome and shows the true evolution of a person who is going through massive change.

At the beginning of the reading, President Sisi presented as the magician: the man who manipulated and juggled power for control. Now we see President Sisi as man changed by a bitter struggle, a struggle in which he had to behave in an underhand way in order to avert a disaster. We see through the reading his emotional introspection and his battered survival. What it has transformed him into is a man who feels very alone and burdened with the knowledge that only he can light his own way forward.

The Hermit tells us about wisdom from bitter experience, the shedding of dogma, innocence, the loss of safety from structure. He stands alone at the top of high mountain with only his experiences to light his way ahead. The Hermit is also a very spiritual card: it is the person who has moved beyond religion to find an individual path to the Divine, a path that has no easy answers.

Interpretation

My original question was *"does he have the interests of the Egyptian people at heart?"* My answer is yes, but it has come at a bitter price, and his understanding of his role, the people, and the path ahead has changed dramatically since he set out of this path to power.

At that start of this process he wanted to be Pharaoh. Now he is in that position, he finally realises what a tremendous burden it truly is. At the start of this process he felt in control, and probably felt very sure about his own 'honour' and righteous intention. Through this journey he has learned the limitations of his honour, and that the world is not so black and white as it appeared. He has also learned that righteous intention is often a fallacy enjoyed by those who have not been pushed to their limits. This process has made him grow up.

We can only hope, with the terrible trials that the Egyptian people have suffered over the last few years, that President Sisi continues to keep himself in check, and that the wisdom of the Hermit truly blossoms within him so that he can effectively guide that large, unruly nation towards a better future, rather than attempting to hang on to power at all costs. If the Hermit turns sour, which can happen if the self-imposed limits are tossed to one side and the unravelling power takes over, then we will see Sisi descend into a self-serving tyrant who will be difficult to get rid of.

Note: The year is now 2024 and the Hermit has indeed turned sour.

When you do your own public figure reading, don't be influenced by what you know about them; let the reading speak. Often what we see in public is only a fraction of the reality: learn not to judge, but to look for yourself.

5. *Task:* Practising this spread

Do several of these public figure readings so that you get used not only to the layout, but also to working without predefined ideas of a person or a situation.
Interpret the reading in direct connection to the question. Remember, if you ask about a person's actions, you will get the information about how that person interacts with the situation. Don't assume the cards only tell you about the person; they can also tell you about the burdens or gifts that affect them. How the person reacts to those burdens and gifts will tell you a great deal about their deeper qualities.

Once you have used this layout for a few public figure readings and you feel confident about your baseline ability to read and interpret it, then widen out your field of reading. Look at situations as opposed to people. (For example, *"what will be the energy flowing through an area this month?"* or *"show me the health of my car"* or *"what is my month going to look like in general?"*)

When you come to doing your own personal readings, or readings for those close to you, try not to frighten yourself. Bad things happen in life as well as good things: look at the year you have just lived through and think of the bad things you experienced as well as the good things. Think about where those experiences took you, what they taught you, how they changed you: sometimes good comes out of difficulties, just as difficulties can come from good things. If you see things you do not understand, simply note them down and revisit them once the situation has passed so that you can get a better understanding of how the cards were expressing that situation.

If in a personal reading you see a lot of bad things, don't panic. Your next question should be *"can I change this through my intentions, direction, or action?"*

If the answer is a good card, then you need to sit quietly and think about what options for change are available to you, even if you don't particularly like them. Narrow the options down to two or three, and then look again at the situation outcome if you made those changes.

If the answer comes back that you cannot change what is coming, then you need to think carefully about the best way to navigate through the difficult situation, how to transform it into something that can bring positive change, and then do a reading to look at *"what will be the long-term outcome for me of this difficult situation?"*

Often what is currently a bad situation is ultimately a catalyst for positive change: if we step up to the challenge, we transform ourselves, our lives, and the lives of those around us.

I speak as someone who has had the readings from hell in the past, and who subsequently went through that hell. But looking back I would change nothing, as each challenge and disaster gave me strength, understanding, and matured me. That is not to say that we should passively accept every disaster that comes our way.

Sometimes it is very necessary to dodge bullets, and the first step of dodging a bullet is knowing that it is coming. From there, you can do readings to look at different options for avoiding or modifying an upcoming situation.

Work with this reading layout often, as it will become a major tool in your future work as a magician. It will also teach you about the profound power of creation and destruction that flows constantly through the mundane in our lives. It is also a very useful divination tool, and divination is as useful on a daily basis to a magician as a knife and fork.

Lesson 3
The Full Pentagram Ritual

As a magician, you cannot work a ritual in isolation: you must work it in harmony with your life in order for it to be fully successful.

A ritual is a final externalisation of inner patterns and powers, and the human is its fulcrum, its enactor, and also its vessel. If that vessel is cracked or badly formed, then the ritual's power will trickle through its cracks, and this will ultimately destroy the vessel. Heavy words indeed.

It is crucial to understand this dynamic at the very earliest stages of your magical practice. If the apprentice grasps this notion and works with it, then slowly the vessel (the magician) will strengthen and come into balance. No magician starts out in their training as a harmonious vessel. Becoming one can take many years, and the process has many different layers to it. But step by step the apprentice can stabilise, tune, and eventually strengthen the vessel. This does not result in a perfect human being; rather it results in a human being who is functional enough to work as a magician.

The first step towards this stabilisation can be approached through the Pentagram Ritual. The ritual itself does not do the stabilising; it highlights what potentially needs adjusting and brings it to your awareness, so that you step into a process of constant evolution.

By now you will have worked with the Pentagram a few times in different forms, so you will understand that it is about 'Man,' not about projecting an external shield. It is the first step of "Human, know thyself."

Just as a body can successfully fight infection if it is balanced and healthy, so too can the magician fight attack or intrusion if they are magically balanced and healthy.

1. *Task:* Working with the Dynamics

Before we get to the ritual itself, we first need to understand and implement the dynamics that flow through the pattern of the ritual in order for it to work. We have looked at the Pentagram in terms of directional elements, tools, time, and Divine power. Now we need to look at it in terms of human action.

The following text may come across as spiritual idealism, but it is not – though the processes it describes are where such idealism, however misunderstood, comes from.

Some spiritual or ethical ideals are formed by culture or religion. But others are actually the remnants of forgotten knowledge about power dynamics which have transformed, over time, into religious ideals. It is important for a magician to be able to recognise which ideals spring from an active power dynamic, and which do not.

So throughout what follows, bear in mind that we are looking at how a particular power dynamic works in relation to the human body and spirit, not at idealism. Do not fall into the trap of taking on board ideals: learn about power dynamics, how we interact with those dynamics, and act accordingly.

Because this particular dynamic is so important to ritual magic and can be very complex, I am addressing it here in detail. And yet I am still only skimming its surface. In later lessons we will address deeper and deeper layers of this dynamic to ensure that you fully understand it for what it is – and for what it is not.

I give

Get out your paperwork from your previous lessons about the Pentagram. Look at the left hand of the pentagram in the diagram you drew. It holds a sword and has the declaration "I give." This is the first dynamic that you need to recognise and work with: that you cannot receive unless you have first given. For a human, a magician, this *give* action is an externalisation of a creative force. The receiving dynamic is already the first stage of destruction. You cannot destroy until you have first created: the magician is the last mediator in the chain of creation and the first mediator in the chain of destruction. Just as the first act of Divine Power is to utter into the Void, to breathe the Breath of life into everything, so too the first act of a human must be an outflow of power.

For the magician there is also an interesting power dynamic: by mirroring Divinity's first creative act, you align yourself with the Divine Stream. This gives you access to a much greater stream of energy to power the work than any human could create for themselves.

This can seem all very mystical and highbrow, but when it is applied to our physical world and our external actions in that world, it becomes very simple. We give and take in a constant dance of moving energy.

Before we can learn how to give at a deep spiritual and energetic level, first we need to be able to give at an outer level. This immediately brings in a sense of defensiveness, as giving is more often than not an issue of resources.

When we humans are well resourced, most of us are generous. When we are not well resourced, we pull up the drawbridge and the archers come out ready to defend. And yet the magical act of outer giving can take many forms, from breathing out, to shitting, to dropping a dime in a hat, to feeding birds, to donating blood: it is about letting go.

Giving can happen in many ways and does not necessarily have to be about resources, but that does not let us off the hook. When an apprentice steps into magic, they step into a pattern that will shape and form them. Sometimes that shaping is painful. I remember when I was very young and had my very first lesson on this dynamic. It horrified me and intrigued me at the same time.

The lesson went a bit like this: each of us in the group of students wrote our name down on a piece of paper. Those names went into a hat. We were instructed that, whichever name we pulled out of the hat, we were to be that person's Guardian Angel for a year.

We were to give them gifts, keep an eye out for them, protect them when necessary, ensure they had what they needed, etc. And then we were to choose something that was very dear to us, an object or a belonging, and give it away. Throughout this we were to remain anonymous, so that the recipient would have no idea who their 'angel' was.

The lessons I learned from this exercise have stayed with me to this day. Some of those lessons were obvious, some were misunderstood, and some took many years to dawn on me.

At first I dived into the process with a great zealous muster. I picked my favourite bauble and dropped it in the bag of the person whose name I'd drawn. I gave them goodies every week, left them food, drink, money, watched their back, averted various fights and conflicts, and so on. I was very self-satisfied. I felt particularly smug because I did not actually much like the person I had found myself landed with. (Ah, those good childhood Catholic morals…)

Slowly this turned into a control issue. I gave, they received, and as I controlled their moods I got a feedback of self-congratulation. Eventually they got 'receiving fatigue' and started to grumble about what they were getting and whether it was on time. (While all this was going on, I was still waiting for my Guardian Angel to kick in… it never happened.) This was not what I expected, and it robbed me of my feel-good factor.

When the year came to an end I was mightily relieved. Not because I could stop giving – I have always loved giving – but because the exercise had become a confusing and deflating experience for me. I had not understood it, which in hindsight was no surprise, as I was too young.

The key to triggering the dynamic of giving, in a magical sense, is to give without seeing where it goes, who gets it, what they use it for, etc. The outer phrase is "I give," but in fact its hidden magical dynamic is "I let go" or "I release." This is really, really important in terms of this magical dynamic and magical development in general. If you cannot let go, truly let go, then you will not make it to become a true adept. So what has this to do with the Pentagram Ritual? Hang with me, we will get there… this truly is important if you want to work real magic with the Pentagram.

Before you can mediate real power without the potential for real corruption, first you must be able to release, from your depths, and unconditionally. That does not come from deep meditation, or from saying "I have no attachments" – yes you do, we all do. Having attachments is part of human nature. The job of a magician is not to suppress human nature, but to focus it and train it.

Remember the engram? True power comes from being able to react at speed, from your very depths, and often subconsciously. That speed and power comes from repeated, slow, deliberate, outer physical actions. So your first job is to learn how to release power through the action of "I give." And that means giving and letting go without reward. That is hard. Giving with acknowledgement and congratulations is actually receiving, not giving. There is nothing wrong with that, and it should be a part of your everyday life. But recognise that acknowledged gifting is more receiving than giving.

But this is an important lesson, and it is not a one-off lesson either: it is a throughout life lesson, and that lesson is about releasing, giving, letting go. And that can be anything, not just resources. It can be an identity, a grown child, your youth – do you get the picture? Many people will try to dodge this lesson, and will try to justify or convince themselves that they are releasing when they are not. Do not fall into that trap. You fool no one but yourself, and this is about you and your own magical development. The deep inner process cannot be engaged consciously until you first begin with baby steps in the physical world. It starts from the outside and works inwards into your depths.

Find something that is precious to you, something of real value, something that you would rather not lose. Put it in a bag. Do not choose something that you like but would not really miss. This is about you, about your ability to truly let go of things that are precious to you.

Now go through your clothing. If you have more coats than are functional,[1] choose a good coat or something similar from your surplus and put it in the bag. Take that bag with the coat and the precious item to the local thrift or charity store and hand it over. Do not get a receipt for it, do not take a tax break on it. Just let it go. Walk out before they can see what is in the bag.

When you get your next paycheck, draw out 25% of your extra food/entertainment/eating out budget for that month. Whatever that amount is, get it in cash and go for a walk in your nearest city. When you see a homeless person, give it to them. Do not question whether they would use it for drugs, do not question whether it would be too much to give, and do not cherry-pick which homeless person you give it to. Just give it to them and walk away. Do not give them chance to say thank you. And make sure it truly is 25% of your food/eating out budget, so that you have to miss a meal or two or cut back on what you buy that month. If however you are on a very low income yourself and have children, go without small food treats or the nice parts of a meal. Ensure your family has what it needs, but you personally should really feel the bite. But if you can afford to get take out, or go out for dinner, or buy fancy coffees on the way to work, or have nice wholesome meals, then you afford to do this. It should hurt, it should make you think.

---

[1] i.e. you need one warm winter coat, one summer coat, and maybe a coat for interviews, funerals etc.

Besides the ethics, emotions, and psychology of these actions, there is a deep and lasting magical dynamic that is triggered by them. You learn to let go in a way that is uncomfortable, that does not benefit you in any way, and that does not give you status or positive feedback. This is true giving/release. This in turn prepares you, and at a very deep subconscious level, for those occasions in the future when you will need to mediate a vast amount of power and release it without question.

This sort of giving should not be a one-off event in your life. Learn to do this every so often, particularly with letting go of things that are very precious to you and that have value. Do not hoard, do not cling. Learn to keep things moving. As you continue to do this in your life, it will loosen you up at a deep level. It will also teach you about what is really precious and what is not. You will also see a deep magical dynamic kick into action, which is that you cannot actually give anything away: it always comes back somewhere, sometime in the future when you need it – but only when it is given unconditionally and without thought for receiving.

It may take you until you are in your adept studies to really, truly understand what is happening here. But when you do come to understand it, truly, in its magical depths, it will blow you away. Giving is a deep magical dynamic that you will learn more about in the coming modules: the releasing of a belonging is just the most surface presentation of a deeply profound energetic dynamic.

I receive

The right-handed dynamic is "I receive." On the surface this can manifest as being able to receive without the need to give something back in return.

Some people (myself included) find the receiving dynamic rather difficult, because although it is naturally balanced by the left-handed releasing dynamic, the action of receiving without giving in return can bring about a deep sense of failure or weakness: none of us like to be in a position where we are in need of receiving without having the power to give back in return. And this ability to receive unconditionally once more takes away our power of control.

The ability to receive without giving back is also a deep magical dynamic. The action of the left hand power releasing unconditionally and the right hand action of receiving unconditionally are two interlinked dynamics that are separated out consciously. This keeps their energies in a balanced tension. When we mix them unconsciously (which is how it tends to work in normal life), we cannot isolate the power of the left or right hand and work with it specifically.

And this gets down to the most basic dynamic of magic: stepping away from the unconscious acceptance of a dynamic, and learning instead to engage consciously with that dynamic's individual, polarised powers in a balanced but unique way.

So we can passively accept a dynamic, or we can consciously engage with it in a balanced way. In between those two approaches lie unbalanced forms of engagement, ones which favour one of the two poles of the dynamic over the other.

This is the result of attempting to engage with a dynamic without truly understanding how it works, and it is what we generally find in religions (and in some magical systems). Some religions lean towards, say, a vow of poverty and non-ownership ("I let go"); others lean towards taking everything to which one feels entitled ("I receive").

Both of these stances are unbalanced and flawed. The most glaring modern example of this is the Western Buddhist's mantra of "I have no attachments," when in fact they are attached to all manner of things and continually wrestling for control. Again, this is something we will examine in more depth and in magical terms later in the course. First it must be learned in a practical, externalised way.

The receiving element of this power dynamic is not just about receiving stuff. It is about receiving stuff *unconditionally*, whether it is something nice or something bad. When the vessel is filled magically, it can be filled with resources and energy, or it can be filled with illness, suffering, and defeat: actually, it will be filled with whatever is necessary to move you forward out of inertia. But when this receiving quality is taken out of balance, away from the left hand power of giving/releasing – i.e. the magician works only with the receiving arm of the Pentagram – you get either greed or glamorised suffering (an example of which is the consciousness of the Catholic Church). As you hopefully can begin to see, receiving and giving is a fine balancing act.

The release/give must be of itself and not connected to receiving. And the receiving must be of itself and not connected to release/giving. But they both must be contained in a balance of action: the magician must do both, but each action must be a complete action of itself and not connected to its polar opposite.

The human is the fulcrum in the middle. If you consistently engage one arm of the Pentagram without the other, you get imbalanced. If you meld both dynamics together and make them dependant on each other, you also get imbalanced.

The task of the magician is first to be conscious of these dynamics (by physical doing), then to understand the dynamics (by personal reflection and magical work), and finally to engage the dynamics as separate energies that are harmonious of each other yet not dependant on each other. This in turn allows the magician to stand in the centre of power and act as fulcrum and conductor to the vast powers of creation and destruction as they flow in and out of our world.

When you engage all of this, first through outer physical action and then through magical work, you will directly engage with the maxim "as above, so below." Magically, this is better expressed as "as is outward, so is inward." By the outermost surface doing, the deepest inner impulse is awakened and begins to grow ready to work with energy and power. You can practise receiving in a manner that is specific to your situation. If you are resourceless, poor, or in need, and you are given the resources you need, accept them. Accept them without the feeling that you need to give something back or that you need to justify the gift, or that you now 'owe.' Accept them without feeling shame or guilt. Accept them as energies that are filling a deficit in the vessel in order for the vessel to function properly.

This can be tougher than it sounds. If you are used to being self-reliant, it can seriously knock your sense of self to find yourself in a position of need. It is important to step away from the cultural and emotional baggage that comes with such a situation, which cuts to the core of our sense of self. This is dangerous in magic and it creates a vulnerability that can seriously threaten you when you are working in the presence and midst of great power. I know, I have been there more than once, and still have the occasional struggle with it.

Another way the receiving dynamic can manifest is in the unconditional receiving of something unpleasant, difficult, or painful. This is also a really important aspect of the dynamic from a magical sense, and it is easily twisted if you are not careful. Sometimes, particularly in the lives of true magicians, the vessel is given energies that are extremely difficult to hold. The magician must be able to hold that energy for however long is necessary in order for a job to be done.

That is a deep octave of a natural dynamic that comes into sharp focus in the life of a magician. Many times you will be called upon to hold power that is painful or uncomfortable. Sometimes it lasts a few days or weeks, other times it can last for years – or a lifetime. Then it really is 'man up' time: that is when the magician is truly tested in terms of their ability to hold and release power, their ability to face a dangerous job or being, and their ability to do what is necessary in order for something to be achieved.

When we experience this in everyday life, it can manifest as a long-term illness or a continuous conveyor belt of bad events. We get swept with the tide and feel helpless in the face of it. When you step onto the path of the magician, you begin to fully and consciously engage with these powers, and that in itself changes the dynamics dramatically.

Corrupt and fragmented magic encourages people to dodge these events through 'results magic.' Corrupt and fragmented magic can also (particularly when it manifests in religion) encourage people to passively accept everything as "the will of God," and then have a massive martyr ego about it. Both ends of this spectrum are unbalanced and unhealthy. In all things that are unbalanced, there is often a grain of truth lurking somewhere in there, but it is a truth that has become massively distorted and is being viewed in black and white.

A magician who engages with a difficult situation correctly will immediately recognise what particular magical or energetic dynamic is in action, and carry out the appropriate work. Sometimes that can indeed mean accepting the situation. But instead of sitting in the shit and feeling sorry for yourself, the way forward is to recognise what is happening at a deeper level, engage it, work with it, and learn from it. Sometimes it means not 'accepting' the situation but actively engaging with it to bring change. The skill is knowing what to do and when.

In magic, and for the magician who is on a magical path, there are no accidents, no coincidences, and no meaningless events. Everything has a purpose: the skill of the magician is to find the purpose, work with it, or learn to work around it.

If something difficult is poured into your vessel, there is a reason for it. (And I do not mean that in the New Age sense of "oh, there is a reason for your suffering." That is just ignorance.) For example... let's get personal. I will expose my underbelly. In my forties I succumbed to a quite vicious autoimmune disease. It runs in my family on both sides, and in reality I had been really lucky (and had worked hard with magic and with looking after my body) not to have had it hit me full blast in my twenties. It has limited a great many things for me.

The reason for the disease being there is that it is inherited. That's it. I had two choices: collapse in a disabled heap and become a victim, or move sideways. So I moved sideways. Nowadays it generally has a minor impact on my life apart from the occasional bump in the road, as I have adjusted my life around it. I cannot do many of things I used to, but that is life. I have also learned a great deal about myself, my body, human nature, and society through this process. It has been a bitter-sweet gift indeed. Magically it is like having an inbuilt early warning system: my immune system kicks off at the slightest magical attack or imbalance. Some would consider that bad, but it is not: it is an annoying but very useful tool, a tool that has come to be extremely useful in my magical work. I have no emotion to it either way; it is what it is.

Do not engage in emotional or energetic attachment, either positive or negative, to whatever difficulty you face: do not get angry, sad, defensive, etc. Looking at the situation without being emotional about it enables the magician to slowly convert their difficulty, whatever it is, into a tool as opposed to a burden – or at least to learn to step around it, absorb it, whatever. The key is not to fight what is poured into your vessel, be it good or bad, nor to blindly accept it. It is vital to learn how to carry on working on your path without being distracted or sidelined by what is poured into your vessel.

If you win the lottery, do not change your path or your life: such a win in real magical terms is the worst curse that could happen to any magician. The key is to continue with your work and trust that the vessel will process whatever power is there in its own time. This is important. When you come to work as an adept (although this can also happen to initiates) there will be times when your vessel, through magical work, will have to hold a very difficult or alluring power, and one that can manifest in your life or body in the weirdest ways. It is not for you to try and process that power in any way; you simply hold it until it is ready to release (this is where the skill of the sword is then aligned with the skill of the vessel: hold/guard, release). The ability to hold energy in your vessel without trying to process it will come once you learn how not to attach emotionally or react to power as it comes and goes within you.

Releasing/giving and receiving/containing are the two major power dynamics that flow in and out of the human sphere, so now we have dealt with them the rest is much easier and less wordy. Sorry that was such a long piece, but it is a key dynamic and it is vital that you understand it if you want to do competent and advanced magic.

In the Pentagram pattern, remember the two directions that engage with the power of the future, and the two directions that engage with the power of the past. Also remember the Divinity above which is air, no substance, a Breath; and the Divinity below which, as a vessel, receives the Breath which enlivens the substance. These directions also work with the two dynamics we have just looked at in depth. Rather than go over how that works here, this is something you can ponder for yourself and take notes on.

Hopefully now you will also be starting to understand why the centre of the magician, and the centre of the directions, is the power of stillness, of the Void, of potential ready but not yet formed. With all of time, power in and power out swirling around the magician, the true centre and fulcrum of all magic and all creation/destruction is this stillness: that is the present. It is the only place in existence and magic where there is a constant 'now.' Everything else is either moving away or moving towards, going into the future or passing into the past.

Physical existence, be it the planet or the human, is a constant dance of movement, vibration and action. Only the very centre of spirit is still and unchanging: that is where the maxim "God is within you" comes from. It is the Breath contained within the flame of life.

So now let's start moving towards the ritual itself (phew). When this ritual is used, it solidifies, roots, and anchors us within ourselves, our existence, and our place within that existence.

In that act of anchoring, if there is any serious imbalance within you, it will rise up to the surface so that you can address it. It is a simple ritual that slowly builds in power over the years, as we engage with the opposing left hand and right hand powers of the pentagram. Notice that this has absolutely nothing to do with the 'left hand/right hand path' identities in magic, which are essentially ignorant bullshit.

The more you work with and engage the left and right hand dynamics in your life and magical work, the more power will begin to flow into your ritual actions: you become a totally rooted, solid gateway for power that stands at the crossroads of power in, power out, future and past, creation and destruction.

This builds and focuses over the years and decades until the magician 'becomes' the pentagram rather than 'does' the pentagram. It becomes a 'sense' or 'feeling' that you recover on nearly a daily basis as opposed to a ritual that you blindly repeat year after year. When you get to that stage, there is very little indeed that can knock you.

That does not mean bad things do not happen; it means that everything is kept in balance and nothing can knock you off that balance. All physical existence has to have good times and bad times; that is how nature works. But you move from "I am suffering," to "I endure," to "I flourish despite it."

If you try to dodge that growth process through results magic, you will not only end up magically weak and ineffective, but you will also start to slide down the long slope of degeneracy as a magician. For example, I have been in magic for nearly forty years, and I have connections with magicians all over the world. I have yet to meet a long-term results magician who is not broke, lonely, sick, depressed, and screwed up. They all do well for a small number of years... and then the backlash comes home to roost.

2. The Full Pentagram Ritual

Note: Eventually as an adept you will do this as a fully contacted ritual with the contacts in the room with you, interlinking with you. But first you must learn to work the ritual pattern, invite the powers in, and then observe how they manifest in your life and work.

Get out your notes from your astrology lesson and your work with the chart and the pentagram. Look up your planets again in relation to you standing in the centre of the chart/pentagram. Focus on the positions of Saturn and Pluto: make sure you know where they are in your natal chart, and where that puts them in relation to you standing in the room (remember that ritual action?).

Set up your work space with the four directional altars and one in the centre. Go around the directions: starting in the east and using the methods you have already learned, light the lights and see the gates opening. With each direction, after you acknowledge it and as you see its gates open, become aware of a figure coming through those gates and standing on the other side of the altar.

Now walk to the east altar. Place your hands upon the altar and close your eyes. In your mind's eye, see the figure on the other side of the altar hold out their hand. Imagine yourself reaching into your pocket and pulling something out. Using your mind's eye, look at it. It does not matter if you cannot tell what it is.
Recite:

> "I, [*your name*], relinquish this
> that has been demanded by the inner contact."

In your mind, see yourself hand over whatever it is to the outstretched hand. Instead of receiving what you have given, the hand closes over your hand and joins hands with you.

Step back from the altar and as you do, see in your mind's eye the inner contact holding onto your hand and move with you, passing through the altar and into the room.

You may now see them with your inner vision more clearly. Do not try to put an identity upon them or communicate with them.

Turn and walk around the directions, aware that the inner contact is walking with you, still holding onto your hand. Finish in front of the north altar.

In your mind, see the inner contact standing beside you. They place their other hand upon your shoulder to support you.

Using your mind's eye, see the inner contact from the north step forward so that they are clearly on the other side of the altar. Stretch out your hand with the gift in it, being aware that the hand of the inner contact from the east is also there. They are supporting you in this act. The inner contact from the north reaches out and takes what is in your hand.

Recite:

> "I release this gift in an act of giving.
> I give it back to my past, back to my ancestors.
> I relinquish all connection with this gift."

Take a deep breath, and blow out a slow, sustained breath, while being aware that you are releasing 'power out.' (This is connected to the 'breathing down the blade' magical action that you read about in a past lesson).

Step back. The inner contact of the east still has a hand on your shoulder. Turn and go to the east. Place your hands upon the altar and wait until the inner contact crosses through the altar and stands on the threshold of the gates.

Now turn, walk around the directions, and stop in front of the west altar. Step forward and place your hands upon the west altar.

See the inner contact emerge from the gates and stand on the other side of the altar. See in your mind's eye the inner contact holding something out in their hand to you. Imagine that you reach out your hand so that they can pour it into your hand. As they do, they then hold their hand over yours to contain it.

Step back, turn, and walk around the directions (north, east, and then to the south) and stop in front of the south altar. The inner contact of the west is with you, a hand upon your shoulder and their other hand upon your hand that contains the gift. You cannot see what it is.

Step forward to the south altar and see the inner contact of the south come up and stand on the other side of the altar. Working with the inner contact of the west, hold out your hand and expose the gift to the inner contact of the south so that they and you can see it. You may or may not understand what it is.

Recite:

> "I accept this gift from the west,
> witnessed by the powers of the south, the powers of the future.
> I will retain this gift for however long is necessary
> and I will willingly let it go when the time comes."

The inner contact of the south steps to one side and holds out an arm towards the gate as if to show you something. You may see past the gate into a landscape, a scene, an image, a person: it does not really matter. You will gain a certain feeling, a deep instinct into the role that the gift will play in your future, however small or great.

Regardless of whether the instinct you gained about the gift was good or bad, now you must absorb it. Take in a slow sustained breath: be aware you are filling your lungs with 'power in.' The inner contact of the south reaches over their hand and cups it under your hand.

Together, you place the gift within you. See the gift, and with your hand and the contact's hand push the gift into your abdomen or chest: the power or energy of the gift is taken into your being.

You may feel a heaviness from the energy of the gift as it is placed within you. The inner contact of the south withdraws back through the gates and stands upon the threshold.

Turn and walk a full circle around the directions, and then walk to the west altar. Place your hands upon the altar and see the inner contact of the west pass back through the altar and stand on the threshold of the gates.

Step back, walk a full circle around the directions, and finish in the north, facing the central altar with your back to the north altar.

Note: What follows is the second part of the ritual, and the part that can be used on a daily basis to embed the pentagram within you.

Hold out your arms to the sides. Throughout this section, keep your arms outstretched, even as you turn. They will start to hurt. Get over it. Keep your shoulders down and your elbows held and that will help. When you stand, stand with your legs apart so that you make the pentagram shape with your body.

See in your mind's eye the sword in your left hand, handle up, blade down. See in your right hand the cup. See above you the hexagram and below you the earth sign. See before you in the south a road going off into the distance with full sun. See people behind you: the ancestors.

Remember where Saturn is positioned in this pattern in relation to your natal chart, and also the position of Pluto.

Recite:

> "In my left hand, the Sword of Justice and balance;
> with my left hand I give to bring balance;
> with my left hand I release to bring balance.
> My left foot stands upon the stone of restriction,
> the Grindstone which forges my future.
> Saturn is my Grindstone."

Now briefly visualise where Saturn would be in your pattern. See a connection, a thread going from your left foot to wherever in the pentagram pattern Saturn is. Take note of whether Saturn falls near an arm, leg, head, shoulder, etc.

Recite:

> "In my right hand, the Vessel of regeneration;
> with my right hand I receive to bring balance;
> with my right hand I accept in order to bring balance.
> My right foot stands upon the Threshing Floor
> which receives the gifts and blessings of my harvest.
> Pluto is my Threshing Floor."

Now briefly visualise where Pluto would be in your pattern. See a connection, a thread going from your right foot to wherever in the pentagram pattern Pluto is. Take note of whether Pluto falls near an arm, leg, head, shoulder, etc.

Recite:

> "Behind me is time past, the ancestors who walked before me.
> I release whatever is necessary to them.
> Before me is the future, the path I will forge.
> I accept whatever is necessary for that path."

Turn around and face the north altar while still keeping your arms outstretched.

Recite:

> "In my left hand is the Sword of balance
> that is given to the vessel in the west.
> In my right hand is the Vessel
> which receives the Sword from the east.
> With me is my past, the blood of my past, and those who birthed me.
> Before you and in honour of you,
> I hold the power of the Sword and the Vessel in your name.
> Beyond me is the future.
> My path is forged by the Grindstone of the future,
> and my past is measured by my harvest upon the Threshing Floor."

Now turn and face the central altar in the pentagram stance (with your arms still outstretched... stop whining).

Recite:

> "Above me is Divine Power, the Father that gives breath.
> To the east is the power of the Sword.
> Below me is Divine Substance, the Mother that receives the breath.
> To the west is the power of the vessel.
> Before me is the future, lined with the Noble Ones.
> Behind me is the past, and the angel who guards me.
> Within me is stillness.
> I Am [*your first name*].
> I Will Be."

Now you can drop your arms.

Sit down on the floor and close your eyes. Meditate for a few minutes and then, still sitting, see yourself standing in the pentagram pattern facing south. Think about the dynamics and powers of the pattern, and think about where the two planets fit within it. What are they near? Ponder on what that means for your life and pattern. Think about the dynamics of these two planets, what powers flow through them, how they affect life etc., and then think about them in connection with their position close to your head, or limb, which limb it is, and what magical tool and power runs through that limb.

Write your observations in your journal.

3. *Experiment:* Adjusting the ritual

By now you have worked with the pentagram in a number of different but basic ways. The pentagram ritual itself is not a dogma; rather it is an expression of the flows of power through and around a human.

In terms of the ritual itself, if you wish to work daily with it, you can either use it directly as it is above using only the recitations, or using the altar work and the recitations. If you stay with that exact pattern, write down your observations, whether it got easier or more difficult – it is one of those rituals where there is elbow room for contacts to join in and put you to work with minor jobs (here, take this, go put it over there). So keep a close note of interactions, what you have to give and take, and write it all down in your journal.

If you wish to be more adventurous and do some experimentation, the first experiment would be to adjust the ritual. This is the first step of creating your own magical patterns. You can include elements from the other pentagram work if you wish, the key when doing that is to think carefully about what you are including, why you are including it, if it is harmonic to the ritual, and at what point it should be put in.

Once you have adjusted it, then stay with it as a set format. The key to building the power of this particular type of ritual is its engram action – its repeated action – which requires doing it in exactly the same way without deviating from the pattern.

As you continue to work with the ritual, and once you can do it calmly, without faltering, and from memory, the first thing you will notice[2] is that power will start to flow around you. You will begin to engage very gently with the flows of power that are constantly moving in and out of the directions. Your placement within that flow of power, in the stance and recitation of the pentagram of humanity, slowly brings you strength and grounding. It also begins the process of awakening the realisation of certain deeper and more powerful magical powers.

---

[2] Besides getting stronger arms – you want biceps, here is how.

When you get to adept level and look back at this ritual, you will understand the ritual in a totally different light and see the power hidden within such a seemingly innocuous ritual.

4. A note on letting go

When you release/give something back to the past, if you see it and know what it is, then let it go, no matter what it is. That means in life, give it away, throw it in a river, etc. If it is something like your house keys (yup, that has happened to me), be willing to let go of the house and move if that is what is needful. Just that willingness to let go sets the action in motion.

And trust me, even though it can seem at the time to be a terrible "oh, shit" moment, it tends to be for the better: it is clearing ground for the future. If what you let go of is a person, again, be willing in your heart to the let them go, no matter how much you love them. Sometimes that can indeed mean a break with someone, but sometimes it can be about a deeper dynamic of not clinging to a person. This happens particularly to people with children who have reached adulthood. You have to learn to let go for their good as well as yours. That doesn't mean you will never see them, it means that you cease to hang on to them.

This also stands for whatever you receive. Whatever it is, be willing to accept it and work with it.

5. *Task:* Researching the Grindstone and the Threshing Floor

In the second part of the ritual, you will have noticed that a new element has been introduced: the Grindstone and the Threshing Floor. (Throughout the course, new elements will be slowly introduced for you to work with and understand.)

The Grindstone is the stone that sharpens the blade (the magician), and the Threshing Floor is the stone that receives the harvest of a magician's life, a harvest that is weighed on the scales of Ma'at as the magician enters into death.

Rather than outline here the deep magical connotations and mysteries woven within this, you can research, discover, and ponder it for yourself. Look up Threshing Floor, altar, and the Dome of the Rock in Jerusalem. Read what you can of the history and mythos of the rock that is now covered by a Muslim sacred building. If you research further, you will discover just how deep the magical action is of setting your right foot upon the Threshing Floor.

Write up your research on computer, and copy across any major inspirations and realisations that have in connection to what you have learned about the stone.

6. When to use this ritual

Use your abridged or adjusted version of the ritual a few times a week for a few weeks so that it becomes second nature. But do the whole ritual at least once or twice in that time.

The whole ritual is excellent to use when you become blocked, stuck, in a rut, or cannot see a way forward from a very difficult or stagnant position. Completing the whole ritual in such an instance, and then doing the abridged version on a daily basis, will begin to shift stuck energies. It gets the power moving, the future opening up, the past falling away, and it stands you firmly on the ground. That makes you very hard to knock over.

Don't be tempted, once the power gets moving and your life starts changing, to do the ritual more and more in the hope of getting better/stronger/faster – that is not the right reason to do continuous work. Do the full ritual to get things moving. Do the daily or at least frequent abridged version to *keep* things moving, and then, once that action begins to materialise in your life, switch ritual focus. You don't need to keep revving the engine once it is going; you need to get it in gear, put your foot down, and go somewhere – which means learning new useful skills, and then putting those skills into action and service.

Lesson 4
The Full Hexagram Ritual

When you worked with the Pentagram ritual, you learned about the power that flows through the life of a human. There are elements hidden within that ritual that will eventually dawn upon you as you progress in your studies in the adept section, which will show you how Divine Power not only flows into the human/pentagram, but also triggers externalisations of power that move you along your fate path.

In the Pentagram ritual, you placed a Hexagram over your head, which is the mark of the Divine Breath as it flows from unbeing into being, from no substance to enlivening all substance (creation). Now we will learn about the Hexagram itself, and how that symbol/filter tells us about that first step of the breath of Universal Power as it breathes out of the Void, out of unbeing.

The Void itself is something that many magicians (and mystical religions) work with and it is something that you too will also work with. The Void is the nothing which is full of potential: it is the cusp, the threshold for the action of creation to begin from.

As the breath of Universal Power is uttered out of the Void ("In the beginning was the word...") it hits its first filter which enables it to pass into form, into creation. That first filter is something we understand via the magical symbol of the Hexagram.

The reason we approach this filter through a magical symbol is that our tiny minds are really incapable of truly understanding the sheer complexity of this creation process. Working with the symbol of the Hexagram, breaking it down into its power dynamics, and then reassembling it helps our brains to process what is actually happening.

This first filter, the Hexagram, is about Divine Power that has done its first division: just like a fertilised human egg starts life by making a first division, so also Divine or Universal Power first divides into two: positive and negative, male (releasing/giving) and female (accepting/containing). This creates an opposition of power, a tension which allows form to exist. Everything in creation is polarised; everything in creation has a tension which creates energy and movement.

The Hexagram teaches us about this basic foundational dynamic. Without that understanding, we fall back upon giving Divinity a human face, emotions, and humanlike reactions. This is a great folly, and it has no place in real magic (or mystical religion). Deities have such qualities, but Divinity does not. Divinity has consciousness, but it is of a nature far beyond what we can understand.

Through working with the Hexagram, the magician slowly learns how this polarised dynamic works, and learns how power can have consciousness without being humanlike. Before we can work with deities as magicians, we must first learn about the powers of Divinity itself. This power flows through everything in creation, and therefore flows through all of magic. It flows through every magical action, every thought, every movement, and once you come to understand these flows of power, how this intricate balancing act works, you can then engage that understanding in advanced magic so that your work flows in harmony with creation and not against it. You work with creation; you do not try to control it.

Whenever as an adept you come to a point in your work where you feel lost, or that you do not understand what is happening, then you return to the Source. And you do that by working with the Hexagram in ritual and meditative thought. It opens the gates in your consciousness so that you can directly engage with its flow of power, which in turn brings your mind back into focus so that you can reengage with your work in a balanced way.

Once the magician has worked with this ritual pattern for a while, they will slowly begin to understand how the Hexagram works, what powers flow through it, and how it is then applied in various magical streams. Its actions are often sadly misunderstood in modern magic, but if you reach back to much earlier forms of magic and magical religions, you will begin to see its use subtly hidden within certain religions and magical texts.

1. **HEXAGRAM RITUAL, PART ONE**
   THE RITUAL OF THE GATES – THE BUILDING OF THE HEXAGRAM

> *The first part of the ritual is about understanding power in and power out, about Divinity in its polarisation and its echo within ourselves. In this section we learn how these polarised powers work with and flow through the directions, and how those polarised forms can be put together and overlaid to create a filter of creation/destruction, power in/power out, a filter of power balance and harmony.*
>
> *This in turn creates a simple but effective flow of power that the magician can then engage with in their work. It is a flow of power that is balanced, and that can be approached from a variety of angles depending on what work the magician is going to do.*
>
> *So first let's go through the first part of the ritual which opens the gates to this power. Learn the ritual, do it a few times, and then we can discuss what is happening, how it works, and what it works with. Then we will move on to the second part of the ritual.*

Open the directions by lighting the candles in each direction in the way you have been trained to, and visualise the gates in each direction. When you have been around all of the directions, return to the east altar and stand before the candle flame.

Place your hands upon the altar on either side of the candle flame and look beyond the flame. With your eyes open, use your mind's eye to see the east gates open. Using your voice, utter the following words:

> "I acknowledge the gates of the east,
> I acknowledge the angelic threshold of the east,
> and I acknowledge the wind of the east."

Step back from the altar, turn, and walk to the south. Repeat the same exercise, using the words:

> "I acknowledge the gates of the south,
> I acknowledge the angelic threshold of the south,
> and I acknowledge the fire of the south."

In the west, do the same and repeat the words:

> "I acknowledge the gates of the west,
> I acknowledge the angelic threshold of the west,
> and I acknowledge the water of the west."

And in the north:

> "I acknowledge the gates of the north,
> I acknowledge the angelic threshold of the north,
> and I acknowledge the stone of the north."

When you have finished in the north, take a step back, turn, and stand before the central altar. Remember the visual of the column of fire and utter the words:

> "I acknowledge the central fire
> that flows through all worlds, all times and all substance,
> I acknowledge the angelic threshold of the Void,
> the Breath of Divinity as it flows through all things,
> and I acknowledge the light within all living beings
> as it flows from the stars to the Underworld."

Close your eyes and imagine the stars in the sky above you. Imagine the earth below you, the east wind to your left, the western water to your right. Be aware of the power of fire in the south before you, and of the power of the earth in the north behind you. Imagine a spark or flame deep within your centre, a light that stretches up to the stars and down to the earth, which meets in your centre in the form of a small flame within you.

Turn and go to the east altar. With your eyes open, in your mind's eye, see the gates of the east wide open.

Turn and face the central flame. You are going to trace a triangle in the air. With your right hand, pointing with your first two fingers, starting with your arm outstretched high above you, recite:

> "In the name of the Great Father..."

Now bring your point down to the right hand corner:

> "...and in the name of the Great Mother..."

Now trace your point to the left hand corner:

> "...and in the name of the Great Spirits..."

Trace your point back to the top to complete the triangle:

"...I give."

Walk a full circle around the central flame, and then go stand before the altar of the west.

With your eyes open, in your mind's eye, see the gates of the west wide open. Turn and face the central flame. Now you are going to trace an inverted triangle. With your arm outstretched, pointing to the left corner recite:

"In the name of the Great Mother..."

Trace your point across to the high right corner:

"...and in the name of the Great Father..."

Trace your finger down to the low bottom of the triangle:

"...and in the name of the Great Spirits..."

Trace your point back to the high left corner to complete the triangle:

"...I receive."

Walk a full circle clockwise around the flame, and then stand before the north altar.

See in your mind's eye the gates of the north wide open. Turn your back to the altar and face the central flame. You are going to repeat the inverted triangle. Starting with the high left corner, recite:

"In the name of the Great Mother..."

Trace your point across to the high right corner:

"...and in the name of the Great Father..."

Trace your finger down to the low bottom of the triangle:

"...and in the name of the Great Spirits..."

Trace your point back to the high left corner to complete the triangle:

"...I Come From."

Walk a full circle clockwise around the flame and stand before the south altar.

See in your mind's eye the gates of the south wide open. Turn your back to the altar and face the central flame. You are going to trace an upright triangle. With your right hand, pointing with your first two fingers, starting with your arm outstretched high above you, recite:

"In the name of the Great Father..."

Bring your point down to the bottom right hand corner:

"...and in the name of the Great Mother..."

Trace your point to the left hand corner:

"...and in the name of the Great Spirits..."

Trace your point back to complete the triangle:

"...I Am Going To."

Walk a full circle around the flame and stand upon the first cross-quarter, the space between the north and east altars.

You are going to trace both triangles, one at a time. With your right hand, pointing with the first two fingers, starting with your arm outstretched high above you, recite:

"In the name of the Great Father..."

Bring your point down to the right hand corner:

"...and in the name of the Great Mother..."

Trace your point to the left hand corner:

"...and in the name of the Great Spirits..."

Trace your point back to complete the triangle.

Immediately use your point to draw a circle from the apex of the triangle and finish the circle at the upper left hand corner, in order to begin the second triangle, the inverted triangle. Recite:

"In the name of the Great Mother..."

Trace your point across to the high right corner:

"...and in the name of the Great Father..."

Trace your finger down to the low centre of the triangle:

"...and in the name of the Great Spirits..."

Trace your point back to the high left corner to complete the triangle. Recite:

"...We Are."

Sit down in that cross-quarter and close your eyes.

Do a simple breathing exercise: imagine yourself breathing in white smoke, and see yourself breathing out black smoke. Do this simple exercise for five minutes. When you have finished, sit still and silent for thirty minutes. You can sit with your eyes open or with your eyes closed. But you must not let your mind wander.

Focus your attention on stillness for a brief period of time, and then imagine the triangle traced before the east altar and remember the Father, Mother, and Spirits' positions and the declaration of "I give." Once you have watched that triangle and studied it, silence your mind once more.

After a period of silence, imagine the inverted triangle traced before the west altar. Remember the Mother, Father, and Spirits' positions and the declaration of "I receive." Repeat the same stillness meditation and breathing, and then go on to remember the action/words for the inverted triangle in the north and the upright triangle in the south.

Sit for a while in silence and remember the double triangle traced in the cross-quarter where you are seated. Imagine the triangle being traced in front of your seated body. Eventually and with practice, you will learn how to instantly visualise the hexagram and feel all of the directional flows of power that come together to make it.

At this point you can close down the directions, or you can continue on to the second part of the ritual.

The meditation aspect of this ritual section is a once-only thing (unless you wish to do it more often). It is to allow a space within your mind for understanding to bubble up. It will not drop instantly into your brain like a file; it is something that will slowly dawn out of the space you have given it. The actual ritual actions of this first part of the ritual are ones that you would combine with the second part of the ritual to make a complete ritual.

2. So what was happening?

In your previous lessons you have learned about the power flows, time, tools, dynamics, and gates of the four directions. The four directions are the pattern of creation: they tell you how power flows into creation and expresses through the magical directions which in turn form the power into particular dynamics of power in, power out, past, future, substance, non-substance, etc.

The Pentagram ritual taught you about how the power that flows from the magical directions is engaged by the human magician, and also how it flows through all of humanity. The difference for the magician is that the power is consciously engaged and worked with, rather than passively accepted. Now the Hexagram teaches you how Divine Consciousness flows through those magical directions, and how it is shaped into specific dynamics by those directional filters.

Remember how in the Pentagram ritual the Hexagram was above you? Now, through the first part of the ritual, you learn how to work with the Hexagram power around and within you as opposed to above you: you consciously engage the Breath of Divinity within you and work with that in your magic. That comes into full force in the Adept level of training, but for now, the simple ritual gestures and meditations will awaken your mind to the structure and filter.

You will notice that when you worked in the directions, you turned your back to the altars. Why? Because you were not talking to or interacting with the power of the direction, you were mediating it through you. This is the very first baby step towards mediating power through you and out into the world.

You face the direction to interact with the power, and you turn your back to it when you are pulling the power through you and directing it somewhere. This is the first step towards training the body to act as a bridge for power. It is a simple action, and you will likely not feel much in power terms at this stage, and that is how it should be. It is like weightlifting: start small, and work up slowly.

In the east, which you now know to be a direction of release/giving, you will notice that the Hexagram's action is 'male.' It starts with the Father, with the upright triangle. This is the output of breath, the output of the sperm that eventually triggers life. This is the direction where you would stand as an adept (male or female, both sexes work this power in the same way), with your back to the east altar, with your mind focused on the male hexagram, and you would utter/breathe out power into existence. Starting the Hexagram action with the upright/male expression defines the magical action as 'outputting' i.e. the start of a power action. The same is true of the south, which is also a male power.[1] The east male Hexagram pattern breathes something into existence (which is why religions of the 'book' tend to face east). The south male Hexagram pattern gives it a future.

In the west, which you now know to be a direction of receiving/containing, you will notice that the Hexagram pattern starts with the 'female' action: it starts with the Mother, the downward-pointing triangle. This is the vessel that receives power just as the egg and womb receive the sperm, just as the earth receives the Breath of Divinity in order to come to life. The west receives the power and contains it. The north, also female, gives it a past. But unlike the Pentagram symbol, which has a distinct 'up' and 'down', which defines the human stood upon the earth, the Hexagram has no 'up' or 'down': it is a composite of the two polarities combined – Divinity with and without substance which together make a whole. Essentially the Hexagram is the 'whole thing' – the symbol of Everything. One aspect is inextricably linked with the other.

When you do the full Pentagram ritual, the Hexagram is above you: it flows through every aspect of the ritual, focusing, filtering, and defining power. The aspects of the Pentagram ritual define the magician's acknowledgement of Divine Power. When you work with the Hexagram ritual, you as the human, in your Pentagram pattern, bring the Hexagram pattern down into your world: it defines your communication and relationship with Divine Power. The symbols and tools in the Pentagram tell you how the human works with and processes the Divine Power through magic. The Hexagram tells you what that Divine Power is, and begins the process of opening a line of communication. Later, as an adept, you will work with this pattern in a much deeper way, but to get there takes work, slow progress, and understanding. The seed is planted here. How you harvest that seed's fruit as a future adept will depend on your own work, development, and maturity as you walk through life.

Hopefully now you will begin to understand how these various magical patterns are inextricably interwoven and interconnected. Do not try to bring them together magically or ritually at this stage – you need to learn the individual steps of the dance and learn to execute each one of them properly before you can put them all together in a dance of creation and destruction.

---

[1] Meaning it is a power that gives, not that it has balls...

So why the execution of Hexagram at the cross quarter? The cross quarter of northeast is the position for all living beings of material substance on the cusp of expression: it is the magical position that defines the step into life. That step is magically perceived as being in the northeast: passing from the deep sleep of the north into the dawn of the east. This is depicted on the Tarot trump the Wheel: the human is draped over the wheel in a ritual position as he tumbles into conception. This is something you will learn more about in the Initiate section.

You work the Hexagram while standing in the northeast because from a ritual standpoint you are placing yourself in the magical position you occupied at the moment just before your conception. You are reiterating your eternal spirit that exists out of time as it is about to fall into life, and you are reiterating your conscious acceptance of the polarised expressions of Divine Power at that threshold of personal creation. It is when those two polarised powers are brought together in ritual harmonics that life begins.

This is why it is important to then sit down and meditate in this position, after doing that action. It is very early days in your magical training, but by sitting and meditating after working the Hexagram, you allow space for deeper understandings that are already embedded within you to find a way to surface.

You can do that once or many times, it is up to you. And don't expect a file download in your brain – this is a deep primal understanding that is held in each of your cells. By consciously sitting down and being silent in the midst of such ritual, you slowly trigger a response from deep within you. It will surface through your dreams, or through sudden inspirations days or weeks later; or it may rise into your consciousness during the meditation.

It will not rise as 'facts' or 'information': rather it will rise as a 'knowing,' a feeling, or a focus of understanding.

Journal

Every time something connected to this bubbles up into your mind, no matter how fragmented or strange, write it in your journal. It is amazing how many times something can appear in your mind and seem to make no sense, or is a mere glimpse, but when you look back in future years, you will see how you were bouncing around the edges of profundity.

3. Hexagram ritual, part two
Born of the Void

Note: To conduct this second part of the Hexagram ritual, take out the central altar and candle. If you have closed down the directions, open them back up and go through the first part of the Hexagram ritual without the meditations. If you have already done the first part of the ritual and you are moving directly on to the second part of the ritual, simply put out the central candle, bow, and then clear the altar away out of the room.

Go back and stand at the northeast cross-quarter. To start with, you are going to repeat the declaration of the two triangles, but with one difference at the end.

With your right hand, pointing with the first two fingers, starting with your arm outstretched high above you, recite:

"In the name of the Great Father…"

Bring your point down to the right hand corner:

"…and in the name of the Great Mother…"

Trace your point to the left hand corner:

"…and in the name of the Great Spirits…"

Trace your point back to complete the triangle.

Immediately use your point to draw a circle from the apex of the triangle and finish the circle at the upper left hand corner, in order to begin the second triangle, the inverted triangle.

Recite:

"In the name of the Great Mother…"

Trace your point across to the high right corner:

"…and in the name of the Great Father…"

Trace your finger down to the low centre of the triangle:

"…and in the name of the Great Spirits…"

Trace your point back to the high left corner to complete the triangle.

Recite:

"…We are, and from 'We,' I shall become."

Walk around the directions, going from the northeast cross-quarter, past east, and all around until you come back to the east.

Stand before the east altar, hold out your arms to the sides and recite:

"I call upon the powers of the east
to witness the giving of Divine Breath into life."

Step back and bow. Turn and go to the south altar.

Stand before the south altar, hold your arms out before you and recite:

"I call upon the powers of the south
to give safe passage to the Divine Breath onto the path of life
as it vanishes into the mists of the future."

Step back and bow.

Turn and go to the west altar and hold your hands out before you in a cupped position and recite:

> "I call upon the powers of the west
> to witness the receiving of Divine Breath into substance."

Step back and bow. Turn and go to the north altar.

Stand before the north altar, hold down your arms with hands pointing to the floor and recite:

> "I call upon the powers of the north
> to witness the release of the Divine Breath back to its source."

Step back and bow.

Turn and walk around the directions and stand in the west with your back to the west altar and recite:

> "Powers of the directions, you are my witness.
> I have announced the passage of the Divine Breath
> from its first aspiration, to its containment in the vessel,
> and then its passage back to the Source.
> I declare that I understand.
> I am a vessel.
> I am life.
> I contain the Divine Breath within me
> and I honour that Divine Breath that gives me life."

Take a deep breath in. Focus your mind on the direction east that is opposite you, and that the air you breathe in flows from this magical direction, and then exhale. Take a step forward and take in another breath, breathing in the air from the magical direction of east, and then slowly exhale. Repeat this action until you are stood in the centre of the directions, where the central candle flame would be.

Turn and face the south, feet apart. Raise your arms straight up above you, arms straight and locked.

Bring your arms down, outstretched to the sides, keeping your arms straight, and follow your left hand with your eyes, so that your eyes and head face east while your body stays facing south.

As your left hand reaches east, it lands palm facing up, while your right arm, without bending, lands west with the first two fingers of the right hand pointed.

Ensure that your hands, eyes and head all move at the same time, in harmony, so that your left hand and your eyes land east at the same time.

Bring your right hand above you (centre, top of the triangle), then bring it down to the east, across to the west and back to above to make the 'up' triangle.

Recite as you do the action:

> "The Divine Breath that brings life to form flows from the east;
> the Father gives."

Imagine the up triangle hanging in the air before you. Bring your hands to your chest (containment – you are the vessel).

Now walk around to the other side of the triangle (passing on the east side of the triangle). Stand facing north.

Extend your arms up above you (inhale as you do that action). With arms straight, bring your right arm down to the east, right hand landing east, palm up, with your head following your right hand so you are looking east.

The left hand moves straight down in front of you to point at the floor with the first two fingers pointed. This is all done as one harmonic movement.

With the left hand, trace the down triangle starting 'down/point' to west. As the hand moves to the west, the head turns to the west, and you exhale and begin to recite.

Ensure the head and hand arrive west at exactly the same time – head stays west. As you recite, trace west to east, east to down. As the hand arrives at 'down' the head is set straight looking north.

As you do the action, recite:

> "The Divine Vessel in the west that contains the Breath:
> the Mother receives.
> The wind that blows from the east finds the vessel of the west."

Drop your arms by your side (release). Close your eyes. See in your mind's eye the hexagram hanging before you.

With your mind's eye, see a flow of power/energy come down from above and from the east at the same time, joining with and filling the east half of the hexagram (along with the east & up section of the space) with a golden light.

As the power settles in the east half of the hexagram it flows out of the east side of the hexagram, flows towards and through you, and vanishes behind you. As it flows towards you it turns red, passes through you, and vanishes through the south gate.

In your mind's eye see the red flow back out of the south gate behind you, and pass into you on your west side.

As it passes through you and leaves you, it turns into a bright white light that dazzles you. It flows into the west side of the hexagram, filling it with a very bright, pure light. It also fills up the west direction and down section of the space.

The bright light flows out into the north before you until the hexagram and the space around you is totally empty. The dark hexagram outline hangs before you, filled with emptiness.

Close your eyes (if they are not already closed for visualising) and take a step forward so that you are stood in the space of the empty hexagram.

With your eyes closed, clear your mind. Feel the nothing all around you. Feel the blackness, the space without time, motion, light, sound: a total black stillness. Stay in that silence for as long as you feel you need to.

When you are ready, take in a deeper breath and hold it, eyes still closed. Take a step forward, open your eyes, and breathe out, all at the same time.

Then recite:

> "I am born of the Void,
> the Breath that breathes life out of the nothing,
> the Breath that contains everything.
> I step into life with the Divine Breath flowing through me."

Turn and face east. Step to the altar, blow out the candle, and bow. Repeat in the other directions going clockwise until the room is dark and silent.

Stand for a moment in the darkness and silence. Be aware that this ritual is about the birth of life, of Divinity breathing life into substance. Be aware that the Divine Breath flows through you. Your breath and your words have the power of Divine Consciousness flowing through them. Use that breath wisely and with balance.

4. *Task:* Learning and practising the ritual

Learn the sequence of the ritual from an outer perspective, without the candles and altars etc. until you can do the movements and recitations fluidly and by heart. Particularly work on the second aspect of the ritual, which has very defined, coordinated actions between your hands, eye, breath, mind, and body. It is a lot to learn and hold in your memory, so if you really struggle with that, record yourself speaking both the instructions and the utterances. Listen to it daily until you have a good memory of it.

Only when you can execute the second part of the ritual with total fluency, by heart, it is time to actually 'do' the ritual using the altars, flames, and intention.

At first, particularly for a beginner, this ritual act can seem fairly easy with not much going on. That is because you are not yet fully 'plugged in.' However for some natural magicians, or older ones with experience, this ritual can trigger deep, powerful connections with the Divinity within and all around you.

Use this ritual as a monthly focus to reconnect with the Divine Breath. Work out a time each month that is right for you, (the most powerful time for this ritual is dawn). It can also be used as a meditative action to reconnect you with the sense of Divinity around you. Keep a journal of your experiences of the monthly ritual, how it develops, how it feels and how that feel changes over time. Have a separate computer file for this monthly exercise that you add to as your practice of it develops.

Note: play to your weaknesses

If you are a patterns kind of person (you like puzzles, math, etc.) do not get engrossed in the patterns – focus instead on the meditative aspect and visualisation aspect.

If you are a creative or visionary kind of person, focus more on the pattern aspect of the ritual. In other words, don't play to your strengths; work to your weaknesses in order to strengthen and discipline them.

This particular ritual, of all rituals, be they advanced or beginner, is the one that can truly tap into the flow of Divine Power in a very simple way. By working with this ritual in order to strengthen your weaknesses, it releases its power into you to guide you and assist you. The moment you engage in the action of development, all the powers and contacts come up behind you to help you and to cheer you along. If you simply play to your strengths, they will stand by and observe, without helping.

The hand/eye coordination, while speaking at the same time, is a very important aspect of the ritual, as it is training your two sides to work in harmony but independently of each other. Remember in the previous lesson the work that looked at the two balanced polarity powers working independently but in harmony with each other? When you start to express that dynamic in simple, physical terms, it changes how your brain operates: it teaches the brain to operate the body in harmonic movements that work separately and yet together. For some people this will be very easy; for others it will not. Deeper magical power dynamics cannot be fully understood by the consciousness until the body itself understands and can act, process, and execute those dynamics in basic, simple physical form. It starts from the outside and works in.

5. *Task:* Mapping the sigil of the ritual

Get a pen and your journal. Draw out a map of the movements of the ritual, first for part one and then for part two.

A straight line where you walked a straight line, a small circle where you turned, a dot for a particular action, and a bigger circle where you circled something. You will end up with a pattern before you. Work with that pattern, adjusting it, refining it until you end up with a sigil that is that ritual. Now look at the sigil and remember the ritual's actions as you look at each aspect of the sigil. Choose one of the ritual's actions that is defined as a line, circle, or dot. Close your eyes and remember that particular action. What is the colour that immediately springs to mind? Don't think about it logically or psychologically; this is pure instinct. When you recover a sense of the action's colour, then colour that mark in the sigil. Do this for all the major aspects of the ritual that jump out at you.

This is the very first stage of learning how to work with magically empowered sigils. First you must develop a relationship with the concept. Eventually as an adept you will be able to 'capture' the essence of a ritual and infuse it into a sigil that is specific to a ritual in a way that is unique to you. You will then use that sigil to keep the power of the ritual flowing in the long term. You will also learn in your adept training how to look at a sigil or sacred writing and 'see' whether it has power within it or not. To do that, first you must learn to fill a sigil with power, and to do that, you must learn how the whole process works. Baby steps. Makes for a safe magician!

Go back over your journal and notes, and sigilise each of the rituals you have done. You will realise that some rituals can be sigilised and some cannot: some power will just not be contained. This is also why writing by hand in your journal is so very important. You need to learn how to use your hand and ink to infuse power. That process is started by using your hand and ink to express power by talking about it, drawing it, scribbling it. General notes, essays, readings etc. can all be done on computer, but there are certain things that must be done by hand in your journal as it is kindergarten training for the greatness that is to come. Ensure that you have journaled your experiences with the Hexagram ritual, and how those experiences develop as you practise it.

6. *Task:* Research

Research different religions, magic, and cultures that have a symbol that depicts a shape upon a shape that is equal and has positive/negative, or up/down (ying yang, for example). Look at the shapes. Draw them out. See by drawing them over and over how that culture is expressing the same dynamic but in a very different way.

Then read the explanations that the culture gives for the shape. As you read different interpretations by different writers on the same symbol, you will begin to see which ones actually understood it and worked with it, and which ones did not. Sometimes the difference is glaringly obvious; sometimes it is not so obvious. Make a point of noting down the different interpretations and what you think of them.

Choose one of the symbols/cultures and write an essay on how that culture perceives the expression of that symbol. What does it mean to them? How do they work with it? What does it appear in relation to? (i.e. teachings, actions, lifestyles, etc.) Don't just go to the nearest Wiki page, make an effort to really look into the symbolism of different religions and cultures, or even magical practices. There are quite a few of these Divine symbols out there in different parts of the world, but it may take you some time to find them. Take the time, as it will surprise you as to how and where these symbols appear.

The shapes that they take will tell you a lot about the power that flows through the land and the people. It will tell you about the dominant elements, how and if they include time in the process, if it is related to human life or not.

You can do this as a computer document or you can do it as a scrap book with pictures and written text, and then scan or photograph it. It is totally up to you. You will get a great deal of knowledge out of this task is you make an effort. You may not understand everything, but taking note and drawing something out, and reading up on it properly can add to your own 'inner library' for magical knowledge. If you don't put effort and curiosity into it, you will get very little back from it. As with everything in Quareia, you gain in equal measure – if you put a lot of effort in over time, you will find you get a strong 'magical wind' guiding you as you learn. If you skip through things and do the minimum required, you will be left alone with no power guiding you.

Lesson 5

The Elemental Patterns and Maps

Note: for this lesson you will need your tarot pack, a bowl of water, a stone, and a candle/flame – and somewhere outdoors to work.

In the last few lessons, you have learned about the elemental powers that flow out of the magical directions. Now you need to know how they express through a patch of land, as that pattern varies from landmass to landmass, and also from small region to region. This in turn will enable you to learn how to draw on local power flows in your magical work, and also how to adjust your magical work to take into account regional fluctuations. This is very important because if you do not take these local flows into account, you can run into some rather difficult power imbalances that will directly affect how you work, what you work on, and also how your body copes with the magic.

This is also the first lesson in the course that begins to teach you 'nature magic.' Magic should never be solely removed from your environment. Magic should be fluid, and should be in harmony with the land upon which the magic is done. There are times for working magic in a temple space, times for working magic out in nature, and times to combine both approaches.

This lesson works with magic outdoors and then brings the outdoors into the ritual space. If you live in a city, pick a day that you can go to the nearest patch of countryside that is close by, to an area where you can work undisturbed, or find a local park, or best of all work in your garden if you have one. If you work at dawn, it is less likely that you will be disturbed, be vulnerable, or look like a nutter.

Before we get to the practical work, let's look at what it is we are actually going to work with. Let's look at how it works, why it works the way it does, and why it is so important in magical training.

1. The magical elements in nature

When I say magical elements, I am talking about air, fire, water, and earth. Some systems and cultures add in other elements or work with a different set of elements entirely. No one system is correct or incorrect, they are just different in how they work with the world around them, and that difference is often deeply connected to their landmass and culture. Western magic works with the four elements, so we will focus on those.

Module II – Patterns and Maps in Magic

The magical element system is a pattern that expresses on the cusp of manifestation. It is a pattern (among many) that is an inner pattern, which is to say it is a deeper expression of power which is then filtered through form which in turn finally expresses itself into physical manifestation in our material world. So wherever you are in the northern hemisphere, that pattern will work in deep magic. In the southern hemisphere there are going to be differences when the direction patterns are being used for the seasons, but beyond that the same pattern works as it is an inner planetary pattern, not a land mass pattern. The basic patterns you are learning at this stage are a foundation for much bigger and more dynamic patterns that go beyond the physical world, so keep everything the same. The sun rises in the east no matter what hemisphere you are in, and the inner larger power patterns are also the same. There will be the occasional surface difference, but at this stage of your training, do not change anything. Later as an adept, when you fully understand all the power parameters involved in making a change, then you can experiment and share your findings with other magicians.

Speculation in magic is useless. You have to have direct experience to be able to talk with certainty; you cannot hypothesise where magic is concerned.

Once that inner pattern externalises on a landmass, it shifts and changes according to the vessel. Each area has its own unique expression of how it externalises the elements, and that can be specific to a small area or a large area. You cannot generalise with elemental magic, as its variant expressions can be very localised indeed.

These localised elemental variants can have a direct effect on your magical work and development. When you work magic, you work with the elements around you whether you are aware of them or not. They are part and parcel of the forces of nature, forces that magic directly engages. These forces can make your work harder or easier depending on how you work and how conscious you are of these power flows.

The inner elemental fluctuations around you, along with planetary influences and the outer elemental expressions around you (rivers, mountains, volcanoes, hot springs, desert, etc.) all affect how you work magically and how your magical work affects you, the land, and everything around you. It can be harmonic or it can be an aggravator. So it is important to know all the variables so that you can work with them in cooperation, modify them when appropriate, draw upon them, or strengthen them. They are sometimes worked with and sometimes not dependent upon what it is you are doing. But to get to that stage, first you must be able to magically identify what is around you and where it is.

So let's have a look at a practical example which will give you a better idea of what I am talking about, and we will look, though that example, how it is worked with by a magician.

2. Regional elemental expression

You know by now the magical expressions of the elements in the four directions. A magician moves to a patch of land he is unfamiliar with and before he starts to work magically, he first needs to identify what type of land he has moved to, what the powers are like, and what elemental expressions are there. He works first to talk to whatever beings are upon the land (something you will learn how to do later in the course). Then he begins the process of learning what elemental expressions are upon that area of land.

The magician will be working with the four magical element system, but he has to take into account the regional expressions of the elements in the directions in order to work harmoniously with the land. If the magician does not do this, he will be working against tides rather than with them.

In his preparation to work magic, the magician must first find out what physical elements are expressing through the directions so that he can adjust his working space accordingly, and also combine the outer and inner elements in his work. The magician goes out on the land near his house and prepares to work in two very different ways, so that he can compare the two results and make a decision based on his findings.

First he needs to find out the gender that expresses through the land. In modern magic we always think of the earth as 'female,' which in a deeper magical sense it is. But within that overall 'female' identity there are small regional 'flips' of the polarisation. Just as with the magnetic polar expression through the planet: there is an overall 'polarity' in the northern hemisphere and an opposing one in the south, but small pockets of the reverse 'pole,' condensed in a particular area, can be found scattered across the planet.

To find out what the gender of the patch of land is, the magician uses divination to ask the gender of that part of the land. After that, he will need to find out how far that 'gender' stretches – it can be a few square miles or it can be a huge area. Also, within that area there can be changes and differences, so it can get complicated. To avoid confusion and making mistakes, the magician defines an area as his working area (within a few miles of his working space) and double-checks through divination the gender power that flows through that space. He then also looks beyond the defined area to see if it changes or if it is constant.

That is important for more advanced work that would draw on a larger area, or for magical work that is intended to support the wider landmass. If you are going to support and work with something, first you need to know what it is you are working with.

So the gender is established. Let's say the magician found that his particular patch is male. As a male magician, that means for him that the power flowing through the land does not compliment him; rather it amplifies his male power. If the magician is fairly young and has high testosterone, he will be aware that he will have to tread cautiously so as not to overwhelm his hormone system or to have the emotional issues that manifest when testosterone is too high or out of control (violence and mental instability, for example).

If he is older, he would be aware that he would be at greater risk of prostate cancer if he is working on a powerful male land for an extended period of time. So he would have to make adjustments to that work by incorporating modifying influences, for instance working with a female deity.

Now that the gender has been established, he needs to identify which elements are the strongest in which direction.

The first method he uses relies on his inner skills (which you started to learn about in Module one). He starts with a candle flame in order to search for the strongest directional expression of fire. The magician has not worked with a compass, so he is not aware which direction is which on the land. This is important, so that you do not subconsciously identify element to direction (i.e. fire/south).

The magician first works the direction facing him. He walks a few steps forward holding a candle flame. Because it is slightly windy, he has the candle in a jam jar to protect the flame. As he steps forward, he holds an intention in his mind to find where the element of fire expresses upon the land. He is totally focused upon that intention and when he steps forward and stops, he 'sees' the inner candle flame within his inner imagination.

The flame does not appear to change. He waits for a few minutes, feeling into the flame to see how it is reacting to the direction. Nothing happens. So then he moves to the next direction, following the same method of walking around the directions that he uses in his magical space. He repeats the same action: waiting, intention, watching, feeling. Again, nothing happens. He then moves on to the next direction. Again he repeats the same action, but this time the candle flame that he is observing with his 'inner vision' leaps to life, growing stronger and glowing brightly. He has found where the flow of elemental fire expresses through a local direction. He places that candle on the floor in that direction to mark it.

Next he takes the bowl of water and repeats the same exercise, going around the directions until he finds one that appears in his inner vision to cause the bowl of water to overflow. The bowl of water is placed on the ground to mark that direction. He repeats the same exercise with a small rock. As he goes around the directions he notices that in one particular direction that the rock seems heavier and denser. He places it on the floor.

So now he must find the last element: air. This one is harder, as there is nothing to hold. So he goes around each direction in turn, faces that direction, and then turns around. He stands, takes in a deep breath, and then exhales slowly. He takes note of how it feels and how it appears in his inner vision. In one particular direction, as he exhales, it feels and looks from an inner point of view as if a large wind is blowing through him. He also has found an added bonus: as he breathes out in this direction, a physical wind suddenly picks up and blows around him. The magician smiles. He has hit the jackpot.

Not only has he found the air direction, he has also found that the land is very responsive, and that the air element is very strong on that patch of land. This will really help him magically in his work. As he mediated magical breath, the physical outer wind responded by blowing all around him: the wind answered the call.

To confirm his findings, the magician then uses a second method: he goes around the directions on the land with his magical tools and observes how they react to each direction. The tools will feel different, they will suddenly but subtly spring to life when they are held in a direction that is elementally compatible with their magical element. This is something you can practise once you have come to the stage of training later in the apprentice section which deals with magical tools.

At this point the magician gets out his compass and marks down which direction is which. If he has been working at cross quarters without realising (for example where he placed the candle is WNW) then he will look at which is the nearest straight direction and will assign that as a specific direction. So WNW becomes west. This is important, as it enables the magician to tie in the outer directional elemental expression with the magical pattern he has built up of the magical directional powers and contacts in his working space: he places the magical elemental pattern and the outer elemental pattern together and brings them into sync.

3. Analysis of the findings

So let's presume the magician's findings were as follows: east – air, south – water, west – fire (WNW) and earth, but in the north – nothing. And his divination told him the land is 'male.'

This presents the magician with a bit of a dilemma. This is not the best place for a male magician to be working magic. But then there are few perfect places, so the magician must adjust how they work to accommodate the local dynamics. But why is this such a difficult area?

We have already addressed the issue of a male magician working on a male land: it can quickly become 'too male' which in turn can seep aggression and conflict, ego and anger into the magic. So he has already thought about working with a female deity that can balance but also match that power (a gentle mother goddess will not cut it).

His second stumbling block is the east/air elemental dynamic, coupled with the magical element of air in the east, all on a male land. It will be very powerful, hence the gust of wind when he breathed out. East is also male, and when used in unskilled hands it can become very fundamentalist and combative. In skilled hands it can be very powerful, but it will be very focused and difficult to keep in check. East wind/male/sword on a land that oozes testosterone can make for a very conflict-ridden mix if it is not worked with properly.

It is tempered a little by the water in the south (a male/female mix) and the fire in the west (again female/male mix). The earth in the west is a double female mix and will help to 'take the fire' out of the male pattern, as will the water in the south.

It also gives him a clue as to which female deity to work with: west is the threshold of death; fire and earth in that threshold is a male/female mix in a female direction. Death, female, fire, testosterone in a female vessel, and earth all point to a warrior or destructive goddess: so for example Sekhmet would be perfect for him to work with. She works with death, disease, the out-of-control 'warrior killing frenzy,' and she also carries the power of the sun/fire. Sekhmet is an ancient deity that is very primal in her power and therefore very stable. She is also a deity that is not tied to a specific landmass: even though she appears to us as Egyptian, in magical reality she appears in the land throughout the northern hemisphere in various forms. Her deeper power has a long reach.

But would that not be too dangerous? No. Would it not be better to have a watery female? No, definitely not. The powerful, focused and unemotional (air) male power upon the land needs a polarity that can match it in battle, a power that has equal strength to keep it in check while also having opposite qualities: she is emotional (angry), she rages, and she is female. The two powers are equally matched in combat. A watery feminine power would be quickly overwhelmed and slaughtered.

So the magician decides to work magically (not religiously) with Sekhmet as a guide and advisor, as a guardian and teacher, and in return he would do 'jobs' for her as requested. He would have to ask her if she was willing to work with him and if she says no, he will have to try and find a similar goddess and ask her. This is where working with deities comes in as an aspect of magical work, something you will learn about further into your apprentice training.

The magician also needs to think about how he works with the outer and inner elements in combination, in relation to his work. So let's look at the elements physical and magical in their working combinations, as they presented to this magician.

East is air, so it is the same pattern as the magical direction. This will make that aspect of the magical pattern very strong indeed. So the magical work the magician does will make use of that dynamic by ensuring that the work engages with a lot of magical utterance and sigil techniques, lots of giving/releasing of new patterns into the future, and lots of creation work. The sword will be totally focused on balance/justice work and not used in a defensive way as it would engage the bloodlust of the overly male power on the land.

The water in the south is a combination of inner fire and outer water that works with the future. The inner fire 'heats up' the water, and south is the future: the magician will engage that direction to 'cook' magical aspects for the future. Heat and water are ingredients for the birth of new lands (volcano/sea), and that very ancient pattern in the land can be tapped into on a land with such an elemental combination to enable very long-term magical projects that will birth new substance in the future.

The fire and earth in the west, which is a water direction, will be an interesting one for the magician to work with. The inner magical element is always stronger than the outer element, so the water will dampen down the fire and nourish the earth element. This again points to perfect conditions to focus magic on long-term projects that will 'birth new substance.'

The north has no outer elemental expression, and it is the direction of earth/female. It is also the direction of past/ancestors. This means that the land is not conducive to ancestor work, death work, or Underworld work: the whole pattern of the land is about the birth of new substance, new land mass, new patterns for the future: this land is a cradle. Think in terms of our planet's ancient history when it was a bubbling mass of hot lava, seas, earthquakes, and the birth of new islands, land-masses, and the beginnings of life. This is the sort of magical pattern you would expect to find in a country such as Iceland, where that process is still happening in a very visible way.

The magician is intrigued. He gets online or goes to the library and researches the history and mythology of the local area, along with looking at the geological outlay of the land. He finds that the geology is very much about 'new land': fault lines, young mountains, and a constantly shifting and evolving landscape. The history of the land is littered with tribal wars, conflict, male dominated societies, and examples of very 'testosterone' men. Now he finally understands the foundation layer of the land that he has moved to and will be working with.

This tells him that he cannot do certain types of magic on the land, as certain types of magical work will aggravate the power flow and be volatile. It also tells him not to try and do ancestor work, any magic that involves conflict, and not to work with any male warrior deities. Once he has engaged the elemental patterns properly, he can work with that elemental pattern to make friends with the local land beings so that he works in harmony with them.

He thinks very carefully about his magical work for the length of time that he will live on this land. He consults through divination to see what positive role he can take while he lives here, and he also consults with his inner contacts to see why he is there from a magical perspective.

He then decides on two courses of action. One is to adjust his regular and ongoing magical work that is his usual project or training work so that it flows more harmoniously with the elemental pattern; the other is to directly engage the volatile creative aspect of the land to assist in that ongoing growth dynamic in the land. He will work as a mediator and conductor for the flows of power: one human directly and consciously engaging magically, in gnosis, with the ongoing land dynamic will have a long-reaching effect far beyond the normal capacity of one human: he becomes a catalyst.

He will most likely never really see the outcome of his work, but he will observe change, sometimes quite big change, in the land and the people as a result of his work. In terms of land/time, his work will be a contribution of less than a second in a time span of a million years. And yet that 'second,' because it is magically focused and in tune with the flow of creation, will be a key 'second': a turning point in a vast expansion of development for the land.

4. Practical work

So now that you are beginning to understand why it is so important to work in harmony with the combination of magical, inner, and externalised elements, it is time for you to experiment and discover for yourself.

You will also begin to see how the course is slowly introducing more and more plates for you to spin in your magical work. This approach does away with the forcing of a generic magical pattern that most magical systems use, an approach that was popularised in the nineteenth century and is still used to this day by magical groups. That approach severely limits the growth, expansion, and power of magic and effectively hobbles the magician.

Learning to work magically by taking all these different aspects and powers and weaving them into a pattern that is unique to the magician and the land upon which they stand allows the magician to truly tap into the vast resources of power that flow through a land. It also works in harmony with the land, the elements, and the dynamic forces around you, so that you jump into a fast-moving river of power rather than trying to dam and deflect it.

5. *Task:* Identifying elemental manifestations

First, find out what externalised elemental manifestations are around you: rivers, mountains, caves, hot springs, etc. and take note of them.

Using the method outlined in the practical example, work on the land upon or very near where you live. If you do this work too far away from where you live and do magic, you might find that you are working with dynamics that are not relevant to your actual working space.

First, work with your tarot deck using the Tree of Life layout to ascertain what gender the area of land is. The final card will give you your answer. The question you need to ask is:

> *"Tell me the gender of this land area where I am standing.*
> *Is it male or is it female?"*

The interpretation may be obvious: a Queen, the High Priestess, or Strength (it is a female card). Or it may not be obvious and may take more than one reading to get a straight answer. If you get a non-gendered card (the Wheel, for example), mark that result down in your journal (keep very tight records of these readings, even if you do not understand the outcome – the information will quite likely will be helpful in the future). Don't forget that almost all of the trumps have one gender power or the other, although many are not obvious at first glance.

If you are not sure about which trumps are male and which are female, look at the depiction of the card, and place it in a direction from the four directional elemental patterns. Remember which directions are male and which are female. So for example the tower would go in the west, which is female (a destructive power that is breaking something down), or the death card which belongs in the north which is also female.

With a non-gendered answer, you need to ask in a different way. You would ask: *"is this land female in its power?"* If you get a card such as the Three of Swords (separation) then it is likely that it is not female. You would then ask: *"is this land male?"* If you still get a *"no"* answer, there is a possibility that the land patch is not gendered. Non-gendered patches of land do happen but they are not common: they are either neutral, which can be easy to work with, or it could be that the patch of land has no gender but has a specific quality of power that flows through it. That can express as the Fool, which tells you it is a young and not yet fully-formed power. That tells you that although it is currently ungendered, it will eventually transform into a gender power. So then you would ask: *"when this land matures into its own power, what gender will it be then?"* Again it may appear as a non-obvious gender, or as a power that has no gender. Whatever your final conclusions are, write them down.

Now it is time to work, as the magician did, outside with the candle flame, the bowl of water, the rock, and your own breath, and find out which elements are the strongest in which direction. Once you have identified the direction where an element is at its strongest, use a compass to identify where the actual directions are. Adjust the direction as necessary so that you end up knowing which elements express through which compass directions (i.e. if the bowl of water you placed on the floor shows on the compass as ENE, then mark it down as east). As the magician found in the example, sometimes you can get more than one element in one direction and none in others. This is unusual but normal. Just work with what you find.

6. *Task:* Mapping

Now that you have your gender and elemental information, you need to map it and look at it so that you can then use that information in your future magical work. Get paper and pen. Mark out east, south, west, and north on the top, bottom, and edges of the paper. Now draw a small pentagram in the centre: this is you. Draw the sword in the east/left hand of the pentagram and a cup in the right hand (keep this small so that you have room to add things in around the pentagram).

Get out your journal notes from Module I Lesson 6. Remember colouring in aspects of your pentagram? Using those colours, colour the top, bottom legs, and side arms of the pentagram in the colours you assigned them in Lesson 6. Once you have finished mapping, have a look at the elements and the colours in your pentagram to see if here is a connection between the elements and the colours of your pentagram.

You need to list the elements in the directions that you found them outside. You can use the words (fire, water, air, earth). If your land's gender is female, draw a down-pointing triangle around your small pentagram to enclose the pentagram, and an upward triangle if the land is male. If the land showed in the readings to be both, then draw a hexagram around the small pentagram (and again think of the magical implications of what that is telling you). If the land showed as being neutral, but of a particular type of power, you need to settle upon a symbol that will tell you what power type it is, using magical symbolism.

If it showed as a destructive power you could use the lightening flash that would pass through the pentagram. If it is a combative power, use a cruciform shape inverted (battle-ready sword) passing through the pentagram. If it is a power of justice/balance, use the upright cruciform (justice). If it is a nurturing power, circle the pentagram (encompassing) etc. There are many combinations, and part of the learning process is to be able to reason, identify, and apply the right shape to the purpose at hand by using instinct and logic. Just think carefully about what you use and why.

Go to your journal notes from the astrology lesson in module one. Remember mapping out your planets around the pentagram/directions? Look at where the different planets of your chart are on the two-dimensional layout. Remember that the centre is you, and the left side is the rising sun/left arm of your chart. Look at your natal chart and your notes. Mark down on the map, using the astrological symbols for those planets, where Saturn, Pluto, Jupiter, Neptune, Uranus, Mars, Venus, Mercury, the Moon, and the Sun lie in this two-dimensional pattern.

Look up the elements assigned to the planets so that you know which ones are fire, water, air, etc. Colour the symbols (draw over the symbol with a coloured pencil) according to their elements: yellow/air, red/fire, blue/water, black/earth. Now do the same with the elemental shapes or words. Study this map for a few minutes and see if there is an elemental/colour cluster in any particular direction or if they are fairly evenly spaced out. Look at those elemental clusters in relation to the magical elemental directions and the natural homes of magical tools (sword/east, wand/south, etc.). How do they match or clash?

In your journal, divide the map into four sections. Look at all the different influences flowing into the space, gender polarities, the elements, the planets, etc. and look where the planets and gender influences strength an area, where the influences compliment each other, and where they are either too strong or too antagonistic. It may take you some time to work out the subtle combinations and how those combinations may affect the power that flows around your working space.

If you have a heavy concentration of one element in a particular quadrant, that could become counterproductive: for example too much fire, particularly if you live in a hot place, can bring a volatile element to your work. A simple remedy for that, when you come to do any magical work in your space, is to place a bowl of water in the work space that is right where the fire is. So for example if you have fire in the south, and Mars and/or the Sun near or in the south, then you are going to need a bowl of water there.

If however you are going to be working magically with fire, then that is the area in your space to work. If you are a man, ensure you are aware that it might trigger latent aggression in you. Awareness is half the problem solved, and learning to control and channel it through physical work like digging, running, martial arts, and mediating it through you will solve the rest (put your hands on a rock and 'see' the fire/aggression flow into the rock or the land).

I hope you begin to see how such a map can be very useful in your magical work. As an adept it can truly make a major difference to your magical work as you learn to gather up and work with all of that power.

If you have the luxury of a dedicated working space and you can mark the floor, then mark it with the elements in their positions, and if possible mark the planetary symbols on the ceiling, sides, and floor[1] etc. That way you stand and work from within the map. If that is not possible, just redraw the map on a good-sized bit of paper, do it neatly, and hang it on the wall of your working space.

Note: If you live in an area where there is no green space fairly close to your work space, i.e. you live in a large, sprawling city with no green space for miles, then as a last resort you can do this in your working space itself. But that is a very poor option, as it truly cuts a lot of the pure elemental connections – you cannot breathe the wind indoors, for example. Even if you have to drive or get a bus out of the city for an hour or so, do that so that at least you get to feel what it is like to connect with the elements out in nature. This is very important for the land magic that you will do later in the course.

By now you should have a map that shows the power flows in your work-space. Each direction should be marked with the magical elements in the directions, the elements that express naturally through the land should be marked in the directions, the gender of the land should be on the map, and the planets of your natal chart should be marked around the map as they appear on your chart. Because you are working in a two-dimensional setting, remember that the 'down' aspect of your natal chart (below the horizon) is the north aspect of your working space.

This map does not become a gospel that you have to work to; rather it is a tool that you use should you need it. If, when you come to do more involved magical work, you are finding energetic resistance for example, then you can look to the map and see if what you are doing is clashing with the power that flows through the space. Similarly, if you are doing some powerful work and you need every bit of energetic support that you can get, then you can look to the map, see where the strongest powers are, and incorporate them into your work. This is something you will learn to do in the later part of the course.

---

[1] The floor would show the planets that are below the horizon.

To get to that standard of work, first you simply need awareness of what flows around you all the time and to know how to interact with that flow: this map is the first step of that awareness. Later you will learn a similar technique for finding the inner contacts that flow naturally around the space where you work, so that you can start to make friends and communicate with them. You will learn that there are 'families' of beings that cluster in particular land areas, and as a magician you can learn to connect, cooperate, and work with them to mutual benefit.

7. *Working:* The ritual communication with the land

Note: you will need ten pieces of paper, a marker pen, a rock from outside near your home, and then rocks, bowls of water and extra candles for the land elements aspect of this work. You will need three good sized sticks or twigs, or a length of string, and a pin to prick your finger. If you have problems with pricking your finger with a pin, then use a lancet, the type that is used for measuring blood sugar.

The extra rock that you find outside near your home is a key element of this ritual, so you need to choose it carefully. The way to do this is: walk instinctively around the land with the intention to find a rock that would be good as a vessel to work with. It does not matter how big or small it is, just that there is no resistance in the rock to working with you. In your mind, talk to the rock and tell the rock that you are about to work magically for the good of the land and ask the rock if it is willing to act as a vessel and mediator of that work. If you feel no resistance, then you are good to go. If not, and you feel resistance, then put the rock down and go find another one.

It is not the substance of the rock that any resistance will come from; it is any being that happens to be residing in the rock. What we call faery beings, land beings, often take up residence in rocks and stones. You have to make sure that the rock is not occupied, and if it is, you need to ensure that the occupant is willing to work with you. Having a pissed off faery being in your work space is not a good idea.

You do not need to do this for the other rocks that will mark out where the earth element is in your space, as they will not be directly interacted with. Just ensure that you put them back where you found them when you have finished the work. Remember this: if you work with rocks magically and directly, remember that there are sometimes beings in those rocks that can assist or block your work.

Read through this ritual and note down the elements and planets in the directions that you are going to identify and work with. Insert their names into the ritual recitation and write out the recitations for each direction with the elemental and planetary variants in it so that you have a ritual script that is unique to you.

(I have only written the recitation for the east; you can do the rest using that same template.)

Warning: the recitations with the inner contacts in the directions are very specific: do not do your own interpretation or add in words. Through the recitation you ask the inner contact to put into the rock whatever is needful for the land. Should you decide to change "needful" for something else, like "regeneration" or "peace," you can trigger untold damage. It is not for you to decide what the land needs; that is the job of the inner contact. Do not be arrogant enough to presume that you know what the land needs.

Do this on computer or in your journal, the choice is yours, so that you have a record of it and can also use it for the ritual itself. If you do it on computer, print it out and place it in your journal afterwards.

In your work space, set up the four directional altars and the central one, and then place upon them the magical elements (fire/south, water/west, etc.): a candle flame in the south for fire, a bowl of water in the west, a rock in the north, and just the usual candle in the east – you do not need anything for the magical element of air; it is all around you. Some magicians use incense, but that is actually a combination of 3 elements, not one (fire, earth, and air).

Each altar will have a candle (which is the working threshold), and a magical element (so south will have two candles at this point). Now place on the altars the inner local elements that you discovered outside on the land: an extra candle flame in the direction where the fire is, a rock for earth, bowl of water, etc. Have three sticks or twigs or a length of string. Remember that south is 'forward and up.' Make the shape of the triangle that relates to the gender of the land that you are on and place it around the central flame. So for example if the land is female, create a downward-pointing triangle with the 'down' pointing towards north. If you are on land that has no gender but has a power dynamic, put on the altar, under the flame, the tarot trump that is closest to the description/image you have of the land.

Get ten pieces of paper and draw out the planetary symbols and their names. Place them on the floor in relation to where they would be in the two-dimensional natal chart. Put the pin on the central altar inside the triangle. Finally, get the extra rock that comes from the land around you and place it on the central altar inside the triangle. Now you are ready to get to work.

Open the directions and gates. Do the Hexagram ritual to tune the space to Divine working. When you have finished, turn to face the central altar. Pick up the rock and hold it quietly. Tell the rock you are about to begin working with it so that any being inside is prepared.

Walk around the directions and then go to the east altar. See in your mind's eye the gates opened and an inner contact standing in the shadows of the threshold. Look at the elements depicted on the altar: these will act as a filter for the work.

Hold the rock out to the inner contact (careful of the candle flame) and recite:
> "I ask the inner contact at the threshold of the east to bridge into this rock whatever is needful for the land upon which I work.
> That power is filtered through the elements of air and [*insert whatever element if any is there*]."

Now stand in silence. See in your mind's eye the inner contact reach out and place something into the rock. It may take only a few seconds or it may take minutes. Wait until the inner contact withdraws their hand.

Recite:
> "The gift from the inner contact resides within the rock.
> The powers of the elements [*say them, air and the others*]
> in this direction fuel that gift."

Bow, pick up the rock and step back.

If there is one of your natal planets close to or in that direction, moving clockwise, go and stand on the paper with the name/sigil of the planet (so at the east altar if the planet is to the left of you/the altar and more than one step away, do not go against the clockwise flow, work with them at very end of the cycle).

Recite:
> "I ask the angel of the planet X, which flows through me in this direction, to help me use my own potential to assist in this work.
> Help me to find what qualities and gifts the planet X bestows upon me, that I may engage those gifts in my service."

Think about the influence of that planet in that direction (i.e. Mars would bring a potential for vitality and energy). Build up in your mind a shape that represents that potential, any shape that reflects to you that energy. Now see yourself within and surrounded by that shape. See energy streaming into you from the planet and filling the shape. Cup the rock in your hands and hold it to your chest. See in your mind's eye the rock being brought into your energy pattern/field. Let it bathe in that pattern/energy.

Now move on to the south and repeat the whole process. Work your way around the directions, working with the inner contacts, with the elements and the planets, until the rock has been filled by the four inner contacts, and has bathed in each of your planetary influences.

When you have finished, go and stand before the central altar with your back to the north. Cup the rock in your hands and hold it to your chest.

Recite:

> "Great Mother,[2] bless this rock, that it may carry back to the land
> all of the gifts, powers, and energies we have mediated in to it.
> May the gifts held in this rock flow out upon the land,
> and bring whatever is necessary to this land.
> I thank you Mother[3] for allowing me to live here.
> I thank you rock for working with me and for being a vessel,
> and I thank the inner contacts for their gifts.
> May this service begin a process of change."

Now pick up the pin and prick your finger, dripping the blood on to the rock. Hold it back to your chest.

Recite:

> "I give of myself to the land, to be a part of the family of the land,
> to be a brother[4] to all beings that live upon this land
> for however long or short a time I will be here.
> Father above me,
> Mother below me,
> beings all around me,
> flame of life within me,
> please help me to be a part of the family of this land
> and not an enemy or outsider.
> Guide my hand, my thoughts, my deeds and my eyes,
> so that I may see, hear, feel, and sense when my family needs my help.
> May my feet tread wisely upon this land
> and may the land uphold my footfall."

Bow and step back. Leave the candles burning (make sure they are safe and cannot cause a fire).

Go from this space and take the rock outside. Let the rock guide you as to where it wishes to be. You will feel instinctively where it wishes to go. Place the rock down and ensure that it is hidden enough that someone will not randomly pick it up. Before you leave, stand before the rock and take in a deep breath, and as you breathe in, see in your imagination the sword held in your left hand, blade down, and the cup in your right hand. Breathe out with intention. Breathe out with the sense that the wind is breathing through you. Breathe out with the magical intention to mediate Divine Breath to the wind. Breathe out as if it is your first breath of life.

---

[2] Or "Father" – use the gender of the land or the name of the power that flows through the land.
[3] Or "Father."
[4] Or "sister."

Now go back to your working space. Put out the flames in the four directions, but see in your mind's eye that the gates stay open and that the inner flame of the candle still burns. Leave the central flame burning if it is safe to do so (if not, put it out but see the inner flame still burning). Get a cushion and walk around the directions until you feel the part of the room where you need to be. Put the cushion down and lie down. Still your mind with your eyes closed for a few minutes, and then allow yourself to drift into sleep or semi-sleep. Stay there for however long or short a time you feel you need to be there. Sleep there all night if you feel that is right. By doing this you are allowing yourself to bathe in the energy of the work you have just done, and it will allow your deeper inner spirit to continue working with the rock out on the land. You may find that you fall asleep and dream wildly. If you do, write down what you can remember of those dreams as soon as you awaken. Do not leave it until later, as you will forget.

When you are ready, get up and blow out the central candle. See in your mind's eye the inner candles in the four directions going out and the gates closing. Bow and leave the room.

Note down in your journal where you replaced the stone and what direction it went into. Ponder upon the choice of direction that the stone took, and see if you get any inspiration as to what the stone is doing: where it wanted to go, what direction it is in, and what it is near will give you clues. Start to keep a close eye on the area and the happenings in the area. The change, if it comes, tends to be slow but defined. What you have done is create a small catalyst, a gentle nudge of power that triggers a process of change. It is like dropping a stone in still water and watching the ripples move outwards.

When I did this work on the land where I live, the change indeed came slowly but in a very specific way. People who were bad for the area moved out, people who were good for the land moved in. Rare local plants started to make a comeback out of seemingly nowhere. Within three years of doing that work (and I used to go and talk to the rock regularly, pour water over it, honey over it, etc.) very rare creatures started to make a comeback. We now have a glut of badgers, we have beavers here for the first time in centuries, ravens, eagles, reptiles, rare butterflies – the local land is really changing and renewing itself.

This small action is like popping a boil that has come to a head: it does not take a major powerful action. It is often better to do a small but well-timed and specific action that is small enough to not trigger resistance, but magical enough to awaken the rebalancing process. It also has deeper implications for the magician: you are learning to start the process of cooperation and giving back with the land around you. Magic does not flourish in a climate of control and hostility. But it does flourish in a space of mutual cooperation, respect and work.

Later in your training, you will learn techniques that work deeper with the land and bring the contact with the land beings into sharp and immediate focus. This action you have just done opens a conversation with the land and all the beings that live around you, and brings you into a more aware space of how everything around you has life, has consciousness and is a family that you are a part of. Guard your land, respect it, tend it and communicate with it.

Lesson 6
The Metatron Cube and the Quarry Mark

| *Note:* you will need paper and pens, and your tarot deck for this lesson.

The Metatron Cube is a deeply magical pattern that is profoundly misunderstood and has been turned into yet another New Age pile of bunkum. If you research the Metatron Cube online, you will find a vast array of sites claiming everything from "it is the root of all Platonic solids" (no it is not, it can contain three of them only), to "it is the Merkaba vehicle that can take you to ascension" (again, not it is not, though it is connected). Sadly this is a result of a combination of ignorance, a wish to make money from the gullible, and the idea that something deep and mystical can be understood and used at the drop of a hat to circumvent the process of spiritual maturation.

Humans love patterns. Humans love to find symmetry in things and then assign meanings into neat little boxes that make the world an understandable place. The world does not work like that and in magic, just as in mysticism, there are no easy boxes and no neat digestible packages of 'truth.' The Metatron Cube is not ancient, rather it is a fairly modern pattern that is constructed cleverly from far more ancient patterns. It is magically coherent, and contains a great many 'subdivisions of power paths' with it, that can be worked with a wide variety of magical workings. It certainly has many magical uses, and filters real power through it, despite the mountain of bullshit that is written about it.

So why have the Metatron Cube in this course? Moving all the bullshit to one side, the pattern is one that points to a deeply profound and powerful magical aspect of creation and destruction. The secrets and keys are not to be truly found in its pattern; rather it is a sigil in the true sense: it is a map to a stage in the act of Divine creation. That stage in the act of creation is something you will observe as an adept and come to understand through your deeper angelic work later in the adept section of the course.

At this stage of your training, you will not work ritually or magically with it, so this will be an easy lesson. And yet it is an important lesson. Just as I pointed out in a past lesson that writing by hand in your journal is the first stage in a long process of learning how to work with power in sigils, so too working with the Metatron Cube in a very simple way prepares the magician at a deep, subtle level for what is to come.

By learning how to draw and observe the Cube, the apprentice slowly begins to embed the pattern into their consciousness where it will stay like a seed, ready to flower later on in your magical understanding. So at this phase of your training, do not try to discover 'truths' in this pattern: simply learn it, draw it, play with it, and get to know it. It becomes something akin to a dream that you cannot fully recall, but tiny flashes still surface in your mind – enough for you to know something interesting or important was happening as you slept.

Working with your hands to draw, write, and create patterns is akin to learning times tables as a child. When I was a kid in primary school, the schools still taught mathematical times tables and we had to chant them each morning before class. Slowly over three years we learned the full tables and we all had a sense of great achievement when, at ten years old, we moved into the 'top class,' into a classroom that did not have the tables on the wall, as we were expected to now know them all by heart.

It was only at that point, when we began to learn more involved mathematics, that it slowly dawned on us how helpful it was to have those tables in our heads. This was the era before calculators; everything had to be done in your head and because of our rote learning we had our own inbuilt calculator that we carried around in our brains. It was also at that time that I slowly began to realise that numbers worked in patterns and worked logically.

So it is with learning magical patterns as an apprentice. First the patterns are drilled into you. Some are easier to understand than others, but slowly, through rote learning, you instil those patterns deep in your consciousness. Later, as you move on to advanced magic, those patterns reemerge as tools, calculators, keys, references, and maps that you have instant and deep access to. First your hand learns them. Then your body learns them. Then your memory holds them and waits with them until you cross paths with an angelic being, an inner contact, an inner realm, or a flow of power that is directly related to a pattern (or rather the pattern related to them).

Suddenly the pattern re-emerges into your consciousness and you finally make sense of it as you find yourself standing in the centre of the power that the pattern is a map for. By having the map in your head, you understand your terrain better and know what to do, where to go, and can spot the door that you hold the key to. And this is how the Metatron Cube works. It is a sigil and map of a particular flow of power in a particular inner realm, and when you come to work as an adept in that place, knowing the pattern of the Metatron Cube will help you to understand and interact with the forces you will stand before.

So why is there so much bullshit around the Cube? Well, humans love bullshit and they love patterns, so put the two together and you have the New Age. A good example of this human dynamic can be observed in the old British movie, *The Life of Brian*. It is silly, dated humour but also very cutting and profound in its observations of human nature in relation to religion and beliefs. If you haven't seen it, if you can find it, get it and watch it. Its message directly relates to our stupidity when it comes to religion and also to magic (which many approach like a religion). If you have seen it, the clamour around the Metatron cube is akin to the 'holy shoe.'

So how are we going to work with the Cube today? First let's start by looking at it. Figure 5 shows an image of the Metatron Cube.

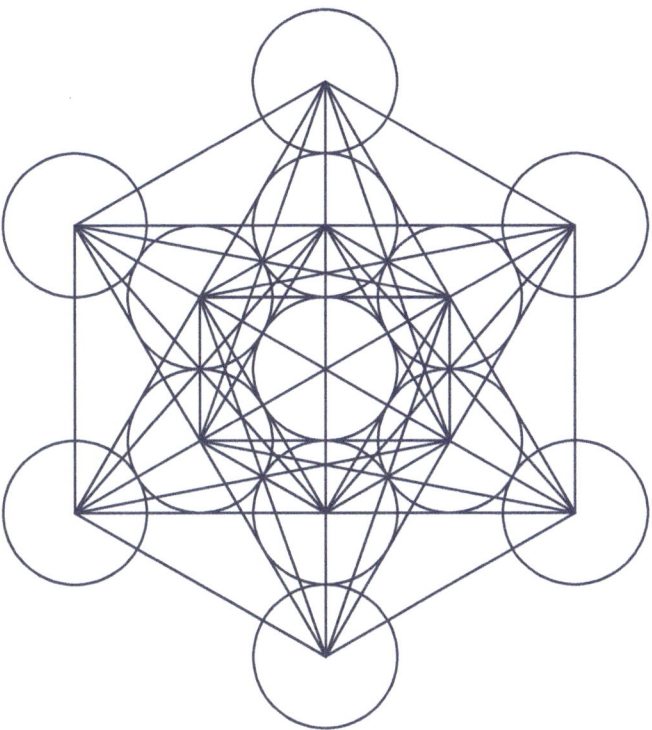

Figure 5: The Metatron Cube

The skeleton of the Cube is the quarry mark, the X with a line running through it. That is the skeleton for many magical patterns and tells you that this pattern, which has the quarry mark, is about creation in its celestial stages. The quarry mark is the foundation pattern for substance. As you will see, there are lots of shapes to be found inside the Cube and most of them are shapes and patterns used in magic. Many different shapes are harmonic with this pattern and some are not. That is a disappointment to the New Agers who like neat boxes where everything fits. What the "crystal licking dolphin kissers" do not understand is that nature is profoundly asymmetric in its symmetry (chew on that one).

To work with and understand the Cube, you do not unravel it like a puzzle; you simply draw it, repeatedly, and see the various patterns emerge out of your drawing. That's it at this stage – that is all you need to do. And you work with that drawing in a number of ways to observe passive resonance into a space. The cube, when drawn properly, because it is a charged sigil, will subtly affect the space that it is placed in. There is nothing deep and mystical about that, it is just how these patterns work. So let's get practical and actually do something.

1. *Task:* Drawing and working with the Metatron Cube

Draw the Cube. That is easier than it sounds, and there is a particular way to draw it that triggers the magical embedding and learning.

You can use a set of compass or a large coin to draw out the thirteen circles. So get a good-sized sheet of paper and map out the thirteen circles. That is the skeleton shape of the Metatron Cube and it is a foundation quarry mark (which as an aside was used in ancient Egypt as a quarry mark). Once you have the skeleton marked out, then you need to mark a dot in the exact centre of each circle.

Now comes the fun bit. You cannot use a ruler or any straight edge to do the next part; it must be free hand. This again is a baby step towards the magical creation of a sigil with the use of your hand – no tool must be used. This has a deeper magical dynamic that will become apparent to you later in your training, and you will find that the closer you come to magical balance and stability, the easier it will be for you to draw 'straight': you learn to draw from the depths of your magical being. To get to that stage, you have to go through the process of learning how to create with just paper and pen. It is the lines and their connections in this pattern that trigger that process, not the circles. Again, this is something that will become much clearer to you later on. And that is something that has to evolve within you, alone, and by your own hand; it cannot be outlined to you by someone else.

So begin by connecting up the dots with straight freehand lines. Many different patterns will emerge as you draw and you will constantly find new patterns that are created by joining up the dots. Once you have finished, sit back and look at it. Look at it in relation to the ritual patterns you have already worked with and see how those patterns interrelate. You will also find patterns within the patterns. Do not try to force patterns that do not fit. As you look at the pattern, one thing you may notice is that in relation to your magical four-directional pattern the Cube has no east/west axis. This is because the Cube is not about humanity specifically, and does not trigger the creation/destruction pattern that is inherent in the Divine act of utterance. Rather this is a pattern that the utterance passes through on its journey into creation. Again, something you will learn far more about in the adept section when you are ready and strong enough to withstand the work.

Repeat this exercise of drawing out the Cube two or three times a week for a month, more if you wish but certainly no less. Once you can draw it accurately, draw it out on a piece of card and place it above your bed. Sleep with the pattern over your bed (directly over your head) for a week and note down any shift in sleep or dream patterns.

After a week, take it down. Whether or not it affects you very much depends on varying factors including your own sensitivity and what else is happening energetically in the house. After your sleep exercise, now it is time to experiment.

We will do this in a few different ways so that if you are not sensitive, it will give you a way to explore the energy of this pattern from a different angle. The sleep exercise and the experiments are something that you can do while you also move on to the next lesson; you can work this lesson and the next one concurrently if you wish to.

2. *Experiment:* Energies

Remember your tarot lesson in module one? Go to your notes in that module's journal. Remember the readings you did for your living space. Identify which area of your living space is the most difficult area energetically. It is likely that you have already taken some remedial action to settle that area, so we need to take that into account. Before you do anything else, do a four-directional reading for that space and write it down in your journal.

Now pin up the picture you have drawn of the Cube on card onto the wall in that area. Pin it up high on the wall in the direction which is the most out of balance. If you feel that it is unfashionable or will spoil the look of the house while you do this, get over it. You do not live in a fashion show. If anyone comments, tell them it is a memory experiment. Your home is not only your safe place, it is your 'magical kitchen' where you cook and experiment.

After twenty-four hours repeat the four-directional reading for that space and see if there is any difference in what the reading tells you about that space. Leave the image on the wall for a full week and at the end of the week do a four-directional reading again for that space to see if having it there for a week made any difference. Note it down and then take the image down.

Twenty-four hours after it has been down, do yet another four-directional reading to see how the space has changed now that the pattern is off the wall. Also note if there was any difference in the energy of that space, or in the house in general, or any odd behaviour of animals in that space if you have pets. Also note down any difficult, out of the ordinary things that might have happened to you that week.

Now move the drawing to the area of the house that shows in the readings you did in module one to be the best, strongest, and most vital area of the house. Again pin it up high and do a four-directional reading for that space before you pin it up, twenty-four hours after you pin it up, and then again at the end of the week before you take it down.

This is a subtle experiment in that you get to see if and how simply putting a magical sigil or map on the wall can change a space. Some can and will, others do not. How a space reacts to a pattern or map depends very much on the land you are on, the house itself, what powers flow through the house, what time of the year it is, etc.: all the power variables define how a space reacts to the inclusion of a magical map or sigil.

It can also be an interesting experiment to put it up in your magical working space for a length of time, positioning it in the south (which is its natural home) and seeing if it affects how you work magically. Later on, when you are in the midst of adept training, it can be very interesting to repeat this experiment, as your inner senses will be far better tuned by that point and you will also be more conscious of how magical energy affects things: you notice the very subtle shifts and actions that would have evaded your attention in the early part of your training.

3. *Task:* Research

Do some internet research on the image. Because there is so much bullshit about the Metatron Cube, and virtually nothing of any real magical sense or clarity, don't even try to research the Cube itself (it will do your head in or you will get sucked into the bullshit zone, which can be very alluring). Instead, search for the foundation quarry mark, and for the other shapes that emerge out of the Cube. Look for them in images of ancient texts, wall carvings, temple symbols, sacred architecture, etc. A particular one is the Flower of Life which is an ancient pattern, and look closely at the small shapes that interlock to make the Flower.

Through researching the patterns and maps that you have already worked with and have begun to understand, you will be able to spot the state of magic in a given time and place according to how those patterns were used, and why they were used. Like all things, this will not tell you the whole story, as it is never as general as that. But it will tell you what stage that civilisation is at.

Each civilisation goes through stages of development; rising to a peak and then descending into degeneracy which then sloughs around in a Dark Age of total ignorance before starting the long climb back to development again. You can track those stages through the use of magical symbolism, magical art, architecture, religion, and cultural expression.

At present we in the West are on a slow, painful descent back into a Dark Age. We see that through the degeneracy and commercialism in our magic, culture, and religions. As always in such a dynamic, there is often an opposing force operating within that pattern, and in each degenerate slide can be found a spark of brilliance or a seed of discovery that will facilitate the next climb. So when in your research you come up against the use of magical patterns in a decaying culture, look more closely at some of the art, philosophy, magic and architecture of that time, and behind the glamorous facade, you will often find new seeds lurking.

In some magical symbols you will see the deeper magical intention, particularly if they are used in a new religion. Look at the early Christian symbol of the Chi Rho, which is a form of the quarry mark that is a sigil for 'foundation.' As you research the Chi Rho (two Greek letters) you will find that it is indeed an ancient symbol that was co-opted by very early Christians and used as a foundation sigil for the new religion.

If you read Plato's Timaeus (do try and make the effort to read it, and if you do, take notes of what 'ah-ha's come into your mind), you will find that Plato alludes to a form of the quarry symbol (the Chi or X) as the foundation of creation, which is exactly what it is. It is the root skeleton from which a pattern is built which in turn acts as a filter that sits in between the Divine first utterance and creation. Timaeus can be tough to read if you are not used to reading the Greek philosophers but it is worth the effort. Not only will you see him struggling to make sense of and find reasons (often unsuccessfully) for things in his pre science world, but you will also come across fragments of very old magical knowledge and working tips that he picked up when he was studying and debating with Egyptian priests, along with his own forays into inner vision which become obvious when reading his work.

It is pointless for me to go into any further depth about this symbolism at this stage in your training, as it would only devolve into an intellectual puzzle-solving pursuit, which is exactly where I do not want you to go with this. I want you to look, see, recognise, and discover – nothing more.

Later, as an adept, you will stand deep in the inner worlds and will see these patterns/maps in operation for yourself, and have direct experience with the angelic consciousness that flows through them. That way you will truly learn what they are about.

But as you read Plato and various other ancient writers, you will realise, eventually, that they too stood deep in the inner worlds and saw for themselves. And that no amount of explanation can sufficiently portray the depths of power and contact that these signs and symbols point to. It is enough, as an apprentice, that you are simply aware of them, that you are aware that most writings over the last two thousand years about these symbols are just intellectual conjecture and religious dogma in the making, and that you will truly not understand some of the deep symbols until you are directly experiencing them magically.

Then you will also understand that they are merely road signs to something that cannot possibly be reproduced, boxed, and understood intellectually or philosophically. Their purpose is to point the way for those who already understand them, to affect the substance they are upon, to focus magical patterns, and to mark the way for other adepts on a journey. As an aside, the quarry mark was also used in classical texts to mark an important passage – like putting a star at the side of text to tell you "this is new and important!"

Spend a good deal of time looking at cultural, religious and magical markings from the ancient world and from far-flung ancient cultures. Look in iconography, paintings, books, buildings, jewellery: do not limit what you look at. When you find something interesting that catches your eye, even if you do not know what it is, save it, print it out, or draw it out. Do not bother with modern interpretations: learn to look and think for yourself.

4. *EXPERIMENT:* MODELLING THE CUBE

If you are truly ambitious and like making models, get thirteen reasonably-sized polystyrene balls and some sticks with sharp points at both ends, and make a 3D model of the Metatron Cube. Again, this is about playing, creating, and then letting the pattern sink into your subconscious. If you succeed, string it up somewhere where you can look at it as you walk past. Most people who try (including myself) will fail miserably, but that is ok... it is the trying that matters.

Don't use a computer program to create the Cube: this is not an artistic or intellectual act; it is about using your actual hands to create something. There is a major difference magically, and you need to know how that magical dynamic slowly develops as you use your hands more and more.

Well that was an easy lesson! This is your little lull and break after a few heavier lessons – enjoy it while it lasts. Essentially this lesson was about two simple things: separating out the bullshit connected to the Metatron Cube, and also learning how to spot magical patterns, which then allows you to ascertain the state of magic in a particular culture and time.

Lesson 7

Combinations

At this stage in your training, you have looked at using patterns and working with directions from a variety of different angles. This is to ensure that you get a good solid grounding in working with the foundational patterns of magic: the work with the elements and directions is the cornerstone of magic. You will continue to look at the same patterns from different perspectives, discovering deeper and deeper layers to them, so that when you really start to engage them magically, they will 'switch on' for you.

Attempting to do magic without a good understanding of these dynamics will seriously limit your capacity to do magic, particularly when you come to do visionary magic, which is a key ingredient in successful magic. The directional ritual patterns anchor and give form to the power and inner consciousness that you work with in magical vision.

In the next module you will learn about the powers of creation in terms of magic. To be able to understand those powers, first you need to know, from a magical perspective, the roads those powers take in our existence as humans. These patterns are those roads. A normal human is pulled along these power patterns like a leaf in a fast-moving river; understanding and working with those power patterns as a magician allows you to swim safely and effectively in that river.

The pattern combinations that we are going to look at, in particular two specific combinations, will show you the skeleton form of the power patterns behind many myths and legends. That in turn will enable you to spot myths that are more than just tribal stories: you will be able to identify those myths that tell of ancient interactions with the directional forces that flow in and out of the world. You will also be able to ritually engage those pattern combinations in your visionary and ritual work.

At this point in your apprentice training, it is important that you focus on standing and walking before you learn to run and jump (and not doing yourself or others any harm). So we will look at combinations that do not involve the future, as that is the aspect of these patterns where most apprentice magicians make the most blinding and dangerous mistakes. Those sorts of mistakes are not easily corrected and can have long-term consequences, so for now you will learn how to operate within combinations that are grounded, well-used in magic, and ritually/magically powerful: it is very hard to move a mountain accidentally.

You will instantly recognise these patterns as they are so deeply established in cultural expressions, myths, and stories. So be careful, as you read the text before you get to the practical work, that you do not allow preconceived ideas to rise into your mind regarding these powers. Like all powerful magic, when it is described in stories and myths, it is often surrounded by dead ends and traps to protect the truth hidden deep within the myth. Those dead ends and traps tend to be the outer expressions of the story.

This is also the stage of training where you will begin to learn about the expressions of the magical tools. You will be learning how to work with the physical magical tools pretty soon in the course, so as an aside, now is the time to start looking for them. Start planning now to find a sword that you can afford. It must be plain, with nothing written on the blade, no faces, no overt ornamentation, and have a cross hilt, etc. You need a plain cruciform-shaped sword that is properly balanced. (Where the handle and the blade meet, hold it there on two fingers. If it balances, you have a good sword.) Start looking, as you will need it a month or two from now. Also look for a plain glass or metal chalice/cup that you can work with. Find one with no ornamentation or imagery on it.

Back to the combinations. We will start by looking at the combination of air/east and water/west. That ritual combination is known as the sword and cup or the Cruciform and the Cup.

The magical pattern of the Cruciform and the Cup is one of the longest-surviving magical patterns known in the Western World. We see the earliest form of this pattern emerging in the burials of the Beaker People (from 2900 BC) in Europe and the Naqada I people in Qena, Upper Egypt (from 3800 BC).

Now at this stage we have to immediately stop and think. Both of these ancient cultures featured vessels and blades in their ritual burial patterns. But we do not know why. And it is really important to realise that we do not know why, and not try to impose our modern ritual understanding upon an ancient culture.

It is most likely that these objects were in tombs/burials because they were key elements of survival: a vessel to hold food/water, a blade to hunt and cut with, or an image of humanity in the form of a cruciform figurine.[1] It is probably that simple: two main tools for survival. But as a modern magician, that in itself holds a great deal of interest for me as to the slow, steady of evolution from objects of survival (and therefore of great importance) to objects that mediate ritual power. We observe those ritual tools evolving to become vessels for power, a power that is an octave of survival and human existence.

Rather than turn this into a history and archaeology lesson, which is not my intention, we will be focusing on the magical aspect of these two implements. We will also not look at the implements themselves, implements that have evolved over time to become the Sword/Blade and the Cup, as that will come in other lessons when you work directly with the physical tools.

First we will work with the actual forces that come through these ritual implements, so that you understand the powers that flow through them. That in turn will give you far more understanding when you come to look at religious iconography and

---

[1] Lempa female figures from Cyprus – look it up.

ritual imagery/sigils: you will know what power they are alluding to and what process they are depicting. And before we go any further, a warning to you about ritual patterns: do not fall into the trap of wishing to fit patterns that you work with onto other patterns. In different cultures you will find similarities in religious, mythological and ritual/magical structures, patterns, and stories. This is often because they spring from the same inner source, but also sometimes they are borrowed.

There are only so many patterns that exist, and we have a common way of approaching things, discovering things, and organising things, so different cultures often come to the same conclusions in their quest to make patterns. Trying to fit different patterns or different expressions into some overarching 'truth' not only leads to fantasy structures, but can seriously undermine the development of a magician. Let things be themselves; nod at similarities, but leave it at that: don't theorise, condense, or delve into ancient conspiracy theories: it is a waste of time and does not allow you to accept that things just need to be what they are. We need to get out of the habit of neatly boxing everything.

1. THE CRUCIFORM AND THE CUP

The Cruciform and the Cup refer to two magical base dynamics: the outputting of Divine Breath into life, and the Divine Vessel that receives that life and gives life. Magically at their root they are male and female respectively. However that is not a fixed, dogmatic structure: the gender expressions are often reversed according to what is being outputted and what is being received. When you come to study the individual magical tools, we will look at that flip of polarity in detail. For now, just file that bit of understanding away in your memory. So let us look at the Cruciform first, and then we will look at the Cup. Then you will put the two together in magical action.

The Cruciform – the Breath of Life

You already know about the use of the sword in the east and the breath that flows out of the east, as you have worked with that structure in your ritual work. But you have not yet worked with the sword itself. First you need to learn how to work with the power behind the sword in a practical but simple way. Later on, in the apprentice section, you will learn the deeper magical dynamic behind this power so that you will then come to fully understand why the breath is depicted magically by a sword.

When you work with the breath magically, it can take the form of simply breathing into something with magical intent, the use of the voice in utterance, a song, a chant, or the use of a word to form magical patterns. It can also be used to call the wind and storms. Look up the use of the *ankh* in Egyptian sacred art: it is a perfect example of the use of the cruciform shape in depicting the mediation of the Breath of Life.

The sword is not an extension of that power; it is a filter that governs how you *use* that power, to ensure that you do not overstep a sacred boundary in the use of a power that is a part of the cycle of creation and destruction.

The magical use of breath, in its most advanced form, can wreak devastation on a person, place, or thing, or it can breathe life into something lifeless. The inner and outer sword acts as the limiter which helps prevent powerful misuse of this magical dynamic.

A historic, mythical version of that action can be seen in the tale of the Sword of Damocles. The king holds Divine power and responsibility, and the sword hangs over his head, held only by a hair. One misstep or abuse of power brings the sword crashing down.

For a magician, this dynamic shifts and changes as they become more adept at magic. In the beginning of training, the sword brings through the power of balance and justice, helping the magician to find their place as a fulcrum in the centre of the elements, and helping the magician to find balance within themselves. It guards the magician from their own stupidity, and guides the magician forward in learning. Later the sword acts as an engine governor to the adept, making itself known in vision and through bodily effects when the adept has overstepped a mark in magic.

Back to the breath.

The first step towards the adept use of this power is learning how to use your breath in a magical way, to transfer something from the 'inner' pattern to outer manifestation: breath both mediates and elicits change. The magical breath when used by a human does not 'create,' even if it appears to; rather it triggers a latent pattern into action. It draws from what is already forming in the inner worlds and gives it a focused pathway to externalise in our world, which you then mediate and release. For example, you may have already experienced this in a very minor way when you were working with finding the elements in the directions: the action of breathing out triggering the wind. If that happened to you during that exercise, it was not that you created the wind; rather you called for its attention.

The magical use of the breath can take many forms. The most powerful and hardest to achieve is the breathing of the Breath of Life into a vessel, an action which enlivens something inert. This was part of the magical process used in Ancient Egypt to turn a statue into a vessel or window for a deity. Another form is the use of the breath in chants or making sounds that trigger angelic consciousness into action in a focused way. Yet another is the recitation of words or sacred languages, done with ritual intent, to effect change in the substance or consciousness of something, or to begin a cyclical unfolding of a powerful event.

One form of working with the breath magically is to bridge something from the inner world to the outer world, something that is a catalyst for change. Often when doing this, the magician has no real idea of what they are bridging, only that it is the right power or pattern for the job at hand. The breath becomes a road that an impulse can travel down as it passes over the threshold into physical manifestation. It is the use of the mind and the imagination, the filters that give shape to power and energy, that form the power within the breath into a working action. When that is done in combination with the sword as a 'governor' to the human spirit, then it can become powerful indeed.

The Cup

The Cup, as you well know by now, is the vessel that receives (and also nourishes). A cup is limited in what volume it can hold, and that limitation depends on what substance it is made from and how big it is. The Cup, like the Sword, is not the vessel itself, but is the governor of the magical dynamic of receiving/containing. Through working with the Cup in ritual, we learn the energy dynamics of how a vessel 'contains,' and the use of the Cup limits the amount of 'receiving' power that the actual true vessel can contain when working magically.

So what is the true vessel? A vessel is anything that can hold and contain. In magic this can be a stone, it can be water, a body, a womb, a tree… anything that is capable of holding energy in a contained way. So a tree/rock/body that has a defined physical shape will hold power in a certain, specific way. Water however does not have the same physically-defined limitations – and here is where it gets interesting. Water carries and contains, but in a very different and deeper way: it holds information, vibration, and very small molecules within its substance as it flows, but it does not have defined boundaries of substance in the way that a rock or tree does.

So it is still a vessel, but a vessel that works in a very different way to most vessels; and the use of the ritual vessel, the cup, gives limitations and boundaries to the water where it has none. That is important for a magician to understand, so that they choose the right vessel for the job. Air does not contain in the same way that water does, but it can move things about and is a good 'bridge.' Fire, too, does not contain, but it transforms.

Air and fire as elements work in similar ways to each other, and so too water and earth work in harmonic ways.

Air and fire transport and transform: they are things that bring the future into being. Earth and water contain and condense: they are things that solidify what has been created and bridged, and then begin the process of sending it into the past. Two elements create and give future, two elements condense and then break down. Only the magician as fulcrum holds the balance of 'now.' So when you as the magician use two of the opposing elements, like air and water, you have a complete cycle. Those two different dynamics are condensed, contained, and filtered through the two root magical tools.

Let's get back to the vessel. An example of this dynamic can be observed in the mythology of Miriam, the sister of Moses, who carried a vessel out in to the desert in the mythical story of the Exodus.

That vessel, depending on which source you look at, is a cup or a rock (It is a rock in the Midrash) both of which provide water in the desert. Incidentally, that magical use of the vessel was in a 'giving' action, not a receiving action. And although the vessel is primarily a container in a magical sense, it outputs as well as receives: it has the power to give as well as to take or hold. In the Midrash, we learn that Miriam had a stone that followed her in the desert, and when she sang to it, it gave forth water. When she died, it dried up.

So here we have a simple but well-known magical dynamic emerging. Air triggering a vessel: the combination of air, water, and earth. The air begins the impulse which triggers the vessel to yield its contents. The stone is the vessel which holds the water: do you see the combination of earth/north and water/west working together as one magical tool? And it is all hidden away in a story.

Note also that when Miriam dies and the stone dries up, Moses asks God for help. God tells Moses to utter to the stone (using the same method as Miriam), but instead, feeling he knew better, he also strikes it with his staff (wand, fire, future... a bad magical decision). The east/west magical axis works well, as does east/north, but using the wand to trigger the stone for water, as opposed to using magical air, took away the future of Moses. File that one in the back of your mind and think about it. Write your thoughts on this in your journal, as you will come back to it one day when you have more knowledge on the subject that is rooted in direct magical experience. And this brings me to the other root magical combination that we will work with and look at, and that is the combination of the Sword and the Stone.

2. The Sword and the Stone

I don't need to go into the sword again, as we have just looked at that. The stone, however, is a very important dynamic that is often missed in magic. In modern Western ritual magic, the North is often depicted as a shield. The shield is used as an altar-top and the ritual tools are placed upon it. This really misses the point of this foundational tool and reduces the ability of the magician to fully engage with this dynamic, powerful aspect of magic.

The stone is a scabbard for the sword: it is a vessel that receives the Breath of Life (sword), and unlike the Cup of the West which is also a vessel, rather than receive, condense, and give as the Cup does, the stone holds and assimilates. And that holding is a completion. Just as the Breath of Life reaches its completion in the stone, so too does the Breath of Life find its home in the completion of an ancestral line. We will look deeper into that later in the course. That is the deepest manifestation of these dynamics: another thing to file away in the back of your head for later on in the course. From a more direct magical perspective, the stone is the scabbard/natural home/protector of the sword; it is also the rock of the ancestors, which in turn is your shield. That is something you have already touched on in your ritual work, so you should already understand it.

When the sword and the stone are combined in ritual magic, you have the sword which governs the magical use of breath, and the stone which guards and guides the magician who wields the sword: the stone is the elemental expression of the Guardian Angel, of the ancestral line whose shoulders you stand upon, and of the female Divinity in substance. It is also the completion of the cycle of life and death.

When used in magic, the stone/earth completes the pattern so that it can be expressed in the outer world. Just as death is assigned at birth, so too a magical pattern, if it is to be stable and effective for its prescribed length of working time, has to not only have its path marked out in the future, but its completion marked out that will take it into the past. The end of a cycle must be embedded in its birth, whether that cycle is life, magic, whatever. So when we look at magical myths that work around the sword and the stone, we know that we are looking at a story of power completion, and an energetic tension between past guardianship and the releasing or suppressing of justice/balance for the future.

In the Arthurian myth, when you wipe away all the additions and decorations from the myth, you are left with this: a sword sits in a stone. The sword that brings balance is embedded in a pattern of completion. It tells of a cycle finished, and the sword is held by ancestral consciousness until the new cycle is ready to begin. The cycle can only begin again when the sword is taken out of its scabbard, out of its stone. Once it is removed from the stone, it triggers a new cycle of the Breath of Life in its journey to bring balance and justice. The sword cannot be used to shed blood, as it is not a weapon; rather it is a governor of the hand of the king (fire, future).

So far in the myth, we have the sword out of the stone and in the hands of a king (fire, future – the south is kingship). It is not balanced by a receiving vessel (the Grail) and once it has been used in battle, which happens in the myth, it ceases to be a sword that is the path for the Breath of Life into substance: it is broken. Another sword is sought, one that can be used in battle (the story of Caliburn and Excalibur).

The battle sword cannot be used magically to balance the elements or operate within a cycle of completion. The quest for the Grail in order to bring balance is fruitless, as first the sword of justice must be held – only a sword of justice can balance the Grail and also fit back into the scabbard/stone. So in the story, the nation is doomed as the sword of justice is broken and the grail is missing.

We see remnants of the use of this pattern in the modern British monarchy, a kingship/queenship that works on a land that is deeply embedded with this magical pattern. At their coronation, the sovereign holds in one hand the orb, which is the sword in the stone, the sum total of ancestral knowledge (completion) within the land; and in the other the sceptre, which is the wand that points and opens up the future. The two are kept separate in separate hands, and the power that they will manifest in the reign of the sovereign depends on which hand they hold which tool in.

Module II – Patterns and Maps in Magic

The Arthurian myth tells us about the deep dynamics of the magical tools as they manifest through humanity, and how they are misused and misunderstood. It tells of greatness given to humanity only for humanity to misuse and destroy it. This is the same story as that of Moses and the Ten Commandments, which is also a sword and stone story.

Moses mediates the utterance (air/sword) from God which is then carved upon/within the stone (the Commandments). Moses brings this great gift to humanity, but it all goes badly wrong, so Moses has to get a much lesser version, a version that does not have the deep, powerful, and beautiful Divine magic within it.

It is a lesser version which exteriorises that deep power of Justice and Balance into a list of simplistic dos and don'ts. The list of rules tells us how to prepare for the deeper power of the Breath of Life to flow into us, so that when we are evolved enough, it can flow freely into the vessel of humanity. Seeing as we have, as a species, still not managed to live by those simple boundaries, chaos continues.

These tales warn us of the breadth of power within these tool/power combinations, and tell us what can go wrong and how to avoid it. As all magic works in octaves, these powerful tales that shaped nations hold exactly the same powers and dynamics as magic done by a single magician; they are just different octaves of the same powers. This is why it is critical to look at these deeper dynamics at an early stage of magical training, so that you realise you are engaging in something that can have far-reaching effects for good or bad depending on what you do with it.

3. *Task:* Practical Work

So let's get down to practicalities. You have already worked with the combination of sword and stone in a very simple form. You don't remember? Lesson five, where you worked with a stone, going around the directions and working by putting things into the stone. That is the kindergarten version of the sword in the stone. It builds from there.

Now we will work with the Cruciform and the Cup. Working ritually with this method for someone else or for the environment can have far-reaching, unseen consequences, and although you are an early apprentice and therefore not yet plugged into power, an apprentice who is a natural magician (a natural mediator of power) can inadvertently, if they misstep, trigger a major reaction across the land or to the genetic line of a person. So you will learn this technique first by working upon yourself.

For many of you, this will simply be learning a technique that is not yet connected to a power source, so you are learning the steps before you eventually 'do the dance.' However if you are a natural magician, it will trigger a response in your body. Because you are limiting the action to yourself, within your own fate boundary, it is very unlikely you will trigger any major response, but you will get some form of response – so see that as an added bonus of the lesson.

If you learn the technique on yourself, you are far more likely to follow the action of the lesson carefully, so as not to harm yourself. This is akin to learning the sharpness of a blade by gently touching the sharp edge for yourself, rather than swinging the blade at someone or something and killing it... and then thinking "oops, that is sharp."

Learn and familiarise yourself with the ritual and make sure you know the visionary and recitation steps very well, so that you do not need to refer to notes as you do the ritual. Practise the actions a few times until you feel ready to do it properly.

For this ritual you will need a glass of water. Use a glass you are happy to bury or destroy at the end of the work. Work with the four directional altar patterns, and the altar in the middle. Do the hexagram ritual first (to tune in Divinity into the space to govern your actions), then do the pentagram ritual to root yourself into who you are and what you are. That prepares the space and prepares yourself.

Once you have finished, place the glass of water on the west altar and remove the central altar from the room. Circle the directions and go to the east altar. Look at the open gates and 'see' the inner contact standing upon the threshold. Bow to them and recite:

> "I wish to engage the Divine power of the Breath of Life,
>   to bring it into myself to trigger regenerative change."

Place your hands upon the altar to steady yourself and close your eyes. You are going to work in vision. With your mind's eye, using your imagination, see the inner contact bow to you, turn, and vanish through the gates. You must stand in silence until they return.

You see movement through the gates, and it seems as though the usual mists that obscure what is beyond the gates clear. You can now see into a library with many shelves stacked with scrolls and books that stretch from floor to ceiling. You see the inner contact looking for something on the shelves. The contact picks up a scroll or book and walks back towards you.

The inner contact walks back out through the gates carrying the book or scroll. The contact walks straight up to you and pushes the book into your chest. Your body absorbs the book and you feel the weight of it within you. This is the passage of knowledge from the inner worlds that is placed into your very substance.

Next the contact tells you to open your mouth. You open your mouth wide, and the contact blows into your mouth. You take a deep breath in, breathing in the breath that has been mediated from the inner worlds to your inner body. Take a physical breath in at this point in the vision.

The contact then points to the west altar behind you, indicating that you now need to go and work in the west. The contact bows to you and you bow back both in vision and physically. The contact retreats back to the threshold of the gates and will stay there while you complete your work.

Open your eyes and take a step back. Turn, and go stand before the centre where the altar would be, facing south with the north altar behind you. Stand in silence, and in your mind's eye remember how you stood in the centre of the directions while doing the pentagram: recover that feeling of being in the centre of all things. Remember the book within you, and remember the breath that was breathed into you. Recite:

> "I am in the centre of all things.
> I stand between the past and the future,
> with the Sword to my left and the Cup to my right.
> I have a book of knowledge within me that is needful for me to understand,
> and I have the mediated Breath of Life flowing through my body:
> I am the vessel for the Breath of Life, I am the sum total of my ancestors.
> I am the earth, enlivened with the breath which unfolds in the future,
> and which flows from my ancestors in the past.
> I wish that the words and breath within me release whatever is necessary
> for my evolution and the evolution of my ancestral line
> as it flows into the future."

Walk straight to the south altar, bow to acknowledge the future, and then walk a full circle around the directions, finishing before the west altar. Stand before the altar, bow, and place your hands upon the altar. Close your eyes.

See beyond the gates, through the mists, and see a priestess walking towards you. You notice that she is walking in a river as she moves towards you. She passes straight through the altar and comes to stand before you on your left hand side.

Open your eyes briefly, and with your left hand pick up the cup/glass of water. Hold the glass of water and close your eyes again. The priestess places her hand on your left shoulder, as she is going to work with you and support you in the mediation you are about to do.

With your inner vision, your mind's eye, see yourself standing before the altar with the priestess standing to the left of you, her hand upon your shoulder and the glass in your hand. As you look at yourself, see a strange yellow light glowing inside of you. It seems to be filling every part of you. This is the breath and the book within you, still in the element of air.

Focus on the inside of your body, on the strange light in your body. Have the intention in your mind that you are going to gather up that air energy, hold it in your lungs, and then expel it into the glass of water. See the strange light begin to turn, like a circle of stars. See the circle of stars get denser as the circle turns, drawing in the light from around your body into a concentrated circle in your chest. Once all of the strange light is circling in your chest, feel the build-up in your lungs.

Take your time. Watch the circling, like a galaxy of stars in your chest getting faster as it turns, getting more condensed and brighter. Look closely at it. See within the condensed light sigils, letters, words, and shapes, all swirling around in a tight, circulating light. Take time: watch and observe.

When you feel your body cannot hold it any more, then it is time to release it. Still working in vision, you notice that the priestess moves from your left side to standing directly behind you, and holding both of your shoulders.

When you get a strong visual image and sense the priestess upholding you from behind, bring the glass up to your lips. Take in a deep breath and slowly breathe in a long, slow, controlled breath over the surface of the water in the glass. In your inner vision/mind's eye, see the swirling light power in your chest flow from your chest, up your throat, out through your mouth, and into the glass. See the light in the glass turning and swirling with the sigils, words, and signs in the light. Put the glass down carefully on the altar (opening your eyes briefly if you have to), and then see the priestess walk through you, placing her hands over the glass.

As you watch, the light in the water changes colour from yellow to blue, the sigils and words change into natural shapes, and the water seems to burst with bright light. She takes her hands off the glass, walks through the altar, and returns to the threshold of the gates. She turns around and bows. Open your eyes and bow to her.

Now pick up the transformed water. Recite:

> "I partake of the river of past and future,
> I drink the words of the ancients, transformed by the Priestess of the West,
> I accept the Breath of Life transformed by the water,
> that it will bring whatever is necessary for my evolution:
> I accept the gift unconditionally and with respect."

Drink the water slowly.

When you have finished, bow to the priestess, who then vanishes back into the west. Go around the directions, starting in the east, putting out the flames and closing the gates. Put the glass inside a bag or wrap it in a cloth, take it outside and stamp on it to break it. Bury the bits. Now go and sleep. Sleep for a few minutes or for many hours, it does not matter. All that matters is that you sleep uninterruptedly and that you wake when you are ready. This helps the power placed within you to settle.

For some apprentices little will happen, as you are still in the early phases of training: you are doing this to learn the technique, not particularly to gain from the ritual. But for some apprentices this will act as a catalyst for major change, a change that can come suddenly or can unfold over months or even years. The change will be to do with your processing, working with, and understanding knowledge.

Knowledge has been placed within you, and then it was mediated into water, transformed, and reabsorbed. It was woven in with the Breath of Life, so the knowledge contained within you will slowly unwind and reveal itself as and when you need it. I did a version of this many years ago and what was placed within me was many books. This was before I started writing. Not long after, I wrote my very first book (a novel, terrible it was). That process of starting to write triggered the inner books within me, and they have served as a wellspring for my work for a long time since.

Another way this can manifest is that you start to make and understand magical connections, understandings, and patterns that you could not grasp before. Essentially, this ritual triggers a download of magical knowledge that can slowly unwind within you, supporting your learning as you study. Sometimes what is put within you has nothing to do with magic but is about something else, but the same principle applies. One thing that is common with all manifestations of this power: what comes out is not only for your own evolution; it is also for the evolution of your family in the future, be they your own children, or the children of others in your bloodline.

What you do need to know is that this ritual action is not just about learning magical knowledge; that is a side product of this work. What you have learned is how to draw upon the power of air, in whatever form that can take that you happen to be working with, and you learn how to contain it within you, transfer it into a vessel that governs it, and then retake it into yourself as the final vessel for it. That action moderates the air power so that your body can take the air power in without it being too powerful or disruptive to your health.

That dynamic that you were introduced to in the ritual process is one of filter and focus. You asked for the Breath of Life to bring regeneration to you. That was in your first recitation in the ritual. Then that recitation was filtered in two ways: first as the formation of a book from the Inner Library (something you will learn about in a future lesson) and then it was also filtered through the inner contact, which modifies it. Eventually you will learn to take in the breath from the whirlwind: the pure element of Divine Breath.

The request for regenerative air, filtered through the book and the contact, ensured that the form the breath would take as it externalises in your life will be through deep knowledge embedded within you. The knowledge passed on to you will unravel through your learning process and is a deeper form of the knowledge mediation that you have already experienced in a previous lesson that prepared you for this (remember?).

The form that the knowledge took in the ritual is drawn from the Inner Library, which holds all knowledge accessible to humanity. But your body would need some help to process this level of mediation, as it is a more powerful way of taking the power of air into yourself. So you worked with a contact in the west. You had to externalise the power and reform it with the help of the priestess from the west, so that it would not only be more accessible to your mind, but less likely to aggravate your body.

Taking in this level of air power in the form of knowledge can impact your body quite profoundly, as I learned in my younger days, so it is necessary to work with inner contacts to modify the power in order for your body not to react to it.

If this process worked for you, you will find it easier to absorb and process knowledge and to recall it. You may also find that you 'know' something without knowing how you know.

If the process did not work for you – and you will not know that for certain until a few months have passed – don't worry about it. The whole point of this lesson is not for the ritual to work, but for you to learn the ritual and let the deeper implications around it sink in to your consciousness at a deep level.

If it does work, that is an added bonus. You will be revisiting this process again in the future in different ways, and there will be plenty of opportunity for success with it. You get what you need when you need it, not when you want it! Keep a diary in your journal or notes on your computer, just outlining any observations you make around any shift in how you process knowledge. Also list any minor bodily reactions to the work, and any dreams that surface within days of doing this work.

4. *Task:* Research

Go online or visit a good library and look at images of different kings, queens, pharaohs, and deities.

Look for the combinations of cup/sword, or cup/sword/stone, or orb (stone and sword), wand, staff, sceptre, or iconography of a deity stood in a cruciform shape in a cup: start with looking for the icon of the *Theotokos as the Mother of God of the Life-giving Spring* or *Life-giving Font*.

Look in Christianity, at medieval coronation paintings; look at Egyptian, Mesopotamian, Roman, and Greek images; and look for the magical tools. Pay particular attention to the combinations of the tools, what hands they are in, and what is around them. Put together a little file or scrapbook so that you can return to this research. Don't try and reason too much; just let ideas filter into your head. And don't skip this task, it is important.

Later you will revisit these images when you understand more about the tools, the inner patterns, and powers, and it will give you a wholly different understanding as to what the images are depicting. That in turn will tell you a lot about the magical power worked with in a particular culture, and you will be able to track what went wrong (it always goes wrong), when, and why. That knowledge will inform your own evolution.

Lesson 8

Natural Patterns of the Land

At this stage of the course you have looked at foundational ritual patterns, the magical elements, the natural local elements, and you have also worked with the foundations of visionary magic. Now it is time to pull these various skills together in order to learn how to work with the landscape, and with those beings within the landscape that are a part of the land upon which you live.

We will start by looking at what major features are on the land which surrounds you. If you live in a large city, you may find that these features are still there on the land, or you may find that you have to reach beyond the city to connect with them.

When I say features, I mean rivers, lakes, hills, mountains, forest, plains, desert, caves, burials, etc. Some areas are littered with these features and some are not: some people live in cities surrounded by mile after mile of flat grassland, whereas others are nestled between rivers and mountains. Whatever surrounds you will have power and contact within it, and you need to learn what is there, even if it is hidden, so that you can engage and work with it.

Many magicians, particularly ritual magicians, fail to understand just how important these features are to their magical work: they operate in isolation to everything around them. This isolationist approach eventually limits the magician severely, as these natural features, and the consciousnesses within them, play a major role in advanced magic. They can also become excellent co-workers in your magical work if your work is compatible with their existence. In return, the magician helps and works with the consciousnesses of these features to maintain a harmonious relationship between the land and the magician – it is always give and take.

To discover what is around you, you can use Google Earth, or any similar software, or old fashioned Ordinance Survey maps.

How far do you look beyond your own home? How long is a piece of string! A mountain that is forty or fifty miles away is likely to have an influence on where you are, whereas a river a similar distance away is unlikely to have any effect on your immediate area. To gauge what has an effect and what does not, draw out a simple map, marking the directions, and mark what is there in each direction: burial grounds, underground cave systems, hills, rivers, etc. Go as far as you need to go in order to mark a feature in each direction and in the cross quarters. Once you have that map, then look up any local faery tales, myths, legends, and old stories connected with any of those features or that focus on a specific area around you.

If you are lucky, you will find local legends about a cave, a hill, a river, etc. and the tale will give you clues as to what is going on in that feature. Just be wary of taking the story literally, as they were often slanted towards a Christian agenda to warn people from connecting with what would have possibly been a Pagan site of focus. That is less common in newer societies like the USA, and more likely in old, established societies in (for example) Europe. And do not assume that a natural feature will connect happily with you: the land beings that inhabit these places are sometimes interesting and good to work with, and sometimes they are hostile.

Some features will have just the natural consciousness of that land and others will have more formed, conscious beings whom you can interact with. So for example you may find an old tree that has a wonderful feel to it and that you can connect easily to, but it has no humanlike presentation or form of communication that you can easily interact with. Other times you will find features that have inner beings residing within or around them: land beings and faery beings often inhabit these places, and they will either work happily with you or they will be hostile to you, or a bit of both.

Remember; you are treading into uncharted territory, so use your common sense. Even if a contact is mildly hostile, gentle forays into communications can turn that around and you can still make enduring friendships: just be aware that some powerful beings always need to be treated with caution. It is like making friends with a tiger: don't do the Disney realm, use your brains.

Here is an example. When I lived in Tennessee, I lived near an area upon which was the Bell Witch Cave. This is a famous cave that is said to be haunted by a witch who would attack people. There are many famous stories about her. So I decided to go and investigate, introduce myself if it was appropriate, and see for myself what was there.

The first thing that struck me was the idea that the contact was limited to the cave was complete bullshit. That whole area of land had a very strange feel to it. I went into the cave, went around the surrounding countryside, into the local graveyard, and just pottered about, trying to get a feel of what was there. The first thing I can tell you is that it is no witch that lives there – in fact, it is not human at all. And it was not one person/being. The whole area was inhabited by strange faery beings that were not overly impressed by humans and were mildly hostile.

There was also an overarching consciousness there, female, that had a similar feel to a deity, but it was not a deity: it was a powerful female land consciousness that was highly intelligent and did not particularly like humans, as they were disrespectful to her. This type of consciousness is often the foundational aspect of a local land deity, in that the form of the deity is a human-constructed interface that then allows the being and the humans to interact. With a being like this, it is possible to open a dialogue, perform a careful exchange of gifts, and establish a mutually respectful and beneficial working relationship, so long as one treads very carefully and is always mindful of being respectful.

Sometimes the contact in a feature is very powerful and destructive towards humanity. Sometimes that is because of the behaviour of the humans in that area, or it can be because they are just not compatible with our species and tend to be either hostile or predatory towards us. Some just ignore us. You need to be aware of these types of consciousness when you work as a magician, so that you do not antagonise or confront them with your magical work. It is better to identify them, tentatively reach out to them in respectful friendship, and tiptoe around them as you work. After all, they have been here far longer than we have and we are in their backyard, not the other way around.

If you are lucky you can fall across a consciousness within features that is very compatible with humans, is not hostile, and is very willing to work with you magically if you are willing to work magically for them on occasion. This can slowly build into a long-term working relationship that is mutually beneficial: they can provide guardianship, warnings about storms or large dangers, and they can teach you land magic – and they often become very protective towards you. In return you can take gifts (honey always goes down well with everyone), sing to them, move things for them, plant things for them, look after the creatures around them, or work in vision with them in various tasks.

Let's get straight to the practical work. You will work in vision and then you will go out on the land. So plan this lesson's practical work in a schedule that will allow you to visit at least one site within seven days of doing the visionary work.

If you only have one feature that is dominant in your land area, work with that. If you have more, visit as many as possible in vision and then physically visit them in turn. You can also use these techniques to make contact with land powers in areas that you are visiting.

1. *Task:* Visiting the site in vision

The first step in this work is to go in vision and connect with the site. Sometimes it is better to visit physically first, but there are many techniques wrapped into this lesson which would dictate that you work first in vision before you visit the site. You will learn why as you go along. This is your first real foray into vision work in this course. Learn the steps in the vision like a story until you know all of the steps and points of contact; then do the actual vision itself.

Do not second-guess yourself or try to prove anything to yourself, just work in your imagination, which is your tool to interface with beings: through your imagination, you will learn to use your mind as a form of communication and as a form of travel. Don't worry that it is 'all in your head' – you will become aware at some point in your vision work, now in this lesson, or in a future lesson, that you have broken through into working outside of your own sphere. Don't force that, it will come in its own time. Don't intellectualise over things or try to self-limit – learn to let your imagination take the reins.

Get the map you have drawn of your landscape's different features. Mark out the directions, and also mark on the map what the localised elements were that you found in your lesson on finding the gender and elemental powers in your local area.

Look at this mix of information and see if anything strikes you about the relationships between the features, the gender and the elements.

Ensure that you have time and space to work without being disturbed. As an experienced magician you would either just sit and do the vision, or you would go to the site, sit down, and visit in vision while also being physically there. But we are going to use a method that is important for you to learn and work in a way that builds magical muscle: this is not just about doing something, it is about learning a specific skill set.

Choose the first place or feature you are going to visit, and know which direction it is in relative to where you live. Have your map with you and place it before you. Work in your ritual space with the four directional altars (no centre altar for this), and start by lighting the directions and opening the gates. When you have opened the gates, do the pentagram ritual to tune yourself and the space to work.

Now sit down in the centre of the directions. Close your eyes and do a few minutes of stillness meditation until you feel ready to work. You are now going to work in vision, similar to the exercise you did in module one. This is called visionary work: it works through your imagination. Before you start, with your eyes closed, imagine yourself looking at the map. See if anything stands out: is there a bright spot? If you do see anything, just file it away in the back of your mind and when you have finished your vision work, mark down on the map what area lit up.

Now see yourself stand up out of your body and walk to the altar that is in the direction of the feature that you are going to visit. Bow before the altar and then see yourself walk through the altar to the threshold of the gate.

Stand on the threshold of the gate and declare (in vision but also use your physical voice, with your eyes still closed):

> "I am going to visit X[1]
> with the intention of paying my respects and introducing myself."

As you look through the gates, see the land outside your house that is in the direction of the gate you are stood in and the direction you intend to explore. Step through the gate and find yourself outside your home. Set off walking in the direction of the feature you are going to visit. If it is a long way away, don't worry about that, just keep focus on the place that you are going to.

As you walk and look at the land, houses, roads, whatever is around you, you notice that they slowly start to fade away as you walk, and nature takes over more and more. You walk and walk, and find yourself walking in a changing landscape, where the footprint of human habitation and farming vanishes, and the land takes on more and more of its primal nature.

You may find that you have to climb over rocks, or push through brambles, dense undergrowth, or high grass, or swim through water that is not normally there.

---

[1] Mountain, river, whatever.

Nature seems to make the path hard for you and you struggle to get to where you are going, while keeping a constant focus upon your destination. This period of walking may take some time: look for creatures, birds, animals, insects, and anything else lurking in the shadows as you walk, but do not stop, do not be diverted from your path: stay very focused as to where you are going. Do not rush this part: take your time.

When you finally get close to where you are going, stop for a moment and look around. Take note of what is around the feature, what other land features are there, or any animals; anything that catches your eye. Now look up. Even though it may be daytime, you can also see the stars. One or two particular stars may catch your eye. Look at them for a moment: they are connected to the land feature you are about to connect with. Keep an awareness of those stars as you continue to walk.

Take a few steps closer to the feature and kneel down. Place your hands upon the ground so that they sink into the earth. As the land feels you out, tell the land who you are, where you live, who your family is, and what you intentions are: to learn, to connect, to be respectful and to serve if that is needed or wanted. Now kneel closer to the land and place your forehead upon the land. Be still. Listen to the land by feeling through your emotions and imagination. How does the land feel about you being there? Take your time and just allow your own spirit to feel into the land, and for the land to respond. You may or may not get a response. When you are ready, get up. Start walking again towards the feature... and sing as you go. Sing a song you remember from childhood while also keeping your mind fixed upon the feature ahead of you.

Something or someone steps out of nowhere onto the path before you. This is the guardian of the site. Do not try to form the image in your mind. It may be very clear or it may just be a feeling. Don't try to force anything, just let the contact be itself. Again, repeat your intention: to make contact, to be respectful, and to be of help if it is needed.

The contact will come right up to you and check you out, or if it is a strong contact, they may ask you questions. Just answer truthfully, always. The contact will then either tell you to leave, or will guide you forward. If they tell you to leave, go straight back the way you came until you see the gate into your room. You will have to try again with another feature.

If they lead you forward, walk with them and answer any questions that rise up in your mind. When you reach the feature, and the guardian stands to one side, you will find yourself before the feature, and out of the feature will come either a human or animal type shape, or you will simply get a sense of a conscious energy. Tell them about who you are, and use images in your mind to show them that you are trying to learn how to live and work on the land as a responsible magician.

When you have done that, wait for an answer, which may come as a conversation or as thoughts/feelings/senses. When the exchange is over, do not go into the feature, even if you are invited. Politely decline and thank them. Tell them you will return in your body soon and that you will bring gifts. Bow, turn, and go back the way that you came. Retrace your path until you see the gate before you that you stepped through.

Step through the gate and through the altar. Stop and look back; you may see that either the guardian or another being has followed you. Bow to them, then go back to your body and sit into yourself. When you are ready, open your eyes.

Write down everything that you saw, using a computer, and what impressions and interactions you had of what happened. Once you have done that, go back to your ritual space and go around the directions, closing them all down except for the direction that you visited. Blow out the candle in that direction, but see the gate stay open. Within a week of doing this work, as soon as you can, go and visit the site physically.

2. *Task:* Visiting the site physically

When you are ready, it is time to go and visit the site. Take with you gifts of honey, chopped up fruit (like grapes or apple chopped into small bits), and take a pin to prick your finger. Leave your phone in the car or turn it off – work without distraction.

When you get to the site, take your time walking about it to get a feel of it and also to allow the land to adjust to your being there. Find a spot where you can sit and not be disturbed. Still yourself and sit quietly. Just listen and observe nature around you: watch the birds, insects, spiders, etc. all doing their work. Once you are nice and quiet, remember the guardian and retrieve the image or feel of the guardian: focus on the guardian and on no other thoughts. Ask permission in your mind, and also using your voice, to make contact with the spirit of the site/feature.

Observe any changes around you, any birds, insects, or animals that appear around you, and be respectful to them (like don't squish a spider that appears at your feet, for instance), as they are all children of the site. Close your eyes and retrieve the sense you had in vision of being before the spirit of the land there. Once you have a sense of that being, or can imagine a shape or image for that being, then once more introduce yourself.

Take the pin and prick your finger. Squeeze the blood onto the ground and once more tell them about who you are and who your family is. They may or may not appear to you in vision; don't worry if they don't, but if they do and you get a sense of their power, and what they are, ask if they would be willing to let you learn how to work with the land as a magician.

If you do not get a visionary connection, don't worry: sometimes the first connect works in other ways, particularly if you are not yet skilled in vision work. Sometimes it is just a feeling, sometimes it presents through the birds and creatures, or the wind. Get up and find a safe place to scatter the fruit bits and to pour the honey. The fruit is for the birds and creatures, and the honey is for the being/land.

Speak out loud, saying that you wish to learn how to work with that land and that you are willing to help the land/spirits in any way that you can.

Move away from where you put the gift and have a wander around. Watch the ground for an interesting stone or a curious stick: if there is something there for you to take away and work with, it will stand out for you.

At this stage, various different things can happen (and take your time in this place, don't rush around, often the contact needs time to unfold). You may find an interesting stone, stick, bone, or feather, or you may come across an injured creature/bird which is presented to you for help. Or you may have an encounter with a bird, insect, or creature: these are all different, subtle ways that the land can reach out to you.

I have had times when virtually nothing happened, and other times where astonishing things happened. It all depends on the power of that land, the willingness of the contacts to communicate with you, and whether there is a need within the land spirits to connect with a human magician. As you wander around, pick up any trash that you find. This is a really powerful thing and is something very few magicians think about.

Trash can sometimes be annoying but harmless; other times it can devastate an area in terms of damage to wildlife, and physical objects are not things that spirits can pick up, but humans can. The simple act of taking a bag out with you and picking up trash whenever you find it is a major service. This simple act tells the local spirits that you care and are willing to maintain an area. Visiting a site regularly and picking up trash, and leaving food for the birds, are all simple, undramatic actions that you can take which make a big difference and are a form of magical service to a land. Later you will learn ways of working magically to help an area be properly maintained energetically, and this in turn will lead to friendships with local beings who will work magically with you.

When you have finished your visit to the site, (stay a while, sing to the land, hang out, lay down and sleep, or just wander about) keep a dream diary over the coming days and weeks to see if the spirits of the site reach out to you in your sleep. Sometimes you get very clear communication dreams; other times it can trigger strange dreams that make no sense. Don't worry about that, just write them down and keep a record that you can go back to in the future.

Learning to connect with the nature around you is a very powerful and ancient magical working method, but because most humans have been cut off from nature for so long it will take time to re-establish lines of communications. Take it slow and steady. Adopt a site, go and visit regularly, hang out, watch the birds, let things talk to you, and slowly build a relationship with it.

When the time is right, which could be straight away or may take time, the land spirits will slowly start to connect with you and show up in visions, magical workings, and dreams. Birds will come and visit your home, and things will start to change around you. Sometimes if the site is very powerful you may get quite immediate communications and a shift in your early magical work. Whichever way it goes, just go with the flow and use your common sense.

If you come home with a feather, stone, stick, bone, whatever, place it on the altar of the direction that the site is in. Don't place them according to the pattern of magical tools (stick/south, feather/east), because they are not magical tools; rather they are gateways to contact. Through the object, you can maintain a thin line of connection to the site, and by having it on the altar when you work it will alert the land beings at the site that you are working magically, which in turn will let them know that you may be someone worth working with. You can use the object as a way to strengthen the contact if you sit with it in your hand during a meditation. You can also use it as a focus to continue visiting the site in vision.

Visit the site in vision once a month, usually near a full moon, using the same pathway that you used in the above vision. Go, say hello, ask if there is anything they need, observe, listen, communicate, and then come back. Don't go and dump on the site by telling them your problems, or asking them stupid questions (can you tell me about god, or how to get power). And physically go to the site once a month or more, clean it up, hang out, take gifts, and just chill out.

Eventually you will learn to step into the inner magical realm of these land beings and commune with them directly in a powerful way. You will also learn to work with the creatures of a site, learn how to look through their eyes, to read the weather from the way the land and creatures act, and that in turn will teach you how to work with the raw elements of nature as magical tools and co-workers.

I wrote a book specifically about nature magic called *Magic of the North Gate*. This might be a good time to get that book and read it. Currently it is on the Quareia website as a free download PDF book, and as we are currently (2024) updating the course, we are looking at ways to also put a lot of recommended and required reading together into a book and free download. *Magic of the North Gate* goes into depth about various ways of working with nature, and I will not be repeating those methods in this course (as there is no need to, it is already in the book). Instead the course will look at nature magic from another angle, so that, along with what is in the book, you will get a whole tool kit of nature magic techniques.

Keep good records of your interactions and experiences with nature, and these notes can be on computer, it is not necessary for these to be handwritten.

3. Module Two Summary

By now you have learned the base foundation skills of ritual, tarot, vision, and patterning, and you should be practising these skills regularly. You have also begun the process, through writing a journal, of learning how to use your hand to transfer power into a sigil or a word. These baseline skills are a rock that you stand on in magic.

Magical training is not about learning an endless ream of rituals and incantations, nor is it about owning tons of grimoires: that is the sign of not knowing how magic works. In reality, the magician has an understanding of base structures and techniques which is often not a large base, but an important one. From there, the magician learns about all the different powers, beings, realms, and actions which inform them about which base techniques to use when, where and why. The module that you have just finished taught you about basic patterns and how they work. From that understanding, you will slowly learn how to construct your own unique working patterns that are individual to you, but most importantly, because you are learning the actual nuts and bolts of patterning, any pattern you do create in the future will work and will work well.

But remember – you have been learning skills, which means they need to be practised by using them and working with them regularly. That way you will have the skill and knowledge to use them practically in magic and in your life. They are not things to learn and then move on from. I am in my sixth decade and I still use those foundational skills on a near daily basis in my life and work. They grow stronger with use and also widen out in terms of power and depth as they are used regularly.

The next module is about deep inner powers. It might seem an early point in training to introduce these powers to you (don't worry, you will not be dipping your toe into the magical depths yet) but without an understanding of these power dynamics you will not fully understand some of the magical techniques that you will learn in modules four and five. You will be introduced to these powers of creation through reading the texts, and then by applying various methods of engagement that work from the baseline of the physical world of your own life before you later go on to learn how to engage with them directly in the depths of the inner worlds: that is the work of an adept.

Make sure that you have by now established a rhythm of work in which you are practising the rituals and techniques that you have already learned and that you need regular practice with, while also studying a new lesson. If you are getting to a stage where questions are arising for you in your training, do not seek to find answers from me or anyone else. Simply write down those questions and think about them. Come to your own solution and conclusion for now, as you really do have to learn to make steps, decisions, and discoveries (and mistakes) on your own.

Well done for getting to here and not giving up. Practise your rituals until they are second nature: you will need that skill in the work that is to come. You are making major leaps, probably without realising it, and while you are learning those base techniques you are also learning how to mature as a spiritual being. Well done!

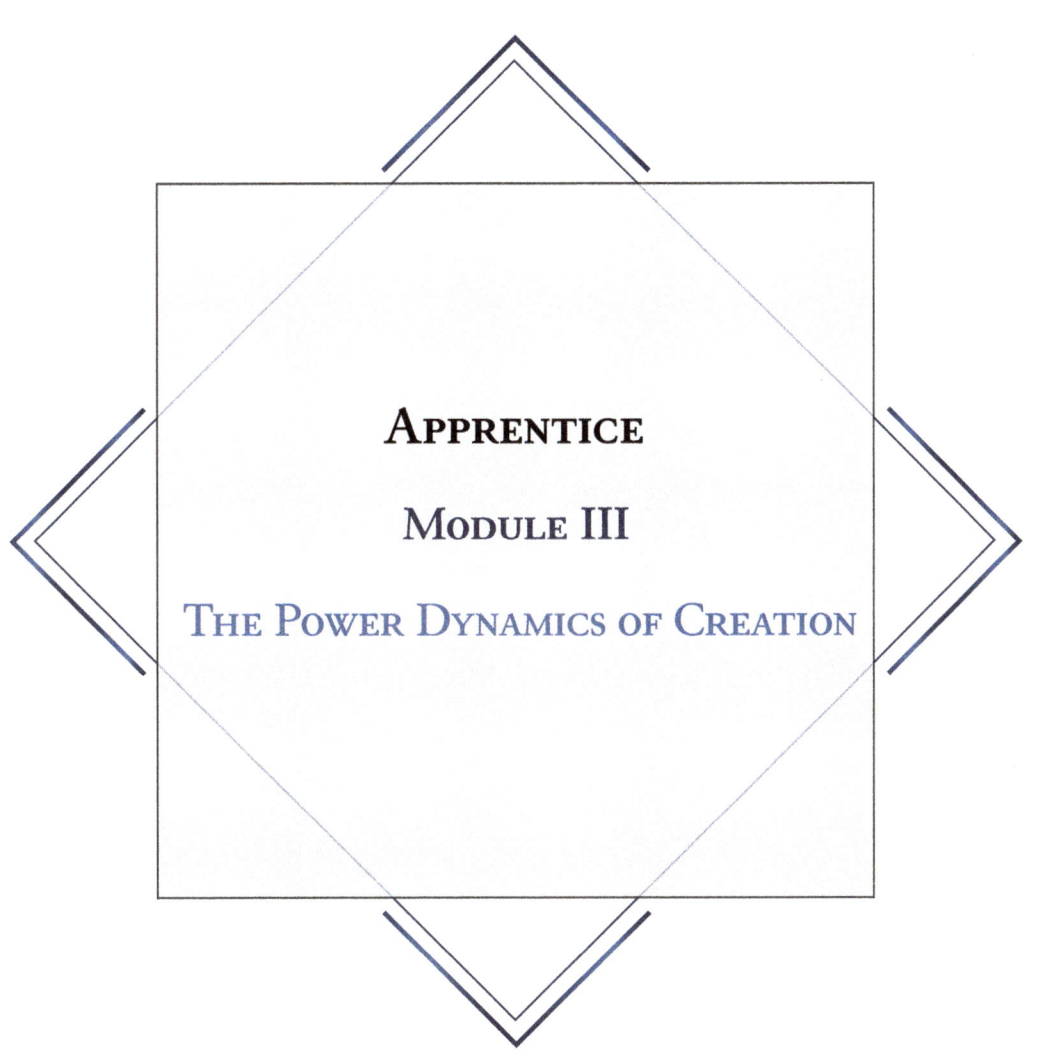

Apprentice

Module III

The Power Dynamics of Creation

Lesson 1
Introduction

This is a reading lesson with no practical magical work, but it does have an essay task at the end of it. So after finishing this lesson, you can go straight on to the next lesson as soon as you are ready. Take your time with reading this lesson, and take notes if you get stuck and do not understand something. At the end of the module, come back to your notes from this lesson and see if you have a better understanding as a result of the practical work.

In the previous modules, you have learned the final exteriorisation of magic, which we call *patterning* or *rituals*: exteriorised physical actions that essentially hold the energy of magic in a particular form and then send that magic out into the world.

It follows the same pattern as human existence: the completion of creation is the birth of a human child. The completion of creation is also a tree, a stone, an animal, etc.: it is the final outcome of something that started as a first impulse which went through a series of energetic processes to arrive at a physical substance or an outer expression.

To be able to operate in magic to any real degree of power, you need to know all the different layers of power, energy, substance, how they operate, where they came from, and where they are going. The first step in that process is to learn the complete exteriorisation of energy (substance or form); the next step is to look at the how that energy was turned into form from a magical perspective. Then the apprentice magician will have far more understanding of the processes in between, which is where magic happens, and will be far better equipped to engage intelligently with magical power safely and effectively.

It would be too much to expect an apprentice magician to fully grasp the true depth of creation powers from the view of a magician, as the real understanding of those depths comes from direct inner experiences of these energetic forces in action. That is a process that begins during the Initiate phase of the training. But to be able, as an initiate, to step into those inner powers and inner worlds to observe the creative act in action, they need a basic background understanding in what it is they are looking at, what they do, and how to interact with them, which in turn gives the magician a mental vocabulary that they can draw upon.

1. Creation and magic

A lot of magical systems give the creation process a cursory nod in the training process. In Western magic that often takes the form of learning the Kabbalistic tree of life system, whereas some other systems look at the creation process through mythology and the acts of the deities. Some forms of magic ignore it altogether.

For many years I taught this aspect of magical learning from a Kabbalistic perspective, but slowly I came to realise that because Western magic has in general so bastardised the Kabbalistic system (in an effort to make it fit the Western worldview and its psychological theories), it is to all intents and purposes pointless to teach it that way: the student invariably wanders off into various offshoots of Western Kabbalah and finds themselves stuck in mindless loops of magical babble. So I had to sit back and think very carefully about how to approach this, as it is a critical section of learning if a magician is to truly reach magical adeptship in a real, practical sense.

I realised that I was simply being lazy: working with inner forms of magic exposes you to key *markers*, or experiences of the powers of creation that are common throughout the human experience. Through those generic experiences, the magician learns the depths of the creation dynamic, and learns how that process affects their magic, themselves, and everything around them in very practical ways. Kabbalah is one method (though not the only one) that systematises those key experiences. I had become lazy in that I had fallen back on already produced and packaged systems as a way to convey magical information in writing. But those ready-produced and packaged systems have baggage; they have fragmentations and also tons of modern-day misconceptions. While it is still possible to operate through that system, I decided it would be better to step away from that vocabulary and look at things in a fresh light.

Writing Quareia has kicked me up the ass and has forced me to stop being such a *lazy* magician. Instead I am making an effort to outline these deep, powerful mystical and magical processes without their cultural/religious structures: I am approaching them by teaching about the key elements that are found in the creation process as they present to a magician, and introducing the student to the beings, powers, and realms relevant to this process. Once you have worked with the creation process in different ways and on different levels, you will immediately be able to spot one of these *keys* embedded within a mythology or a religion. And you will be able to recognise it *because you will have seen it and experienced it in action* for yourself. That experience is one of the hallmarks of the Greater Mysteries.

To get to that stage, you first need a background understanding. This module is the start of gaining that background understanding, and more modules around this subject matter will appear in the Initiate and Adept section of the training as you slowly inch your way deeper and deeper into the realm of creation. You will also learn the polar opposite of the creation process, and that is the process of destruction and of death (the next module). Together, those three key energetic dynamics tell us everything about how real and powerful magic hangs together.

2. The use of visionary technique

Unlike the more externalised forms of magic, i.e. rituals, sigils, utterances, forming of objects, talismans etc., the energetic powers of creation are best understood, interacted with and observed through visionary magic. Only once the magician has worked in vision will such powers be accessible to be worked with through more externalised methods.

This is because the magician must first have direct and unique energetic experience of these powers in order for the understanding and power resonance to settle within the mind, spirit, and also the body of the magician. The magician works with the inner and outer worlds together when they engage with power magically, so the understanding from both sides of the fence must be active and based upon direct experience in order for such magic to be successful.

The inner worlds, where energies are formed and patterned, can only be experienced and interacted with through the use of the imagination. This expresses itself through dreams and through visions. In some kinds of magic, those dreams and visions come spontaneously and are uncontrolled. In other forms of magic the magician uses their imagination consciously as an interface to trigger, work with, and to an extent control the visionary act. Dreams are best left to unfold themselves naturally, so the magician uses controlled and disciplined vision, and uncontrolled, un-interfered-with dreams. That allows both sides of the human mind to express themselves in their different ways.

As we discussed in Module I's lesson on visionary exercises, the imagination is used by a magician to create windows in their consciousness that the human spirit can step through in order to interact with beings, spirits, and powers in the inner worlds (worlds that have no physical manifestation). You have worked with your mind/imagination in various lessons so far, learning slowly how to build up images using your mind's eye in order to 'see.'

In future, in all lessons, I will no longer use the term 'mind's eye,' as you should all now know what it is I am referring to. From now on we will call it by its correct name, *inner vision*. You will be using inner vision a great deal more in your magical training from now on, and using it in balance with exteriorised magic so that your mind and body become used to the balance of working in both inner and outer forms, often at the same time.

The inner dynamics of creation are observed using inner vision. The magician interacts with various beings by using inner vision, and once they have acquired a good grasp of the inner dynamics of creation, then they can slowly start to connect the inner and outer dynamics together in magical acts. The combination of the two properly plugs the magic into a power source, and gives the magic an energetic focus, a pattern of behaviour, and a stable way to complete that magic successfully.

A magician would not plug into these deep dynamics to do simple or 'surface,' everyday magic like protection, etc., but they would most certainly plug into these powers to varying degrees when undertaking long-term powerful magical work that will have a lasting effect.

This method is very similar to the pathworking that is used in psychology, the only real differences being that inner vision is not about 'you,' is not venturing into your own inner self, and is not a constructed story. The realms exist outside of yourself, and the images used in vision are key steps that describe things which other magicians have also seen repeatedly over thousands of years: it tells you what is there, and you also have your own unique experiences. The images we see in those visions are a collective human interpretation of what is actually there: they are very real and exist independently of us.

In our modern world of science, the model of 'proof' is to measure the veracity of something by the ability to reproduce findings. That modus operandi has become the gold standard for everything in our lives. Magic does not work quite so neatly and cannot be measured using that paradigm. However, there is one gold standard that does shine in magic, and that is that there are key elements that appear in inner vision to everyone who stumbles into the inner worlds, regardless of whether they were aware of those keys or not. They are not widely discussed, and are therefore unlikely to be in the subconscious mind or memory, waiting to resurface as an 'experience.'

These key images, interactions, and experiences are a hallmark of *inner contact* for magicians, and help us psychologically by telling us in quite plain language that we are on the real and right track. Often they have slightly different presentations, but the overarching power and communion is the same. And some major keys are not written into the course so that you can find them for yourself – once you have experienced them, you will then be able to research them for yourself and track them down in ancient images and texts. This is one of the hallmarks of the Mysteries, and one of the ways the Mysteries protect themselves.[1]

I could write reams on these different keys, but it would not forward you an inch as a magician, because you will not have experienced them for yourself. True, direct experience changes you at a deep level, and that direct experience and the subsequent change is the chariot that carries you deep into magic.

There will be many times you will have self-doubt about your visionary experiences, and that can be very healthy, so long as it does not limit you. If you see something in vision that does not compute, do not automatically dismiss it: you may very well find that what you saw was a real power contact. So if you experience something that does not fit with what you think should be there, do not dismiss it, simply write it down in your computer log. It can be sometimes be handy to research what you have seen after you have seen it: often you can come across ancient references buried deep

---

[1] And the Quareia adepts will be looking for those unmentioned keys in your submitted work for mentoring: it will tell us that you are on the right track.

in stories or myths that exactly (or almost exactly) describe what you saw. That tells you it is not just in your own head, but that you were connected with something that magicians saw thousands of years ago.

There can be times when the imagination 'plays out' in the visionary process and what you see is simply coming from you and not from the inner worlds. There is no easy way around that, unless it is really obvious in its presentation. Slowly you will learn, through work and practice, to differentiate between what is really an inner world experience and what is your own mind amusing itself. That only comes from lots of practice, having direct experiences, and having those direct experiences confirmed in retrospect, either by other magicians or from ancient texts.

The best of all confirmations come from situations where, for example, an inner contact tells you something is going to happen (someone is going to die, something specific is going to be given to you unexpectedly, etc.) and then it happens, and there was no way you would have been able, even subconsciously, to effect such an outcome.

I write more about this type of process in my book *Magical Knowledge One*, but in truth, the best way to work with vision is to treat everything as real until you slowly start to be able to differentiate for yourself, and that time will most certainly come with work. That stops you inadvertently shutting down a contact by ignoring or blocking it from your mind. Such an action will have a far more long-term negative effect on your magic and training than accepting everything, even if that means accepting something that is simply your own mind. Every magician goes through this process, and as you develop it will become less and less of an issue. Just also be cautious of accepting everything you see and hear as 'truth' while working in vision, particularly as a new magician, as that too can take you down a not-so-good road. The key is simply to take note of your experiences, be respectful of the experience, and then wait and see.

Let us have a quick look at the stages of this creation dynamic that we will be looking at in depth through this module.

Through the module we will start the journey into creation by stepping backwards through the creation process. We will look at the first layer of beings that most humans come into contact with in magical vision or work, beings that stand at or near the threshold between our manifest world and the deeper inner worlds. We will start with the outermost manifestation of creation, and that is the physical world.

3. The garden

The *garden* is a name for the physical world that pops up a lot in various ancient texts and temple structures. The physical world encompasses everything: the land/earth, the plants/trees, animals, insects, humans – and it also includes the moon, sun, and stars.

This is something that many magicians forget or do not think about: the planets and stars around us are also a part of the manifest world – they are not separate, nor are they a deeper or higher expression. This is one of the mistakes that magicians make when using the Kabbalistic Tree of Life: they place the moon, sun, and stars on different Sefirot on the Tree, not realising that most of the tree is actually inner worlds, not outer worlds.

Now you start to see why it is a good idea not have anyone working with the vocabulary of Kabbalah in the course: it has become too confused and fragmented when used in Western magic. It is badly misunderstood when taken away from its mystical religious roots.

The *garden*, or physical world, is the peak of the creation process. The *inner garden*, that is to say the inner expression of the land, shows up as a balanced and harmonic landscape and it is this 'ideal' that crops up in ancient and religious texts. This is the pinnacle of creation and is the inner template for the outer land. The outer land is not balanced and it is far more dynamic in its processes of creation and destruction, depending on the interactions it has with the creatures/humans etc. that live upon it.

As soon as anything manifests physically, it moves beyond its peak and begins its slow march towards degeneration and destruction, as everything has its death programmed into its birth. So like everything else, it is a constantly flowing process of in/out, life/death.

This peak at the outflow of creation is also the point where magic exteriorises into a ritual and goes out into the world to 'do its thing.' In the last module, you learned the four directional ritual pattern that works magically with the world. In this module, in the next lesson, you will learn to take a step deeper into the magical mysteries of the physical world so that you gain a better understanding of your own 'ground zero' (the land upon which you live) before you start to work magically with any power in the physical world.

Throughout history we have found ways of ritually reiterating this peak of creation, this inner garden that upholds the outer manifest world. We see it in the biblical Garden of Eden, and we see it in the mystical Pagan history of Kaaba in Mecca (Paradise on Earth).

The pre-Islamic Kaaba was said to have been built by Adam to the specifications given to him by angels in order to recreate Paradise on Earth. The original cubic building housed different expressions of the deities and their combined energies mirrored the inner garden in balance.[2]

We also see this recreation ritual action in the botanical sanctuary at Karnak in Egypt and also at Göbekli Tepe in Turkey. These are just some examples of the ritual mirror of creation that were worked with.

---

[2] Quick hint on reading the symbolism of old myths: "Adam" equals people/person in the far distant past from the time perspective of the writers of the myth.

This point in creation is where the magician stands: stepping into the inner garden, the magician steps out of time and begins to backtrack through that creation process to observe how that creation came into being.

4. The inner threshold

The *inner threshold* is the first step inwards from the creative process. This is the realm of the imagination, and the group consciousness of every living thing. It is the inner body of the land (the *inner garden*) and of every living thing. This is where the first magical interactions happen for the magician as the magician learns to work within their own imagination.

Just before creation exteriorises out into the physical world, it first creates the inner pattern of each living thing. This is the stage where we find the inner spirit of a tree, a dog, a river, a human; and the stage where the mind, consciousness, and dream world are formed. We step over this threshold to go into physical life, and we step over this threshold again at death as we begin our journey back, deep into the inner worlds.

For a magical apprentice, this threshold is the training ground for inner magic, and at some point the magician has to overcome the challenge of the threshold guardian that stops an ordinary person from wandering beyond their dreams and imagination and into the deeper inner realms themselves.

The apprentice learns to use this part of 'creation' through visionary magic, learning to step through the imagination in a controlled way in order to pass beyond this threshold and gain access to the deeper inner worlds.

This threshold is often referred to as the realm of the moon, not because it *is* the realm of the moon, but because the moon affects our minds and dreams; the description is therefore a planetary association. The physical moon itself is a part of the physical world. So be careful that you do not tie too much of an association with this realm and the moon, as it could end up confusing you and leading you up a dead end. Rather, we can study old myths, stories, and attributes connected to the moon to get a glimpse of the powers of this threshold and how that power expresses itself to us as humans.

The lower parts of the creation process (which is what this module is about) have planetary connections which do influence aspects of the creative process, but as you tread deeper into the inner worlds you will find the planetary associations fall away.

5. The polarities of creative power

Once we step beyond the threshold of the imagination and the inner spirit of the outer being, we reach a second energetic threshold beyond which is the deep cauldron of creation with all its inherent angelic powers, deities, beings, and Divinity itself. This energetic threshold is not so much an inner space or realm; rather it is a tense, polarised power filter that the patterns of creation flow through and past on their way to physical manifestation.

That is vocabulary that will leave many an apprentice staring blanking at the words, because we are getting into areas of power that there is no current vocabulary to describe.

Imagine it a little like this. We have an energy barrier between two powerful magnets that create a magnetic or energetic tension. This energetic tension acts like a filter: it slows things down and filters out anything unnecessary. It also acts as a catalyst that triggers the formation of shape, gender, bloodlines, race/species etc.

In the depths of the inner worlds, the creative process of something (tree, person, etc.) has been forming and has started its movement towards taking shape into a solid form. It goes through a series of changes as it interacts with the inner powers around it (something you will learn about in the Initiate section) and finally it reaches this energetic barrier/filter. Once it passes through this filter it will pass into spirit/mind form (the inner threshold), and then finally be birthed as a physical living thing.

When that 'something' that is destined for life passes through this barrier or filter, it is changed quite dramatically. It starts to take on both aspects of a polarisation at a very deep level and that polarisation or energetic tension allows it to physically manifest (every living thing has this polarised aspect).

This polarisation in its depth expresses through positive/negative energy opposites. But this is not the only polarisation that happens: the 'something' that is destined for life also takes on feminine/masculine polarisation (every living thing has an aspect of both within them). It is akin to the first division of the cell as it begins life. And the octaves of this polarisation are layer upon layer that are interwoven in the consciousness, substance and spirit of the living being.

When we as magicians, and as living beings, backtrack through magical visionary work and step into this filter, we are confronted by this polarity of power as a field of energy. How we react mentally, physically, and spiritually to this energy field very much depends on how the current health and balance of that polarity is within us. Now this is where it starts to get interesting. You would think, because this *filter* or barrier is a deep inner energetic field, that it would be wise to ensure our deeper consciousness and spirit is fairly balanced so that is it not badly disrupted by stepping into such a powerful field. And so many magicians work on their 'psychological deeper self' through counselling and self-analysis in order to maintain and strengthen that balance. But that is not how we are constructed. We work from the outside in, not the inside out. What we change on the surface triggers deep change within.

When we work in the depths, it triggers surface changes: again, energy working in tension and opposition.

So what on earth does all this mean for the magician?

If the magician is happy to only ever work in non-powered outer ritual (ritual dramas) and not tap into deep, underlying inner powers, then all of this deeper work is meaningless. However, if as a magician you wish to become adept at effecting change in the outer world using magic, then you must be able to work in the deep inner realms using your consciousness. To do that, your consciousness must be able to pass through this energetic barrier without triggering a cascade of physical and mental reactions, which is essentially the first line of defence that protects the inner world from stupid people – and protects the stupid people from the impacts of the inner worlds.

So how do we find that balance in order to pass through this barrier?

We find that balance by first understanding and then working with the two polarised, opposite power dynamics that create and uphold that barrier. Those two polarised powers are within our cells, our deeper spirits, and express through our daily lives. They also express externally around us through fate – and how we interact with that externalised power in our life radically changes us. It brings us more into balance.

The externalised forms of these energies that are around us express themselves as catalysts for our individual and collective evolution. As magicians we learn to work harmoniously and consciously with these energies rather than being dragged through life by them. By working consciously with these dynamics, in their most exteriorised form, we begin a process of deep inner individual change. This in turn leads to the process of rebalancing within which allows us to work with deep power, energy, and to pass over thresholds safely.

This all sounds very deep and meaningful, and a tad complex, but in real terms it manifests in very simple ways. You have already been working with these two polarised powers in ritual without realising it. In magic they manifest in their most outer form as the sword and the cup, the two tools that guard the power impulse as it passes into the magical space.

The sword is the most outer form of a limiting power that we will call the *Grindstone*.[3] The Grindstone limits and slows something so that it can become stronger, denser, and more 'manifest.' That is its deepest power, and we see that in how particles and cells work. In human fate, a totally different octave, it manifests as life events or conditions that limit and shape the individual, a nation or a race.

In magic this manifests as the 'engine governor' which stops power coming through too quickly – many commercial vehicles have 'governors' or limiters on their engines which limit the speed they can be driven at. The magical Limiter also stops

---

[3] These powers also manifest through everyday life, which you will come to recognise through the lessons in this module.

the magician from misusing power by stopping the magician reaching too deeply or accessing power when they are unbalanced – Remember the Sword of Damocles?

The opposing power to this is one that releases power and we will call that the *Unraveller*. As the Grindstone limits and polishes, the Unraveller frees things up and then dissolves them. As the Grindstone limits in order for something to solidify, the Unraveller allows a free flow of power and energy which in turn eventually brings degeneration and death.

When we die, our energies are released from the bondage of the body, for example. And we all know what happens to our living bodies if we allow free rein to our senses: we over-consume which in turn brings about our downfall.

The deepest energetic function of the cup is as a cup of the *Scales*: the sum total of your actions, development and evolution is "weighed upon the scales," that is to say, the way you develop as a spirit in life governs how the spirit travels back into death from life.

The *Threshing Floor* (remember that from your pentagram ritual?) is an octave of the power of the Unraveller or the cup. The 'harvest of your life' is placed upon the Threshing Floor and governs how your spirit interacts with the transition process into death and beyond.

You will discover, through the in-depth lessons on these powers, that within each opposing polarity there is also an inherent dualism: the complexity of the octaves of these powers are within everything, from a single cell to a city, to an animal, to a life event or a work of art. When you step into the inner worlds, if your *body and spirit* has these two opposing influences in more or less a state of conversation if not balance, then you can pass into the deeper inner worlds without too much of a problem.

The way to achieve that is first through understanding, and then through direct conscious engagement in your outer and also magical life. Taking that first step of direct engagement triggers a whole cascade of change within you. And the lessons of this module will take you through this initial direct engagement. The way the body and spirit balance these two opposing influences will be discussed in depth later in this module, and you will be able to work in a series of different ways to trigger that balancing/conversation process.

At this point you will be beginning to see just how complex magic can be once you get past the surface presentation. And yet it still works with very simple principles of power in opposition, tension, power moving in opposite directions, and the maintaining of balance in the centre. The universe, the body, the mind and the inner worlds all work the same way: just as a muscle needs opposing actions, so too does the mind and spirit. The role of the magician is to work as a fulcrum, as someone who stands in the midst of the opposing powers and who conducts the orchestra of power from a place of stillness in the centre.

In today's world of commercial magic, many training groups have apprentices using counselling, psychological analysis, and drama rituals to make or even force themselves to be 'more balanced' – which of course does not work (though they are almost on the right track): these are all actions that still obviate responsibility from the magician for his or her own actions (and they tend to come away from self development rituals and go back to treating everything around them like shit).

Rather, magical balancing occurs through a subtle shift in how you live your daily life, how you understand your own body and mind, and how you first recognise, and then engage with the various beings and powers of creation as you learn to spot them active in your own life and the world around you.

6. The Inner Beings

At these thresholds, there are a variety of different inner beings that will work with the magician in order to first find and then maintain that inner and outer balance in opposition, and who act as threshold guardians, teachers, guides and workers. In the latter part of this module, you will meet these guardians in vision and ritual and learn how to connect and work with them.

7. *Task:* Researching *Ma'at*

The tasks for this lesson are easy and are simple study ones.

Look up and research everything you can find on the ancient Egyptian concept of *Ma'at*. Don't just find the deity and stop there: the deity is the face of a deeper power dynamic. Ma'at is the ancient Egyptians' version of this polarity power filter that creates balance – power in, power out, always working to keeping the Scales balanced.

The reason you are looking at it from an Egyptian perspective is that it is one of the few cultures we know of (they left behind a huge body of work) that engaged that inner threshold dynamic in their cultural and religious lives. And what they painted and wrote about is the closest I have ever come across to what is experienced when you step into the inner worlds. Essentially, they knew their shit.

Once you have researched and read up on Ma'at, write a short essay on what you understand Ma'at to be, and reflect in that essay how you feel Ma'at does or doesn't operate in your own life, and your country, culture, legal, and spiritual system. Do this as a computer essay and keep it in your folder. You will be coming back to this essay to reassess and compare with how your understanding has changed as a result of your magical work.

8. *Task:* Researching the Scales

Look at ancient Egyptian depictions of the Scales of Ma'at: you will notice in ancient pictures (not modern reproductions) that the feather is on the left hand scale (if you were the Scales) as is Djehuty, who is the deity of the transmission of knowledge (air). On the right hand side of the scale is the vessel which holds the person's heart, which is the harvest of their life and deeds.

Also look up the image of Themis, goddess of Divine Justice as depicted in Union Station, Washington D.C., USA. Whoever made that statue knew their Inner Mysteries. Note the nod to the Threshing Floor. Then look at various depictions of the goddess of justice from various ancient cultures. What you will quickly see is that some hold the sword in their left hand (to the right as you are looking at the picture) and some are reversed.

This reversal has two reasons: one is that as the Mysteries within a culture begin to degenerate, often the power depictions become lost or reversed, and this happens in all different cultures. Whether it is deliberate or not I do not know: it could be to protect the Mysteries or it could be out of a loss of knowledge.

The other reason for the reversal could be to do with the two forms of justice. One is the Divine power of Justice, which is the two opposing polarity powers of the threshold that protect the deep Mysteries (sword in the left hand), and the other form of justice, which shows the reversal of the tools, is human justice, which is flawed. The Scales held in the left hand show the weighing up of the words (air) of a person rather than their deeds (which is weighed in the right hand/west).

These are keys that are symptomatic of the state of the Mysteries at any given point in a culture. If the powers are depicted correctly, you know that at least someone in that culture at that time was clued in to the Inner Mysteries. If the keys go missing or are reversed, cast to one side, etc., then you know it is a mystical sign of the slow descent into collapse of a culture or religion. The depictions of the polarised powers of the thresholds are ones that can teach us a lot about the gnosis or lack thereof in a culture or religion. And the way that you as a magician work with these powers and tools will dictate how successful you are at penetrating the Deep Mysteries as an adept.

These two polarised powers are summed up as *power in* (to life) and *power out* (to death). The sword/Grindstone limits and shapes, the cup/Unraveller weighs and measures, and then releases.

Look through ancient art, statues, and wall reliefs, and take notes on any ideas or revelations that bubble up into your mind as you research this topic. These tasks will help to cement the outer keys into your mind and also embed the understanding of Ma'at deep within you: by experiencing these powers through magic and then externalising through study and writing, you will gain a balance of understanding that you can then work with as a magician. Spend time looking and thinking, and do not skip this task.

9. Summary

For those who find this whole concept and discussion a far cry from their ideas of magic, don't panic – although it is seemingly advanced or obscure, it is a vital part of the early stage of learning how to work in magical depth, and it is a cornerstone of adept magic, a stone which is laid in the foundations. These dynamics play a major part in the formation of life and of magic, and without accessing these powers and energies the magician barely scratches the surface of their magical potential. These polarised dynamics are the power stations of magic, of mysticism, and of life itself.

Lesson 2

The Inner Garden and Outer Vessels

The physical world around you is the biggest source of stability, learning, power, and strength for a magician, and yet it is sadly overlooked by many a magician. It is also the most powerful gateway to inner realms, beings, and spirits if a magician knows how to operate a space productively. All magic needs a vessel and a power source: first you learn to use what is already around you (the vessel of creation) before you then go on to work with magical tools (vessels) and powers.

Magic is everywhere: it is an expression of Divinity in substance and we as humans can mediate that power, raise it, and work with it. Everything around you has the creative and destructive powers flowing through it, and everything has consciousness in one form or another. Part of the work of a magician is to tap into that flow of power and also to communicate with everything around them. This opens the door for the magician to a path of cooperation, co-working, and mutual guardianship.

This is done in a variety of different ways, of which some are highly ritualised, others deeply mystical, and some very simple. The process of learning these skills starts with the apprentice magician doing a simple act: talking to everything. This has two actions from a technical point of view: it opens the door for power sources to flow, and it triggers natural 'vessel' actions. Why?

When as a magician you talk to something with magical intent, you mirror, at a very low level, a fundamental power dynamic of creation: the utterance. In its very deepest form, which you will learn about as an adept, it is a vibration, a sound that flows out of the 'nothing' that triggers a chain reaction that results in substance/consciousness. In a mystical form, we know this as the Word – *In the beginning was the Word.*[1] Everything in creation works in octaves, in patterns, and it is these octaves and patterns that a magician triggers when doing magic.

By talking to something with magical focus *and intent*, you recreate that act in a very small way and even though it is the simplest, tiniest form of the action, it triggers a magical flow of power: it is a catalyst. As an apprentice you learn to talk to everything while also learning the outer actions and tools that engage with this magical creative power, along with meeting some of the beings involved. As an initiate, you build on that experience and learn to engage with the beings that work with the process. As an adept you learn to utter into life.

If you talk to natural living things like plants, trees, creatures, insects, rivers, storms, you are talking to a consciousness that is already there. By talking to them, you are taking the first step towards the threshold of the inner garden: the physical manifestation of something is only the outer shell for something far more powerful and

---

[1] John 1:1 New Testament King James Bible.

profound that fills that shell. This *inner garden*, or to put it more technically *the inner landscape*, gives you immediate access to the power source that is already partially formed and is therefore stable to work with.

By talking to everything living around you, you also signal that you are waking up; that you are willing to be an active part of the world around you, not just a passenger. And slowly you will find that things start to talk back to you, using your mind and also the physical world around you as interfaces. This begins a conversation that grows into a friendship based on mutual respect, and from that friendship the magician gains support, learning, fellowship, and companionship.

Often, working in that harmonic way eventually catches the attention of larger land beings, deities, and ancient ancestors in the area, so that over a period of time your working team becomes bigger. That also results in learning how to work magically as a team of beings, so that it is not always about you and your work, but is also often about the needs of everything around you.

This team acts like a power substation and allows you to plug into a power source that is already managed: it is like the fuse box of your house as opposed to the power generating station. So although at a magical technical level you are intentionally seeking a source of power to work with, it manifests as communicating and then working with the beings around you.

1. Talking to vessels

The same sideways view is also true of the *vessel*. In magic we often think of the vessel as a cup, or in advanced magic as a golem or an enlivened statue that holds consciousness and/or power. And yes, those are examples of magical vessels. But the building where you work magic and the inner landscape around you are also vessels: the inner landscape is the natural vessel and the building you work in can be turned into a vessel that can receive and hold power.

Before you learn to turn a vessel into a magical vessel (a skill which you will learn later in the apprentice section), first you must learn about the more expansive vessel potentials around you. The way to start that learning process is to 'switch on' the building vessel and then also learn to pass into the inner landscape as a vessel and work with it. To switch on a building as a vessel, you talk to everything around and within it (opens the door for the consciousness and power), and then you tune the frequency of the space though ritual magical action (working the directions and the gates). If you think of that switch action as like a dimmer switch, these two simple actions are akin to turning a light on, but very dimmed. Later, you will learn to fully integrate a building with the inner landscape, create and open gates (both inner and outer) for that building and then join everything up. That turns the building into an enlivened vessel: the first stage towards turning it into a true power temple.

There are two basic types of vessels; those that mimic species and those that do not. Let's talk about the sort that do not (you will learn about species vessels in another lesson). The vessels we are going to work with are buildings, cars, jars... basically anything that does not have a face and is man-made. There are also natural versions of this type of vessel: rocks, mountains, etc., which we will learn about later. But the man made ones tend to surround us the most. Anything that has physical substance can be a container. A container for what?

They can contain extensions of your own consciousness (a thought-form, for example) or they can become places of habitation for spirits. You can achieve this through the use of magical patterns, which is something you will learn later on, or through a more natural route, which you will learn first.

The natural route is triggered by talking to something as if it were a being. This creates an inner doorway for a spirit or consciousness to step into the vessel. Straight away you can see the good side to this, and also the bad side. The good side is having a being which is not parasitical step into the vessel (a parasitical being is only there to eat your energy) and which is willing to work with you in return for a home, interaction, companionship, and entertainment. The bad side tends to happen if the vessel is not properly tuned, and as a result becomes filled with parasites and low-level beings.

The way to avoid a parasitical or unhealthy being stepping into a vessel is the focused intent and approach of the magician. You will learn about beings later on in the apprentice section, but before you get there you need to know how beings operate around us. Focused intent is a major part of the skill set of the magician, and by focused intent I mean talking to something with the intention that the 'something' is a vessel for a being that you intend to interact with magically.

Let's have a look at some practical examples, which will demonstrate to you these dynamics far better than a theoretical exploration can.

2. Random inhabitation

An inexperienced magician spends a couple of years doing regular magical work in their home. He does rituals, calls, visions, experiments, alchemy, etc. but in a haphazard way, without any true, defined intent or focus other than curiosity, and he does it in isolation to everything else around him. He may cast a circle, do a banishing, and then get to work.

Over a period of time the magician starts to weaken, have bouts of depression and low energy, he gets a string of minor illnesses, and the house always feels 'uncomfortable' to those who visit. It always seems dark, no matter how many lights are on; it feels sticky, and no matter how much he cleans, it never quite feels right. This is the outer manifestation of working in such an isolated and haphazard way.

Now let's change perspective and look at the same situation from an inner point of view.

When our magician moves into a house and begins doing magic, it 'turns on a light' in the inner world and he becomes visible. Spirits are curious and draw near.

But the magician does a circle and banishing, which appears in the inner world as "fuck off to everyone except the person I call." So the spirits draw away, disappointed and sometimes offended. The parasitical beings, however, see the energy being generated and draw nearer. They are not bothered by the magician's hostile approach and they watch him, looking for a way into that yummy scene.

The magician casts a circle and does a pentagram banishing. But such a system pattern is weak and ineffectual. The initial resistance that the parasites get from this banishing action is quickly overcome as they get used to it and see a way in.

Every time the magician does this action and then goes on to do magic, it generates energy that the parasites are drawn to. They all gather around and feed furiously upon the magician's own energy and the energy he is generating. They dress up and pretend to be the entity the magician is trying to summon, and a relationship is formed. Eventually they move into the house and begin to multiply. Think in terms of ticks or fleas.

Soon the word gets around that there is an easy source of food, and the word is passed along as to how to dodge the weak defence created by the magician. Soon the house, the magician's body, and his energy sphere are full of small, low-intelligence, low-life beings who feed happily on this new food source. If these beings are lucky, the magician uses sexual power, drugs, adrenaline, and god knows what else in their magic, which in turn creates a wonderful buffet of food for these beings.

All the while the more intelligent spirits, who feel insulted by the rejection (the magician's banishing ritual) and who do not wish to feed off the magician, watch in amusement from a safe distance. They were willing to make friends, do work, and live alongside someone who could potentially see, hear, and work with them. But the magician had, through his banishing, made it very clear they were not welcome.

That scenario is a very common one and is propagated by innocence and poor training. The first mistake is to assume that everything needs banishing; the second mistake is to assume that the magical casting of a circle and a banishment actually works and works powerfully. Most of the time they don't. And just as an aside, bear in mind that the pentagram ritual taught in the original Golden Dawn training – and virtually all subsequent ritual magical schools/groups – was never meant to be a powerful banishing technique: it was a beginner exercise, just as the ritual work in Module II is beginner level. The GD version just looks flashier.

If a powerful being wants to get into your space, it will do so and no amount of banishment will stop it. Why? Because most methods of basic banishing draw upon the individual strength of the magician (regardless of the use of Divine names). This way of working also rejects beings that would be very helpful: it does not stop them getting in, but the unfriendly attitude turns them off. And it also does *not* stop beings that are looking for a dinner...

Think of it like security guards at a nightclub. If you are the manager, your job is to manage everything, not handle the security. For that job you employ large, muscled people who are well-trained in conflict resolution, defence, and restraint techniques. They also usually throw a mean punch, and in some countries will be well-armed. The same principles apply in working magic. You are the manager, and you outsource the security to those better able than yourself. And for your own safety, you also learn hand-to-hand combat, weapon use, and keep well muscled: for magicians, that comes from working with different power patterns.

So what is the answer? Let's have a look at a different scenario.

3. Magical inhabitation

A magician moves into a house and begins to work magically in the space. He works with magical patterns that root him in the role of fulcrum: Divinity as the breath (no dogmatic religious form), the tools of balance, the rooting in the ancestral line (buffer and shield), and the working with the inner and outer directions (power sources).

The space begins to 'tune' to a certain energetic frequency, and an inner energetic pattern starts to build in the house. The four gates begin to appear in the inner landscape of the house, and through those gates, deeper inner beings that are tuned to specific powers and contacts begin to leave their energetic signature in the space.

This turns all the inner energetic lights on, and the spirits, beings, and parasites in the area become aware of the magician and start to draw near. They get to the house, but the parasites are stopped from entering the space by the guardians of the thresholds in the four directions. Also, the energetic frequency of the space (that has been generated by the focused magical work) shifts and tunes to a point where the space becomes uncomfortable for these low-life beings to stay in. It is like one of those high-frequency noises that humans cannot hear but which is unbearable for mice.

The more intelligent nature beings find that they can enter the space, usually through the gates, as the guardians of the thresholds see that their presence would be mutually beneficial for the magician and the beings. They pass into the space, join in energetically with the ritual work, and some decide to stay. Their inclusion gives the magician access to a group power from the beings who work in cooperation with him. They stay, live in the space, and earn their keep by guarding, assisting, and teaching/learning. They embed themselves into the substance of the building (which has now become a magical vessel) that is now compatible with that type of being, or they come and go from the land outside like friends popping in for tea.

From the magician's perspective, he builds the magical patterns in the house, and he talks/works regularly with each of the four gatekeepers by lighting the directional candle, communing with the inner contact, bowing, and then getting to work. When the magician meditates, he acknowledges the gates and the gatekeepers/

contacts, and that regular interaction keeps a door open that allows those guardians to have a constant presence in the house.

The magician also talks to the house itself. He tells the house when visitors are coming, or when there may be a threat, or if he is going to be away for any length of time: he talks to the house in the same way we would talk to our pets. By doing this act in a focused way, it creates a doorway for interaction and informs the beings in the vessel of changes to the space's energy, which in turn makes it a lot less likely that they would be triggered adversely by a visitor or shift in the routine of the magician (and talking to the house as the vessel, rather than addressing just the beings, helps to solidify the structure of the house as a vessel for power).

Slowly but steadily the right beings move into the house or visit regularly. The beings communicate through the mind of the magician, though sometimes also through physical acts (for example, moving things to get the magicians attention) and they begin to teach the magician how to do certain magical acts better or more productively. They also alert the magician to things that the spirits or the land may need help with, so it becomes a mutual relationship. This is a very old way of working, and has many layers to it.

The magician introduces certain working deities into the space, and eventually the house becomes a collective of humans, deities, spirits, and land beings, all of whom work together to a collective goal. That is a vessel filled with power and which mimics an octave of creation. The first step of that is the healthy and tuned magical patterning in the house, and the second is talking to the vessels: talking to the house which allows the house to become a vessel for beings to inhabit.

4. The Inner Landscape

The second part of vessel/creation learning is the inner landscape. I don't want to go into too much depth here, as I want you to get on to practical work. Essentially, the inner landscape of the land is the inner spirit and template for the creation of the manifest world, including all beings/species. And that is where it gets interesting. When you go out onto the land in vision, you pass into the inner landscape, which is like the default template for that land. So it often looks like how the land would have appeared in that area before humans started inhabiting and changing it.

Now we get to the weird bit. Humans have a template of creation as well, but when you pass into one of these, it does not appear as an 'inner human'; rather it, too, appears as a landscape. For the longest time I assumed that this presentation was something to do with how my own mind worked. But once I got into deep discussions with other magicians who had also found out how to access their own inner templates, they too found that they had broken into an inner landscape. It appears that the inner landscape is the inner vessel that our spirit is poured into as we pass into life: our pattern and the pattern of the land are inextricably linked.

When you work magically you stand, from a spirit and energetic sense, in the inner landscape of the land. If the temple is tuned, it will also appear in the inner landscape, as will the gates. You can do that passively, or you can draw upon that inner landscape to further fuel and balance your magical work. So let's get to practicalities.

5. *Task:* Connecting with the inner landscape

The first exercise is to connect with the inner landscape around you. You can do this either in a passive way or in a magically defined way. You have already stepped into part of the inner landscape in a passive way when you went in vision across the land to connect with a river, a mountain, etc. As you walked, you passed from civilisation to wilder land. That is a simple, natural crossing of the threshold into the inner landscape in a very simple way. The way the land presented in that work is very similar to how the landscape reveals itself to you in dreams and through traditional shamanic vision quests.

As a magician working from a magical space, there is a more technical way to access this inner landscape that brings it into focus with your ritual work and space. This method still uses vision to start with, and then once you have established the ability to work with vision you introduce ritual and combine the two together to make a whole magical act. That enables you to begin the process of learning how to align with, and then tap into, the stream of creation as it flows into the world.

For the practical work of this lesson, you are going to do a vision, then a ritual, and finally a ritualised vision. Then you will do tarot readings to check your progress and the results of your work. Let's work first with the inner landscape. Read the various steps and keys for this vision, and once you are familiar with them, then it is time to do the vision for yourself. The more you do this formed visionary method and practise it, the more your mind will begin to step into the inner worlds in spontaneous vision and dreams: it gives your mind a method of working that it will begin to play with in its own time.

The ritual: Working with the inner landscape

Work in your ritual space. Put a pen and paper on the east altar and also on the west altar. Put your tarot cards on the central altar. Get a piece of white thread that will fit and tie loosely and comfortably around your ankle. Place the thread on the south altar.

Go around the directions as you have learned, light all the candles, see the gates open, and then go sit down in front of the central altar, with your back to the north.

Still your mind with a brief meditation. When you are ready, with your inner vision, see the room around you. See the gates in the four directions and see them open with inner contacts standing on the thresholds.

In vision, stand up and walk around the directions, acknowledging the contacts in the four directions, and then stand before the west altar. Step through the west altar and pass through the gates and walk until you find yourself standing out on a landscape.

Look back and see your work space with the four gates surrounding a flame. Stand for a moment and just look.

As you watch, you will slowly start to see other beings appearing at the gates and standing on the threshold, looking at the flame. Watch how the guardians react to these beings. You will notice that the guardians allow some beings to pass into the ritual space and reject others. The ones who are allowed near the flame will be faery beings, land beings, or ancestral beings from your area.

If you can get a sense of how they look or feel, try to remember that, as it will help you to identify them later in your magical work. But don't worry if you cannot fix on how they present. Don't try and force it: you will pick up the necessary signatures in your own time. Now turn away from the ritual space and start walking. You will find yourself walking in a natural landscape. Walk on the land in a large circle around the ritual space, but keep a reasonable distance.

As you get into an area of the landscape that aligns with a gate, have a look around. What does the landscape look like? Is it healthy? Is it rocky? Is there water? Sea? Hills? Caves? Go around and look at the land that is beyond each gate by walking the inner landscape around the outside of the ritual space.

Can you see buildings made by humans? If so, they are either tuned, consecrated, or have been there for a very long time. You may see buildings that do not appear in the outer world: those are buildings that slowly became vessels for one reason or another, and when the outer building was torn down the inner pattern of the building stayed. But bear in mind it is unusual to see a building in the inner landscape.

If you want to, at another time, you can use these visionary steps to explore the landscape in the wider areas around where you live: this will help you find local ancient temples, ritual burials or natural power vortexes. But for now you are going to work in a magical, systematic way.

Turn and go back to the west threshold, but instead of seeing yourself step back into the room, step over the threshold of the gate with the intention that you are going to reveal the inner landscape that runs through the ritual space (what is there in the inner land where your house does not show).

As you step through, let the landscape extend into your work space: see the land, the trees, water, whatever as they emerge, and see it appear in the ritual space until the four gates and the flame in the centre of the room appear to be in the wild of nature. Walk around the ritual space and notice if any streams of water, ancient trees, or any sort of feature appears within the ritual space.

Go to the central candle and step into it. Stand within the flame in vision: you will realise that you do not burn; rather the flame energises you. Stand facing south, with the east gate on your left and the west gate on your right. Feel a wind flow straight down from above onto you and flow through you: this is the Divine Breath.

Hold your arms out in vision, feel the rock beneath your feet and the wind flowing down over and through you.

See ahead of you, through the south gate, the road into the future with the Noble Guardians standing there, and feel a gathering of spirits/ancestors behind you: these are most likely not your blood ancestors, but the spirits of people still sleeping in the land.

Turn your head to the left and look. A large and strange-looking being steps through the east gate and stands beside you. The being is much larger than you, and they stand slightly behind you with one hand on your left hand and one hand on your left shoulder. Now turn your head and look to your right. You find that your hand is on the rim of a large stone jar that is almost as big as you are. You can see in to it. As you look into it, you see lots of things that you recognise but cannot quite get a fix on: a bit like waking up from a dream where the memories quickly fade. The jar may be full or half full.

You keep looking at the jar, as it fascinates you. So many things in it feel and look familiar, but you are not sure what they are.

As you watch the jar, a being, once again large and strange-looking, steps through the west gates and picks up your jar. He looks down at the floor beneath the jar, and you notice that the floor is smooth, solid rock.

The being takes your hand from the rim of the jar and tips the contents of the jar onto the stone floor. He stands the jar back up and begins beating its contents on the floor with a thin stick. The contents break apart: some of it turns to dust and blows away, some of it stays behind.

The being then squats down and picks through what is left. The large being to your left pushes down on your shoulder to make you kneel on the stone floor so that you can touch the contents left on the floor. Both beings signal for you to touch one of the remaining contents.

You reach out and touch something. Immediately you have a memory of an experience you had in the past. It is a strong memory, maybe something you had forgotten about, but it comes back to you and you remember the situation, your emotions, and your actions.

Spend a little time thinking about your actions and think not about the effect your actions had on others, but the direct effect it had upon yourself.

Take as long as you need to if you wish to touch the other fragments, and think how that situation affected you in the short and long term.

The being from the west blows upon all the contents on the stone, gathers them up and places them in your pocket. In your meditations you can take one out a time and explore a situation/memory to ascertain what you learned from it, how you have

Module III – The Power Dynamics of Creation

potentially matured from it (or not), and what insights it gives you into yourself and your own path.

The jar is now empty, or so you think, until you stand back up and look into the jar, and you see that it is filled with water: it is ready to receive new energetic memories. The being from the west stays with the jar: he is the guardian of the vessel. You stand, looking at the south, with the large being to your left, who is the guardian of the sword, and the guardian of the vessel to your right.

Now open your eyes while still retaining a sense of the beings in the space with you. This is time for a break. The walking through the west gates and surveying the land is something you can do a lot if you wish.

Now it is time to get back to work: have a stretch and then sit back down. This next part is a working technique of visionary ritual, so practise it and remember it (see notes below).

6. *Task:* Visionary ritual of mediation

You are going to work with a foundational visionary ritual method that in this instance is for a specific task: the mediation and birth (creation) process of the two main ritual tools. Although the way you are going to do this is specific to two different tools, the actual baseline technique can be used for any form of power mediation, something you will work with again in different forms.

Once more sit back down facing south with the central altar before you. Close your eyes. See with your inner vision the four gates around you. See the large being to your left and the being and vessel to your right. You are going to trigger a faint flow of creative power. Do this by seeing a line of bright light come down from the stars into the room. As it hits the room it triggers a similar line of light that passes through the east gate into the room.

As it flows from the east into the room, the large being to your left holds out their left hand and slows the flow of light/power down until it changes colour to a bright yellow. The being emits a sound as the light hits his hand. Remember that sound.

The yellow light passes through the being's hand and flows into the central flame. From there it travels from the central flame to the south altar and passes through the south gates, vanishing into the distance.

Watch the south gate. The light returns as a red line of power, flows at an angle from south to west, and is held in the western flame. You see the being in the west holding the vessel full of water, and the flame sits on top of the water. There it changes colour again, taking on a deep blue colour. The blue light then travels back to the central flame, changing to black, and immediately flows north but also straight down below the central flame, passing deep into the earth. You have worked with this pattern before, and it is the inner energetic template for creative and destructive energy in its completed flow.

Now open your eyes and stand up. Walk a full circle around the directions and then walk to the east altar. With your eyes open, be aware through inner vision/imagination of the constant flow of energy flowing into the room from the east and from above.

The large being moves in front of you, standing within the east altar. The being places a hand upon your chest and you reach out, both physically and in vision, and place your left hand upon their shoulder.

Take in a deep breath. As you breathe in, a symbol appears upon the forehead of the large being. You may see it in your imagination, or you may 'sense' what it looks like. Take your time with this and do not try to force anything. When you have a good idea of the symbol shape, pick up the pen on the altar and draw it on the piece of paper.

Everyone works slightly differently with this technique. If no symbol appears in your inner vision, then simply pick up the pen and let the being guide your hand. Draw out whatever comes. After that, mark the paper with an L shape but where each side is equal length (half a two-dimensional square) above the symbol.

Once you have written that down, with your inner vision see the large being move to the right of the altar, so that he stands on the south side of the east altar. He places his right hand on the altar and stays there. Every time you work in this ritual space, keep an awareness of this being: he will now stay there until you complete your work with your soon-to-come magical sword.

Now bow, turn, and go to the west altar. With your eyes open, stand before the west altar and keep an awareness of the large vessel that is upon or within the west altar, and be aware of the being there.

As you look at the vessel, the being draws your attention to shapes, patterns, or symbols on the vessel. Close your eyes. Use your inner vision to look carefully at the patterns on the vessel and one in particular, a symbol, stands out and is bright. Remember the shape of it, open your eyes, and write down the shape of the symbol on the paper that is on the altar.

Above the symbol write a reversed capital L (so the foot of the L points left instead of right) and again write it as half of a two-dimensional square (each side is equal). These symbols are the sigils that will be unique to your magical tools and to the beings that will inhabit them (the beings you are working with).

The being stays in the west altar, holding the vessel, and will stay there until you complete your work with your magical cup in an upcoming lesson. So from now on, every time you work in this room, see both of these beings standing there, waiting. Step back, bow, and walk a full circle around the directions.

Go and stand before the east altar. Be aware of the being. Close your eyes. See a wind flowing through the east gate and blowing over you. Take in a deep breath. Turn your head to the right (south) and breath out with the intention of passing to the south the breath you took in from the east. A priest or priestess appears on the threshold of the east gate. See them with your inner vision. Do not ask their name, just acknowledge them with a bow of your head.

Take note of how this person is dressed. Do not try to dress them with your own imagination, just let them appear as they want you to see them. If you do not get a clear sense of how they are dressed or what they look like, don't worry: just be aware that they are there. They are there to simply witness your words.[2]

Take in another deep breath from the wind of the east and feel the large being at the side of the altar place a hand upon your right shoulder (right when standing facing east is future deeds).

Breathe out and recite:

> "I strive to honour the Divine Breath
> through my breath, my words, and my songs.
> I accept the guardian of the Sword
> and I am willing to be taught by the guardian of the Sword
> in whatever way is necessary, in my magical life and my daily life,
> so that I learn to work in a balanced way with power."

Step back, bow, and go to the south.

Stand before the south altar and with your eyes open, use your inner vision/imagination to see the south gate, and beyond the south gate a road or pathway in full midday sun. Pick up the white thread and hold it in your left hand. Now close your eyes. Using your inner vision, see the Noble Ones on the path before you. These are men/women who shine brightly. One of them walks towards you, passes through the gates, and holds out their hand. See yourself handing them the white thread. Physically hold out the thread over the altar (be careful of the candle flame).

The Noble One pulls a white thread from within themselves and places it into your white thread: through this thread, you will be connected to them, and when you work in vision and stand at the inner threshold, they will recognise you (don't worry if the thread falls off before you get to that vision in a future lesson, once it has been on you for however long it needs to be there, it will fall off but leave an inner imprint upon you).

When the Noble One steps back, withdraw your hand and open your eyes.

Tie the white thread around your left ankle, and do it slightly loosely so that the thread can stay there for a prolonged length of time without restricting your ankle when your ankle flexes. Step back from the altar, bow, turn, and circle the directions, and finish in the east. Be aware of the being there. Leaving the gates open, blow the candle out, bow, step back, and repeat by putting out the candles in each direction, and the centre one last.

---

[2] See note two: the importance and power dynamic of the recitation, below.

Note one

The emptying of the vessel is a one-off event in vision. It is not something you repeat (you get one chance as an apprentice when you step into magic to have the being assist you in the emptying).

However, should you wish to do a regular (once a year) look over your *Harvest* (also known as your deeds in the Book of Judgement), it can be useful and insightful (and can be profound at times) to spend a couple of weeks of each year meditating upon your actions (regardless of good and bad), pondering on the effect they had upon you and whether you have learned from your mistakes. In Judaism there is a form of this known as Yom Kippur. We will look again at this concept in lesson four in a more practical and magical way.

7. What just happened?

First you connected with the inner landscape which made you more visible to the inner beings around you, and you learned what inner powers are in the land upon which you live.

The work with the sword being and the vessel being taught you the flow dynamics of creation. Power *in* from east/above, power *existing* through east to south via the centre (the centre axis holds the Void that everything flows in and out of), power *breaking down* from south/future to west/threshold of destruction, power *composting* from west to north via the centre and down. You have already worked before with that pattern, but now it needs to build in your understanding from an abstract flow of power into patterns of shape, beings, and tools.

From this understanding, you will start to fully understand the tool/direction/elemental families and the patterns and combinations they work through. Through that understanding, you will then be able to see such patterns used in ancient magic and mysticism. You will also start to see the constant dance of creation and destruction as it flows in a constant pattern in manifestation.

You connected with two beings of the tools: the two guardians and governors who oversee and work through and with the magical tools. These two foundational tools always have beings working within them. You will learn how to operate with them through the tools, and in turn they will guide you by putting learning in your path, and they will protect you from serious danger – but not from your own stupidity or arrogance.

The white thread upon the left ankle is a connection with the Noble Ones of the future, also known as the Sandalphon: these are angelic beings that guide and work with magicians deep in the inner worlds, and who also act as magical companions as you work (you will learn more in another lesson in this module). The white thread is your first connection to one of these beings and begins a very quiet, slow process of adjusting your body to their power, so that when you come to work with them in the inner worlds, your body will not be impacted by their communion with you (and they will recognise you).

It is placed on the leg that stands upon the Grindstone, something you will learn a lot more about in the next lesson. This energetically connects the companion/Noble One to the energetic flow of the Grindstone power that will flow through your outer and magical life. You will learn to work in combination with the Noble One, the inhabited sword, and the Grindstone power in order to learn, mature, and strengthen as a magician.

The vessel is the scale of Ma'at and is the vessel that records and weighs your deeds. You will slowly learn, by working with the vessel and the being, to weigh your own scales and keep your own balance in your life and magical work. The symbols from the east and the west will be inscribed upon your magical tools and will seal the connection between the tool and the beings connected to them.

Note two: the importance and power dynamic of the recitation

Done in visionary ritual, this is not a 'feel-good' or psychological affirmation: you are starting to tune into the power of the east as an apprentice magician and certain responsibilities come with that. These responsibilities are nothing to do with ethics or morals, but about how the power of utterance works for a magician. The more you tap into power, the more your utterances will become conduits for power. Your written and spoken words will slowly gain power and will mediate power and energy. Because of this, you will have to learn to guard your words for yourself. That is a complex learning curve and the guardian of the sword will guide you when necessary, but it is better to do it for yourself (your own lessons are easier than those of the sword).

This does not mean "you must never speak a bad word" – that is an unbalanced misunderstanding of the power. Sometimes harsh words are necessary, sometimes destructive utterances are necessary. You will have to learn what, when, and how to mediate this utterance power through trial and error, as it is unique to you. Just know that you cannot switch it on and off: it is constant.

In your everyday life, from this point on, if you misuse your voice in some way you will know about it. You will be either physically, mentally, emotionally, or magically affected. What you have done by reciting in front of the witness, and engaging with the power of the sword, is that you have given permission/accepted the dynamic of governance from the inner worlds. This speeds up your evolution, learning and fate. Every time you do something that is badly imbalanced, you will get an almost immediate reaction, to teach you (not punish you) and limit you until you get back on track. Without this dynamic, you cannot step into deeper magic, or if you do you are far less likely to be guarded and taught, and far less likely to stay in one piece mentally or physically. You will essentially be on your own.

It can all seem a bit scary, but this process started for me at the age of sixteen and I can tell you, the backlash of power misuse is almost instant. But it was a good teacher and also an excellent guardian.

My writing springs from that dynamic, as did a lot of my learning. The process is not temporary; it is with you for life, and it most certainly helps to form you into a better, stronger, and more mature vessel.

8. READINGS

You are going to do three readings.
For the first one, use the Tree of Life layout and ask the question:

"What is the power of the being that is the guardian of the Sword for me?"

The last card tells you what type of power runs through the being, and that in turn will indicate to you what sort of power focus will flow through your magical sword when you come to enliven it and work with it.

For the second reading you will use the four-directional spread and your question will be:

"Show me the health of the inner landscape of the land where I live."

That reading will show you if there are any unbalanced, destructive, or unhealthy energies in the inner landscape (not just the outer land). If you see problems, just note them down for now.

The third reading also uses the four-directional layout. You will ask:

"Show me difficulties in the inner landscape that I should work on, but only show me ones that I am currently capable of working on."

If something appears in the reading that is a problem, do the vision work where you go through the gates and out into the inner landscape. See what you can find, and work according to your instincts and what you know. If it looks dirty, clean it up. If an aggressive being is there, ask it to leave. Don't put yourself at any great risk, but do what you can.

If you don't know what to do, think about what you would do if the images presented to you were something you encountered in your physical life, and go from there.

Write down all of your findings in your computer log and also take note of what you did. Make sure you write it down while it is still fresh in your mind, including any strange details.

9. THE TOOLS AND SYMBOLS

Leave the symbol drawings on your altar if you leave your room permanently set out. If not, put them somewhere safe in the east and west of the room. You will get them back out when you come to enliven and work on your magical tools, something which is coming up soon in the course.

You should have already have ordered, bought, or found your sword by now (remember you were told to start the process of getting a sword). If you have not, now is the time to do it. If you have it, place it in the east and tie the paper with the symbol on it around the blade of the sword. Keep it in the east of the room, and do not use or touch it for now.

Also now is the time to get a vessel. You will need a cup or bowl that is metal, thick ceramic, or wood. When you get it, tie the paper with the symbol onto it and put it somewhere safe in the west. Now is also time to start looking for another magical tool, a lesser-known one, and that is a set of scales. And by scales I do not mean cooking electronic weight scales, but old-fashioned scales with a central pole and a cup on each side. Make sure you get ones that actually work, and where the T bar can move and the scales stand upright (not hanging ones). Scales like those shown in Figure 6.

Start looking for them now, as it may take you a while to find them. Look in online stores, junk stores, anywhere that you may find them. When you get them, wash them and place them either on your west altar, behind the west altar, or in the middle of the west wall in the room where you work.

Figure 6: Scales

Lesson 3

The Grindstone

You have already begun to look, in small ways, at the polarised threshold powers that act as a barrier to the deeper inner worlds, and therefore to deeper magic. For an apprentice magician to try and engage directly with these powers would be folly: they are non-emotional angelic powers that simply fry anything that reaches too far across the threshold if that reaching is done in ignorance.

So first the apprentice is introduced to these powers through simple outer ritual and understanding that has no power behind it, and through basic magical and non-magical acts. Then they inch in a bit more in vision, but still staying within their own realm. You have done both of these, even if you did not realise it at the time. This step-by-step approach allows you to strengthen, become aware of, and learn the rules of engagement before you stumble across the power lines.

The next step in your learning about these threshold keepers is to learn how their power expresses through the human life and mind, so that by learning consciously your subconscious also learns, adapts, and develops. The mind, emotions, actions, and energy drives in a human are the filter through which these powers express first.

By approaching these aspects of our own existence, we are then better armed in our subconscious to be able to walk in a balanced way between these two powers in order to enter the depths of the inner realms safely and productively. Once you have seen and recognised how these powers operate in your life, you will come to see how they operate magically and mystically. The key words of the Grindstone in its manifestation through life are *restraint*, *labour*, *perseverance*, and *patience*: the qualities of Saturn. Through engaging these qualities with magical intent in our everyday lives, our deeper spirit also engages these qualities, and they subsequently flow through our magical acts. That in turn allows us to work with far greater amounts of power without serious risk of damaging our minds and bodies.

1. The angelic power

Although we will look in depth at angelic beings later in the apprentice section, it is useful to look at the angelic powers that flow through, and are the source of, these two polarised powers: the angelic manifestations of the Grindstone and the Unraveller.

These two powers are not the type of angelic beings that we have been exposed to through religious or magical teachings. Rather they are a step removed from the material and human world, and they do not have the dressing that we usually associate with angels. In essence, they are strong powers that each do one specific job, like two giant magnets: they create a barrier.

In the inner worlds that barrier appears as guardians who challenge you, and also as an unseen energy that bounces you out of vision. In life their power expresses through fate patterns, and they trigger events or they pour power into events. In magic, those two presentations become more immediate, more powerful, and more direct in their actions.

Each of these two polarised powers has many different expressions; hence each one has its own lesson in this module, so that we can look at them in depth. Some of you who already have some experience of magic (or who are magicians revisiting training) will already have an understanding of what I am saying. For those who are new or relatively new to magic, what follows may all seem a bit difficult to understand, but stay with me, as we will approach this from a human perspective which you will indeed recognise.

Although these are powerful, deep angelic beings, and they operate in depth throughout creation from a single cell to a species, landmass, or nation, how they directly affect you as an apprentice magician is best viewed, understood, and worked with through life experience and visionary ritual. This way, your conscious mind, subconscious mind, and physical body can slowly absorb the knowledge, adjust to the power flows, and learn to be around and work with these vast beings without getting fried or going mad. It is also a much more direct way to learn than to sit and try to philosophically or intellectually understand them.

This lesson looks at the Grindstone, the left hand side of the polarity.[1] In magical ritual, this power is externalised in its weakest form as the sword and as the Grindstone that your left foot stands upon. That is the baby step. But then we need to grow up. So the next stage is to look at the dynamics and effects this power has on our lives. The Grindstone does not just flow through the lives of magicians; it flows through all life, and in humans you will instantly recognise its influence once we get to look at it.

The only difference for a magician is that the magician learns to consciously engage and work with this power, first through their life and outer ritual, and then in deeper vision and direct contact as an adept. To get to that adept stage and be able to have that direct contact without being destroyed, first the magician must recognise and understand its weakest, most outer influence in human life. That awareness opens the doors within you, and starts a deep energetic conversation with your subconscious and with your eternal spirit.

First we will look at the actual power dynamic of the Grindstone, and look at why it does what it does. Then we will look at the practicalities of how that expresses through your daily life.

---

[1] Which has nothing to do with the 'Left Hand Path' in magic.

2. The Role of the Grindstone in creation

In its deepest role, the Grindstone slows down the speed and vibration of energy so that it can be formed into matter. Through restriction the energy becomes denser, stronger, and more able to be contained in a vessel. The Grindstone's opposite is the Unraveller, which frees up over-restriction or breaks down the density of something in order either for it to become more fluid or to break it down and compost it.

At a magical level the Grindstone creates barriers that protect the inner worlds from stupid humans, and protects stupid humans from the onslaught of power that is inherent within the inner worlds. It limits your magical actions so that you become more solid in your power as a magician, and also helps to prevent you overreaching (unless that overreaching is necessary for you).

In terms of magical power, it is the dynamic which shapes power and gives it boundaries in order for it to be contained: a ritual is an extension of the Grindstone power, as is the sword, the key steps within visionary magic, the use of a sigil, etc. It is the power that constructs a magical form that is then filled with contact and energy. So you begin to see why it is so vital for a magician to understand it. But it cannot be understood intellectually; it has to be experienced both magically and through everyday, conscious life – that way, you truly understand it on every level. Once you understand it, you can engage it magically.

On an individual level, for humans, this power weaves into your fate pattern, which is a dynamic pattern that is constantly shifting and evolving (it is not a fixed, rigid path), and drops the energy of restriction into that fate weave. This is to slow the person down, and to present them with barriers that they must overcome in order to strengthen and mature them physically, emotionally, and mentally.

It can present though life experiences, external influences, cultural restrictions, physical restrictions, disciplined training, or through mental or emotional issues. A developing magician learns to spot that action and engage it by applying the Grindstone power consciously and directly to their lives where it is needed. The presentation of the Grindstone in the fate pattern is energy, not events: how that energy expresses itself in your life is very much dependant on your choices, actions, the society you live in, your body, mind, and the state of the species. It is both personal to you and also impersonal; it affects the individual and the collective. The task of a magician is to recognise this energy when it is present and active in your life and work, and to work with it, fully engaging it rather than being swept along by it. That is one of the major differences between a magician and a non-magician. When the Grindstone is expressing through the collective, through your society, it is important as a magician to spot that and work with it so that you are neither its victim nor 'swept up' by the current as it passes through. Rather you recognise it, and then see where you can work with it or side-step it – whichever is appropriate to the situation.

At a creation level, this power also dynamically works through nature and is part of the constant change and evolution of the planet, the landscape, and the elements: it is one arm of the re-balancer. Once you learn to recognise this power in action in your own life and in your own society, then you will more easily also spot it in action in nature. Throughout history, religion and magic, or aspects of such, Man has sought to control, limit, or deflect this power, which has always simply resulted in disaster at some level or other. You cannot control this power and you cannot stop it: it is a part of life itself. Once we look at the aspects of this power in everyday life, you will start to recognise where magicians throughout history have tried to dodge its power or have been swept along by it unconsciously, in ignorance. And yet, to understand this power and to work with it in your life and magic is to tap into one of the greatest resources of power known to man. But to do that and not be destroyed, the magician needs to tap into this power with gnosis. So let's look at how this power expresses itself through the human life.

3. The Grindstone in life

In a non-magical life, the Grindstone presents through life situations which prevent you from doing what you want to do or which force you to do something you do not want to do. That is the simplest way to put it.

That power triggers the energy on the fate path, and how that presents depends on the person, their situation, and their culture. It is much stronger in some individuals than in others. If a person does not need that power in their lives to restrict them, or if they overly self-restrict, the opposing power is more dominant in their lives (the Unraveller). Essentially, one major way this dynamic expresses is to teach you the difference between what you want and what you need. That in turn highlights to you your weaknesses and vulnerabilities.

This same dynamic that appears in the life of an individual is also mirrored or appears in a society or culture. This power, like all powers in creation, works in octaves: the deepest pattern of the power repeats at different frequencies as it steps down and becomes more formed and personal. But the actual underlying dynamic stays the same. When we look back in history and we come across powerful and dynamic shifts in a society, we can often spot the activation of the Grindstone, or the Unraveller, or both. People who have little internal strength or are 'switched off' are often swept along by these power tides, and the result is a huge shift in how a nation thinks or behaves. When a nation is involved (1930s Germany is a good example), there are often many different types of beings involved that are mediators of the powers of Grindstone and Unraveller: they work behind the scenes in various manifestations. An adept magician can often spot these manifestations and either get out of the way or work carefully to clear the road ahead for that nation.

In a magical life the same dynamic applies, but it is recognised for what it is: a necessary step that needs to be understood, learned, and worked with. As the magician gets deeper into magic, one of the two dynamics may (though not always) engage more powerfully than the other, the result of which being that fate is 'sped up,' or, that is to say, that the lessons come thick and fast.

So for example, an apprentice magician engages the Grindstone by being aware of where they need to apply self-restriction or patience in their life, and rather than fight blocks in their life, they learn to engage them and work with them. The initiate learns to use the magical sword in ritual/vision to create a restrictive pattern that contains and limits power in a magical act or project. The adept learns to mediate or *bridge* through themselves the raw power of the Grindstone into a magical pattern, a land area, a person, or an event.

In order for the initiate and the adept to do that powerful work safely, their mind and body must already be tuned to working with the Grindstone in their outer and inner lives so that they hold a better power balance within them. This is because every power you mediate or bridge passes through you first, affecting everything in your sphere before it is then externalised into its vessel, pattern, or project. If an adept attempts to bridge this power and they have not reconciled the Grindstone within themselves, then it will get to work on them before it works on anything else. The adept will find themselves confronted by the Grindstone power in their health and in their everyday life.

The safest and most successful way to tune to the Grindstone power as an apprentice is through its actions in your everyday life. It is a lifetime process, and at first the apprentice magician struggles to first recognise and then reconcile themselves with the power. As they progress, the power re-presents in ever more powerful ways, working through the life pattern, the body, the mind, and the emotions. At some point (hopefully earlier than later) the magician learns to spot the triggering of this power, recognises what it needs to do, and then instead of waiting for the life bomb to drop, steps voluntarily into a situation or pattern that would obviate the need for the lesson: the step of letting go, self-limiting, or self-releasing.

Let's have a look at some practical examples of the Grindstone activating in life. We will look at some very different situations that nevertheless all have the same dynamic, and look at the outcomes relative to the way the person dealt with the power. Bear in mind that life is a very complex weave indeed, and although these two opposing powers are very present in all of life, there are also many other lesser and greater dynamics, powers, energies, and life patterns that flow in and out of a person or a nation's life.

4. Examples of the Grindstone in action

These following short examples are not here to bore you silly (they will be obvious to some and not to others), nor are they anything to do with moralising: morals have no place in magic. They are simple, externalised life expressions of the Grindstone which in turn prepare us to work more deeply with the inner aspects of this power.

Human society's conditioning

Each society and religion has its boundaries of 'good behaviour' and 'bad behaviour.' Some grew out of mystical understanding and devolved down to dogma, and some are simple societal control methods. The hardest thing for an apprentice magician who has grown up in a religious society or family is to step away from such dogma in a balanced way. Usually as a young, budding magician, the person carries the dogma with them as a mode of thinking, and simply transplants it onto another dogma: we see this in many magical systems and alternative religions. They are simply rehashing the same issue. This stems from their as-yet-inability to spot and then disengage from the inappropriate restriction and engage a deeper, more magical one.

This dogmatic restriction, which often appears in magical systems as a 'code of ethics' or patterns of self-development rituals, continues to trap the young magician in an unproductive cycle of destructive restriction. The magician feels comfortable in the safety of the dogma, but is unable to truly progress to any power as a magician. The unbalanced restriction triggers the opposing power in the magician's life, and they slowly unravel.

Once the magician spots this and steps away, they restrict their desire for a predictable system with a set of rules. They learn to recognise that the true power of the Grindstone comes from the restriction of *not* having predictable walls and rules: you have to actively engage it and understand it for yourself, alone, and without guidance. That means falling back upon yourself as the maker and keeper of your own limits. That is an example of magical engagement, in the first simple step, with the Grindstone.

Alternatively, the young budding magician walks away from the dogma they were raised with and rejects all boundaries. They immerse themselves in self-indulgence, emotional and physical experimentation (Left Hand Path magic, for example) and they either self-destruct through that process or they learn to self-limit from direct experience. Again, this is engaging the Grindstone magically and consciously, but this way is reached through immersion in the power of the Unraveller.

A third way is where the magician steps away from the dogma they were raised within, and steps into a discipline of some sort, be it martial arts training, sports, or arts training: a discipline that is hard, long, and challenging. Through that process, the young magician learns to self-discipline, understands the necessity for boundaries, be they physical, emotional, or otherwise, and learns how to transplant that learning into their magical practice. This is why it is easier for lone magicians who have intensively trained in some form of discipline over a long period of time to progress well in magic.

Drama/emotional conditioning

The Grindstone can also engage through emotional dramas. When we are young, many of us project internal imbalance through emotional swings and dramas: it is the body and mind's way of trying to release the toxicity of imbalance. Think hormonal teenage outburst.

As we go through life and we have hard knocks (the Grindstone in action) we either degenerate down into a life of victimhood, or we get to a point in our life where we see that our reactions often come not just from outer situations, but also from our own need for emotional expression:

"I am angry/sad and I don't know why, but it's not your fault."

The ability to get to that stage of self-awareness, to acknowledge imbalance and not project a reason onto someone or something else, is the first step of engaging the Grindstone. For an everyday person it is a step towards emotional maturity. For a magician it has the added bonus of alerting us to some imbalance, be it in our own minds, our own bodies, or because of some power imbalance somewhere.

The next step a magician would take is to find out, usually through divination, where that imbalance is coming from. Sometimes it is something within us that needs physical rebalancing (hormones or depression), or it is coming from unbalanced magical practice which needs changing, or it is the result of magical interference from outside of the person.

The magician would identify the cause and act accordingly. If it shows up as a necessary process, the magician would then decide to 'suck it up,' tread water, and see what is coming out the other end of it. Often this happens if a lot of power is due to come into the magician's practice and they need either to go into a phase of withdrawing and waiting, or to adjust their life ready to accept the power in a balanced way when it arrives. This is the Grindstone being engaged with: it is limiting the magician in order to prepare them for something.

Through working with the Grindstone in these simple ways, the deeper aspect of the magician's psyche learns, through sideways application, how to self-limit for necessity when it comes to deeper magic and power: it becomes a second nature. That in turn allows the magician to work with large amounts of power and not go mad or get greedy. That then opens up a whole new aspect of magic for the magician, as they are stable and self-disciplined enough to work in depth in the inner worlds without temptation.

The Grindstone of magicians

Once the magician is working with the Initiate level of training (though this can also happen to an apprentice) and the powers are being consciously engaged, then the Grindstone presents around the magician in a constant dynamic I call the *Sword of Damocles*.

Here is a way it triggers for me, so that you can see it in practical action. I do a lot of magical writing and I write from my own magical experience, not from other books. I believe in 'hiding in plain sight' methods of writing and not holding information back. Occasionally though, I inadvertently cross a line. I will start to write something without realising that it should not be written about. When I do that, I begin to burn – literally. My skin, my organs; they will all burn furiously. My face will go red and I will feel very ill.

When that first started to happen, I would do a reading to see if I was ill. The answer was always the same:

> "No, you are not ill, but you have triggered the Sword
> by acting in an unbalanced way."

The sword would appear in my health reading with it hanging over my head – this type of situation is where the story of Damocles comes from. It is a deep magical dynamic that has nothing to do with systems or dogma; it is an energetic response to crossing a power line that should not be crossed.

When this happened, I would look back over what I had written and would then see how that text could be badly misused in a powerful and destructive way. Sometimes it was not that it could be destructive, but rather that I had, by writing a magical detail, taken away the student's chance to find out something deep and powerful for themselves; I had potentially short-circuited the magical development of another human being. As soon as I deleted the text and then began writing with more care, the burning would instantly stop and peace was restored. That is the Grindstone in action in a magician's life.

A completely different magical application of the Grindstone is one where it is purposely engaged. Here is an example. A magician is being attacked by another adept (sigh, humans are such dicks sometimes) powerfully and dangerously: the curse or attack is to the death. An inexperienced magician would lash back, but the adept knows better – not because of ethics, but because they understand how power works. The adept does not retaliate. He simply cleans the attack off himself and carries on about his business. The attacker becomes enraged that the victim has not died, and so piles more and more magical power into the attack.

The adept on the receiving end still does not respond. Nor are they badly damaged by the attack (usually bruised but not battered); they simply clean it off again, patiently and without emotion.

The adept on the receiving end is intentionally engaging the Grindstone. They may also work with the Grindstone magically, not on the attacker, but upon themselves: ritual/vision work with the sword to guard their own temper, stay their hand, and draw strength from Saturn to persevere. This is a part of the adept dynamic known as *the Adversary*. For every magician who evolves and strengthens, the power of the Adversary appears in their fate pattern, and it can flow through anything or anyone within the orbit of the magician. The power of the Adversary is a higher octave of the Grindstone, and serves as negative polarity to the magician in order to strengthen them and teach them through direct experience. The power of the Adversary can flow through a magical attack on a magician, and a wise magician spots that Adversary power in action and takes a step back. They will learn how to defend more and more powerfully, and they will learn patience. They will also learn that the bad things that happen to them through the action of the Adversary are nothing to do with punishment, but through the dynamic of cause and effect. The magician learns to move away from the mentality of *reward and punishment* and move towards the mentality of *cause and effect*. The magician learns to hold power gently and to wield it only when necessary.

This approach does two things. The first thing is that it slowly grinds the attacker down: they are outputting a lot of their energy to use magic to kill someone – that takes a lot of energy, a lot of work, and a lot of focus. Soon they begin to obsess and pour all of their magical resources into the attack: they are emptying their inner and outer resources. This in turn weakens them considerably and eventually kills them (the effect is usually in relation to the magical intention).

The second thing that happens is that the Unraveller is triggered for the attacker. When you attack magically, you set up an energy relationship or line of energy contact. The attack travels down that route and the attacker and victim are connected energetically. As soon as the adept on the receiving end consciously and magically engages the Grindstone, it sets up a see-saw effect. And the Unraveller is the opposing power of the Grindstone: if the Grindstone appears at one end of the energy connection, that will automatically trigger the Unraveller on the opposing side.

So the attacker has the power of the Unraveller flowing through him in an unconscious way. That manifests as the magician finding it harder and harder to hold a magical pattern, and they mentally, physically, and emotionally begin to unravel as a result of their own imbalance. And if the attacker had intentionally used death magic, that triggers the death aspect of the Unraveller and speeds up their own death.

The adept on the receiving end does nothing at all towards the attacker; they simply work on themselves and let the attacker blow himself up in his own time. By not engaging with the attacker, the adept has not bound themselves up in yet more energetic loops with the attacker, and has not outputted any energy that would potentially feed the attacker. It can be a long and laborious process, particularly if the attacker is a long holder of grudges, but the strength the adept on the receiving end gains through such restraint of action is considerable indeed.

The end result is a dead or seriously weakened attacker, and a stronger, wiser adept on the other end. In the next lesson I will look at a similar situation from the perspective of the Unraveller, and also look at a slightly different way of dealing with the same issue.

5. *Task:* Grindstone tarot readings

Your life

Using the four-directional reading layout, use your tarot cards to look and see if the Grindstone is in action in your life. To focus the reading on your outer life, use the centre for your health, the east for education/writing/learning or daily work, south for creativity, west for relationships, and north for family/home. Then look at your inner energies using the same layout and use the 'magical directions' attributes of: east, with something coming in, the use of utterance, or a new cycle, the south would be the future, fire, or angelic contacts, the west would be something falling away into the past, thresholds of endings, or connections with water, and the north would be the Underworld, ancestors, the dead, and ancient powers.

If you identify the Grindstone in action (it will show as a difficult restrictive card), sit and think about how instead of fighting it or trying to avoid it, you can first recognise where in your life it is playing out, why it is playing out, what you need to learn from it and then engage it through your actions, common sense, emotions, or mind. Remember the key words for the Grindstone and apply them.

An event

Choose a time in history where something major happened that changed a culture, religion, race, or land. Do the same readings that you have done for yourself: look at the outer manifestation and then the inner one to see if the Grindstone was in action. It may or may not have been.

If it was in action, read up about the history of the event, people's eyewitness accounts, and pay close attention to any art that came out of that time. See if you can see an unconscious or conscious expression of the Grindstone in the writing, thinking, art, or poetry of the time.

What you are looking for is major restrictions or disciplines that brought major growth, strength, or change to a nation. If the change was a restoration of balance, the Unraveller will also be seen in the events. If the change ultimately brought imbalance, look to see if the Unraveller was absent from the dynamic.

Write up your findings on computer, and also log your readings.

6. *Task:* The Grindstone in your chart

Revisit your astrology chart and look at the natal position of Saturn and the current transit of Saturn. Look at where it is in action in your chart: see if there is any correlation between your chart's transits and the reading you did about your outer and inner life. Think about where that transit of Saturn sits in your personal pentagram pattern, and take note of the nearest direction and tool, and what power flows through them.

Bring all of the information together and see if there is a need to consciously engage the Grindstone in your life in some way.

7. *Task:* Grindstone ritual

If you are embarking on a new course of study (Quareia, for example) or college study, a new job, anything that is a major project, work ritually to draw the power of the Grindstone into that path in order to help you learn better, apply yourself consistently, and to strengthen you.

Design your own ritual to invite the Grindstone power into your life to work with you. In the design, draw upon what you already have learned about ritual and use the four-directional pattern to open the gates and directions. Look at aspects of the Pentagram work you have done and choose key aspects of that ritual work to construct your own personal ritual. Include in the ritual a recitation to call upon the Grindstone power of the east, the Noble Ones of the south, and the Unraveller in the west to guide you in the engagement of the Grindstone in your life: invite that power to work with you.

Write down the ritual in your computer log and keep diary entries over the coming weeks of any observations you may have about that power triggering in your life.

Lesson 4
The Unraveller

What I call the Unraveller is the polar opposite of the Grindstone.

Where the Grindstone forms, limits, and strengthens, the Unraveller disassembles, loosens, and begins the process of weighing and dispatching energy back into the Void via the power of the Scales (A.K.A. Justice).

At this point, I want to state that in this module and subsequent ones that tackle creation and destruction, I have purposely stayed away from the better-known magical and mystical names used in magic and religion for these powers.

This is to move away from the cultural and religious/magical dogmas that have built up around these powers, and subsequently only serve to trap the magician in a series of dogmatic, inaccurate patterns that serve as dead ends for true magical progression.

We are at a time in our human evolution where we want to get to the *dynamics* of things: the growth in science over the last hundred years is staggering, and that comes from a wish to know 'what is there' without overlaying supposition – and superstition. We are at a phase of magical evolution where we need to step back and look with new eyes. Hence the movement away from established vocabularies. This in turn allows the aspiring magician to learn, experience, and observe in an objective way without preconceived ideas. Like the Grindstone, the Unraveller's influence permeates every aspect of creation from the smallest particle to the mind of the human and the lay of the land. For those students who think in a very 'science' way, view the Unraveller as the power that triggers the self-destruct process in a cell. For those who work in a more poetic way, the Unraveller triggers the start of the composting process, or literally, the mental/emotional unravelling process. In a magical sense, the Unraveller is the power that is worked with for unbinding something, releasing something, or for magical work that is involved in the slow destruction of something large or long-term.

Its action is slow, deliberate, and loosens power/energy to a point where it becomes vulnerable to any destructive power. So the Unraveller does not in itself destroy, but it *prepares* something for destruction. Its positive action is to loosen something enough for it to be worked with better, to free up energy trapped in something, and to help reshape things. So you can begin to see why it is such a pivotal power in magic. The two opposing powers of Grindstone and Unraveller are powers that form/disassemble just before or on the cusp of physical manifestation, a place where a lot of shorter-term magic is worked with.

As an apprentice, you will first approach the Unraveller from an everyday perspective, from your own physical, mental, and emotional experience. From that base understanding, you will then be able to recognise this power in action around you in nature and in magic. From that awareness, you will learn as an initiate, and then as an adept, how to consciously work with, process, and create/destroy in harmony with these opposing powers.

When the Unraveller is properly engaged in your life it can be a very powerful and positive force, particularly in a culture that is obsessed with control. If the Unraveller is plunged into without due thought, its actions will destroy. Like everything, it has good and bad, balance and imbalance.

A good way to look at this process from a training perspective is that before you break the rules, you must first learn them. The Grindstone is the discipline and limitations that train you in a conformed way: this gives you technique, discipline, and strength. It also gives you a major reference point for power, and allows you to see the weakness in yourself that needs reigning in, and in the technique you study. At that point, by engaging the Unraveller, you learn to step away from the conformity, the restrictions and barriers. You step into your own individual path as a magician, knowing what can be loosened, released, and played with, and what cannot or should not.

That wisdom comes from training, so that you learn how to engage the Unraveller in a way that does not unravel you, but which simply loosens whatever needs loosening, freeing up your potential. If the Unraveller is worked with by someone who has not first undergone and understood the power of the Grindstone in one form or another, they will swiftly unravel mentally and physically. Again, the Mysteries protect themselves. By working with these two powers through your own life and body, *your body and mind* learn how to cope with the power. This in turn allows you to work with these powers in the depths of the inner worlds without being unduly or adversely affected by them: you are already used to them in a small way.

So let's look at the Unraveller first in its action in creation, then its action in magic, and finally its actions in our everyday lives.

1. The Unraveller in creation

When we looked at creation via the Grindstone, we thought about how the first breath travels energetically towards manifestation, and how one of its last filters acts to slow down and solidify that energy. It then manifests as substance: a human, a tree, an animal, a rock. The moment something becomes physically manifest, it starts its march towards destruction and death. The Unraveller energy kicks in and programs the self-destruct mechanism in the physical substance, so everything that manifests already has its 'destruction button' ready. But that self-destruct is also a part of creation: cells are constantly renewing themselves and can only do that if the self-destruct is active: as the cell completes its task, it self-destructs and new ones are created. A failure in that self-destruct process is involved in cancer, for example. The cells just keep reproducing and not destructing.

In science, specifically in biology and genetics, we are starting to realise that when a person is born, their genome already has deviations that dictate a potential for disease and death at around a certain age (excluding accidents, murder, etc.). This is the Unraveller. Our pattern of fate and our genetic pattern are interwoven, and the weave has 'hotspots' of Unravelling energy imprinted within it. How these manifest depends on how we engage with this power. So for example at a human level, say someone was born with a predisposition to heart attacks at an early age. They can adjust that pattern to some extent (but within limits) depending on how they live their lives: they either engage the Unraveller and the Grindstone to shift their pattern, or they do not and they are subsequently at the mercy of these powers.

Similarly, in deeper aspects of creation from a magical perspective, the Unraveller is ever-constant wherever there is creation. Wherever you find a powerful being that works on the manifestation of physical being, an angelic being for example, there is always a counterbalance of a destructive being that will break down that creation when the time is ready. This is why it is so important to work across the board with all beings in the inner worlds. Magic that focuses only on creation/good/nice is unbalanced and potentially corrupt. The same is true of magic that focuses only on destruction/bad/evil – there always has to be a balance. This polarity of creation and destruction, male and female, light and dark, runs through everything in our world and in the inner worlds. Bear that in mind in your future studies.

2. THE UNRAVELLER AND MAGIC

In magic the Unraveller takes on the role of disassembling. When the Unraveller has disassembled something and completed its work, it then passes on whatever has been unravelled to the next power. That may be a power of rebalancing (such as the power we magically call *Justice*) or the power of Binding, the power of releasing, or the power of rebuilding. It all depends on the magical act that the power of the Unraveller is being used for. How this power affects you while you work with it all depends on what magical work you are doing, why you are doing it, and how well you have attended to your own baggage. The following are examples of magical use, outcome and consequence. You will not work with this level of magic yet, but it is important to understand how it affects you and why: the work that is needed to ensure your successful engagement with this power starts during the apprentice level of training. First you work on yourself so that the power does not need to as it flows through you in future work.

3. UNRAVELLING MAGIC: EFFECTS

If the Unravelling is done to restore balance, as you work with this power, it will also unbind within you things that need unbinding or unravelling in order to restore balance. The same goes for magic that calls upon the power of Justice. For example if you are clinging to a job, a partnership, a way of life, etc. that is ultimately unhealthy for you, the power of the Unraveller, as you work magically with it, will pass through you and begin that unravelling process.

Don't forget that the true power of Justice is to restore balance, not to 'get justice' or 'revenge.' It is more akin to the Egyptian concept of Ma'at, which you have already looked at. Often we fight against this restoration of balance, as it can be hard for us to see far enough into our own future to see where our true balance lies. As an adept magician you learn to trust this power, to go with the flow, but also to truly understand balance – a process of understanding that begins at the apprentice level. When you have triggered this unravelling process in your life through magical action, it is best to simply 'go with the flow,' trust the power, and actively let go of things that are unravelling around you.

If the unravelling magic is done without a goal of balance, without the need for rebalance, then it starts a new process of events. To work with the Unraveller in a magical act where there is no real unbalance draws the magician into a new cycle that will trigger uncontrolled imbalance both in the magical situation and also in the magician themselves. If the magician does not understand the process, their attempts to restore their own balance would likely make the situation worse.

Everything you do magically passes through you before it then goes off to do its job. That is the pay-off for working with deep inner powers. Ultimately, if the magician works in an intelligent way, it gives the magician access to huge reserves of power to work with. It also serves to strengthen, mature, and enlighten the magician as they allow the deep inner powers to flow through them. This is where the tradition of magical training making you a better person comes from. It doesn't come from ritual affirmations or initiations; it comes from directly engaging with the powers of Divinity as they flow through our world.

If those deep inner powers are worked with in ignorance, it can trigger all sorts of problems that eventually destroy the magician. So you can see why it is important to know how these powers work, and also to know yourself (the first requirement of the Mysteries).

There are ways of doing magic that do not engage these powers, but it is magic that is very limited in its power resources and therefore limited in its action. That type of magic is not what this course is about.

So let's look at a practical example of the Unraveller in magical action, which will then help you to see how it could affect you magically. That in turn will help you spot where you need to look to your own life and body so that you can work powerfully and effectively with this dynamic.

4. The Unraveller in action

A magician is contacted by someone who has been powerfully magically bound and is dying. The magician first looks, using divination, at the wider picture, and sees a number of things. The first is that the binding is quite vicious and is done by an unbalanced adept. The second is that the binding is interfering with the fate expression of the victim. The third thing the magician sees is that the binding has been done from a place of vengeance: the victim had left a magical lodge and, being an adept themselves, had decided to set up their own lodge. Some of the old lodge members had left with the victim, which had enraged the lodge leader, who is a skilled but imbalanced person.

The magician then looks at the health of the victim and sees that the binding has triggered a cancerous predisposition in the victim: by binding the life expression of the victim, that binding magic had found a way to express through the physical substance of the victim. The self-destruct mechanism in the cells of the victim was already predisposed to stop working. The binding magic was enough to nudge that action into full imbalance: the self-destruct was inhibited, and the cells started to proliferate. The victim became cancerous and was very ill.

The next step the magician takes is to self-examine where they themselves are in life: is there something in their own life that needs unbinding and unravelling? The magician realises that their own 'day job' is becoming unhealthy for them, but they enjoy the good wage and work stability that it gives them.

Before he begins the magical process of helping the victim, he opens all the gates, talks with the inner contacts, and agrees to work consciously with anything within himself that could need unbinding. He also agrees to be willing to lose his day job if that is what needed to restore balance: he puts the option on the table and asks the inner contacts to work with him.

Then the magician gets to work. He works in ritual and vision with the victim, and engages the power of the Unraveller in conjunction with the power of Justice. He creates a pattern and magical construct, pulls the power of the Unraveller and Justice into the pattern, and then places the victim within the pattern so that the power will flow through them. The Unraveller power begins to unbind the binding magic and the power of Justice gets to work on rebalancing.

It is a long process that takes a couple of weeks, but slowly, the Unraveller starts to engage in the life of the victim and a number of things happen. On a physical level, the victim begins to respond to the medical cancer treatment – in fact they respond very well, and their prognosis is changed from okay to good. The new lodge group feel a shift from feeling uncomfortable about starting a new lodge to feeling very good about it, and they all get an inrush of energy and enthusiasm for the new project.

The lodge leader who did the binding starts to Unravel. The power works on everyone involved just by the nature of how it works. The lodge leader was not directly targeted magically, but as a main player in this chess game they are a part of the pattern, so the magic will also flow through them and affect them. They begin to become more neurotic, to display unbalanced emotions, to overeat or engage in behaviour that is self-destructive. As a result, the remaining lodge members pull away, and the lodge collapses.

The magician prepares to lose their job by starting the job hunting process, as they figure that is where the Unraveller will work through them. However that does not happen. Instead they get a promotion and are moved to a new area that is healthier for them. Also, something that the magician was eating that was mildly irritating their system suddenly becomes a major problem, and the magician has to stop eating it. It is one of those minor intolerances that if left unchecked can do longer-term damage to the system. By going with the flow and allowing those changes to happen without resistance, the magician engages both the power of the Grindstone and the power of Justice in their lives to restore balance. The Grindstone is engaged through self-discipline with the food issue, and the power of Justice puts the magician where they are supposed to be.

So you can see how these powers affect everyone involved, and how through the skill of the magician, 'many birds can be killed with one stone.'

A lesser type of magic would not have engaged with the deep power of the Unraveller, but would have involved different individual magical acts: unbinding the victim and attacking the lodge leader, which takes a lot more energy and is less effective. It would also not have triggered the renewal in the life of the magician.

5. The personal Unraveller

So before you get to work magically with this power, you need to learn how to spot your own need for, or vulnerability to, the Unraveller, and be able to engage it consciously. This is not glamorous or exciting magical work, but it is very necessary work that you will be glad you did when you reach adepthood. For some of you this will all be very obvious; for others of you it will not. But no matter how obvious this work may be, take the time to do it and do it properly. Because of the very personal nature of this work, do two different records of this work, one on computer for the mentor if you want to be mentored in the future (just put in an overview), and the other more personal handwritten in your personal journal. Don't skip the record keeping of this work: it is important to log it and keep it so that you can refer back to it in the future.

6. *Task:* Looking in the mirror

Often what we think needs releasing or unravelling in our lives can be different from what *actually* needs unravelling or letting go of, or loosening up. Because of this, you will approach this work in two different ways. This is not something that can be done in a month and then moved on from: the process starts now if you have not already engaged with this process in your life, but it will be a continuous process throughout your magical life.

Do this work immediately, and then plan to revisit this process every year. A version of this can be seen in Judaism which is known as *Yom Kippur* or the *Day of Atonement*, something you were introduced to in lesson two. It actually spans a couple of weeks each year where the person reflects on their actions over the past year and atones for their 'sins.'

Looking in the mirror is not the same process: it is a similar but more profound action (a deeper octave). Pick a time each year where you plan to think about what aspects of your life you are clinging onto, or what aspects of your life or personality need loosening and freeing up. Spend that time in reflection and meditation, and think of practical ways that you can positively engage this power in your life. During this time also think about where the Grindstone may need engaging or disengaging in your life, and where the power of Ma'at needs to flow better through your mind and actions.

None of this is about 'atonement'; rather it is about learning to *know yourself* and to know the powers active around you and how you have responded to them. Your reflections are not about other people, but about yourself: what powers were active in your past, how you responded to those powers, and how your response potentially created weakness or imbalance within you.

Also look at how any unbalanced, immature, or unwise actions created chaos or unbalance around you (the effects upon others and upon the land). Spot them, learn the mistakes, understand what when wrong, why, and why you must not go back into that pattern of behaviour again. Again, this is not about societal or religious morals, but about self-maturing through wisdom in hindsight, responsibility, and learning to engage your own Grindstone or Unraveller where necessary in your future actions.

For a period of two weeks after you have done your meditation, work on the process of 'Looking in the Mirror.' Choose an aspect each day and think about your personality, your everyday actions, your relationships and responsibilities, your job, your magical studies and interests, memories and past events, and any other aspect of your life that comes to mind. Think about things that may need freeing up, where you are too controlling, or clinging onto things, or where things are starting to break down and need conscious engagement to bring change. Think about past imbalanced actions or behaviour and use the power of hindsight to think about your past mistakes.

The most important aspect of looking in the mirror is to not only spot present and past imbalance and mistakes, but to actually do something about it and not repeat the same mistakes in your life. Evolution is not making the same mistakes, but learning from past ones and making new mistakes that you will learn from. Eventually the process leads you to spot mistakes before you make them, engage the right polarity dynamic, and side-step them.

Write down on a piece of paper the most personal and revealing aspects of this exercise and clip the paper into your journal (so it can be taken out if you have to submit Module III journal to a mentor). This is private to you and you alone. Then type up an overview of the experience in a way that it is okay to submit to a mentor should they ask for it.

7. *Task:* READINGS

Using the same method and layout as you used in the previous lesson, look at the aspects of your life, and also of your body, to see what areas are already in the process of unravelling. They will appear in the reading as 'going away' types of cards or of separation or loss.

With the results you got from your previous readings from lesson three and the results you got from this set of readings, put the two notes together and see if they match up with what came to light during your meditations. Write down the similarities and differences.

8. *Task:* THE UNRAVELLER AND YOUR ASTROLOGY CHART

Look at your chart and your current transits. See where Pluto is in transit in your chart. Take note of the house it is transiting, and also what astrological sign it is transiting. If you are using `astro.com`, look to see if there is a current major Pluto transit listed in your chart. If there is, read up on it. Look at your pentagram pattern/seal and see where in the pattern Pluto lies. Because Pluto is slow-moving, it will most likely be in the same place. See what magical tools, powers, etc. it is near.

Compare everything you have found with the conclusions you came to from your meditations and readings. You should now be getting a good idea of where your weak spots and strengths are, and a good idea of what needs working on and what doesn't in your life. Once you have identified areas of your life that you feel need proper engagement with the Unraveller, write them down and set yourself tasks and goals that will allow the Unravelling and/or Grindstone power to flow through you in a practical conscious way. Keep notes on your progress.

9. *Task:* UNRAVELLER RITUAL

In the previous lesson you designed your own ritual to connect with and invite the powers of the Grindstone into your life. Take another look at that ritual and expand upon it. Write into the ritual a second part that calls in the power of the Unraveller. Aspects to be included in the ritual: work with the magical direction of west, work with the gates, and the inner contacts at the gates.

Work at the west altar and allow whatever needs letting go of to flow energetically into the west. Also work with a mirror in the north to look at yourself and to be brutally honest with yourself in a ritual setting (and think about why the mirror belongs in the north). Everything you do and say will be witnessed by the inner contacts, and you will be held to it. Make no promises, *make no vows* (that is very important). State your reflection, understanding, and what you intend to do about it.

Once you have reworked the ritual to be balanced, and have practised it from memory, then it is time to do it. Do it at a new moon and take a ritual bath beforehand: a fresh start. Write down your notes afterwards. These notes will be private to you and will never be looked at, but it is important to write them down so that you can refer to them in the future, as you will need to.

Once you have completed that task, rewrite the ritual so that it is not specific to you: ensure that it can be used by any magician regardless of age, gender, culture, etc.

Remember, this is not a psychological act, but a ritual magical act. So don't get into flowery language or showy psychological actions. Keep it sharp, to the point, and magically relevant. Some may feel that it is early days to be writing your own magical ritual, but doing so will make you think about how ritual is constructed. No matter how much you study ritual construction, it is only by actually having to *do* it that you start to see all the subtle implications.

Do this on computer and copy it somewhere safely; it is likely that it will be used by other magicians in the future when you finally come to teach or work with other magicians in some form or another.

10. Study

Look into the history of the Peasants' Revolt of England in 1381. It is a classic example of the interplay between the Grindstone and the Unraveller, and how complex that interplay can be. From that time of events, a slow but subtle long-term change happened within the people, the Monarchy, and the land for both good and bad.

Looking at the powers flowing through an event in a way that has nothing to do with magic allows you to look at the complexity of these powers without falling into the trap of stereotypical magical or ethical thinking. You will see the weave of how good and bad intertwined to produce massive change in a society. It also begins the process of understanding how important it is to look at things beyond magic to see the forces of Divinity in action. Some of the greatest magical wisdom can be gained from history, art, music, poetry, science, etc. that have no direct magical links. This is why many adepts read widely on subjects such as history, philosophy, geography, medicine, music, sciences, etc.

Lesson 5
The Inner Guardians

Now that you have begun the process of working with the Grindstone and the Unraveller, it is time to begin to understand the other inner powers that guard and work with the thresholds of the inner worlds. Like the previous two powers you worked to understand, I have taken away the better-known names of many of them and given them titles according to what they do.

The names that have been used in magic in the past for these beings have become so distorted in the misuse and misunderstanding of these powers that it is time to step away from those names and for the magician to learn through direct experience. Even though this is an apprentice level, it is important to learn about these powers from the outset of training, which will not only prepare you for working properly with them, but will also give you a deeper understanding of them – an understanding that is sadly lacking in modern magic. These beings can be recognised in ancient Egyptian texts as well as many other ancient texts: once you know their function and character, you will instantly recognise them in sacred texts around the world.

Why do you need to learn about these beings? Without knowledge of these powerful beings, there is no access to deeper and more profound magic. These are the powers that work behind the scenes of creation and work at the threshold of material existence, a threshold where magic begins its flowering. Most of them you only need to know about and read up on at this phase of your training, but there is one contact within this group of guardians that you will need to meet in vision and learn to work with (and one you will also come to meet shortly in another lesson). Relationships with the rest will flower as your training progresses.

Let's have a look at these various contacts and learn a little about them: some you will recognise if you have read ancient mythic or theological texts; others you may not. First let's have a look at the realm where they reside. This realm is called the Desert, something you will learn a lot more about in the months and years to come.

1. The realm of the Inner Desert

Knowledge of the realm of the Desert had sadly fallen by the wayside in modern magic, and yet it is a key realm for any powerful magic that uses inner vision and inner contacts. Fragments of this realm can be seen in Greek mythology, where an aspect of the Desert is known as the *Lethe Plain* – the death realm, an aspect of the Desert, which you will learn about as an apprentice.

When a magician reaches deep into the inner worlds without the heavy filters of modern magic, they invariably hit a place that seems devoid of life: a vast desert with a great crack in the earth at one end (the *Abyss*) and a river at the other end (*the river of death*).

This desert is hinted at in many magical texts, but because of the dangers that can potentially threaten a magician if they wander into this realm without preparation, little detail is written about it in texts and grimoires. This danger results from the lack of knowledge of the guardians that stop humans blundering into this realm unprepared. That is why you, as an apprentice, must go through various preparations before you step fully into this realm.

Just as the Garden of Creation teems with life, so the opposite is true of the Desert. It holds no living or growing thing. It is void of life and full of knowledge. The Desert is the home of a vast array of angelic beings that are involved in the act of creation: the Desert is where pure Divine Breath and power is formed into the pattern of physical manifestation and begins its journey into life. Stepping over the threshold of the Desert, that pattern of life becomes a person, a tree, etc. – a concept you have already briefly looked at.

The Desert also houses the collective knowledge of all beings that have manifested in our world at some time or other. It is a similar idea to an inner landscape: where an inner landscape expresses the inner form of a land or person, so the Desert holds the inner temples, adepts, priests and priestesses, and deities: the inner forms of the outer manifestations.

When Crowley was told by an inner contact that he could only access communion with Choronzon in the desert, the contact did not mean an outer desert, but was talking about the inner realm of the Desert. This is a place where the Abyss can be accessed as well as the knowledge of the ancient temples and priesthoods, where demonic and angelic beings can be safely met on their own territory, and where, as an adept, the magician can witness the true power and beauty of the pattern that is partially expressed through the Metatron Cube, in action. For a magician to safely access and work in this place, he or she must first get to know and be accepted by its guardians.

If you are a person who works well through imagining something, imagine the desert appearing as a vast, lifeless plain scattered with ancient temples, the Abyss, the river and mountain of death in the distance, and the mists that shroud Divinity on the other side of the Abyss. Mists also appear to obscure areas of the Desert that the magician is not yet prepared to step into. There is also an area of the Desert that is a 'holding area' where powers or beings that should not be manifest in the outer world at this present time are held in the sands until it is time for them to be released.

If you read the Old and New Testaments of the Bible, you will also, once you have become familiar with this realm, recognise many aspects and contacts of this place in the various writings.

Now let us have a look at the various types of beings that stand on the threshold between us and the Desert. Not all of them are guardians; some are deities or sub-deities, some are workers – many beings work on this threshold to bring final form to the Divine Breath as it manifests as a physical being. They are the weavers, connectors, balancers, as well as guardians. Let's start from the closest to us and work in from there.

2. The Weaver

The Weaver is a deity power, female, that takes all the strands that are flowing out of the Desert and weaves them into final form to produce a specific life. The Weaver takes the strands from the Three Fates which have defined the length of life, the time of death, and the time of birth of the person or creature, and weaves around those key points more subtle aspects of the life that is to be lived. In some cultures the Weaver goddess is also a battle goddess, such as the Egyptian goddess Neith, and in other cultures they are female spirits such as the Norns in Norse Mythology. However the power of the Weaver presents in a culture, it is always female and expresses its power to humanity through the visual vocabulary of weaving or knot making that is connected to fate.

For example, we learned about the energies of the Unraveller as energetic hotspots in a life: the Weaver connects those 'hotspots' into the pattern set out by the Fates, and weaves a place of birth, and key moments within a life. At this point let me say that these images and descriptions are how our consciousness can understand and interact with these powers. In real terms, these powers are truly beyond our understanding in their full expression. As a species, we have learned to use common imagery and have 'humanised' how we perceive lot of these beings so that we can interact with them safely. The depictions we use are essentially energetic filters that allow us communion. Without these filters they would be beyond our ability to communicate with: it is a common vocabulary of concepts and images, so bear that in mind. You will see varied versions of these powers in cultures and religions around the world if you look closely enough.

As magicians, we work with this vocabulary of concepts and images in order to build an interface that we can work through. This vocabulary is something that has been deeply embedded within human consciousness for millennia: hence if you find these beings or places accidentally and without prior knowledge, you will see them in the same way the ancients saw them: a collective interface built up over thousands of years.

Back to the Weaver. The Weaver appears to us as a goddess who weaves life into being. She is only occasionally interacted with directly by magicians, but she is known, acknowledged, and respected. If, as a magical adept, you wish to specialise in magical work connected to fate and the formation of nations, then you will learn to work more closely with this goddess.

Most of the ancient Mysteries around the world have their own version of this goddess: in ancient Egypt she is known as *Neith* (pronounced 'Net'), one of the most ancient deities in the Egyptian pantheon. An aspect of this power is known in Greek mythology as Athena. These goddesses are known for being warriors (so much fate is determined by war) and also as weavers of creation.

Sadly, as the Mysteries of the ancient world began to degenerate, the understanding of the aspects of these powers also degenerated. Neith became known as a weaver in a day-to-day sense, as a basket or cloth weaver. This is a total misunderstanding of the vast powers this goddess wields, and we can often, as magicians, track the degeneration and collapse of a nation by tracking how the understanding of the deities fell apart.

So if you come across a goddess of weaving and she is thought to be the patron of weavers, dig a little deeper and you find that in fact it is a goddess who is the power of the Weaver of creation. As the outermost being on the threshold of the Desert, she is very well known around the world.

3. The Three Fates

The Three Fates figure extensively in many of the ancient Mysteries. One is involved with taking the thread of life that flows from the Divine Breath and has been formed into a pattern of a particular expression (human, animal, etc.), the second one determines the length that life will be, and the third is the one who determines the point of death.

These three beings essentially form the birth, length of life, and death of a human. If you read up on the various mythologies from ancient texts about these beings, you will notice that over the generations, more and more powers and attributes are added to their mythology (humans do have a habit of elaborating; they cannot keep anything simple). From a magician's perspective, we work with these beings in their core, original roles as the three intertwined powers that determine the *timing* of a life.

Again, few magicians would work directly with these powers unless, as an adept, they were specialising in an area of magic that would bring them into direct contact with these beings, but all magicians need to be aware of these powers, what they do, and how they operate.

Gnosis of these beings is important, as it will help you understand the mystical and inner aspects of a life, and how that life operates in the outer world. An adept working with fate or as an exorcist would need to have a deep understanding of these beings and how to interact with them when needs be.

If we take all the mythological dressing away, what we are left with are beings that work in a very narrow and specific way with time and manifestation. Without physical substance (a body), there is no time. These beings are the ones that sit on our side of the threshold and 'midwife' the human into conception.

At a deeper level of understanding, they are the powers that flow through the stars: the powers that come together in harmony to create a measured window through which a human soul can step into conception and birth.

Their power can be looked at through astrology, through angelic patterns of conception and death, and through tarot. They decide the 'when,' and the Weaver defines the 'how.' That does not mean that a human has a set, locked fate; a path that cannot be changed. What it means is that there are certain key points in time where 'hotspots' are active. How we are affected by those hotspots largely depends on our own choice of action.

However, I have found over the decades that there are certain patterns of fate that cannot be dodged or avoided (though some can), and these key moments in time do, indeed, seem to be set before our birth. How we react to them and what we take from them (or give to them) determines our deeper development and maturity.

This is important to understand as a magician, as it directly affects how long-term magical projects are approached, and it also affects our understanding in regards to divination when we look at longer-term events. Some are mutable and some are fixed: as we mature as magicians we learn to spot these hotspots in advance so that we can approach them in the most productive and wisest way possible.

What I have observed personally as a magician over the decades is that as far as death is concerned, there seems to be a final 'fixed' time, but there are also other times that crop up as a result of the 'weave' hotspots and also through our own actions and the actions, usually magical, of others that can potentially take us out. These we can avoid if we know how to.

So in a way, we can potentially not make it to our 'fixed' time, but be taken out earlier through different influences. But I have also observed that when that fixed time comes, nothing can dodge it. Often when I have been around magicians who have come to that fixed point in time, they feel it, recognise it, and understand it. They start to disconnect from the world around them and go with the power flow rather than fight it.

My findings over years of magical exploration tell me without doubt that these beings exist and have a direct influence upon us, but the 'known wisdom' that we have about them is rudimentary. In real terms I have seen and experienced that the influence of these beings upon us is far more complex that it would at first seem. But for you as apprentices, starting from the rudimentary understanding will suffice.

As an adept, you will interact with these beings for yourself and will over time observe their influence in the world around you. From that, you will come to gain your own personal knowledge of their power and action, which is the true way the Mysteries work: you experience the depths of the inner worlds in a way that is specific to you. That in turn matures and develops you as a spiritual, mystical being.

4. The Keeper of Justice

The Keeper of Justice is a power that many will be familiar with: it is a power that is still depicted at courthouses throughout the Western world. Again, this power appears to us as female and is well known to us as, like the Weaver and the Fates, it is a power that resides on our side of the threshold. This means it is easy for our consciousness to tune in and connect with this power. However, the deeper powers and meaning of this being are, like the others, often misunderstood, and are expressed in our culture in their simplest and least powerful forms.

The Keeper of Justice is not a goddess; it is an angelic force that is akin to a fulcrum. It is the centre of two opposing forces, and its job is to keep a balance between them. So for example, the Keeper of Justice acts as a narrow filter for the powers of the Grindstone and the Unraveller, and also for the deeper powers that are behind those two polarities: the Keeper ensures a necessary balance between the two, whatever level of balance is needful for a particular soul to manifest physically.

Another function of this being is to act as a gatekeeper or filter that magicians encounter when they work in the Desert realm. This being maintains the tension of energy, like a membrane, that the magician passes through as they step deeper into the inner worlds. If the magician is working towards maintaining a semblance of balance in their lives, that balance will be strengthened and assisted as they pass back and forth through this membrane.

If the magician is working in a very unbalanced way, or is very unbalanced within themselves, then passing through this membrane will either push them back out of the inner worlds or will create yet more imbalance within the magician. We see this manifesting as things so extreme as magicians becoming increasingly mentally unstable as they try to force their way into the inner worlds in an unbalanced way. Another more simple and protective way this membrane can affect magicians is to push them out of vision if their body is harbouring disease, or if they are in an energetic space that is not conducive to inner work: it has a protective action.

If the magician is, for example, infected with a flu virus but not yet showing symptoms, the energetic pattern of the virus will already be making the magician energetically vulnerable: if they gained access to the deeper aspects of the inner worlds while incubating an illness, the energetic impact of the work would most likely enable the virus to attack the magician's body more successfully.

Similarly, if the magician has some event coming into their very near future that would need a lot of energy (pregnancy, a major life change, etc.), the Keeper of Justice will not allow the magician to pass deeper into the Desert. This is to ensure that the energy reserves of the magician are kept at their optimum for what is to come.

Another octave of the Keeper of Justice is the *Keeper of the Scales*: the being that oversees the power of Ma'at in our world. In a mundane life, the Keeper has minimal interactions with a human life. If, however, that human is a magician or a priest/priestess, then the deeper that human steps into the Mysteries, the more and more the Keeper will engage in order to guide the human on a path of balance. We see this through the Mysteries of the Threshing Floor, something you will learn a great deal more about in future lessons. It is also a power that is heavily involved in the action of the Sword of Justice (the Sword of Damocles).

The deeper into the Mysteries the adept goes, the more the Keeper engages with them and flows as a governing power through their lives. This enables the magician to learn how to maintain balance within an unbalanced physical existence (all physical life is unbalanced in some way – it has to be for physical manifestation to happen), and how to govern themselves and their magical work in as balanced a way as possible.

You have already, through your previous exercises and lessons, learned the beginning of how this power flows through magic, and the deeper you go in your magical studies, the more this power will crop up in your life. If you are willing, as a magician, to learn the lessons laid before you by the Keeper and to work closely in conjunction with this power, then as a magician you will mature into your own power and learn how to wield it wisely.

The power of the Keeper not only works on the threshold of the Desert, but operates throughout creation and nature: once you learn how to recognise and understand this power, you will see it in action in everything around you. It is the power that keeps polarities tight and balanced, it maintains the flow of creation and destruction in the manifest world, and it maintains opposing energies and powers within every living thing.

So now you begin to see that the Keeper of Justice has little to do with the maintaining of cultural or moral laws that are disconnected from the deeper powers of creation. The Keeper does not judge or moralise; the Keeper simply triggers the process of rebalancing that which is unbalanced, and helps to maintain balance where it exists.

5. The Keeper of the Threshold

Now we are getting to the layer of beings that are not so well known in mythology and stories. The Keeper of the Threshold is the first being that works in creation that is only really known to the mystics and magicians throughout time, and was not written about much. Whereas the outer beings involved in creation who resided on 'our side of the threshold' were often communicated with, interacted with, and were widely known, the being on the threshold and the beings beyond were reached only by priesthoods and magicians working beyond the threshold.

The culture that did penetrate the threshold and pass on pertinent information that we know of was Ancient Egypt. The early kingdoms (pre-dynastic and Old Kingdom) really knew their stuff, and as a magician wanting to learn the true depths of magic, it would be wise for you as a student to study the texts and wall paintings from these amazing people. For many years I did not fully understand the depths of their knowledge. It was only as an adept and visiting Karnak that I finally realised just how knowledgeable these people were of the inner worlds and of magic.

The Keeper of the Threshold is a vast angelic consciousness that transforms the deep inner pattern created from the Divine Breath and gives it the *inner form* of the outer being that it will become. The Keeper of the Threshold does not determine what those patterns will become; rather this being is the catalyst that triggers the transformation, takes the information from the pattern, and moulds it into shape as per instructions. Some cultures do depict this being, often in the form of a potter who takes raw materials and gives it shape. So if you are looking for reference to this being in ancient texts and myths, look for a depiction of a potter (the ancient Egyptians called this power *Khnum*).

As a magician, you would not work directly with this power. As a power that sits on the threshold, it is too vast a power for a magician to attempt to communicate with, and it is not a power that human magicians should attempt to work with or harness. But an awareness of this being, as a working adept, will help the magician to not make inadvertent dangerous mistakes.

6. The Utterer and the Wheel

Before we get to the being that you as an apprentice can meet and work with, there are two other powers found upon the threshold of the Desert that it would be pertinent for you to know about. One is the Utterer, and the other is the Wheel. If you have studied tarot, the Wheel will be familiar to you, and for those who have studied theology, the Utterer will be known to you.

The Utterer is an angelic being that operates through the element of air and works within a narrow field of action. That action is the use of sound to affect change. This angel mediates the Divine Breath of God from the inner world to the outer world.

> "In the beginning was the Word, and the Word was with God, and the Word was God."[1]

The Utterer mediates this *Word* out into the world in various forms, the most natural expression being particular storms that effect change.[2]

Another more commonly known action of the Utterer is to mediate wisdom and knowledge to humanity. This comes in the form of revelations, inspired writings, prophecies, and the teaching of humans who are treading a path into the Mysteries. The action of this angel can also been seen through inspired music, poetry, and stories, all of which bring change to the world and to the minds of humans.

---

[1] The gospel of John 1:1 New Testament King James Version.

[2] In my book *Magic of The North Gate* I talk about these storms that have 'intent.'

A non-mystical, non-magical example of this is something that the composer Igor Stravinsky (1882–1971) once talked about.

He said:
> "I heard, and I wrote what I heard.
> I am the vessel through which the *Sacre* passed."

He was talking about the composing of *Le Sacre du Printemps* (*The Rite of Spring*) which premiered in 1913.

This music was particularly discordant to the ears of that time, and was described as "sending listeners to hell" and driving people "to eat ashes and fill their bellies with the east wind" (Jean Cocteau). Indeed, not only did this piece of music change music in the west forever – it also foresaw the First World War.

When Stravinsky wrote this music, he did not alter it, refine it, or edit it. His notations show no working upon the composition; rather he literally wrote it out in one draft as he heard it. This is an example, of which in history there are many, of the Utterer speaking through a human. Don't forget that sound and vibrations are the main powers through which the angelic beings of creation work: the mediation of words is very much a secondary thing.

The Utterer was also responsible for the revelations of the Prophets, and this angelic being stands behind humans who speak with an inspired voice, a voice that changes nations.

The Wheel is fairly well known to most magicians, and is an angelic being that brings change. The Wheel constantly turns and powers the cycle of birth and death, creation and destruction, and the shifting sands of fate.

As an initiate, you will learn to spot the action of the Wheel in your life, and learn how to work directly with it to facilitate that change in a conscious way: you will learn to actively participate in your fate rather than be swept along by it. The Wheel is one of the driving forces behind major 'hotspots' on your web of fate (which you will learn more about soon).

7. THE NOBLE COMPANIONS/THE NOBLE ONES

The Noble Companions/Ones, also known as the *Sandalphon*, are a collection of angelic beings that act as guides, companions, teachers, and protectors of humans who tread the road of the Mysteries. Some teachings connect the Sandalphon to the Wheel, but they are in fact different, but similar, powers. Like many angels, the Sandalphon are a hive being: when all the bits are brought together, you have a massively powerful archangel. What we work with as magicians appears as one angel, but is in fact a fragment of this greater being (hence they are often referred to in plural). We get a small bit so that we can withstand the communion and work with them. This is why often a single angel is referred to as 'them': they are both an individual power and a group of many.

The Sandalphon, known in Egyptian texts as *The Noble Ones*, are beings that assist in the mystical evolution of humanity. They guide us along the road of the future, and walk with us as we step into the inner realms of the Desert. These are beings that we can talk to, ask questions of, and who will accompany us as we stretch deeper and deeper into the inner realms. They will not protect you from your own stupidity: you are responsible for yourself, for your own safety, and your own learning. They will point things out to you, show you things you would not have necessarily found by yourself, and will guide you to scenes where you can observe and learn. But they will not spell things out for you, and they will not stop you from making mistakes that you can learn hard lessons from: they are true teachers.

As a magician, as you learn and mature, your interactions with the Sandalphon will expand beyond the inner realms, and they will become more apparent in your outer life as you learn to externalise your mystical development. As you cross from doing magic to *becoming* magic, the Sandalphon will walk beside you and a subtle interplay will develop between you as learn, grow, and mature. The first step towards developing this relationship is to meet them in vision. From that first meeting, you can then begin to work with them as you learn to step into and carefully explore the inner worlds.

Do not think of these beings as parents who will indulge you or overprotect you: they will not. If you do not tread with respect and caution in your visionary work, they will not protect you from the consequences of such immaturity. As a magician, you are responsible for yourself, and yet if you are in true danger and have acted to the best of your knowledge and ability, they will nudge you to safety.

Building a relationship with these beings is of the utmost importance for a magician, as they are beings that can guide you into the Deeper Mysteries and will show you things that you must experience for yourself. For you as an apprentice, the best way to make this connection is through vision. For the following vision in your practical work, learn the vision first by reading it a few times. Note in your mind the key points, as they are the triggers that will put you into the realm of the threshold, and will also trigger these beings into action. Don't worry if in the midst of vision you forget a minor detail: as long as you follow the key steps, you will be successful. Working in vision this way, alone and without a resonant adept working with you, is harder and takes longer to truly trigger power in vision. But it also makes you self-sufficient and allows you to progress at a rate that is healthy for your body and mind. So don't feel like you are a failure if at first it is difficult to make any powerful connection: it can take time and practice. Eventually you will start to feel the power shift happening, and like all skills, the more you practise, the better you will get at it.

8. *Task:* **The Vision of the Sandalphon**

Light a candle in the east of your work space, sit in the centre of the room, and meditate until your mind is still (east is the magical direction of the threshold).

Once you are still, see with your inner vision the candle flame burning. Stand up in vision, and walk to the candle flame. Bow to the powers and contacts in that direction, and then step into the flame. Bathe in the flame, which is the flame of life, and feel things being burned away from you: things that no longer belong with you. You are cleansed and energised by the flame which flows through you and all around you.

When you are ready, step forward beyond the flame, with the clear intention of stepping to the threshold that joins the inner and outer worlds. You find yourself in a place of stillness and silence. Beneath your feet is sand, a flat desert that stretches off in all directions. Most of the landscape is obscured by mists, and you can only see a small area of desert around you.

Call out, both in vision and with your physical voice:

"I call upon the Sandalphon,
if they are willing and it is right,
to allow me to meet with them."

In time, a figure will walk towards you out of the mists. The figure is tall, with long hair stretching down their backs and flowing into the sand behind them. They walk in the sand, their lower legs and feet deep in the sands of the desert.

(If they do not appear, simply wait and meditate. If they still do not appear, do not retrace your steps, simply open your eyes and finish the vision: this will keep the inner pattern of the vision going. Work with the vision every day until they do appear. Don't rush it: this works in the timing that is right and safe for you.)

As the figure comes to you, hold out your hand. The Companion 'reads' you through touching your hand and feeling your hair. If you have no hair, they will lay a hand upon your head. The companion will indicate for you to walk with them. Walk alongside them into the mists. The mists may fade, and you may see some of the landscape of the Inner Desert. They may show you things, and if they do, take note.

Take as long as you need in vision to walk with them until they indicate it is time for you to walk back into the mists. You may not see anything for the first couple of times you walk with them: being in their presence is often sufficient to begin with.

The Companion will indicate that they are now going to leave you. Bow to them, turn, and walk into the mist with the intention of walking back into the flame of life. The flame will appear before you. Step into the flame, bathe in its power, and then step forward, stepping through the flame, through the east altar, and back into the room where you first started. Sit back down into your body, and when you are ready, open your eyes. Have your journal before you.

Before you can forget (and you will), write down what you saw, what happened, and draw out any buildings, beings, or signs that you were shown. Later, type up your notes on computer so that they can be submitted if needed.

You may have a long encounter with them or a short one. Neither is preferable; it is whatever is needful for you at that time. Do not try to force any aspect of the vision, do not try to 'imagine great things,' and do not ask them questions or converse with them at this stage. Simply be in their presence and look at whatever is shown to you. Take this contact a step at a time, so that your mind and body can get used to the contact. This is important advice for your own wellbeing – so take this advice and do not get into talking with these powers at this stage of your training.

9. *Task:* Visiting with the Sandalphon

Work with this vision two or three times a week for a month. Keep good notes of each encounter, regardless of how interesting or uninteresting the encounter is. Do not try to filter what you have seen: it is common to see things that you do not understand or that you do not feel belong in that vision. Write everything down: some strange aspects will become better known to you as your skills progress.

Also, do not move on to another lesson until you have worked with these beings for a month. It is a crucial point in your training, and it is important that you gain the skills to connect with these beings properly and get used to working in vision with them. If you find that nothing is happening, keep working with the vision beyond the month: it will connect, as and when it is right for you.

And remember, you see everything in your own mind and imagination: that is the interface that these, and all inner beings, work through to communicate with you. Eventually you will be able to converse with these beings, but such conversing can be a major strain on your energies (their voice carries great power), so be content to simply be with them and look at what they show you. Once they begin talking to you, then you can talk back: let them initiate the first conversation.

When you do begin conversing with these beings, don't ask silly questions that you should find the answers to yourself. And ensure that any question is directly related to your own personal development as a magician and as a human: they are not an oracle, nor are they the Utterer. Keep notes in your journal of the questions that you ask, and type them up into your computer notes.

After you have worked with these beings in vision for a month, make it a routine to visit with them on a fairly regular basis, for example once a month. Keep writing down your encounters, and also note the date, location (both the visionary location and your own physical location), and any time when the Companion appears to you in other visions unexpectedly. This will happen when they are ready to start working with you through your training.

The reason to mark down the time/location details is so that you can then run a chart to see what astrological powers were flowing around you at that time. It can be quite revealing. You would look at the chart of the encounter, and then also at your own transits for that time.

10. *Task:* Stravinsky's Rite of Spring

Lie down and listen to Stravinsky's *Rite of Spring* (find a recording that Stravinsky conducted himself if you can). Listen to it a few times over the month that you are working with the Sandalphon/Noble One. If you are not used to listening to classical music, it will take a few times of listening for you to adjust to the taste. And even if you are used to classical music, the Rite of Spring is not easy to listen to. It is a mediation of the power of destruction that was building up and was about to spill into the physical world in the form of World War I. It was written and first performed in 1913, and World War I broke out in 1914. For Stravinsky, it was a music based expression of sacrifice; a year later the young men of Europe were sacrificed on the battle field in the most terrible war the world had ever known. If you listen with all of this in mind, then you will hear the power that was flowing through the composer.

If you fall asleep, take note of any dreams you have as you doze, or any dreams you have that night. Also note down how it makes you feel, how it affects you, and how it affects the room and the land around you. You can ascertain the effects on the room or land either by your own sensitivity, or by doing a Tree of Life reading with tarot, asking:

"How does this music affect the land around me when it is played?"

11. *Task:* Research

Read up on and research the following: Meskhenet, Shai, and Renenutet (Egyptian mythology), the Norns, the Moirai, The Parcae, and also search for deities of fate in different ancient cultures. Similarly, look up Weaver goddesses around the Ancient world and in mythology. Read their descriptions and see if you can spot where attributes have been added over the ages. Don't attempt to force any of the deities and fates into neat little boxes for your own understanding: cultures approached them in different ways, and their understandings of these powers reflect a lot about their culture and the understanding of that time.

12. *Task:* Working with an image

Once you have a good idea of the different expressions of these powers around the world, choose one of the fates and one of the weaver goddesses and read about them in more depth. Find ancient depictions of your chosen subjects (wall carvings, stone carvings, wall paintings, statues, etc.) and print out the images. Either use the printed out image or create/paint your own image using the original as reference. Don't elaborate on the image or add things in, this is not playtime nor an artistic exercise: you are slowly learning how to transfer power into a window of contact. This is the first step for the apprentice magician.

Once you have the image you are happy with of the Fates and the Weaver, put those images in the northeast section of the room where you work magically. They do not need to be on display if that causes a problem (partner hates them, or there is no room, etc.), they just need to actually physically be in that direction of the work space.

What you are doing through these art actions is learning the first action of enlivening objects (a simple baby step), but you are also slowly introducing these powers into your work space. Many magicians have lots of images and statues dotted around their living or working space. Some do that because it looks good, others do it to psychologically connect with them or they are copying something they have seen on social media. None of those reasons are why you are doing this.

By having images of key, specific powers in your space, you are learning how to live and work in a magical pattern whereby powers and contacts have 'windows' into your life and work. As an adept, you will learn how to connect the powers of the deities, angelic beings, and contacts to images, and enliven them so that the power can connect through that image to work with you in your realm.

It acts like a window, and also like a power filter that keeps the power levels low enough for you to operate around safely. That skill does not suddenly download into you as an adept: it starts right at the beginning of your training.

This first step triggers a deep cycle of learning: it is equivalent to a toddler learning how to draw a face by scribbling a round shape, sticking arms on the side and drawing eyes and a smiley mouth. Although primitive, it is the practice of that scribbling that enables the child to develop fine motor skills.

So, too, the apprentice magician must learn to create and live with images that have the potential to carry power. They learn to choose wisely and not randomly or through dogma, fashion, or will. Each image present in the space of a magician is there for a specific reason, does a particular job, and often is unseen or unnoticed by the uninitiated.

As the magician progresses in their studies, they slowly learn how to gently 'turn on' these images and work with them. Some will not be worked with: their presence in the life of the magician is enough to trigger change and development (the Weaver and the Fates are good examples of this passive presence).

Lesson 6
The Laws of Fate

At this stage in the module, it is time to learn about the underlying laws (dynamics) of fate. This is something that very few magical schools look into or discuss, and yet it is of paramount importance to a magician, as it affects everything you do in magic. Every magical act is governed by these laws, and both its long-term outcome and its effect on you as a magician is dependant on you operating within these laws, both for your own safety and for the safety of everything around you.

The laws of fate are a complex weave indeed, and the culture around many parts of the world (which is Abrahamic-based) is unbalanced in its modern understanding these laws. This cultural overlay is often a major stumbling-block for magicians in their training and practice, hence it is important to address this early on in the training of a magician.

The power dynamics of fate pervade everything that we do, everything around us, and steer us through many lives. Knowing how to navigate this maze, to the extent that we as magicians can know and understand it, enables us to live powerful, fruitful lives as magicians. That does not mean that we live lives free of worry, pain, stress, and disaster; rather it means that the ups and downs of life become a training ground for us, and the 'hotspots' (remember those?) do not take us out or destroy us. We become co-drivers of our fate rather than passive passengers. That shift is a major one for magicians and is a shift that truly defines us as magicians and separates us from the world of non-magicians.

There are three basic dynamics that the magician needs to know about in fate.

They are:

1. The dynamic of self and one's own personal relationship with fate.
2. The family web and how we are deeply connected through blood in our fate.
3. The rest of the world.

Those three sections are very clearly defined in our fate, and each one has its own peculiar dynamic. Before we look at those dynamics, let's first look briefly at the issues of cultural overlay that act as such stumbling-blocks for magicians.

The first is what I call the Disney sentimentality. This is a nice but heavily unbalanced way of viewing the world that has no real bearing on how the world works. It is amplified by New Age sentiment and ends up twisting our understanding of a deep, enduring power dynamic that runs through every living thing. The first thing is that nature is *not cute*. It is not cute simply because everything in nature fights to survive and fights for resources.

When a being (human, animal, plant) is well-resourced, the deeper qualities of sharing, caring, patience, and communion surface in many (but not all) beings. There seems to be a disconnect in our modern thinking: we think such qualities come from being a good person, when in fact they come from being a well-resourced being (barring severe mental illness or severe mental disorders).

A lot of destructive behaviour comes from being under-resourced, be it food, shelter, community, education, or expression. I know this is simplifying the situation, but I don't want to have to write a whole book, which is what it would take, to outline the complexity of this issue. So the issue of being under-resourced (or serious mental health issues) should be something in the forefront of a magician's mind when he or she comes to work on a magical project that involves the fate and behaviour of an individual.

The other mistake that is also often made in issues of fate is that if the magician means well, then all will be well. More damage can be done to a fate pattern by being 'nice' than by being relevant. Sometimes pain, destruction, being under-resourced, etc. is what is needed for a situation to move forward in a balanced way: good or bad can balance the Scales, and the magician needs to know what is needed and when.

Now you begin to see the complexity? Most of this can be navigated through divination and inner sight.

The other main issue that comes up in magic is the misunderstanding of *Karma*. It has become a dogma in the East and the West that everything is locked down in fate and you can do nothing to change your lot: it is your karma. That is total bullshit. There are indeed tides of cause and effect that do run through fate, but they are not fixed: they flow and ebb according to how you act and react, the choices you make, and the choices of those around you. You are, for the most part, in the driver's seat of your own fate, with the inner powers of fate sometimes taking over the wheel at important spots in the road: it is a joint effort.

1. SELF

The understanding of fate in respect to you as an individual is a complex and slowly evolving skill set that usually develops over time depending on our life experience. So for those who are reading this that are young (below 35 years old) much of this knowledge will have to be taken on trust: the true understanding of fate and its actions in the life of a magician depends on personal experience and the ability to spot and recognise the dynamic in action.

Those who are older, and particularly those who have been practically involved in magic for quite some time, will recognise much of what I am about to discuss. I don't want to sound condescending (though I probably will to some), but for most (not all) people it takes a few decades of events, challenges, and knocks before we begin to understand our fate: it was certainly like that for me, and for most people I know. At thirty I knew it all. At fifty I realised I knew very little indeed.

That recognition will help you better understand your own experiences and put them in context of fate and magic. This section on 'Self' will be a bit long, as the subject matter is complex, but I will try to keep it as succinct as possible.

Let's first look at the wider picture of fate in the life of an individual magician, and then we can narrow it down to practicalities. Magicians are *born*; it is not something you wake up one morning and decide to do.

When in the life of the magician they choose to engage in magic largely depends on their individual fate weave. Some wake up to magic in childhood, some trundle along later in life. Some feel like they have done it all before and are simply remembering, and some step into magic as total empty slates ready to be filled. But one thing they all have in common is that the interaction with magic *was already in their pattern before they were conceived.*

If magic is in your pattern, you cannot run away from it. Wherever you turn in life, it will be there waiting for you. However, magic in the pattern of an individual does not always express in ways that we would today consider a 'magical path': it can express through arts, literature, music, science, or religion. Once you work as a magical adept you will instantly recognise someone who is a magician, who is working magically, but is not 'doing magic' (remember Stravinsky?). That in turn makes us stop and think about what we define as 'magic.'

A good example of people who have magic in their fate weave but do not 'do magic' in terms of outer understanding was a person like Nikola Tesla. Tesla was a scientist, but he was also a magician in that he connected to the deeper aspects of creation in dreams and visions, mediated that contact into his work, tapped into (without realising) the Inner Library, and worked instinctively with the energies and powers of creation: he was a magician who expressed that role through physics. We can also see it in people of religion, of the arts, etc.: it is not just a matter of being inspired; that is not the same thing. It is the ability to reach into the inner worlds, mediate that power to the outer world, and in turn effect change. That is essentially all that magic is.

But with that understanding we can immediately see how such action crosses paths with the powers of fate: to act in such a way is to consciously engage with the powers of creation, the powers of life, of time, of substance; and such action can alter the vast weave of fate and creation. If you are going to engage in such activities, which is what magic is all about, you need to understand a bit about how it works so that you do not blow yourself up – or others around you.

Recognising the fate path

Some have stronger, more defined fates than others; that is the first thing to understand. A strong fate path will have very clearly defined hotspots, clearly defined actions, and these will find a way to manifest in the life of a person one way or another. A weaker fate path will still have defining 'ingredients,' but it will be less fixed and more fluid (and there are lots of variants in between).

When you are born, you will have a tool box of qualities and potentials (which can be seen in your natal chart), you will have specific hotspots in your future life path (as defined by the fates, which can be seen through divination), a framework for the soul to operate through (the body, both in genetic make-up but also in how it develops, which in turn depends upon nutrition, physical illness/accident, etc.) and you will have a set of inherited skills, qualities, and problems (from your bloodline).

All these create a framework through which the soul expresses itself in life. The soul also comes into life with its own collections of experiences and skills gained in previous or future lives (unless it is someone's first time around). Already we can begin to see the complex weave that we call fate and how intricate it can be. So we have a picture building of a soul, a vessel for the soul, a context for that vessel, and a place in time/location that the soul and vessel can operate in. The time and location for manifestation is ultimately chosen by the soul at a deep level, and that choice is then translated by the Weaver.

How that complicated weave of fate plays out largely depends on our actions, choices, and how we respond to the events that happen to and around us. Most people are blown along their path of life in this fate weave like tumbling leaves. The magician, however, learns and then engages with the dynamic to ensure that their choices and responses upon this path are clear and are made in gnosis. This in turn allows the potential for the magician to reach to its fullest extent.

Action/reaction

Most magic is born out of a need or wish for action or reaction. Sometimes it is our own wants/needs; other times it is requested of the magician by a third party. Those actions can be anything from simple magic that is involved in healing, issues of money, relationships, protection, etc., to magic that is involved in longer-term issues to do with exorcism, the development of a group or nation, tending the land, or affecting major change that will have long-term consequences for individuals or large groups of people... you get the idea.

All those varied types of magic fall into two categories: *action* or *reaction*. Clearly defining which is which, and understanding which category one is actually working with, has a profound effect not only on the outcome of the magic but also the effect such magic will have on the fate of the magician and of all those involved.

Action magic is where the magic starts a new cycle. *Reaction magic* is where the magic intervenes in an already ongoing situation. Being able to clearly identify which is which is of paramount importance to the magician, as the outcomes will be very different for all involved. Sometimes such identification is easy; sometimes it is more subtle, and the magician should always take the time to investigate and also use divination to ascertain exactly what dynamic it is they are about to work on.

Action magic

Action magic creates a whole new cycle of events. This in turn engages directly with fate powers and also, in certain circumstances, with the powers of creation itself. Immediately you begin to see the potential for huge amounts of power to flow through a magical act regardless of the intent of the magician.

When you instigate a new cycle or triggering of fate, which action magic always does, this can draw deeply on the energy reserves of the magician and affect their own fate pattern at a deep level. The level of effect this will have on the magician can vary widely depending on the long-term implications of the magical action.

Let's look at a simple, practical example of action magic and its effect on the magician. Bear in mind that everything you do as a magician is going to have some sort of effect and you cannot dodge that. What is important to understand is that some effects are worth it for all involved, and some are not. Being able to identify the differences is a skill all magicians need to have.

Let's look at very simple, low-grade magic – which is the most commonly used form of magic. The magician is approached by someone (we will call her Helen) who wants help finding a job by using magic.

An inexperienced magician would immediately get to work and use the methods they know well to trigger a situation where Helen gets a job. If they know what they are doing in terms of magical technique, it will most likely work. But the inexperienced magician did not first step back and look at the overall situation and personality of the person. The magician does his work, Helen gets her job, and immediately the magician begins to get tired and feel energy drained. A few months later, Helen loses her new-found job because she did not do well at it, and she was soon back at the magician's door.

The magician then either figures out something is wrong, or if they are really dumb, they repeat the magical act again. If the magician fails to learn from the direct experience, and continues to do such magic for Helen, the magician will slowly, over time, become ill and poorly resourced in their own life.

So what went wrong? It is simple magic, with good intent, and should not really cause any problems, right? Wrong.

The first mistake the magician made was that they did not investigate *why* Helen could not get a job. If Helen was a hard worker, willing to do what was necessary to find work, but was in trapped in an area of high unemployment, and they had few marketable skills, then what the magician should have done is to use divination to look and see if the magic would indeed *help her fate along*.

Notice the question was not about looking to see if the magic would get Helen a job. If the magician is good at what they do, of course Helen would indeed have gotten a job, but it may not have been in harmony with her fate pattern. For example, Helen could have possibly needed to move out of that area in order to start a new cycle of their fate somewhere else. The only way for that to happen is either for Helen to realise that (and some people also 'feel' it), or the other option is for fate to force Helen's hand by blocking every avenue for work until she *has* to move elsewhere in order to support themselves. By blindly creating a magical pattern for a job, the hapless magician stalled the fate of Helen, which in turn burned up a lot of energy, energy that is drawn directly from the blockage in that fate path: the magician.

Another example of this sort of scenario is where the client does not really want to work and cannot be bothered making the effort to find a job: this helpless victim 'please do it all for me' is a common dynamic in people who seek out magicians to help them. (Not all people who seek help are like this, but many – too many – are.) This would result in a situation where the magician does the work, the client gets the job, loses it, comes back to the magician, and the same thing happens over and over again until the magician either stops the process or becomes too weak to be effective any more.

This constant 'opting out' of personal responsibility pushes the energetic burden back on the magician, and they literally energetically carry the client along a stalled fate path.

The various fate consequences of not checking before instigating action magic can be minor or major: for an extreme example of major consequence, say a client (whom we will call Fred) was a sexual deviant, a rapist by nature. In Fred's fate path, there are hotspots along the way that would force Fred to change or face his behaviour (or would have taken him out) which in turn moves him along a path of learning and maturing. If magic had not intervened in the life of this rapist, he would have been forced, by lack of jobs and poverty, to move to another city.

In that city, the Fred would have been caught, convicted (his Grindstone hotspot in action) and through that conviction and subsequent imprisonment, he would have begun a process of facing his actions and learning both to understand and control his actions; or he may have gained treatment for mental illness, or hormonal instability. Or he would have entered into a cycle of offence and arrest – the hotspot set up the conditions for evolution, but it is up to the person to respond and engage, or not. This in turn would have moved Fred along a fate path that could be one of maturing, or one of total degeneration depending upon how he chose to respond.

Any key hotspot in this complicated weave could have been the one that, if magic had not intervened and Fred had been forced by circumstance to move to a different city, would have saved the women around him in his present location from his attack. By using magic to keep him in a job, there is a potential for a woman to be raped and murdered in a situation that would not have happened if the magician had not intervened.

And as the instigator of that process, the magician bears the full weight of the energy imbalance. Also, the twists and turns of fate can be enormously complex, and if you stall that process through magical intervention, the consequences for all involved can be limitless. It is not all doom and gloom, though.

An adept magician would have seen all of that in a first round of readings about the client, and would have refused to do the work. It is that simple: that is the difference between the actions of an inexperienced magician, and of a true adept.

Another example of a situation in a similar vein is one whereby the magician looks at a client, sees that they are indeed doing everything they can to help themselves, and/or their fate flowers massively if they are helped to get a job. In that sort of case, the magic is done, it is successful, the client blossoms in the job, and the magician has no side effects.

The key to such action is in knowing the long-term consequences of that action, and whether that action is compatible with the individual's fate path and the paths of those around them.

And that in turn is arrived at through interviewing the client, and then doing readings to look at their fate path.

A simple interview with a client can tell you a lot. Are they stupid and lazy and just want a quick, easy solution with no personal effort? Are they drama queens that are trying to stretch beyond themselves? Are they not doing everything in their lives first to solve the problem? (That self-responsibility, or lack of it, is a big flag for a magician.) In a world where people think they can buy anything, magic is often badly misused, and that misuse can rebound in the long-term fate of a magician. They may not feel the impact straight away, but it will catch up with them at some point.

What has this to do with creation? Everything. One of the roles of a magician is to facilitate the fate path of themselves and others, but it is not the role of the magician to interfere in a way that would short-circuit a fate path. The same rules apply to ourselves as magicians. It is very tempting to use the skills of magic to make our lives much easier and obviate our own fate events because we might not like them. And indeed, the magician must not be a victim of their fate; rather, they should be the drivers of their own fate. Consider it like driving a powerful car. If you are irresponsible, you can do a lot of damage; if you are sensible, you can move swiftly down a road while also being safe.

Reaction magic

Reaction magic is magical intervention in an ongoing situation, and often, but not always, where magic is already in the picture. If a magician is wise and knows what they are doing, reaction magic is the easier of the two to deal with: it is simply a matter of rebalancing scales. But even that is not so simple... If, for example, someone has been magically bound, it would make sense to unbind them magically. Sometimes that is all that is needed. But there are times that such a hostile magical act of binding is a part of the learning process of a person, and in those circumstances you would not unbind them; rather you would work magically as a catalyst for the person to find their own solutions magically, which in turn helps them to develop as magicians themselves: the best learning is from direct experience, not theory.

As you are beginning to see, these fate twists and turns can be very complex at times, and dipping into them magically in ignorance can make life a lot harder than it needs to be. The best way I have found to step around those difficulties is to use divination in the form of readings to look specifically at the long-term implications and consequences of particular magical actions before I do them. It has taught me a great deal.

However, it is also important to develop your own intuition, understanding, and wisdom. Do not just rely on one source of information: learn to use your magical skills along with your own common sense and understanding, and also your free will of choice. Some people reading this might not agree with me (that short-term magic like jobs/money magic causes any problems) and my answer to that is, sure – find out for yourself through long-term direct action and experience. Now you will be beginning to understand why good tarot skills are important for a magician, and why it is important that you learn them step by step in order to be a successful, safe and healthy magician.

Guardians and guides

Before we move on to looking at fate in families and the world in general, I would just like to cover a word or two about guardians and guides. When you step onto a magical path, your fate immediately 'wakes up' and can often accelerate, which can be uncomfortable at times but is ultimately worth it.

The other thing that happens through your stepping into magic and magical training is that you become, at some point, consciously connected with your Guardian Angel and the inner guides and beings around you. This in turn enables you to feel, hear, smell, see, or dream them when they are trying to warn you, connect with you, or teach you. These are all inner senses, something you learned about in your early lessons.

Their job is to help you, guide you, and open doors a crack for you on your magical and spiritual path of development. They do not carry you, or protect you from your own stupidity: they do not interfere with your learning process. But they will intervene at crucial moments of danger, or at times when it is really important that you stop and make a careful decision. They may speak to you through your mind, your dreams, or you may feel them around you.

There is a lot of talk in magic of "communion with your HGA," with long and elaborate processes for opening communication lines. You do not need to do that. What you need to do is learn to be still, to be aware, and as you develop as a magician, so the communion develops naturally.

The first step for an apprentice magician is to know that 'the team' is there and that it is your job to be ready to listen, take note, and act accordingly. Often it is like a whisper at first, or a 'feeling' or instinct. If you learn to recognise that, it grows, develops, and becomes eventually a relationship of communion.

If you try to force that communion through ritual, you will potentially short-circuit the natural development of the relationship: the communion will constantly be reliant upon ritual to open the doors rather than allowing the doors to open naturally, in which case they stay open all the time. It can be more frustrating to let it develop in its own time, but trust me, it is worth it.

And when you are aware that a guardian or guide has just saved your ass, thank them. I have been saved from disaster by guardians more times than I care to admit, and the process of saying thank you, and being aware of them, normalises the process of communion at a deep level within us, which in turn strengthens it.

2. Fate web of the family

The relationship of fate with families is a curious thing. We are heavily interwoven with those of our blood, whether we like them or not. And it does not need to be in a direct line: childless aunts can affect nieces and nephews and pass on skills sideways down a line through the children and grandchildren of their sisters.

Ten years ago I thought I had the family fate thing sort of figured out, only to find more recently that it is even more complex than I realised. Rather than write yet more volumes on the subject, suffice it to say that blood ties are strong, and when you do magic, it can amplify them. It does not mean that the tie is strong to every one of your family members, but it does mean that key people within your line will be oddly connected to you in strange and energetic ways: you can have what I call 'collective fate' which is fate paths of a similar nature, or ones that are dependant on each other. You may not have anything to do with these family members, but even so, the connections can run deep, and waves of fate can wash through a family line like a tidal wave.

Because of this, when you work magically it can affect family members at a very deep level. Usually this is good. When you develop as a magician, you also develop as a soul and as a human. That development spreads out through your bloodline, and those who are linked strongly to you through fate will also benefit from your development. And that also is true for past family ancestors: the magical work you do today affects those who came before you as well as those around you and those who will come after you.

This is something to keep in mind when you make magical choices. It is healthier, however, for your family to benefit as a side effect of your magical work, rather than trying to work directly on your family, something which is fraught with potential pitfalls. A lot of benefit comes from the passive backwash from balanced magic: it positively affects your bloodline, the land you live on, and also you as a magician.

And this is another thing that you as a magician will find: if you do what you are supposed to be doing magically, you will never need to do magic for money, housing, or any other minor outer need: if you do your work in the way you are supposed to, what you need will come to you through outer means.

It took me a long time to trust this dynamic, but when I finally let go of the control (I am a control freak) and focused on what I was supposed to be doing, what I needed came to me as I needed it. It is all part of the fate weave: learn to work with your fate, get on with your work, and the guardians of your fate will do their job also. If you try to control it yourself, they will step back and let you get on with it, but they are far better at the job than you can ever be.

3. Fate and the wider world

In this day of internet and global communication, we are constantly bombarded with events and issues that are far removed from us. As magicians there is a great temptation to step in and work magic to affect world events in some way or another. This is folly for so many reasons, and yet to do nothing goes against our instincts. Those instincts were formed as the result of our cultural upbringing, and we have to recognise when that is surfacing: we assume our caring and compassion is our nature, when in fact it is our conditioning and being in a culture that is well-resourced.

When you step out of Western culture and live in a different country, you come to hear mantras like "it's not my problem". This is in an under-resourced country: the people focus on what is immediately around them. Start to see how simple facts of nature have a bearing on our expressions of culture at a deep level?

What I have found is that if you are meant to do something about an event or situation that is far removed from your family, land, and community, the job will be placed before you in no uncertain terms. And that job may often not be what you expected. Cultures, people, and landmasses all have their own fate paths and patterns, and to dabble with them, regardless of good intentions, can have disastrous long-term consequences for everyone involved. And you will be carrying the energetic consequences for the rest of your life. This is not theory: I have seen and experienced this for myself many times over, and am myself carrying the consequences of my own ignorant past.

But there are times when it is within your pattern to intervene, and if so, you will know about it very clearly. It is very unlikely to happen to you before you reach adeptship, as such work involves many different skills. The basic rule, which many do not like to hear, is simple: sort your own backyard out first. Once you are capable of working further, and it is right for you to do so, you will be placed in the midst of the situation so that you can effect change.

And that is all that you tend to usually do in these circumstances: you either mediate whatever is necessary to bring balance to a situation, or you mediate change. Sometimes, rarely, you are given a specific job to do, and when that happens you rarely get to know what it is you are doing until it is over. This is to ensure that you do not inadvertently make stupid mistakes through misplaced emotion. I have been dumped into the middle of war zones, revolutions, contested elections, and epidemics; given a job to do, and then immediately taken back out of the situation.

Most of the time I had no clue what I was doing until after the fact. Then it slowly dawned on me what I was working on.

This way of working seems alien to us in a world of 'knowing' and control, but it is precisely those dynamics of our modern world that short circuit deep magic. You have to learn to trust: we are simple workers in a vast, complex weave of fate, and we need to be humble enough to just do our jobs without wanting control or to be 'saviours.' Some people see that as being weak: I would say that is someone who does not know power.

A note on the practical work

Most of the following tasks are tarot readings. The skill of tarot has a major part to play in the work of a magician, particularly when working around fate, so lots of practice is a good thing. Because you are going to be looking at various fate patterns it will take a lot of energy, and you will need to spread these tasks out over a few days: don't do them all in one day, as it will drain you energetically.

Take your time with them and maybe spread them over a week or more. Expand out from the set questions and experiment if you wish to; just keep tight records, snapshots of the readings (or write down the cards in their positions), and type your notes up on computer so that you can go back to them or compare them in the future with other Quareia magicians who have done the same exercises. Ensure that you wash your hands well with liquid soap, salt, and water after each reading session: you do not want to be carrying around fragments of the readings.

4. *Task:* Fate recognition

After you have meditated for the day, sit and think about your life from birth up to this point. Think about the places you have lived, the events that have happened to you, the choices you have made for good or bad, and look carefully at how certain key points, decisions, and actions have led onto better or key things in your life. Learn to recognise where fate has swept you along, and where you have had a defining input into your fate.

This simple exercise can start a process of learning and understanding within you of how fate operates around you. Obviously the older you are, the easier it is going to be for you as you, are more likely to have had major experiences in your life that are easily recognisable (though some youngsters do have a lot packed into their short lives!). Look for events out of your control, maybe ones that you fought at the time but that you eventually realised led to better things or to learning. Look for events that were a direct result of your own decisions. Think about how different (or not) they felt.

Also think about whether there were any signals you were given that you spotted.

For example, I have been moved around (from town to town and then country to country) a lot by fate ever since I was a little girl, and sometimes I moved by my own choice. Each time this happened, before I had made any decision or an event had happened that moved me on to another home, I would find it difficult to clean my house. No matter what I did, it always looked untidy or did not feel right. It took me a long time to recognise this fate signal, but that is what it was. At a deep unconscious level somewhere, my fate weave 'pinged' to me that I no longer belonged where I was, and that it was time to move. That 'not belonging' manifested for me as the house not feeling comfortable, and for me not being able to keep it balanced.

Everyone will have their own unique 'pings' or signs that they will discover if they look back over events. Some are common ones, and some are totally unique to the person. So take the time to look back over your life to see if any have emerged for you yet. This pondering upon your own fate path is a very good exercise for you to do. It is good to look back through your own memory before you start to look using tarot: see what you can for yourself first, and then the readings will fill the picture out for you.

5. *Task:* Looking at historical fate patterns using tarot

Do a search for well-known historical stories in which someone within the event had a pre-warning of what was to come: Cassandra and the fall of Troy is a famous example. Once you have chosen the event, read as much as you can about it, any small details, oddities, etc. Now get your tarot deck.

1. First do a reading using the four-directional pattern, and ask the question:

    "What inner forces were flowing into the event that triggered the person to have a precognition of the event?"

Look at what powers are showing in the east (coming/air/forming), south (here, at their height/fire) and west (starting to fade/population/water). Write them down, and look at the information the cards give you. What is your overall first impression? Is it obvious what was coming (the inner worlds shouting) or was it a subtle power that could still do a lot of damage once it manifested?

2. Then ask:

    "How did the event affect the fate of the person who had the precognition?"

Sometimes people have a precognition of an event that will not personally affect their fate in a negative way, but which will affect those around them badly (it is a precog of service to others). Other times the precog of an event is not just a warning for everyone else, but also for their own fate as well. Sometimes they are warned to get out of the way but not tell anyone else, and sometimes they are told what will happen, and that it will destroy them personally (they are given warning of their own death within the disaster).

When this warning of their own, as well as the collective doom, is pending, it is usually a major part of their fate and it will be ultimately productive for their soul/spirit: the warning is to prepare for the death, not to avoid it. See if you can discern which, if any, of these dynamics were playing out.

3. Now do a reading using the Tree of Life layout and ask:

*"What was the ultimate outcome of this fate pattern:
was it for the good of the nation/people involved or was it to destroy them?"*

Go by the last card in the reading (position number 10). Sometimes disasters are ultimately to push evolution forward, and sometimes they simply destroy and compost in order to make way for something different.

6. *Task:* Looking at your personal fate pattern with tarot

1. If you, in the past, have had a pre-warning about something in your life, a precog of something that then happened, do similar readings to the ones you have just done. Do a reading to look at what it is you were shown at that time (your keyhole/fragment view of the event), then look at the actual event (you get a wider picture), and then do the reading to look at what the ultimate long-term outcome was/will be for you. If you have not had an experience like this, move on to part 2 of this task.

2. Now think about your previous lessons in this module, and think about the dynamics of the Grindstone and Unraveller, their actions and effects in life. Think back to times in your life when these powers may have been active in your life, either through your own engagement/actions, or through fate inflicting them upon you. If you can identify times in your life when these powers were active, think about the situation. Then do a reading, using the Tree of Life layout, and ask:

*"This situation, what was the longer-term outcome for my fate pattern,
did it help me along or did it hinder my fate?"*

If the reading showed that the action of one of these powers hindered you, then do a reading using the same layout and ask why. It may show that it was because of your own action/reaction, or it may show some force outside of you hindering your fate. Write down the readings and think about the end card. The rest of the reading shows how the outcome came about.

3. Use the four-directional pattern (with the relationship card crossing the first/central card) and ask:

*"The situation I just looked at in my past, what were the deeper and longer
term powers that were flowing through my fate pattern at that time?"*

It may show harsh powers, regenerative powers, ancestors, deities, etc., or a mix. What it will show, as you are looking at your own fate pattern in a simple way, is what was needful then to get you where you are now. Read it in that context.

Lesson 7

Working with your Past

1. Crafting notes

The Cloth

For this lesson you will need a large white piece of cloth, either big enough to act as a cover that you drape around yourself, or large enough to cover the working space of your temple/work space floor.

If you want to work in the future with a magical shield that is placed around you, choose a simple, plain white cotton bed-sheet that will drape over your shoulders and that is big enough for you to wrap yourself up in. If you want to learn how to stand upon your shield (the magical floor), then choose a king-size or bigger piece of white cotton cloth that covers your working space. You can roll it up and put it away when you need to work magic that should not involve your own fate pattern.

The Cord

You will also need a length of cord. Measure it with you arms outstretched at your sides at shoulder height: it should be long enough to stretch from hand to hand with your arms held out, but it should be no longer that your outstretched arms: any length beyond your hands should be clipped off. During this lesson, the fabric and cord will become 'tuned,' and then in Module V you will learn how to turn them into an enlivened magical tool: the Shield.

Altars

You should also have four altars for the directions and one for the centre by now. If you have been using bits of furniture etc. in the directions, that is fine, but it is coming to the time when you will need an altar for the centre that is only used for that purpose.

The cheapest and most mobile way to do that is to get a small but tallish fold-up table, similar to the ones used for camping or for garden furniture. Whatever you use, make, or buy, make sure you can stand before it and touch it with your hands without having to bend over, that the surface is big enough to accommodate five candles laid out in the directional pattern, and that you can put things under it. It does not matter what it is made from, though wood or metal is best. If you are really broke, make it yourself out of scraps of wood or even cardboard. If money is no issue, do not buy some fancy wild magical altar: it needs to be simple, clear, and mobile.

2. On the rest of the module

Now that you have had to plough through lots of reading and not much action, the final two lessons of this module will be more doing than reading. It was important for you to get a good understanding of some of the powers, dynamics, and beings involved in creation and fate before stepping into the work that you are about to do. To dabble in your own or anyone else's fate without any understanding can have all sorts of implications, some of which you will be now familiar with: that understanding will act as a caution for you, and make you think carefully before you step into any magical act that can trigger or change a fate pattern.

Before you begin to look and work with your own fate pattern, first you must learn to magically look back over your life so far, and learn how to *time jump* into sections of the life you have already lived. This can be a very interesting magical act that, once you have worked with it for a while, will change your view on spirit encounters, your view on time, and your understanding of how time does, or does not, affect inner actions.

This "going back before you go forward" is part of a power dynamic that roots you, grounds you, and slowly begins the process of stretching your spirit out like chewing gum until it becomes more fluid and your boundaries less rigid (it is an octave of the dynamic of "going down before you go up"). This in turn allows your spirit and vessel (body) to be able to work without too much impact when you start to work forward in time: it is like muscle exercise for the spirit, while also teaching you a great deal.

3. Passing into the past

In this lesson, you are going to learn how to go back into moments of your life and intervene if needed.

If you think of time as a linear path, this work will tie you up in knots trying to understand what it is you are doing. Time and events are very fluid and heavily interwoven: just learn to flow through time, and don't try to take it apart to analyse it until you have worked a great deal in the methods of flowing back and forth through time. That way, when you do come to analyse it for yourself, you will be able to draw on a good reservoir of direct experience that will help you understand it in a way that you can work with.

This method uses ritual as a gateway and vision as an interface to allow your consciousness to flow back through time within your own life pattern in order to observe, interact, and commune with yourself at an earlier age. This is not a psychological act: it is an active magical act that effects change beyond ourselves.

Think of your life not as a path you walk, even though we often magically work with 'paths' as an access point to the future. Think instead of a large fishing net with shiny things dotted around the fabric of the web. Think of time as spreading out from the centre, which is your conception, and the rest of your physical life flows around, upon, and within this 'net' like water. There is no real 'back' and 'forward'; it is more like, 'over here' and 'over there.' Changes made by revisiting events you have already enacted trigger the whole net to change in a constant evolution – your past, present, and future all change.

Learning to be more malleable with your understanding of time will stop you from blocking yourself by overanalysing – just do it, and then let the impact unfold slowly. Then you can think about it, and let your deeper instincts and the guardians around you gently nudge your understanding.

In the last few lessons, you have been casting your thoughts back into various events in your life so far, and have potentially done some readings about them. This has tuned you in a bit to remembering and recalling past events, what they felt like, what was happening, etc. Go over your notes from those lessons, and then sit and think about times in your life where you may have felt total despair, helplessness, or a great deal of pain or anguish, fear, etc.: it does not matter how far back in your life you go, even if it was early childhood.

Once you have identified a key moment in your life when you were really suffering or were vulnerable, try to remember everything you can about that event: smells, sounds, what you saw, what you heard, what impressions you have of that time. Write them all down. Build up the image of that incident/time in your mind until you have a clear feel or snapshot of it that you recognise.

A warning

This really is not a psychological working that you are going to do. It is active magic, and if you are successful you will trigger change in your life and the lives of others who were involved with you at that time.

The warning is not about danger, but about respecting the power that you are working with. Do not instigate an action thinking "oh it doesn't really matter, it's only all in my head and no harm will come": that would be a great folly. For example, if you were the victim of an attacker in your past and you are going back to that point, the attacker and his/her fate and actions have nothing whatsoever to do with you: they are not your responsibility, nor is it valid to do an act of revenge, punishment, whatever.

Do not misuse this technique: it is solely about you, your own fate, your own life, and nobody else's. Overcome any temptation to meddle with anyone else.

Now it is time to get to work.

4. Practical Work

You will need your cloth, your personal pentagram pattern (with your planets, names etc. on it) and the length of cord. You will also need a cushion and a blanket to have a sleep on.

Leave yourself plenty of time to do this work, and ensure that you will not be disturbed. Set up your working space with the altars in the directions, and place the pentagram pattern image inside the fabric (wrap the fabric around it) and place it under the central altar. Position the cord around the central flame in a loop.

Sit and meditate until you are still and settled, and think about the point in your past that you want to work with. Throughout this working, keep that time foremost in your mind. The process of stretching starts now. When you are ready, get up, light candles in the correct manner that you have learned, open the gates using the method you have learned, and acknowledge any contacts stood on the thresholds: throughout this ritual keep a mental focus of intent to pass into a specific time situation.

Now go and stand before the central altar. This is your fate ground zero: everything you are, everything you have been, and everything you will be all begins here in the centre of the pattern, and the flame that is tuned to the centre of the pattern is resonant with the flame that burns within the centre of your being.

Spend a little time tuning in to the central flame in the magical space, and the central flame within your own centre: they are one and the same flame. The outer flame is an exteriorised 'twin' of your inner flame. The temple space is an exteriorised 'twin' of your own magical consciousness.

Once you feel fully tuned to the centre, circle the room, starting (as always in ritual action) in the east. Stop at each altar briefly to bow, while keeping awareness that east and south are the powers of 'future' and west and north are the powers of 'past.' When you reach the north, bow, and then stay in that direction.

Be aware of the contact at the threshold of the north gate. It may be ancestral, it may be faery, a land being, or an angelic being: whatever being it is, acknowledge them and state, using your physical voice, that you intend to pass through the gates of time and work with your younger self. Ask for guidance from the Noble One, the Sandalphon who stands behind you beyond the south gate.[1] Place your hands (or fingertips if it is low down) on the altar as you need to have physical contact with the altar.

You will do the vision aspect of this work standing up with your eyes closed (to stop you falling asleep and getting into hot water inadvertently).

---

[1] Now that you have made visionary contact with them, they are likely to turn up in a lot of your workings, particularly key ones.

Close your eyes, and with your inner vision see the gate and the threshold of the north before you on the other side of the north altar. See the flame before you, and feel your inner flame: be aware of it resonating with the outer flame in the north. Remember that point in your past that you are intending to visit.

When you are ready, see yourself step *through* the altar of the north (it is important that you do not walk around it, but pass in vision through the body of the north altar) and cross over the threshold of the north with the intention of going to a particular time in your life that you have already pinpointed in your mind.

As you cross the threshold, you will find yourself standing in mist. Keep a mental focus on that point/incident in time, and keep focus on the intent to visit that time. Once you have total focus on that intent, start walking forward into the mist. You may walk only a few steps, or you may have to walk for a while until you come to a state where the mists begin to clear.

As the mists clear, you will find yourself stepping into a scene. It may take you a little time to orientate yourself, and it may also take you a little while to recognise your younger self in that scene (we often appear different in spirit than we do in body). If you have arrived at a scene from your past that is not the one you intended, but is still an aspect/event of your past, stay with it: you will have been directed to that event in particular because you were more needful of work at that point in time than the event you had intended to go to.

Watch the scene passively as it unfolds around you. Do not get drawn into the emotion of the situation or the memories. This can be hard, but it is vital that you do not connect emotionally with the memory. Observe yourself in that scene, observe your inner energies (which may appear to you as lights or colours around and within you), and watch your emotions. There will come a crisis point where the lights within the body seem to dip as the full impact of the situation hits your younger self. It may be in the midst of the situation, or it may be the time directly after: just stay with the scene until you see that dip. Some magicians observe it as a dip in vibration, or sound, light, colour, scent: whatever shows around and within your younger self that is fluctuating. When you see that dip, that is the time to get to work. As soon as the dip happens, that is the deep impact in your inner energies at that time, a dip that can be dangerous for you in terms of longer-term damage, and weakens the web both at that time and in your future.

Step over to your younger self and place your hands upon their shoulders, standing behind them (always behind them). If it is a particularly traumatising event, stand behind them and wrap your arms and your energies around them. Now allow your own vital force/inner flame to brighten and to spread around and within them: share your current strength and vitality with them.

Whisper into the ear of your younger self: tell her/him that it is okay, they are not alone, that they will flower, grow, mature, and go on to great things. Tell them they are guarded: let a feeling of safety, protection, strength and endurance flow into them from you. They may or may not hear you: it doesn't matter. What matters is that the dip is rectified by filling them with strength, and letting that young spirit know that they are going to be okay and that they are not alone.

Once you feel they are more stable, step back and immediately walk away back into the mists without staying around to see how they do: it is important with past work to leave immediately after you have finished what you are doing.

Walk through the mists with the intention of stepping back over the north threshold. When you reach the gate/the gate appears, step over the threshold, through the altar, and open your eyes. You or may not feel very tired after that working: if the event was a major hotspot in your fate weave, your intervention will have taken a lot of energy.

But you cannot rest just yet.

Now go to the central altar with the south beyond the central altar and the north behind you, and pick up the cord. Hold the cord out so that it stretches across your chest from east to west with the ends in your hands – your arms should be out at your sides, at shoulder length, with your left hand in the east and your right hand in the west.

Close your eyes, and see with your inner vision the gates of the south. Two figures immediately step through the threshold: one is the Noble One and the other is a mature woman in ornate clothing. The Noble One puts out an arm for the lady, and they walk together to the other side of the central altar and stand before you.

The lady is Lachesis, the Measurer (also known as Decima). She closely inspects the cord you are holding, and then she pulls out a cord from her robes and measures it against your cord: she is checking that your cord is indeed the right length. She indicates to you to give her your cord. Drop your arms, and hold out the cord over the altar (careful of the flame) to her side of the flame (the flame is always a threshold).

Lachesis places her cord into your cord so that they become one and hands it back to you: now lay it back down in a circle around the central flame – your ground zero and your measure are together. Lachesis steps back, and the Sandalphon steps forward. The Noble One bends down and places his hands upon your sheet and pentagram pattern that is under the altar. He waits as something passes into the cloth/pentagram, and when he has finished he stands up, bows to the central flame, and then steps back.

Bow to Lachesis, the fate who measures life and to the Noble One, and watch as they withdraw back over the south threshold. Once they have gone, open your eyes.

Starting in the east, go to the east altar, bow, pick up the candle, and place it on the east part of the central altar. Do the same in the south, west, and north until the four directional flames closely surround the central flame. Now lie down and have a sleep while the cloth, pentagram, and cord are cooking – and really do try to sleep: it helps to 'fix' this action in your spirit.

Once you have rested, however long or short that time is, get up, and before you put the candles out, take the cord, the pentagram, and the cloth. Roll up the cloth around the pentagram. Now tie it with the cord by wrapping it around and around the cloth, and tying a knot. Take the bundle and hold it to yourself for a moment: it will be charged with energy. Let your body and the bundle be in the same space for a few moments.

Find a safe place to store the bundle where it will not be messed with at all (you only take it out to place it under the altar when you work on your own fate). In Module V you will transfer the images on the pentagram pattern onto the fabric. Before that time, they both have to energetically 'cook' and tie in to each other. The cord is the binding of your own personal time, and it will hold and protect the fabric and image until they are fused together to become a specific form of shield.

If you feel up to it, and feel a need for it, this is something you can repeat at other times in your past if it is necessary, but only if it is really necessary – and if you do not observe a dip in the energies, do not take any action at all, simply observe. Watching your past experiences from this inner standpoint can be very interesting and revealing indeed: you sometimes see things from a totally different point of view and can often see how an event was a necessary occurrence that guided you towards something else in your future, or gave you strength or an experience that was needful for your development.

Spend a week or two experimenting with this method of stepping into your own past. Just don't overdo it, as it can take a lot of energy. Each time you do it, simply put the bundle under the altar (so that it gets more charging) and ensure the Sandalphon are standing at the south threshold.

You would not work with Lachesis again (she worked with you just to trigger the cord). You would simply light the directions, open the gates, go around the directions, and then step through the north gate with your focused intention.

5. *Task:* The Egyptian Book of the Dead

Note: Don't do the following task until you have done the visionary work. Always look up after the fact, not before.

First, read the following translations of Spells 153A and 153B from the ancient Egyptian Book of the Dead:[2]

BD 153A

Spell for coming forth from the net.
Let he who sees behind him, who has control over his heart,
Who unravels and tangles when it is time to join the earth,
Split open the ground!
You unravellers, who are your divine fathers' children,
You catchers, while ever you catch,
Encircling on the embankments of the lake's waves,
You cannot catch me in that trap of yours
Wherein you catch the dawdling dead;
Nor will you snare me in your net
Wherein you snare those who would avoid the grave,
In that net whose floats go to heaven and whose weights go to the ground.

For I have come forth from its plumb line
And have rejoiced in a rising boat;
For I have come forth from its cupped hands
And have surfaced like Sobek;
For I have made the hemming and hawing arm go against you:
I am a loosener and tangler with hidden fingers.

I know the net's reel:
It is the thumb of Sokar.

I know my stake that goes through it:
It is the ankle of Shesmu.

I know my door through it:
It is the hand of Isis.

I know what will slice me through it:
That sword of Isis which cut the umbilical cord of Horus.

I know the identity of its floats and weights:
They are the knee and thigh of Ruty.

---

[2] Translations by Michael Sheppard, from the copies of these spells found in the papyrus of Nu (Publication: Lapp, G. (1997), *The Papyrus of Nu (BM EA 10477)*, Catalogue of the Books of the Dead in the British Museum, I, London: The British Museum Press).

I know the identity of the netting with which it catches:
It is the web of Atum.

I know the identity of the unravellers who catch with it:
They are earth-serpents, Ancestors, eaters.

I know the identity of its two arms:
They are the two arms of every god
Who hears the complaints in Heliopolis
On the night when the moon is half full,
In the temple of the shimmering moon.

I know the identity of the water above, which tightens the net:
It is the part of the firmament that the gods stand upon.

I know the identity of the orderly who receives the net's fish:
The fish-skewer is the orderly of the god.

I know the identity of the offering-mat on which the orderly offers himself:
It is the offering-mat of that Horus alone in darkness,
The unseeing one whom those who shall not exist fear,
To whom those who shall exist give praise.

And just as when I arrived, when I surfaced as the senior one,
So shall I be drawn landward when I fall back to earth:
By two great teams of rowers,
And by the great one whom I put in the old god's house.

And just as I came, as an unraveller with spear in hand,
With knife in hand, with sword in hand,
So I shall go forth: I shall encircle and tangle through the net.

I know the identity of the knot which stitches up the open wounds
On this great finger of Osiris,
And the identity of the two fingers which seize it:
They are two fingers on Ra's hand,
And a fingernail on Hathor's hand.

I know the identity of the threads caught in this knot:
They are all the cords of the multitude of people.

I know the identity of its bolt/book:
It is the hand of Isis.

I know the identity of its draw-ropes:
It is the safety-rope of the oldest god.

I know the identity of its cords:
They are the day's threads.

I know the identities of the unravellers who trap with it:
They are snake-gods, Ra's ancestors.

I know the identity of the Finished Ones:
They are Geb's ancestors.

Just as you have caught, so have you eaten,
And just as I have caught, so have I eaten,
For you have swallowed that which Geb and Osiris have swallowed.

So, he who sees behind him, who has control over his heart,
Who unravels and tangles when it is time to join the earth,
Split open the ground!

So, unravellers, who are your divine fathers' children,
Hall-occupants in Denderah:
You cannot trap me in that trap of yours!
You cannot snare me in your net
Wherein you catch the dawdling dead
and snare those who would turn back from the grave,
For I know that net from its topmost floats to its lowest weights.

Behold how I have come:
With my reel in hand,
My stake in hand,
My bolt/book in hand,
And my sword in hand.

Just as I came, so I have entered: by hammering myself in!

Do you know who I am,
knowing the name of he who tangles his place's fledglings/children?

I shall bore in what is extended; I shall hammer it in; I shall put it into its position.

Regarding the stake that is with me, it is the calf of Shesmu;
Regarding the reel that is with me, it is the finger of Sokar;
Regarding the peg/book that is with me, it is the hand of Isis;
Regarding the sword in my hand, it is the cleaver of Shesmu.

Behold me having arrived!
And behold me as I sit down in the boat of Ra.
As I cross the choppy lake to the northern sky,
I shall act through what they have done: praises;
Through their praises for my life-force,
For I live through their lives, there.

BD 153B

Spell for coming forth past those who catch fish/the obliterated.

O impeders, O weavers/snarers,
O unravellers, who are your divine fathers' children,
You do realize that I know the identity of this great big net?
Its identity is Uniter.
You do realize that I know the identity of its netting?
It is the cordage of Isis.
You do realize that I know the identity of its stake?
It is the calf of Atum.
You do realize that I know the identity of its spool?
It is a finger of Shesmu.
You do realize that I know the identity of its peg/book?
It is a fingernail of Ptah.
You do realize that I know the identity of its knife?
It is the cleaver of Isis.
You do realize that I know the identity of its weights?
They are the iron in the sky.
You do realize that I know the identity of the floats?
They are feathers of the Falcon.
You do realize that I know the identity of its unravellers?
They are the Qefednu Ape.

You do realize that I know the identity of that area that is pulled tight above it?
It is the Moon's temple.
You do realize that I know the identity of the one who uses it for fishing?
It is the great elder sitting on the eastern side of the sky.

A great divine one does not eat me;
But will a great divine one digest me?

I did not sit (like) those who are over the river's two banks;
Rather, how I have eaten is by digesting through its mouth.
The dregs of the dead are in my stomach!

I am the divine guinea-fowl: I am Ra as he emerges from the Nun,
And the god is the Ba.
I am who creates the authoritative utterance: imbalance is abominable to me!

I am Osiris who makes Maat, on whom Ra lives every day.
Just as I rejoice as the Bull, so I mourn as the Ennead,
Through this identity of mine of the guinea-fowl.
Just as I developed myself with the Nun in this identity of mine of Khepri,
So I develop into him each day:
I am the lord of the sunlight!

Since I have dawned gloriously as Ra, the East's lord,
Life is given to me through these Eastern comings-forth of his.
The youthful ones and senior ones in the fields are those whom I have preserved,
My having been born in those who are at peace.

I have eaten Shu!
I have digested Shu!
I have shat Shu out!

Both kings are within me!
Khonsu is within me!
Those whose heads are bound are within me!
I envelop the body heat of a multitude!

Now, use the internet to search for examples of the vignettes (images) that often accompany these spells. BD 153A's vignette shows a net being drawn by several men; BD 153B's vignette shows three apes drawing a fishing net.

In the Egyptian understanding of the cycle of creation and destruction of life, an understanding which was considerable, they considered rebirth as a lesser existence, and something that affected the common people. The king[3] and the senior priests & priestesses of the Mysteries[4] studied and practised hard within the Mysteries to avoid the net of souls upon their death.

Just as the individual has a web/net of fate, so too does a nation and a species (and everything else): like all creation, everything is octaves of everything else. Everything in creation works along the same patterns (recycling, I like it). The net of souls is the collective web of fate, and the hapless soul upon death becomes trapped in a cycle of rebirth (trapped by the net of souls).

The king and other highly initiated ones learned how to sidestep that pattern: the king in particular, along with other major players in the Mysteries would, upon death, go through a process whereby their body and spirit was carefully prepared in order to stay upon the land for a protracted length of time while also simultaneously 'residing with the gods' (hence a mortuary temple was called 'the temple of a million years'). Some details of this process will be covered later in the next module and again later in depth as an initiate.

This is just one example in the ancient cultures of a deep understanding of the fate process, and of also the process of the passage from human to deity. When you search the texts, you are not going to find much (there is not a lot), but you will find some things. If you then search the terms in Google images, you will start to see hidden things in the images that you will begin to understand and recognise.

---

[3] The title Pharaoh did not come to mean the head of state until the Amarna/eighteenth dynasty in Egypt: before that, they were kings.

[4] Not all of the priesthood worked within the Mysteries: some were royal officials or basic temple attendants.

It is not all spelled out for you: these are the Mysteries hidden in plain sight. There will be objects, stances, hand positions, symbols, and much more that you will begin to recognise from your training.

Also do a search (sometimes an image search is helpful) to look at different ancient cultures and their knowledge of patterns (like the web of fate/net of souls) in relation to weaving creation and destruction. It is known in Tibetan, Greek, and Hindu Mysteries, for example. This research is not for an essay, it is for yourself: finding aspects of the Mysteries in different art, religions and stories will trigger deep memories, and can start opening many sleeping doors within you. Because it is for yourself, do not just skip over this search – it is important for you to learn about different cultures and how the deeper mysteries run through many of them.

Regardless of what culture a human is from, if it is a temple culture, then it also has the Mysteries, and although there are slight differences in interpretation, the core essence, patterns, contacts, and powers are the same. A temple culture is a culture that has a defined belief system that builds temples, has formal priesthoods (male or female or both), uses script of some kind, creates images and statues as vessels and doorways, and has activities that at times include the populace in sacred processions, reenactments etc. A non temple culture would be defined as a culture that is more nature based and does not build temples, or an egalitarian culture that has no defined religious or spiritual belief that we know of – Mohenjo Daro[5] is a possible candidate for such a culture.

This is why I keep saying to you, that as you learn and experience things, so you will begin to finally see the Mysteries all around you in paintings, poetry, ancient temples, stories, legends, etc. They don't need to hide, because you need to understand the keys to see them. When you are an adept, you will revisit the ancient Egyptian texts, and other texts from all around the ancient world, and then you will really notice and recognise many of the magical techniques that you have learned.

---

[5] A city of approximately 40,000 people that was situated in Sindh province, Pakistan 2500 BC to 1700 BC.

Lesson 8
Working with your Future Fate Pattern

Again, this is less of a reading lesson and more of a doing lesson. Get out your journal notes from when you were working with the Pentagram pattern in Module II (the one you now have wrapped up in the bundle), and reconstruct the pattern by drawing it out: the tools in the hands of the pentagram, the hexagram, earth sign, your name, your planet positions, etc. Map it out on paper.

What you are going to work on is the dynamic that opposes that of the past: you are going to do the early step of working on your future, working within your web of fate. This is not about changing your future, but about learning first how to recognise the inner aspects of your web of fate, the beings, powers, and aspects that flow through it and then tune into it. This visionary ritual exercise is also about meeting your Guardian Angel: the tentative first step in learning how to work as a team with your Guardian Angel.

Because of our modern culture, we think that changing our future directly will make things better, but because of the complexity of fate, it can often make things worse. It is wiser to fully optimise what is before you by recognising it, trusting it, and simply keeping an awareness of it. That conscious awareness of the weave, what it looks like, and being aware of the beings that work through it triggers deep shifts within you that lead to you being a co-driver of your own fate and not a helpless passenger.

This method works with ritual and vision combined, and is not an easy task to do, particularly for an apprentice. But some heavy lifting is good for you. It teaches you more respect for magic once you experience just how powerful and complex (and beautiful) it can be.

This visionary ritual works far more powerfully when done with a group energy around you; however, working alone with this is better for your training in the long term. Easier is not always better, and before you enjoy the boost of power levels that group work can bring, first you must slowly develop your own strength and independence, so that you are fully self-contained as a magician and are reliant on nothing but yourself.

We have looked at how fate operates like a web (or net), and how it has various hotspots, bumps, dips, etc. Those features are the tides that push humans along the process of life. But they are also potentials as well as drivers: potentials for development, self-ruin, destruction, renewal, learning, or vanishing into ignorance. We can become victims, or we can become active participants. The magician is the participant who connects with the raw material and joins in the process of turning it into something beautiful and unique. Before you can learn to participate, you must get to know your materials and know your co-workers.

One of the most powerful magical ways to participate is not to manipulate or craft; it is to observe with intention, which by itself enlivens the potential of the weave: your observation becomes a catalyst which triggers necessary change into action.

When you come across a difficult bump in your fate weave, before you look to see whether you can dodge around it, first look to see if it is a bump that can ultimately strengthen or teach you. Often difficulties are what help us evolve, and we must step up to those difficulties, find the gems hidden within them, and flower despite them.

One way to approach this is through the magical observation of your weave in action, and the other is to commune with the beings involved, observe your outer situation, and allow your Guardian Angel to guide you (without obviating responsibility for your own future). Sometimes a magician would use both.

Note that direct results magic is not used: not only is that silly, but it is also weak magically. This is one of those magical situations where less is more: a slight nudge triggers a huge movement, or an observation enlivens a sluggish pattern and triggers it back into action.

1. Hitting the blocks in the road

Sometimes you can come up against walls in your fate path: these can manifest for the magician as literally seeing in vision a wall or block that they cannot get around, or they can manifest in outer life by having every step forward you try to make being blocked.

When you see this or it happens, or you detect such a block in the fate weave, do not take on the mentality that you have to crash your way through it. Be more intelligent: step back, look at it, see why it is there, and from what you find, you will know if you have to just sit and wait, or if you have to find a way around it.

The way to step back and look at it is to use the visionary ritual method you will learn in this lesson: you will get a much wider view in terms of energy and weave as to what you need to do.

If you are in a truly dire or overly dynamic situation in your life, doing the visionary ritual of *Viewing the Web*, observing, and from those observations, while you are still in vision and have your Guardian Angel stood before you, thinking of an option for life action (or choosing a path forward at a crossroads) will trigger a response.

If the option is the right one, the beings and the web pattern will light up and become fully of vitality, and you will get a favourable response from your guardian (usually in the form of a smile). If it is the wrong option, the web will dull down, the beings will slow down, and the guardian will tell you by his facial expression that the option is not a good idea. As an alternative to working in ritual vision, sometimes simply sitting and waiting is the best option. These blocks can act as a 'stop' or 'give way' sign: they are there to keep you in a holding pattern while something comes into form. Once that form is ready for you to interact with, the wall falls away.

The other reason the wall can appear is to stall you while your 'energy tide goes out.' Sometimes for magicians, if major changes, work, or developments are on the horizon, your energetic tide goes out in preparation. The wall serves as a block to protect you from overreaching your low resources until the tide comes back in. Sometimes the block is there to teach you how to be mutable and move sideways. As my mother used to say, "when the door shuts, a window always opens," and she was right. When you come up against a block, first look to see if there is an alternative route or action: be like water and find a channel that you can flow down.

As a magician, the way to discern what block is doing what is to engage a variety of skills and tools. The first one is your own intelligence and common sense. The second is meditation and vision, the third is divination, and the fourth is patience and a sense of trust in your guardian.

Here is an example from my own life. In 2007 I hit a major wall in my life and magical work. I lost my job and thus my home after being 'outed' as Pagan in a heavily Christian community, I was very ill, and my magical work ground to a halt. I went in vision and all I could see was wall after wall. I saw that some of those walls were a natural part of my fate, and others had been put there by another magician in order to block me.

I had huge responsibilities (supporting my daughters and a grandchild) and yet every resource was whipped out from under me. I had three choices: use magic to remove all of those obstacles, wait, or 'be like water.' I sat and thought about the overall picture of what was going on. Every resource was blocked and taken away from me: something big was going on that was beyond a simple magical aggression from a disgruntled ex husband, and it was something that was important for me to recognise, understand, and work with.

I talked to my guardian and said that I did not want to shirk any lesson or challenge, but I was so under-resourced that I could not even think straight – yet it was critical that I made the correct decision. I was too weak to observe my weave, so I asked the guardian to help me see which direction I should be thinking about going in.

The day after, I had an enquiry from a company in Houston, Texas regarding a potential job. I flew from Nashville, where I was living, to Houston for the interview. Two minutes into the interview (which was an all-day interview) I started projectile vomiting. Not a good first impression. I was supposed to conduct an apprentice ballet class for the company, and I had to run to the bathroom every few minutes to throw up. My body would not work properly, my mind was fogged, and I could not properly demonstrate my skills and knowledge in classical ballet. Needless to say I did not get the job, and I had just wasted precious financial resources to get there.

I was too weak by this time to work in ritual vision on my fate pattern to discern what was going on and what was coming, so again I talked to the guardian. I said that I had gotten the message that I was no longer to work in my art form, but that I had no qualifications to work in most other jobs. I was too weak to take off the magic upon me, and combined with my own fate events that were unfolding, it was all too much for me.

That night I had a dream about the moorland where I was born. I finally got the message, and it made total sense: I had to go home to Britain, and take my youngest daughter and grandson with me. Every other possible option was firmly closed to me. We landed back in Britain with nothing but a couple of bags of personal belongings, a few toys for the baby, and enough money for a few months. At my age, and after a lifetime of working hard, that is not a good state to find yourself in. We were essentially homeless, penniless, we were all sick, and I felt defeated.

But the land immediately responded to me, came into my dreams, and I felt I was where I was supposed to be, however hard it was. I also noticed that by going with the flow of change, however much I felt defeated, the action of leaving the country voluntarily had loosened, and then cast off, the magical blocks upon me: I had essentially moved into the impact, not pulled away from it or tried to remove it. That had taken the power out of it.[1] This is a dynamic I knew well, but in my addled state I had not thought about it.

I talked again to my guardian.

"What next?" I asked.

The answer I got back was another question.

"Are you prepared to work hard?"

My answer was, "I am always prepared to work hard."

The guardian asked the question again, and I answered the same. After the third time, I simply answered "yes."

I felt the shift in my pattern immediately, and knew that no matter how hard things were, they were hard for the right reasons and I just needed to suck it up and get on with it.

It took nearly three years for the new path to come together for me and my daughter, and when it finally did form itself, I then understood why the wall had been so severe, and why the new path had taken so long to come back together.

The energy tide needed to go right out in preparation for the very long-term, powerful, and productive pattern that was about to come back in. Throughout that time, I had to stay my hand magically and not intervene: I was clearly made aware that I would have what I needed, so long as I focused on the future. The sheer force of the fate tide had washed away many things that did not serve me well, and when that tide came back in it brought wonderful things with it that I could not have even wished for.

---

[1] Using fate tides already in action can remove or 'burn up' magical blocks or binds: this is something you will learn about later, in another module.

The outcome is that I now live exactly where I need to be and in a situation that is optimum for me: a secure, affordable home in a wild and beautiful, quiet, powerful, and magical place. And I am doing what I am supposed to be doing: writing, teaching, doing magical art, and magically tending the land. I got all the health care that I needed so that my body could get back on its feet, and through a variety of interesting fate quirks, I connected up with all the people I needed to be in contact with for my future.

My daughter also ended up just where she needed to be, and is now a post doc academic scientist. If we had not been forced back to Britain, there is no way she would have stepped into such an education as was available for her here in Britain, and her subsequent important and life saving work would have not happened. It was a very tough time for her with a small baby in a different culture and with no resources, cut off from friends and familiar things. But she rose to the challenge, took advantage of the cheap education, and worked her ass off. She, also, trusted all the powers around her.

I tell you this so that you can see how major problematic bumps should not always be avoided (and often the really important ones cannot be dodged anyhow), and how you should not be terrified if you see large difficult obstacles in your path: learn to trust. Sometimes they are there to shift you dramatically, to change what you do, where you are, and who you are with, so that you can flower into who you are supposed to be. If I had done magic to force my future into a picture that was to my liking, none of my books nor this course would have been written (and biology would not have gotten a talented researcher). You have to learn to trust, to always be willing to do your best, and to let the inner lot pick up the slack where you cannot. I was shown the edge of the cliff, but I was not allowed to fall off it.

This is why results magic can sometimes badly stall a wonderful future: short-term fixes can close many long-term doors. The key as a magician is to be able to look, ascertain, understand, and then act accordingly. Some disasters are not vital experiences for you to go through; but some are, and you need to slowly learn how to tell the difference. So let's get to work.

If you feel you need to do this work more than once, do not do it too soon after the first time. Keep it at least a month apart, do it on the new moon, and think carefully about the timing of it: if you are working on a Quareia lesson that is involved in destruction, exorcism, or is a lesson that is energetically hard work, wait until the next new moon after such work. Even though the work is simple observation, it can be a major stretch for your energies, and it would be easy for you to burn out. Learn to respect the fact that sometimes, seemingly simple magical acts can actually be very powerful indeed, and will take a lot of energy to do (conversely, you will also find that sometimes what can appear to be a major magical working uses little energy at all).

Resist any temptation to interfere with what you see: you must observe only, learn from the observation, recognise and acknowledge the beings and your guardian, and then leave it at that. Read through the ritual more than once and familiarise yourself with all the keys, images, actions, and aspects: ensure that you know and remember it, then do it at the next new moon once you are ready (day or night, it doesn't matter).

2. *Task:* Viewing the web ritual

Note: after the visionary ritual there is a task to draw or paint something straight away. When you prepare to do the actual vision work, make sure you have the time and materials to get straight onto painting/drawing.

The following visionary ritual relies a lot on your own deep inner instincts. Because of this you need to let that instinct and inner sense rise to the surface. This will be easier for some than others: if you tend to overcontrol and/or overanalyse, be aware of that quality within you and keep it in check. This is about learning how to have visionary experiences that, besides imagery, also trigger energetic impressions. If you are too busy trying to interpret what it is you are feeling or experiencing while in the vision, you will kill the work. Sometimes those tight qualities are needful in your life, but like all things, the magician must learn to be the driver of their vessel, not its passenger.

Setting up

You will need the four directional altars and candles (but no central one), your bundle, and your sketch of your pentagram pattern.

Place the bundle directly in front of the south altar (future), ensuring that it is touching the bottom of the altar. Place the pentagram pattern you have drawn out just south of the centre of the space (so you have the copy before you and the original wrapped in the bundle).

You will be standing in the centre for some of this work (and looking down at the pattern for reference), so make sure the direct centre is clear. Put your art materials to one side, but within the magical working space (for energetic resonance).

Part one of the ritual

To start the work, because you are going to be working with and observing deeper powers, you need to properly tune and plug in the ritual space and yourself to the Divine powers and contacts that run through magic. This brings the room and yourself to the right frequency so that the work can be done. To do that, use the second part of the *Hexagram Ritual* from Module II, Lesson 4: light the four directions, see the gates open, visit each direction, bow to the contacts on the thresholds, then begin part two of the Hexagram ritual. Do that visionary ritual up to the point where you step into the empty Hexagram. Bathe in the silence.

Part two of the ritual

Turn a full circle clockwise on the spot, slowly, and end up facing south. Close your eyes, and in your inner vision see the south gate and the Noble One standing on its threshold.

The Noble One steps over the threshold, passes through the south altar, pauses to touch your bundle briefly, and then stands before you and bows. Bow back (physically and in vision). The Noble One then walks behind you and places his hands upon your shoulder – or he may place both hands upon your spine, just below the nape of your neck.

Open your eyes and look down at your pentagram pattern briefly, noting the positions of the planets. It does not matter if you cannot at that moment remember which planet is which: just let go and be aware of the positions around the pattern that the planets are in. Now close your eyes again. Remember the Noble One still behind you, and be aware of the planets' positions around your space.

Hold out your arms (physically and in vision) to the sides, and 'see' the sword in your left hand and the cup or bowl in your right hand. Be aware of the power of Divinity above you and the land and ancestors below and behind you. Be aware of the path that vanishes into the distance through the south gate, and be aware of the beings of the sword and cup by the left and right altars. All the powers are now in place, and the space is tuned.

The Noble One places his right hand over your eyes, and tells you to look through their hand: the filtered vision of an angel. All of the beings, planets, tools, and shapes you had visualised shift and change to bright lights upon a web that you are standing in the centre of. They all have a similar energy colour of light to them, and they are all around you. Now you can drop your arms.

As you look, you notice other lights and shapes that are scattered all around your web. There may be many of them, or there may be only a few. Some will have a uniform shape, and some will be misshapen. Some will have bright lights and some will have dim lights. As you look, you begin to notice faint, ethereal beings with long fingers working in clusters around the shapes and lights: these are angelic beings that are constantly working on your web (and also on the web of every living thing) in a constant act of weaving, repairing, and disassembling aspects of the web.

The closer you look, the more you see, and you begin to notice that every single aspect of the web is a vital component: if one thing was taken out, the web would collapse. You also notice that the weave hooks into, and is a part of, the path that flows out to the south and into the mists of the future.

Focus your attention back to the beings working around your web. One seems larger and brighter than the others. As you watch this being, you notice that he is directing the others, guiding, helping them, and teaching some of them how to work on your individual web. As you watch him, he realises that you are focusing on him. The being finishes what he is doing and then walks over to stand before you.

As you look into his eyes, you see something you recognise at a deep level within you: you know this being. As your understanding begins to dawn, the being smiles at you: this is your Guardian Angel. You now begin to understand that the interventions, nudges, whispers, dreams, and feelings that you had were translations of this work that is being done constantly on your web of fate. As the angelic being worked on key hotspots, dips, and bumps, that work translated to you as warnings, protection, guidance, and advice.

Now that you have an understanding of your Guardian Angel, every time this being works on a critical point in your fate, you will become aware of them and what they are doing. That in turn will help you to make better decisions when you come to crossroads in your life. Before you can try to communicate with this being (they must always initiate the first conversation), the being steps away and gets back to work.

Turn your attention back to your web, and every time you look, you will see more and more tiny aspects, weaves, beings, and actions happening: your fate is complex indeed, which is why it is usually best just to let the beings who work in your fate get on with their job and you get on with yours. The Noble One takes his hand away from your eyes and steps back. He walks around you and stands before you, smiling.

Bow to him, and he bows back. He turns and bows to your Guardian Angel, and between them passes a recognition and understanding of fellowship. The Noble One walks back through the altar to the south gate, and as he walks, you realise that the ground, web, and pattern beneath him lights up: he is a guiding light for your future. He vanishes into the mists beyond the south gate, and the room once again appears to you in vision as your working space with the four altars and the candle flames.

Now open your eyes. The power is still going, the beings are still working away, but you bring your consciousness back to the living, physical world.

Go first to the east altar. Place your hands upon the altar, and be aware of the web connections that flow out of this direction and their connection into your fate weave. Step back, bow, and go to the south. Repeat the same action in the other three directions of placing your hands on the altar and just being aware of the connections these thresholds have to your fate weave.

When you step back from the north, go back to the east, bow, and put the candle out. Close the other three directions also. Place your bundle back in its resting place, and put the pentagram drawing into your journal.

Keep notes of any dreams, intuitions, or feelings that arise in the days after this working, those that you feel are connected to this work and to your future.

The working you just did is simple, and yet as you get used to it and repeat it, just to observe and nothing more, it will become more powerful. At some point in your magical training you will realise that you are becoming more aware of that weave around you all the time, and of the angelic beings that work with that weave.

As an adept, you will develop enough focus to be able to tune into the weave instantly, without ritual support.

If you feel a tremor or shift in the weave, you will feel it in your energy, which in turn will alert you to the fact that something is happening, or is about to happen, that will directly affect you in some way or other. This tuning ability comes with practice, and with learning how to work in vision, not only with images in your mind, but also with feelings in your emotions, your mind, and your body: your deeper senses develop in a way that cannot really be described in text; rather they have to be experienced. But you will begin to recognise them as they develop.

3. *Task:* Painting the spider

Paint or draw (and do this as quickly as possible after your visionary ritual work so that the energetic resonance within you can pass into the picture) a picture of a spider in the centre of a web that has the bright spots upon it: the web that is your fate pattern.

The spider has the weaver power and is deeply connected magically to the weaver goddess and the angelic beings that work on the web of fate. This is why many magicians, including myself, have a great deal of respect for spiders, and treat them with care and respect. A magical house will attract spiders, and they will take up residence in directions around the house where the most energetic threat tends to come in from: they start working with you in a passive way.

If you live in an area where some spiders are dangerous, and yet you wish to work magically with them, mark out a territory. What I used to do when I lived with black widows is that I developed a routine whereby the floors, corners, and low places where they could inadvertently cause harm or be harmed would be constantly cleaned, vacuumed, and have cleaning products put on them that spiders don't like. But the high places, crevices, disused storage spaces, etc., in the house were theirs, and they were not disturbed. They figured this out pretty quickly and stayed off the floors, furnishings, etc., and hung out in cracks and crevices nearer the ceiling and roof space.

Whenever I was under threat, or a dangerous tide of energy was coming in, they would all appear and would gravitate to the north wall in the house: they guarded the death threshold, and their weaving/hunting power stopped things coming into the house from that direction that should not be coming in.

Back to the drawing. Place the finished drawing or picture in the south of your working space, either on the wall or hidden somewhere. It does not matter if it is displayed or not; however, it is important that you remember it is there, and that you keep that awareness. The energy that is around you from doing that visionary working will flow into the picture. You are placing her in the south to focus her power on the weaving of the future – your future.

It is a simple, passive form of magic: the resonant image of an old power is placed in a direction where you wish that influence to flow. South is your future path. North is protection against death.

Move her around as needs be, but only put her in the north if you are truly under real threat, either from death magic (which will come once you are an adept and you manage to piss off enough magicians), or if there is serious illness in the house. Simple, passive magic like this does not stop things altogether; rather these things act as filters by downing the power levels of incoming energies: they slow things down, which then gives you enough time to notice and deal with the issue.

The fact that you have met Lachesis in vision, have observed your own web, and have stood in full consciousness within the resonant power of that web, enables you to pass on an echo of that power into a picture if it is done straight after the working. It is another step towards enlivening and empowering objects fully.

4. *Task:* Research

Look up myths and legends to do with spiders and the web/weaving of fate. Take notes, and see what you are drawn to.

Appendices

The Quareia Apprentice Study Guide

Introduction

When I first started writing the Quareia course, my intention was for it to be a simple first-stage training that people could then use to launch themselves into the hot waters of magic. However, the universe had different plans, and the course turned into a complete, long-term magical training akin to doing a university degree, and then some.

As the Apprentice section has no mentoring, it is the most difficult part of the training, and it has now become apparent that students need a bit of help here and there with basic questions, and with understanding certain concepts. I also felt that it would be helpful for Quareia students to have a better understanding of the dynamics behind the course and how it is structured.

This study guide is aimed at Apprentices studying the course. I hope it gives you a deeper understanding of the path you are walking, while also addressing a lot of the more common questions I have been asked by students.

It is not a 'cliff notes' type of guide; nor is it a bullet point summary of the Quareia course. Rather its intent is to shine some lights into the less obvious corners of your training. Hopefully it will help you along your path.

"What is a magician?
'One who does magic' is the Magician's reply.

What is a magician?
'One who stands at the centre of everything' is the Developing One's reply.

What is a magician?
'One who reflects the golden rays' is the Foremost One's reply.

What is a magician?
'One who is I,' replies the Divine."

— Josephine McCarthy

Appendix A
How Quareia Works

> *"Our virtues and our failings are inseparable, like force and matter. When they separate, man is no more."*
>
> — Nikola Tesla

One of the first things to understand about a course as vast as Quareia is how it works. This is more important that it first appears, as knowing how a course works will tell you how best to approach it.

Most people's experience of approaching a course is rooted in high school and university education, and those learning approaches are very different from a classical magical education, just as they are different from any serious classical art form education. So for many, the way this course is structured and worked with will be a major learning curve. Many magical schools, particularly self-learning courses, are written in ways that reflect modern college learning techniques – and for smaller courses that can work well. But for a full classical magical education, the student is likely to run in to problems almost straight away.

The Mysteries in any culture are complex and difficult to learn. The aspirant is required to engage all their human skills, not just their intellect. It is this need for drawing on every aspect of yourself in order to move forward in magic that many find difficult early on in their training. People are used to compartmentalising their learning, viewing it as something separate from the rest of their lives. Also, their learning generally consists of small bites taken out of various unconnected subjects. The shift to total immersion into learning can prove difficult for many, and impossible for some.

Properly studying magic requires hard work, some sacrifice, and the willingness to change and adapt how you think. And yet, though that sounds tough, it is one of the most rewarding, exciting, and fascinating journeys you can take through life. It also requires that you be fully responsible for your own learning. In today's world of commercial teaching that has become the norm in many cultures – and in almost every aspect of learning, not just magic – students have become used to treating their education as a commercial transaction. As a result, they have developed an unhealthy attitude to their learning environment: they expect to be able to dictate to their teachers what they will learn and how they will learn it. Certainly, in some cases this has forced teaching establishments to smarten up; but overall, it has caused standards to drop as institutions water down courses, or tailor them to demand, or make them more 'appetising' in order to attract more paying students.

While a young student may enjoy an easier, more 'fun' course that has been made tastier with appetising but ultimately useless additions, in the long term the student will suffer from a lack of training, as the most important aspects of serious training in any subject are often the boring, difficult bits. On a deeper level, such a dumbed-down course disengages the ability of the student to learn effectively: they do not learn how to learn, but instead how to consume.

Some of the issues raised in this guide will be relevant to some, and not to others. Quareia is studied in many different cultures and countries, and in this book I have to address the various questions that have been asked from far-flung corners of the earth.

Some of the general queries I have been receiving, as students progress through this course, are issues I had not really thought about, but are quickly becoming apparent, hence this guide. Many of those issues are faced particularly by students who live in different countries around the world, issues that have to do with things like the difficulty of translating certain concepts or approaching the study of magic itself. There are also some simple yet annoying problems like broken links. I was stupid enough, when I started the Apprentice section, to quote web addresses. I was not thinking for the long-term about how links come and go, nor about the difficulties of accessing websites from certain countries. For that you have my deepest apologies.

In this chapter we will look at the underlying structure of the course, how it was built, why it was built that way, and what that means to you as a student. With that knowledge, you will be better able to understand the issues that come up for you in your study. It should also help you engage better not only with Quareia, but also with any classical magical training (and indeed any classical art form). In later chapters we will look at more specific issues, at various dynamics of learning, and at the most common queries that we have had.

1. The ethics and code of Quareia: *Ma'at*

At the foundation of the Quareia course is the philosophy of Ma'at, an Ancient Egyptian way of thinking that underpinned the whole ethos of Egyptian society, religion, economics and so forth. This philosophy was personified by the goddess Ma'at: the goddess of Truth.

I chose Ma'at as Quareia's foundation because it is the most stable, coherent magical dynamic out there. It will open the doors of magical and mystical under- standing in their truest, deepest forms. Mysticism and magic become bedfellows as soon as you scratch below the surface of everyday magic. The deeper you get into powerful magic, the closer you step into mysticism.

Because Ma'at is so foreign to how our modern societies function and think, it may be worth spending a little time outlining this concept, as it is often misunderstood by modern minds. We tend, as humans, to relate and compare the unknown to what we know, and translations of unfamiliar concepts like Ma'at, which is often rendered in English as "justice" or "truth," can often confuse people further. Another translation of Ma'at in English is *balance*. Ancient Egyptian words, just like English words, often have various layers of meaning to them: what layer you pay attention to depends on context. (An example in English to make this clear: the word "spirit." This word can mean a human soul, the presence of the Divine, *any* supernatural being, boldness of character, a distilled alcoholic drink, and so forth. Most of the time, context makes it clear which meaning is meant.)

In English, our understanding of 'truth' and 'justice' are often coloured by our societal norms, our inherited religious beliefs, and our cultural patterns. If the two pans of a set of scales are in perfect balance to each other, this would be expressed in English as 'balance,' and in Egyptian, as Ma'at. In the Ancient Egyptian way of thinking, balance is truth, and lies express 'imbalance.'

Most magical students who look at Ancient Egyptian texts tend to concentrate on just two texts: *The Book of the Dead*, known to the Egyptians as *The Book of Going Forth by Day*, and a collection of late Greco-Roman Egyptian spells called *The Greek Magical Papyri*, which is a collection of magical spells that date from between the second century BC to the fifth century AD. Unfortunately, though these are very different texts from different periods in Egyptian history, both of them often lean more towards *Isfet* than Ma'at. Isfet is the disharmony and imbalance brought about by bad choices and actions, and the word is often mistranslated today simply as 'evil' or 'chaos,' terms that would be better applied to describe Apep, the chaos-serpent of the Egyptian mythos. (Also remember the earlier point about words having layers of meaning: I am using the term *Isfet* here in the layer of its meaning which has to do with 'bad choices' and imbalance.)

As the outside influences of Greek and Roman culture increasingly ate away at the old ways of Egypt, so the sense of Ma'at retreated and the dynamic of Isfet emerged. This is particularly apparent in the Greek Magical Papyri.

This can all get very confusing for an Apprentice student. My advice is to approach all of this as you would any new subject: understand that there is far more complexity in the subject than at first appears, and the way to develop your understanding is to take small steps forward, one at a time. First learn the surface presentations of things, and the deeper aspects will emerge as and when you are truly ready to see them.

Ma'at is balance. This is expressed in Egyptian religious and magical texts as the balance of powers, and it was expressed in the code of the king and priesthood by the need to uphold the balance of powers, and also the balance of their day-to-day conduct. For the people, it was a simple code of ethical behaviour, a way of life, and a rule book that they could follow. So Ma'at had many different levels of expression, and all these levels are relevant and present in the Quareia magical training.

Ma'at was used both in the initial construction of Quareia and in the whole magical path that developed as a result. This was simply because it is the one philosophy that gets to the heart of how magic actually works, not because it comes from one particular culture. Ma'at is the dynamic that nature is based on, and the dynamic that allows the human to become an integral part of nature at a conscious level.

Ma'at is the harmony of cause and effect, of one thing rebalancing another, of the balance of light and dark, day and night, and of a harvest properly weighed and checked. As you progress through the course, you will be exposed more and more to the complexities of balance, both in magic and in nature. Every magical act has a counterweight to balance it out, and everything is upheld by the fulcrum of the scales. The fulcrum in magic is like a pillar that magic revolves around, and so long as everything is balanced out, the powers flow well.

Ma'at, or balance, gets to the very heart of magic, and once you understand this dynamic principle in action, then you will truly begin to understand magic. Ma'at is not an 'Egyptian thing,' rather it is an Egyptian word to describe a natural order in the mortal world.

You will notice, as you progress through the course, a lot of Egyptian magic and religious dynamics in the work. This is not because I favour Egyptian magic above all else, but simply because it is still, to this day, the most balanced and accessible profound magic that we can still work with and study. You will also come across lots of other different cultures and religions in the course, and that will be discussed in a later chapter. So let us move on and look at the various substructures in the course, so that you can understand why some things are put together in a particular way, and why some lessons are as they are.

2. The rule of absolutes

The rule of absolutes is a very old way of teaching that is still used occasionally in the teaching of classical art forms. When I was a ballet trainer who worked with professional and pre-professional dancers, I could always tell which of them had been trained using absolutes, and which of them had not. Those who had, displayed a solid technique and were able to grasp, absorb, and translate complicated movement concepts, and fully understand how those concepts related to their work. Those who had not, however, often quickly became confused, and could not easily absorb methods and concepts into their technique. The lack of absolutes in their training caused them to overthink and overanalyse their technique, which restricted their progress.

For my first couple of decades of teaching magic, I saw similar patterns in my students: a tendency to overthink and an inability to absorb what was necessary and integrate it into their work. It struck me then – I can be slow sometimes – that magic should be taught as a classical art: ballet or magic, the same foundational rules apply.

So what is the rule of absolutes?

The Rule of Absolutes is a method of teaching that includes barriers to contain each stage of the syllabus. These barriers allow the student to learn what is necessary at that point in their education without their consciousness constantly stretching forward and wondering what will come next. Students can focus purely on the step before them, and that becomes their world, their rule, their absolute.

Once everything that is necessary has been absorbed, the barriers come down and the student progresses to a new phase of training.

A good analogy that I often use to explain this method is as follows: a toddler picks up a metal fork and goes to stick it in a plug socket. In the UK the voltage at a plug socket is 230 volts, which could kill a child. The mother takes the fork out of the child's hand, knocks their hand away from the plug socket, and says 'no' forcefully. The child is taught an absolute: they are not allowed to touch the plug socket. They do not know why, but they do as they are told.

When the child is about seven years old, the mother tells the child that the plug socket is dangerous, and they must never stick anything metal in it, as it could kill them. The mother then shows them how to plug something safely into the wall socket.

When the child is ten or eleven, the mother explains what the plug socket does, how the mains work, and where the fuse box is to turn off the electricity in an emergency. She then gets her child a kids' electricity kit, so they can learn to wire a board and make a light bulb come on.

As an older teen, the child learns in depth how wiring works, what its dangers are, what a ring main is, what amps are, how to change plugs, what happens with electric shocks, and how to administer first aid.

The 'absolute' for the child at seven is that the wall socket is dangerous and must never be played with. They don't know exactly why or how it works, but they know to stay away from it. As far as they know at that point, they must never, ever touch it, *ever*. Pertinent information is given at each stage of the child's development without swamping them with information they cannot understand.

This teaching method can be applied in many different ways, and for lots of different reasons. In Quareia it is deployed a lot, particularly in the Apprentice section and to some degree in the Initiate section. The student is contained by an absolute "this is it!" or a black and white, immovable rule, to allow their current stage of understanding to properly grow and deepen. Then, later, this boundary is removed, and they are exposed to another layer of understanding. This enables the student to take sure and solid steps, forming a foundation they can stand on, and their understanding and magical evolution grows at the pace that is right for them. Succeeding and learning within a containment is rewarding: you have a limited pot of learning to achieve, an achievable goal, and a nugget of knowledge that you did not have before. Learning in defined steps is what develops an artist, not sitting in front of a piano railing at having to do your scales, frustrated that you cannot learn to play Chopin's works in a week. Learning to master the scales while taking pleasure in that ability is the reward of the absolute. It is the path, not the destination, that gets you there.

3. Repeat repeat!

True classical training is taught in a repetitive manner, and in a manner of *return*, and this method is also deployed in Quareia. In the early days of their Quareia training, the apprentice has many exercises that they must repeat *ad nauseam*, to the point of, at times, utter boredom.

This is not done to bore the pants off the student, but to get them to achieve two important things: one is to get rituals, exercises, and recitations into the deeper part of their mind. They stop having to think consciously about them and can do them without thinking: the actions become *engrammed* into their consciousness.

Engramming through rote learning is one of the foundational skills of magic, and it must become second nature so that it can be called on suddenly in times of need. First you must learn the skill of engramming, how it works, and what it feels like. Once you have practised that skill in some basic exercises, you can then choose to deploy it later in the course as and when you feel it is necessary.

The second skill that repetition teaches is patience. Being able to focus on something and to repeat it and practise it until you have become competent in it builds inner 'grit.' You get used to persisting with something, even when it is difficult, until you have achieved what you need to achieve. This is another necessary skill in magic. It is often overlooked, and yet it is a cornerstone of the craft. Being able to step up, practise, and repeat, even when you don't feel like it, silences the side of you that wants a constant input of new, glittery, and interesting things, and awakens the side of you that builds determination, forbearance, and discipline.

A magician without discipline is no magician at all: they are simply playing at it. The skill of discipline is critical to so many aspects of magic, and it must be present not only in one's actions, but also in one's thoughts and emotions. The mind is a major player in magic, but it is not matured by focusing directly on it. Rather it is strengthened and matured as a side effect of other work. The dynamic of one thing being strengthened by working on something not directly related is another major aspect of early magical training. It also plays a large part in other classical arts. In ballet, few students realise that the passive limb is actually being strengthened when that passivity is approached in a certain way. Dancers at the barre work first on one limb, then on the other. While the left leg 'works,' the right standing leg is being strengthened, if the training is correct.

All these threads of foundational training are woven together to create a solid base on which the magician can stand. Every lesson, and every aspect of a lesson, has all these elements woven into it.

4. From the outside in

The teaching approach to magical rituals, visions, and patterns is 'from the outside in.' First the student learns the outer aspect of a magical act, and they perfect that first before they step into any power at all.

Every magical act has two parts: the structure, and the power that fills that structure which essentially turns the magic 'on'. To stay with the electrical wiring analogy, first the wiring is laid, the fuse box is put in place, and the switches are mounted to the walls. Then they are all linked together for the power to flow through them. Then the power is switched on.

Similarly, the Quareia student builds a structure of magic within them before they access any level of power that could harm them. This structure-building also teaches them, passively and without them realising it, that any magical trainee should have a basic vocabulary and structural understanding before they are introduced to power or contact. This understanding does not come from book reading; it comes from learning practically the early basics of magic such as rudimentary tarot and astrology, rituals with no contact or power, moving around in vision without leaving the mundane world (which some people call remote viewing), and so forth.

So the beginner develops a basic vocabulary of divination, ritual, and vision, the three foundation skills, and that slowly builds up to a solid basic understanding. As the student progresses in their training, power begins to flow into those foundation skills and fills them. In the Adept section there comes a point where the student starts to realise that once you have a solid competency in the foundation skills, the outer structure of those skills becomes less rigid: they become more fluid, more flexible.

This leads the magician to the understanding that once the structure and rules are learned properly, they can strike out and develop their own forms and methods of work. If a student attempts this too early in their training then they will flounder, as they are not anchored properly in the work. They will not fully understand the deep dynamics behind a unit of work or a method, which will make them vulnerable to damage and even catastrophe. In magic, as in any classical art, you must learn the rules and structures before you can learn to break them successfully. And that is the point at which evolution occurs in magic, and in any classical art.

Too often these days in any form of serious education, people reject or throw away their rules and structures far too early. This creates a dumbing-down of the system, and it ends with the blind leading the blind.

So this course is heavily structured towards the apprentice learning the foundations, learning the patterns, the basic rituals, etc., without power being connected to them. Later the outer patterns become more complex, and this pushes the student really learn how to 'pattern make' – which is to say, to create and work with rituals. Once this skill is in place, the work is connected to contact and power. Later in the course the student is shown how to connect with ever-deepening powers and contacts. If they have truly worked with the system as directed, then they will be ready for everything to switch on, and for the power to truly flow.

However, it is also important that right from the early days of a student's training they understand what power and contact feels like. So the rituals and visions they learn are not empty: they do have passive contact and power within their framework. Though the apprentice magician cannot yet trigger that power and contact for themselves in any depth, that contact and power does wait on the thresholds, and some of it washes into their work.

5. THE THREE STAGES

The three stages of the training – apprentice, initiate, and adept – are not just labels, nor are they there simply to divide the course in three. They are three distinct phases of development in magical training: being torn apart, being reassembled, and finally 'rising in wholeness.'

In magical terms, this follows an ancient inner pattern: before someone can truly step into the stream of magic, everything within them that no longer serves a purpose – all weaknesses, vulnerabilities, and immaturities – must be stripped away. This is not done by focusing on those weaknesses; rather the apprentice's work triggers deep and ancient patterns of power that flow into their life, often unseen, and find every weak spot in them.

The Apprentice

The magical work done as an apprentice, besides learning outer structures through practice, is also a series of catalysts. Because the student has no real access to magical power, they have no control over the process. This really speeds up their fate and maturation and prepares them for the power they will step into as an adept. In a mundane life, it usually takes a lifetime, sometimes many lifetimes, to develop such maturity. But the moment anyone steps onto a serious magical path of training, that process speeds up. Lessons in life are learned quickly, and if the apprentice steps up to the process and realises what is happening then they can engage with each situation that arises, and know that it a necessary process.

This can manifest in an apprentice's life in many different ways, depending on their weaknesses. It can trigger illnesses to slow them down and make them change how they live their lives, what they eat, what they do, etc. This is linked to a dynamic I call the *Pots of Resources*, which I will discuss in a little while.

The triggers in the Apprentice section can change where the student lives, who they live with, what they do for a job, where their interests lie, or how they behave as a human being. Regardless of how the catalysts affect the apprentice, once they understand that what is happening to them is a necessary process and stop fighting it, and rather engage with it, then they find themselves at the end of the Apprentice section, a bit battered, but wiser for the experience and in a better, fitter place.

It is like cleaning house: all the rubbish is thrown out and the windows are cleaned, and the place is washed down, fixed up, and properly prepared for what comes next. This dynamic also filters out those who have no place in magic.

Three main types of people are drawn to magical training. The first type came into life with magic in them: they have done it before, in some other life, and have come back to remember, advance, and mature into deeper magic. The second type are new to magic, but have been prepared, again through other lives, and it is a path that burns like a creative fire within them. Both these types are born to be magicians, and one way or another they will find their way through magic, regardless of the path they take.

The third type is a person fascinated by magic, but not truly able to take up its burdens. This is a long, tough, and often unforgiving path, but it polishes you from a rough stone into a diamond. But some people are unable to cope with the rigours of magic, or they are too unstable to cope with the power that flows through it.

The apprentice training, the 'being torn apart' part of the course, will unravel the third type out of magic for their own protection: fate will block them from it. One of the functions of the apprentice training is to act as a filter against those who are not suitable, for whatever reason, for deeper training. It will also block a person from stepping deeper into magical training until the right time comes. Timing is everything, and there are times in our lives when putting magic into the mix is not such a good idea. But when a student is really ready to try on the heavy mantle of magic, then the blocks will disappear and the path will open up.

This is an ancient way of training magicians: those who truly need to walk the magical path may have moments of being discouraged, of feeling overwhelmed, but they will not give up, or they will pause and return when they are ready.

Before I go on to talk about the processes of the Initiate and Adept sections of the course, I want to talk briefly about what I call *Pots of Resources*. From a magical perspective, each person has, at any time, a finite amount of energy 'stored' in different aspects of their lives.

To make this easier to understand, I always talk about various 'pots' of resources such as 'the pot of health,' 'the pot of magic,' 'the pot of emotions,' and 'the pot of the home' (food, housing, money). Over the decades, as I have observed my life and the lives of other magicians, I have noticed that if you use too much of the energy in one 'pot' and it is important that its store does not run out, then it will start to draw energy from the other 'pots.'

So for example, if you are engaged in a long round of powerful but necessary magic and you exhaust your 'magic pot,' then it will start to draw from your health 'pot.' This is often seen in magicians who commit to magical service at a powerful level: their health starts to suffer as energy is repurposed for their magic.

How fate and our actions affect the distribution of our energies is a complex topic, too complex to get into here.

Suffice to say that one of the functions of the Apprentice section is to teach a person about their 'energy pots' through direct experience as opposed to theory. You will learn where your strengths and deficits are, and with this knowledge, you can walk your path wisely and healthily, employing the fullest reserves of your fate.

Finally the apprentice stands on the threshold of the Temple of the Mysteries and request entrance to the outer court of the true Mysteries. Many modern magical schools these days consider the very basics of magic to be 'outer court' training. In fact, that level of work does not even approach the steps of the threshold of the outer court. The reason for learning those basics first is to prepare the student to stand at the threshold of the outer court of the Temple of the Mysteries and request access. Only when the student is properly prepared will the threshold appear. At that point the student has to decide if they are really willing to take that step. Once one crosses the threshold of the Temple of the Mysteries and enters its outer court, there is no going back to a mundane life. Even if you decide to cease your magical training and leave magic behind, if you have crossed that threshold then magic and the Mysteries will follow you wherever you go. It is a step towards the Divine, and a deep awakening: what has been awoken can never be truly put back to sleep. So the apprentice student who stands before that threshold is challenged to consider whether this is truly what they wish to do, and if they are willing to take up that mantle.

The Initiate

In the Initiate section of the course, the student steps out of the ashes of the Apprentice section and begins the process of being put back together. As they learn the knowledge and skills necessary for a true initiate of the Mysteries, they are also given the tools and skills to heal and rebuild themselves, and the strength to forge forward to the threshold of adepthood. When the initiate reaches the cusp of their adept training, they will be able to look back at their apprenticeship and see how everything that happened to their lives was necessary for things to have worked out as they did.

The path of the magician is the Path of Hercules indeed: it takes courage and strength to forge forward in the face of adversity, and this process polishes the student in every possible way. The Apprentice section is a tough one indeed, not because of the outer study, but because of the inner transformation that comes from that work. That inner transformation that happens as a result of the apprentice work prepares the ground and foundation for the house of the initiate to be built.

What was willingly relinquished as an apprentice is now transformed and returned to the initiate in a new and better way. What was withheld from the apprentice is released, and the final act of the initiate, as they stand on the cusp of adepthood, is to be reborn. The apprentice section is the death of the old; the initiate section is the conception, pregnancy, and finally the birth of the new.

The Adept

The Adept section of the training is where the magician truly steps into the Temple of the Mysteries and begins to learn the skills necessary to be accepted within the inner court: the company of the deities and the Justified Ones.

The Adept section takes the reborn one and trains them in the skills and knowledge of the adept. It weaves together the mystical and the magical, and puts the student in the midst of many of the aspects of the magical Mysteries so that they *become* those Mysteries. It is the direct experience of something that teaches you, not the study of theory.

As an adept student, the magician begins to realise the complexity of magic and the Mysteries, and begins to understand the enormity of the Mysteries: you can work for a lifetime in the magical Mysteries and still only scratch the surface. Once the adept has the skills, tools, and knowledge to properly face true power, they are cast into that power while confronting themselves. There must be no hidden weakness within an adept. We are all human, and we all have weaknesses and strengths, but the adept knows themselves: you know your weaknesses, which ones can be strengthened, and which cannot. You know how to compensate for any weakness, and even how to turn them to your advantage when necessary.

The difference between a mundane person and a true adept is that the true adept strengthens every weakness they can, and knows which weaknesses cannot be changed and must therefore be integrated into their life and personality. Hence the ancient maxim of the Mysteries: Know Thyself. In Latin this is *nosce te ipsum*, and in Greek γνῶθι σεαυτόν (*gnōthi seauton*).

The final aspect of the adept training is stepping from the last remnants of the mundane and being born again into the life of the Justified adept. This title, and its attendant form, is to be completed at the death of the adept. The completion of the adept training is the beginning of the magical mystical life, where you have all the knowledge, tools, and skills necessary to walk a magical and mystical life in service.

6. CIRCLES WITHIN CIRCLES

One of the major aspects of classical training is the *circling* of knowledge. Each part of magic has many hidden depths and layers. Just when you think you have learned everything you need to know, another layer reveals itself and you find yourself back on your journey of experimentation and learning.

This can confuse or trip up students who approach magic with a 'tick box' mentality: studied that, got it, now I move on. Magic and the Mysteries do not work like that. Each form, aspect, and dynamic of magic has endless depths which, when studied in depth and worked with, repeatedly reveals yet another layer. The surface layers are only the basic 'magical knowledge.' Beneath them are endless hidden layers that can take you into the adept aspects of your studies, until you reach the Deeper Mysteries.

Once you arrive at the layer of the Deeper Mysteries, a lifetime of discovery awaits you. As you mature and evolve, those levels of Mystery will reveal themselves as and when you are ready to integrate them into yourself. And so it goes on, layer after layer. At some point the adept mystical magician realises that you can never reach the bottom of the pot of learning.

Each aspect of magic has many different faces, and behind those faces are the complexities of the weave of fate, time, power, and consciousness. On their journey, the magician realises that the True Mysteries are not about histories, systems, beliefs, rituals, or religions. The True Mysteries are the same the world over, and they can be penetrated and understood only through inner transformation.

This is why classical training in any major art form is taught in a circular manner, or a *manner of return*. First the apprentice learns about the top layer of a subject by looking at it, touching it, 'sniffing' it: tentative exploration. As the student develops, matures, and gains knowledge and direct experience they circle back and reexamine the subject. This process of returning to a subject and looking further and deeper is neverending: it continues throughout a magician's training and throughout their life as an adept.

Quareia approaches magical training in the same way. The student, at each stage of their development, circles back to a subject they have already looked at and examines it more deeply, with more mature eyes. Over the many years it takes to complete the Quareia course, the student begins to realise that every aspect of magic and the Mysteries is indeed a bottomless vessel that can be reexamined throughout a lifetime. An adept should constantly be rethinking and reassessing what they believed were certainties, so that they are constantly evolving and developing as a magical being: they become The Developing One.

When the two opposing methods of Absolutes and Circling are brought together in training, they create a tension of learning, a balance of two dynamics that can at first confuse a student, but which will ultimately give them a mind that is flexible, astute, and grounded.

7. The good and the bad

Magical training in the West has mostly become an unbalanced education of 'only good' (or 'only bad'). This applies on many levels, but in terms of course structures and syllabuses, what has happened is that the student is only exposed to all 'good' experiences in their practical work. While this makes for 'happy consumer units,' it does nothing to prepare students for the onslaught of real magic, what it entails, what can happen, and most importantly of all *what it feels like, for both good and bad*.

Magic is an experiential art form, not a collection of spells and knowledge. Magic works with raw powers that can hurt you and beings that can trick and even destroy you. What keeps a magician safe through their developmental years as a student is not muttering banishing spells at every shadow, but the deep inner radar that they should be developing. And that can only develop from direct experience. The sanitising of magic is another byproduct of the commercialisation of magical training which has slowly crept in over the last few hundred years.

Everything now has to be a positive experience to 'keep' the student. And the root of the problem is wishing to keep the student, either for ego or for money. It is absolutely vital that a teacher never tries to keep a student; rather the teacher must give the student the best possible magical education they can. Whether the student stays or goes must be irrelevant to them. This means giving the bad with the good.

This dynamic of giving the bad with the good is not mentioned in the course, but it is there. I thought for a long time about the wisdom and implications of revealing this dynamic to students, as doing so can somewhat affect their resolve, and may prejudice how they approach their training. But given the rapid worldwide decline in educational delivery and the increasingly destructive and dangerous atmosphere now making itself known in various countries, I felt that it was probably, on the balance of things, more useful to outline this than to stay silent.

Eighty percent of the course's work is practical, and the student is given tasks to complete. Some of these tasks are directly magical, and some are not. Once the student has got some way into the course and has a good foundation of apprentice and initiate skills, then the course switches gears and sets tasks in a different way. The early stages of the course put a lot of magical protection around the apprentice, and the steps they are given to take are safe, secure, and will trigger an experience of one kind or another.

Once they reach the Initiate section, the training wheels start to come off, and the dynamic of bad versus good is slowly eased into the work. The student is given projects or tasks to do, some of which, while not dangerous, may or may not trigger experiences that are not exactly healthy in magical terms. This is not explained; rather the student is simply told to do such-and-such for some number of weeks.

The tasks and projects themselves are valid magical acts, and the skills learned are invaluable, but it is important for the student to learn how a repeated act over time can change. The nature of the contact can change for good or bad, and the energy can change for good or bad. When the student starts to feel more and more negatively affected, they are eventually driven to fall back on something they learned in their apprentice training: divination. They will check to see what is going wrong. This way, they learn what something feels like, they learn how to make a decision when they do not know all the variables, and they learn what it feels like when a situation is corrected.

Such experiences are invaluable. A physically unpleasant experience is something you never forget. But the student must never try to avoid such experiences: rather they have to learn what they can take and what they cannot, and to act accordingly. I do not exaggerate when I say that such experiences can save a life later on. They are necessary and an important part of the training.

They also teach the student something which is increasingly lacking in modern education and general wisdom: *anything* can be poison, it all depends on the dose. The same is true in magic. Because of the commercialism in the West and the concurrent dumbing down of our education systems, people are growing up with a very black and white view of the world. They think that if they pop a vitamin every day without fail, then they will be healthy. But some vitamins can be toxic if they accumulate. More is not better, and the idea of thoughtlessly doing the same thing every day has no place in magic. A magician must learn to weave their way through the path of fate. This is a complex skill to learn, as fate's dynamics flow through every aspect of a magician's life, from what they eat and where they live, to what magic they are doing at any given time.

The student will learn this through trial and error in their work, and they will learn it by their magical actions in training. After the first few experiences of this kind, they will start to realise that there was always a very quiet voice of warning within them, or a feeling of slowly building imbalance like a whisper slowly getting louder. The moment they recognise this is the moment they discover their own inner alarm system. That learning alone is the most precious thing in magic.

This method of teaching is not used in the visionary work, as it would be far too dangerous. Of all the aspects of magic, focused visionary work is the one that can truly open powerful doors, and because of that, the student is exposed only to those visionary structures that will help them grow and strengthen.

In terms of the further reading suggested for the student, however, a similar dynamic of good and bad is employed. There is little actual outside magical reading matter that is part of the course study, which can confuse students who feel that to learn magic, you need to read lots and lots of magical books. This is not correct, for many reasons, one of which is that a student who constantly dips into the all-you-can-eat buffet of modern magical writing can end up very confused. Certain magical texts are studied, some in depth, but mostly the student is given ancient Greek, Roman, and Egyptian texts to explore (they are also given supplementary research tasks on world cultures, myths, and religions). These texts are the foundations of Western magic, and they are still strongly relevant.

The 'bad' side of the scales, in terms of reading material, manifests in two ways, and only in the adept section, as the student needs to know enough of the rules before they can spot these underlying dynamics. One way is to expose the student to magical writing that 'is' magic: the text itself becomes a magical embodiment of power, and as such becomes its own consciousness. This is an ancient form of guardianship: the book acts not only as a vehicle for knowledge, but also as its own guardian. Poke it the wrong way and it will bite you.

The other way is to suggest that the student read one or two texts that are, basically, magical gibberish. It is important for the student to be exposed, without prejudice or teacher comment, to an example of a type of magical writing that is still produced today. This is work that is commercially driven, has little real magic in it, and simply repeats older texts that were themselves repeating texts invented simply to part superstitious and ignorant readers from their money. It is important that the adept student discovers this for themselves: they must develop their nose for bullshit and dressing-up, and learn to draw conclusions based on their own knowledge and experience. This cannot happen much before the Adept section, but once you are skilled in an art form, you can quickly spot inferior and counterfeit work for yourself. This is an invaluable lesson for a magician, for discernment is an important tool.

8. Learn the rules first

This is one of the most ancient principles of any classical training, and again it runs contrary to how a lot of people think today. You cannot break the rules until you know them completely, and thus know why you are breaking them, what effects this will have, and where it will lead you.

Students often mistake 'learn the rules first' to mean that they can never experiment or self-discover, and that they have no control over their education. This is generally the result of the sort of education they received as a young adult: 'do what you want' and 'anything goes' are principles that have become all too commonly and unthinkingly applied in many Western education systems. Such an approach will set up a student of magic for ultimate failure: they may learn some interesting things and feel more in control, but they will remain stuck on the first few rungs of the ladder of magic.

In magic as in ballet, if the basic and intermediate training is not solid and intelligent, then the advanced work will have no foundation to sit on. Proper magical training gives the magician not only knowledge and skill, but wisdom and safety. It allows the ancient patterns of magical dynamics to grow within the person so that they will have a good 'compass' for power and contact. Once the dynamics are learned properly, then the magician can apply their skills and knowledge to any magical or mystical system, and they can begin to experiment in a way that is rooted in *gnosis*. If you know that putting a 240 volt cable in your mouth is dangerous then you will not do that; but you will know what voltage is safe to work with, you will know that copper wires are good conductors of electricity and plastic wires are not, and you will use fuses in your experiments to stay safe as you explore how things work.

The training structure of Quareia works with the 'rules first' dynamic, and the basic structures and dynamics are laid out to give the student a flexible and intelligent basis for their magical knowledge. As the student progresses deeper into the course, more and more opportunities are presented for experimentation, tinkering, and invention. When something could be dangerous to them, such play is not encouraged. As an adept, once all the structures are learned, the student then understands why it was important to follow the rules and not break them. And with that knowledge and wisdom, they can plunge body and soul into magical experimentation in a way that is unique to them and their skills. That is the stage of magical evolution. That is the breaking of the rules in *gnosis*.

I am amazed at the number of students who want to play about with patterns, tools, and actions in the early stages of their training, usually on a whim or from something they have read in a book. They are doomed to stay on the apprentice rung of magic until they give up that approach. The basic system presented in the Apprentice section is there for a good reason, and unpicking and altering it will disengage the student from Quareia's magical pattern – and from its inherent protections. The current fashion of 'my ignorance is as good as your knowledge' cuts no ice in Quareia.

Of course, Quareia is set up in a way that people can do what they want with it, but if you truly wish to succeed in magic, then learn the rules first and gain a good level of competency. That is the way to evolve and develop as an intelligent magician.

What trips up early students, I think, is that they learn parts of a set system – Golden Dawn, Druidism, OTO, etc. – without realising that the magic in that system is structure-specific and does not translate well into other forms of magic. Quareia does not work in that way. It builds and works from the structure that underpins all the different forms of magic. You learn the underlying patterns and fully understand them, then you can see for yourself how these other forms developed, why they developed, and what they are working with. Such an approach allows you to work magically with any other magical system in a coherent and intelligent way.

9. Conclusion

I hope this chapter has given you a basic overview of how the course was approached in its creation, and how its outer construction worked. Now that you know a bit about some of the dynamics and principles which underpin the course, you should have a better understanding of why the course is as it is, and how best to operate within it. This knowledge may be particularly important for students from Eastern cultures, as their approach to learning can be very different indeed, particularly with respect to the Mysteries. The rest of this book will look at more specific aspects of the Quareia training, common questions that have been asked, and ways to approach certain aspects of the training. With a course as vast as this one – it is similar in scope to a university degree – it is appropriate to offer guidance without disengaging the student from the basic steps, struggles, and decisions that they have to make for themselves.

"Then the Lord God formed man of the dust of the ground, and breathed into his nostrils the breath of life; and man became a living soul.

And the Lord God planted a garden eastward, in Eden; and there He put the man whom He had formed.

And out of the ground made the Lord God to grow every tree that is pleasant to the sight, and good for food; the tree of life also in the midst of the garden, and the tree of the knowledge of good and evil.

And a river went out of Eden to water the garden; and from thence it was parted, and became four heads.

And the Lord God took the man, and put him into the garden of Eden **to dress it and to keep it.**"

— *Genesis 2:7, The Tanakh According to the Masoretic Text* and *JPS Hebrew/English Bible*, 1917

Appendix B
Common Study Issues

> *"If the doors of perception were cleansed everything would appear to man as it is, infinite."*
>
> — William Blake

Subsequent chapters will deal with those aspects of the course about which students have been shown to need some in-depth advice and guidance. But in this chapter we will look at some general issues which have come to light, issues that I had not thought about or been aware of when I was writing the course.

1. Magic and modern life

There are a few aspects of modern life (and in various places around the world) that can clash with a magical path of study. Here we will look at the ones that seem to be causing the most problems for people.

2. Distraction and commercialism

The world has become a place of distractions. We are surrounded by constant noise and stimulation, and a lot of this stems from commercialism. Commercialism has its place and serves a necessary function, but in some countries it has become an overarching monster that infects everything it touches.

You cannot get away from it; and anyway to run from it would be counterproductive. You are in the age you are in, and must learn to function in whatever society you live in. The key is to make it work for you, not for you to work for it.

The neverending stream of media that pours from phones, televisions, and computers encourages people to be constantly plugged in to whatever devices are around them. New technology that makes things easier for you is exciting, particularly when you are young, but magicians have to be constantly aware of what is happening in their surroundings and why. Commercialism needs a consumer, and that is all you are to it: a person to be manipulated into buying things so that companies get your money and you get a dopamine hit from your acquisition.

This aggressive commercialism taps into an ancient human defence mechanism that we might call our 'inner squirrel.' A squirrel spends a lot of its time finding food and storing it for the winter. It gets *pleasure* out of this – a hit of dopamine squirted into its brain – and for a sound biological reason: its sense of satisfaction at keeping a full and ever-expanding larder ensures that it will survive the winter.

Our two most basic instincts are the same as the squirrel's: breed and store food. Those two root survival instincts are abused by advertising, which presents you with things that trigger either your breeding instinct or your instinct to store food. 'Sex sells.' 'More is better.' The more you buy, the better you feel, the safer and more in control you feel. But if you step back and realise this, then you can turn commercialism on its head and make it work *for* you.

The positive side of commercialism is that it makes a lot of useful things easily available. As a magician, it is very important that you spot and understand all the dynamics surrounding you in your modern life, so that you can engage with necessity rather than desire. The key to a lot of magic is simple necessity; but knowing what is necessary and what is not can be difficult for someone who has spent their life being marketed at all day, every day.

The biggest problem this sort of environment poses is its lack of silence. There is no downtime for the mind, and a constant unseen battle is being waged between your subconscious and the marketing machine. In such an environment it is difficult to get past the first few steps of a magical training, and this can prevent many sensitive people from ever progressing.

Let's treat this issue practically. The two main distractions are the TV and the smartphone. Both serve useful purposes and are now part of everyday life. But they can begin to rule your life and block you from magic if you are not careful. You have to learn to use them and be around them *as a magician*. There is a relatively recent notion that you can have it all, that you can keep enjoying all your consumption and your distractions and still be a true magical adept. That is not true. However, there are ways to balance things so that you can still enjoy the fruits of modern living while walking an ancient path. But you have to be careful and pay attention to your mind and everything around you.

3. Television

Many people keep a television going in their house day and night. They have it on as background noise during the day, as a source of entertainment at times, and as a companion as they sleep. This creates a constant background chatter in their home. Not only is this bad for magicians, but it is also bad for children.

Magic, development, and learning all need quiet times when your mind can wander and wonder. Quiet is also necessary when you need to focus. The needs of a magician are similar to those of a developing child. A child needs to have silent times when their imagination is the only thing that entertains them. Silent boredom is an important part of their development, for it is the breeding ground of the imagination, and the imagination is the key to magic.

My advice is not to have a television playing while you sleep, or while ever you are not actually sitting down and watching a program. Besides the constant noise it creates, passively letting all sorts of programs play in the background of your life can affect your mind and imagination: their content will settle deep in your imagination and can affect your inner vocabulary.

Your inner vocabulary is the language that inner beings/spirits will use to communicate with you. If it is passively and subconsciously picked up from reality TV shows, horror films, and god knows what else, then it can cause problems for inner contacts when you are trying to connect with them.

4. Smartphones

Smartphones can create similar problems. The instant and constant narrative available through social media can quickly become addictive. People constantly check their phones, and even take them to bed with them. They are often used as alarm clocks, but this can often slide into the person checking their phone if they wake up in the night; and they check it again the moment they wake up in the morning. This can cause creeping problems for a magician or magical student. Waking up in the middle of the night and having to lie quietly and think, is great exercise for your mind and imagination. It is also a time when the world around you is still and silent – hopefully – and this can allow deeper thoughts and analyses to surface.

This in turn affects how you dream and what you dream about. Dreaming for a magician is not only the brain processing its daily intake: it is also a time when the deeper spirit of the magician can get to work. A lot of magical work is done in dreams, and it is a time when warnings, communications and insights can surface. Anything that affects your dream state – television, phones, medications – can have a direct effect on your ability to dream deeply and magically.

So buy a simple alarm clock for the side of your bed, and keep your phone out of the bedroom. Learn to unplug and not be ruled by these devices that can deeply affect your mind in so many different ways.

I get many emails from young student magicians who have severe problems with meditation, stillness, and silence; the majority of them are plugged into devices day and night. Their minds have become trained to constant noise and input, so meditation and silence can be a real struggle.

It can be a good exercise to keep a tally for twenty-four hours of how many times you engage with a media device for passive noise, companionship, or entertainment. It can come as a bit of a shock to people to realise just how much of their day is spent connected to one media device or another.

Learn to use these devices to your advantage. A phone is primarily a source of communication. Be wary of allowing it to become your constant entertainer and companion. When you cease to use your smartphone passively, and start using it only for its real purposes such as communication and research, then at first you will go through a withdrawal and loneliness. But afterwards you will be driven to books, art, music, and your imagination. That is the fertile ground that breeds a strong magician.

Modern advances can be wonderful things, if you do not allow them to completely take you over. A good film or program can inspire you, uplift you, or inform you. Lying on the floor listening to a complex piece of music can fill you with emotion. Staring into the distance, deep in thought, is how great things are born. And leafing through books to find what you want gives you the opportunity to stumble across hidden gems, which a focused internet search does not. There is also the magical bonus that the book, as an object, can become a doorway. A computer cannot. Books and computers are different animals, and learning to work properly with both of them can really help you.

5. Sleep

Sleep is really important to magicians as it is when a lot of magical work happens: it is a time for learning, speaking, and communicating, and a time when spirits, deities, and inner contacts can get messages or warnings to you.

Currently, many magicians like to try to control their dreams to trigger lucid dreaming: this is simply fashion and nothing more. The more you try to control what happens in your sleep, the more you end up blocking real magical connection. So don't do it!

The length of sleep you get, and when you get sleep, are also both important. A lot depends on whether you are a night person or a day person, and whether your sleep patterns are dictated by work or, for instance, wanting to stay up late and play games. If you are a morning person then make sure you get to bed in plenty of time (I know, I am starting to sound like your mother), because the problems for magicians start to show when they do not get enough sleep. If your body and mind cannot get through their clearing-out process and still have to do their magical processing, then you will start to feel it.

In some countries there is competition between peers about how much work they can do and how little sleep they need. For a magician this is a lethal combination. Magicians need more sleep than most people, as they are processing more and often working or learning in their sleep.

Sometimes when I am doing a heavy round of magic, I need twelve hours sleep – nine at night and three during the day. I slept a great deal while writing the Quareia course, as I was processing so much contact and information. But normally, seven or eight hours a night is about average for a magician. Any less than that, and your health will likely start to suffer.

You should not sleep in a room with a television going. And the deeper you get into magic, the more you will have to watch what you have in the room where you sleep, as certain objects and images can have troublesome effects. This differs between magicians, but generally the deeper you get into magic, the more important it becomes to take care over your bedroom.

If you are the type of person that I call 'see through,' i.e. you have a thin inner skin and are easily affected by spirit contact, and find you are having troubled sleep, then sleeping with an eight-hour safe candle burning at night will help you. If it is too bright, then try putting it in a hanging sanctuary lamp or in a dish with tallish sides to block some of the light. Some of this is discussed in the course, so I do not need to go into it too much here.

Most importantly, get a good night's sleep. Don't watch movies just beforehand, as this can affect your inner narrative. If you are currently exploring a certain culture or mythos and you find an old film that connects with it, then that is an exception, as watching it just before you sleep help you tap into that stream of myth. But be warned, watching violent, aggressive, or badly unbalanced programs before you sleep will embed their narratives deeply into your subconscious, and this will affect your magical contact. Being a skilled magician means taking extra care of your mind, imagination, and emotions. They are the tools of your trade.

6. Time restraints

When the life of magic and the life of work clash heavily it can make for problems. Some people have two jobs and a family to support, and that can make magical study and practice difficult. If you have no spare time at all, it is best to wait for something to change before embarking on magical study.

However if you do have some spare time, but have time constraints, then being disciplined yet flexible will help a lot. For example, meditation. If you are not simply avoiding doing meditation, but really do not have twenty minutes to sit and meditate, then doing a few sessions of five minutes each, scattered throughout the day, will start the process off. I used to meditate on the bus to work, and when I had a lunch break I would eat, then find a quiet space to sit and meditate in silence for ten minutes.

When it comes to ritual acts, that can take up time, so plan ahead and manage your time properly. Once you have decided to do a ritual act and set a date, the process begins at that point. So if you set a date, stick to it.

If life is continually getting in the way of practising your magic, and it is not just that you want to watch a movie or play a game but you really are being blocked by your responsibilities, then you are probably being held back from magic for some reason. This happened to me a lot in my early days, and looking back, it saved my ass. I was too unstable and immature in my teens to be delving too deeply into magic, and the constraints of work and ballet kept me waiting for quite some time. I am a natural magician, and when that natural ability is mixed with the idiocy of youth, bad things can happen. The secret is to be honest with yourself and not make excuses, and to be serious and disciplined about your intent to study. Either do it and fully engage with it, or don't do it.

7. Family

Having children is another restraint on study, and you may have to put your studies on hold until your children are old enough. Magic does not happen in a bubble: it affects all aspects of your life and can also affect your children adversely. Each situation is different and you have to think carefully about what you plan to do and why. The magic in the Apprentice section is unlikely to harm any children you are connected to, but deeper study may.

The general rule is, do not do magic if you are a mother until your child reaches seven years of age. There are always differences unique to each individual, but in general, it is best to wait. I had to stop most of my magical practice when I had kids: I did not so much as pick up a tarot deck until my youngest was about two. I did not really start to resume my magical practice until my youngest was seven, and I have to say, it was the longest seven years of my life. But it was worth it. And in truth, you really don't lose all your magical connections: it is still around you, and beings will still connect with you, but any actual magical work should wait.

If you find that your child is magical – if they are clearly picking up on things and seeing things, then they may do very well around magic once they are about five, or you may find that magic affects them no matter how old they are. With such a child, the type of magic you do is important. Balanced magic rooted in the balanced Mysteries should not harm them, but they may need extra care and protection. Imbalanced or aggressive magic could affect them very badly indeed. When you take on the responsibility of having a child, as their mother, their wellbeing takes precedence over everything else. It does not matter how depressed or isolated it makes you feel, you have a responsibility to nurture and protect them above all else.

If you are a father, it can really vary as it depends upon your inner connection with your child. Some fathers have a deep inner connection with their children, regardless of how attentive or inattentive a parent they are in everyday life, and some do not. Your inner connection has nothing to do with being a good or bad father, it is simply either there or not. If you have a deep connection, then you have to wait until your child is old enough before you can continue your magical work. If you don't have a deep connection, then experiment with carefully continuing your studies, and watch closely how your child reacts. If you do some magical work and the child then starts having nightmares or getting sick, or seems to know what you have been doing, then they are being affected. If they seem just fine, then continue carefully, but remember that each magical act is an individual thing. Your child may be fine with some things and not with others.

The easiest way to find out if you have a deep inner connection with your child is to watch what happens to your inner energy when they are sick, injured, or disturbed. If your energy suddenly goes right down, but you are not ill and there is no other cause for your lack of energy, then it is likely that your inner energy is upholding them. In that case, you are deeply connected to them and you will have to be careful.

8. Resources

This can be a problem for people in some parts of the world. There are some things that the course states that you need, usually for a ritual, that can be hard to get. With things like cloths and candles, improvisation is good. Bed sheets can be cut up to make cloths. With candles, you do need a living flame when a candle is indicated, because the element of fire needs to be present, so an electric fake candle will not work. But tea lights can be used, as can small ghee or oil lamps that produce a flame. But be wary of oil that smells of paraffin, and of perfumed oil, and don't use scented candles. Certain scents, particularly synthetic ones, can close contact down. Inner contacts and spirit contacts can be sensitive to smells.

With recommended books, it is often only part of a book that you need, and often these books can be found online, as a lot of them are in the public domain. Some of the necessary texts are embedded into the course for you, and we will also be producing a collection of the classical texts you need so that you can get them cheaply. They will also be available as a free download.

If you cannot get oils, resins, and so forth, then work without them. It is usually a matter of do your best, use your imagination, and when there is something that is impossible to get, then work without it. Later, as a mentored student, if you really do need them, and cannot afford them, if we can, we will send them to you.

Once a student reaches the Initiate level of training and has been accepted for mentoring, if they cannot afford a Magicians' Deck then we will send them a free one. I also keep an eye out for secondhand books that are from the Quareia reading list, and when I find them cheaply, Quareia buys them to give for free to people who need them. In some countries even small amounts of money can be difficult to come by.

All these things are done for mentored students: they have demonstrated their ability to study the course by reaching Initiate level, and the mentoring shows commitment. If someone wants mentoring and they cannot afford to donate, it is done freely for them, and resources are given to them if they need it and we have what they need.

This is all done on an honour basis. Quareia is ruled by Ma'at, *balance*, and we take our responsibility to our students seriously. We expect them to be truthful, and we give freely where there is real need. If someone decides to ask for freebies because they want to spend their money elsewhere, then the dynamic of Ma'at will kick in. It is a living magical power, and it will flow through the life of the student. It gives where there is need, and binds where there is untruthfulness. Two of the cornerstones of Quareia magic are honour and fellowship, and we will always make sure that any seeker genuinely walking the path of magical study has what is necessary for them.

We work closely with mentored students to make sure they are fully supported in their work, and as people help Quareia, we help students.

9. Ethics and culture

It has come to my notice that some countries' cultural and ethical concepts are so very different from those from which Quareia sprang that our students from those countries can easily become confused.

The stew that is Western magic was brewed in a cultural cauldron which stretched from the Eastern Mediterranean to the tip of Northwest Europe. The ancient Egyptians, Babylonians, Greeks, Romans, and Celtic tribes all added ingredients to that stew, as did many other peoples.

While countries like India have much in their ancient history and culture that is similar to that which produced Western magic, once you move further east into countries like China and Vietnam, the common language of magical reference points changes. Also, where countries have been Communist for some time there can be some difficulty in understanding the basics of magical thought. In an atheist society, it is difficult for someone to think about deities and so forth.

For example, in a conversation with a student from China, I tied myself in knots trying to explain the power dynamics of the Tree of Life. When a person has no cultural concept of Divinity, things start to get complicated.

I have no idea what the solution to this is. The only advice I can give to someone studying the Quareia course from a radically different culture is to go into the course with an open mind, and deal with each step as you come to it. Don't try to analyse ahead, as you will only get more and more confused. Learn what is directly in front of you, and as things start to trigger and work, then inner contacts will draw close and help guide you. Think of it as learning a whole new language. Don't try to read and understand the highest level of literature at the beginning: learn the baby steps, one at a time, and you will get there.

I think what will happen is that people who come to Quareia from different cultural backgrounds will study it in their own way, and out of that, as they complete the course, a whole new genre of magic will develop. Once a student has the actual magical vocabulary and has adapted some ways of magical working to their own cultural context, then their magic will evolve down a whole new road that is perfect for them. Also it will trigger the inner contacts, spirits, and powers of their land, and it will start to take on a life of its own. It will still be the same magic, just with a different accent.

In practical terms, I would also say that you should adapt and be flexible. Don't worry about not fully understanding something, particularly in the early days of your training. Often in magic the understanding catches up with you when you are ready.

10. Myths

At various points in the course, students are given small sections of particular mythologies to look at, read, and discover what is going on magically under the surface. It is important to study Egyptian, Roman, and Greek myths carefully, as they contain many hidden dynamics that need to be understood.

However, there are also points in the course where students are given various Northern European mythologies to look at and analyse. If you are from a radically culture and you cannot make sense of these European myths, then find a similar ancient myth with the same theme, – not a modern work of fiction – from your culture and use that instead. To do this, look at the techniques used to analyse the myth, and at the general subject matter, for example sleeping kings and queens, or warriors who are said to not be dead but sleeping in a cave or hill, and who will emerge when the nation is under threat. Similar stories can be found in the Far East, but where there has been Communist suppression of myths and stories you may have to work hard to find what you are looking for. Old songs and old children's stories can often be good places for a culture's mythology to hide.

Once you move beyond the surface of magic, you will find that the deeper undercurrents and dynamics are the same in every culture, as they are inherent to humanity; as such, a culture's myths and stories often hide these deeper undercurrents.

The key is to look at how the myth is approached in the lesson, what tasks are given, and what the lesson is trying to teach you. Once you understand the approach being used, you can use that approach on a myth from anywhere: you are learning how to learn.

11. Fear

This is a major stumbling block for a lot of students, and an issue that had not occurred to me. We live in a time of conspiracies, media propaganda, and social manipulation; untruths, fantasies, and bullshit ideas all flourish in our social media, news, and entertainment.

As the education systems of some Western countries degenerate, more and more people cannot tell the difference between fantasy and reality or fiction and non-fiction, and they believe anyone who speaks with authority, even if they are talking total nonsense.

This is a particular problem in magic, as one of the main tools of the magician is their mind. The mind and the imagination are regulated by hormones to some extent, and when a person is kept constantly in a state of fear it begins to affect how they think and imagine. This sets up a pattern of behaviour that becomes the norm, of being constantly in a low level of fear and stress.

Not being able to trust the media narrative, yet lacking discernment themselves, some students – particularly younger students who have grown up in this odd environment – develop an outlook on the world in which everything is perceived as a threat.

Inner contacts, spirits, beings, and deities are all perceived, consciously and sub-consciously, as threats. So you have a young student with a deep desire to study magic and mysticism, but who is also terrified of everything that goes bump in the night. (This can be particularly exacerbated by watching a lot of violent horror movies, which often weave aspects of the occult into their narratives.)

I have had many emails from distraught individuals terrified out of their minds because a spirit tried to interact with them, or because the door creaks too much, or because they think demons will attack them and eat their eyeballs (I shit you not). Healthy caution in magic is one thing; adopting the narrative of the violent American horror movie genre as your inner vocabulary and magical narrative is quite another, and it is not healthy.

I am at a loss as to how to remedy this issue, and can only suggest that people take greater care over what they expose their imaginations to. If you do feel something is happening to you, and some of it is similar to something in the movies, then it is likely that either your mind is playing tricks on you, or you are interpreting a genuine attempt at contact as something hostile.

There are magical protections woven into the course's structure to protect you from unnecessary bad experiences: if you are following it as prescribed, then you are safe. Just learn to interpret what is happening around you. Common sense is always the reference point when you are not sure what is going on.

And when a magical 'expert' touts a horror narrative, know that they are not an expert; they are an unethical person who is either mad, bad, or stupid. Usually what lies behind such behaviour is a wish for authority – pedestal standing – or money. Ego and money are always the bedfellows of such behaviour.

12. Dead Ends

This can become a serious problem for students, and being trapped in a dead end of study will likely block you from reaching deeper into magic. The dynamic of the *dead end* is an inherent part of the study of magic: its purpose is to unravel out of the magical arena those who are unsuited, mentally or physically, for it.

However, it is also a dynamic that suitable students can get stuck in if they are not careful. Students stuck in dead ends stay in their comfort zone, or focus on one aspect of the training alone, or repeatedly go back to an earlier lesson and try to perfect it. All these things stop students moving forward and developing, and instead keep them trapped in a loop of repetition.

Some get trapped in the tarot dead end, doing lots of readings, and reading as many books as they can find on the subject, instead of simply doing the step they were assigned to take in a lesson and thus securing a building block for their path ahead. Instead of securing that building block, the student delves into the depths of tarot, trying to learn everything they can about it. But tarot is not truly learned that way. It is learned by practice *alongside other magical practices*. You are like a juggler keeping plates spinning: you have to pay attention to all your plates equally, not focus on one in particular.

It is the same with astrology and ritual: these are things that people feel they can learn a lot about simply by reading and playing at it a little bit. But by not paying attention to the other aspects of their training, they miss how the powers are interwoven, and end up locked out of the system.

In later chapters we will look at the dead ends found in each of the foundation core skills that can particularly trap and hold the unsuspecting student. Often a student will rationalise their dead end by saying they want to get something exactly right before moving on. Magical training really does not work like that. If the student cannot trust the course's steps to take them where they need to go, then they will find themselves unable to penetrate the evolving aspects of the training. This course needs to be studied in small but frequent steps, not by crash studying one particular aspect.

The other general dead end that will unravel a student out of training is becoming an instant expert who seeks to lecture everyone in their magical group of friends, taking on the mantle of authority before they have even got past a few beginner modules. This is an example of the *messiah trap*, an ancient trap in magic in which an immature ego is glamoured into becoming a saviour or expert when they know nothing and cannot help themselves, let alone others.

It is also a symptom of projection. When a person cannot cope with something, they rally to others who also cannot cope and set themselves up as saviours. This gives them a little circle of acolytes, but it locks them out of the training. A person who gets stuck in this dynamic cannot begin to move forward in gnosis, as they have no self-awareness.

When you first learn a skill, it is understandable to want to use it to help others; but a student must know *why* they want to do that. Do they really want to help others, or do they want some modicum of authority?

13. Hitting a wall

This is the most common issue of all, and it is inherent in all forms of classical training. Intense long-term study has its own tides, and this is particularly true of magical training. There are times in the training when you will hit an energetic wall. You cannot seem to make progress, you are exhausted and demoralised, and you feel like a failure. You are not. Not at all. It is a good sign, though a painful one.

There are various reasons why this happens. One is that it is normal with any intense training to hit such a wall: it is part of the process. And with magical training, there can be an awful lot happening in the world to cause inner 'bad weather' which will either pull you into action in your sleep, or lock you out for your safety. If you are pulled into working in your sleep, then all your magical energy will be used up with such work, leaving you with nothing for practice. And if you are locked out, then no matter what you try to do you will not be able to access any sense of magically 'moving forward.'

If you are hitting the wall constantly and do not feel that you are moving forward at all, then put your current lesson on pause, and move on with the course. Come back to the stuck bit when you are ready. We do not all develop the same way, and magic tends not to work in straight lines. The course's step-by-step training is important for its overall coherence, for anchoring the foundation, and for developing a proper sense of training. Its steps will be in the right order for ninety percent of its students. However, ten percent always develop in a different way. Do not use this as an excuse to skip forward if you are just bored or feel that a lesson is beneath you: a lot is hidden in even the easiest of the lessons. However, if you are seriously hitting the wall... then move on. Just don't forget to come back soon and finish off the stuck lesson.

If you are finding that you are stuck *and* exhausted all the time, then one of two things (or both) is happening. Either you are working in your sleep, or you are being stretched.

Working in your sleep happens naturally with a lot of students without them realising. Having lots of weird dreams and broken sleep? This is a symptom of your deeper self having taken over and started working in your sleep. A lot of the work in Quareia is about service, and sometimes you can get drawn into service work in your sleep, particularly when the situation is critical. At the moment the Western world is struggling with a dangerous buffoon of a leader with his finger on the nuclear trigger, and with the rise of fascism in various parts of the world. This situation can develop into a nasty long-term scenario for the whole planet, so it is no wonder that people are working hard in their sleep.

It is important to recognise this when it happens. If your tarot skills have developed enough, then do a reading to see what is happening in your sleep. It will likely show work, conflict, or struggle. Whenever you are working in your sleep, you must make sure that you are not overworking magically in your waking life. So don't overdo the training work: take some time out. Be mundane. It is important to learn to manage your energy, and to recognise when you have been working in your sleep without realising it.

Being stretched is a more difficult thing to explain. It is akin to being rearranged, and it often happens to people on magical or mystical paths. Again, you will feel blocked and tired. When that happens, rest, slow your magical work down (but don't stop), and be as normal as possible. You will feel when the stretching is over, as your energy will come rushing back in.

If you have exhaustion and *physical* symptoms, then go see a doctor to make sure you are not ill.

For the most part, hitting a wall means that you are backing up in preparation for a major leap forward. You will be blocked from moving forward properly until everything is in place around you, and you have processed internally what you have already learned. The key to hitting walls is to wait patiently. Continue your basic practice, and don't overdo it or push yourself. View it as treading water while you wait for the sluice gates to open. When the timing is right, everything will suddenly leap forward, and you will be back in the fast lane.

Remember, real magical training is not a short one or two year jaunt. It is a long marathon. There will be times for sprinting, times for resting, and times for time out. Find your pace and your limits, and don't ever feel you have failed because you get stuck... that is just bullshit. We all get stuck, we all take time out. I still do, after decades of magic. It is called being human.

14. Cherry picking

Cherry picking happens when a student not only looks ahead at the more advanced modules (which is not a problem in itself) but decides that there are elements of the course that are beneath them, so they skip them and instead dive into the more advanced work that has grabbed their attention.

There are various problems with this approach, and the student often ends up getting damaged, or getting the attention of hostile beings. I get endless emails from terrified student magicians who are being hounded and who have made themselves ill through their actions.

The roots of this problem are not trusting the structure of the course and not taking the work seriously enough. Ego can also be a factor: the student feels, because they have done some previous study, that it is okay for them to pick and choose.

One of the overarching problems in magical training and study today is a lack of foundation skills: if those are not rock solid, then the whole 'house' of a person's magic is built on sand. Everything is fine until real power or real contact happens, and then everything goes down the toilet and the student is in a mess.

To be honest, I am not willing to clean someone up and put them back on their feet if they have harmed themselves by ignoring advice. That might sound harsh, but I don't have the time it takes to help such people, and learning from your bad experiences is either a really good teacher or a really good filter: you either drop out of the course, or you learn to sort yourself out. All the skills you need to help yourself in such situations are outlined in the very first Apprentice module. You either apply them and learn a harsh lesson, and thus mature a bit so that you can study properly, or you drop off the magical path: you are filtered out. Magic takes no prisoners, and the earlier a student realises that and takes their study seriously, the better.

This course is built in layers. Each layer has aspects of protection, strengthening, and knowledge acquisition. If you miss a vital part of a layer, then you will likely have a serious weakness in your magic. Everything stands on what was done before. This course is built like a pyramid with a wide, solid base, and as the pyramid rises, the structure becomes more condensed and complex. When you look at a pyramid from the outside, you do not see the internal architecture that distributes stress and upholds everything. So it is with Quareia.

If you are curious and wish to look ahead in the course, then do so. But keep in mind that what you read is not the same as what you experience when you actually do the work. Do not be fooled into thinking that because you have read something, you fully understand it. This is not a theoretical course alone. All the theory has its root in the direct experience which constitutes seventy percent of the learning. Most students will walk the path a lesson at a time. A few will be prompted to engage in a practical lesson a step or two ahead, usually for a specific reason. Do not do that unless you get a serious prompt, and you must also still continue with the given sequence of lessons and *redo* the more advanced step when you get to it. Needing to do a lesson early is rare: do not let your curiosity or your whims be a reason for doing so. Magic sometimes has its own timing, but the steps must also be done in sequence to make sure that all aspects of the pattern, the protections, and the learning are in place.

15. Broken links

I have mentioned this earlier in this guide, and I have to apologise for putting internet links in the course. They vanish so quickly. None of them are critical: they are just there to make your research easier by giving you somewhere to start. Use a search engine when you come across broken links: you will certainly find something useful, and even if you do not find what we were trying to show you, it will not affect your training in any way.

I learned a lot of harsh lessons from writing the apprentice section, and I had to smarten up with how I approached things to make sure that the course and the information in it would last in the long term.

A final note: the internet is becoming increasingly commercialised, locked down, and threatened. It would be worthwhile for any serious student of Quareia to download and store, or even print out, the whole course. The course is also available in book form: the cheapest form is the three large paperbacks, one for each section. We have produced them as cheaply as possible to make sure that as many people as possible can access them, and they should also be available in UK and USA libraries on request.

Various people around the world are also working on translating the course into different languages, and these translations will also be distributed in as many ways as possible to help people access Quareia.

> *"I am striving to give back the Divine in myself to the Divine in the All."*
>
> — Plotinus

Appendix C
Approaching Magical Study

> *"The seeker is as a cracked vessel.*
> *Through direct experience, the cracks are filled*
> *first with copper, then with silver, and finally gold.*
> *Then, and only then, the vessel can hold the Water of Life."*
>
> — Josephine McCarthy

In this chapter we will look at general advice, and some general pitfalls that a student can tumble into. I hope it will give you the advice you need to be clear about how you are going to approach your magical training.

1. Discipline

The first and most important skill to acquire if you wish to train seriously in magic is discipline. For some this comes naturally, for many it is a struggle, and for some it can become a barrier: too much discipline and you end up locking yourself down by obsessing over achievements and goals; too little and you are left floundering around the edges of magic.

The first step towards developing a healthy discipline is to see it as a method of approach that gets you where you wish to go. Some people can become obsessive about discipline, so that without noticing the discipline itself becomes their goal. This sets the student up to 'fight' the course, which will result in them constantly hitting walls they cannot get beyond.

A healthy approach to developing discipline is to approach the course within the rule of absolutes: work on what is in front of you, enjoy it, and explore it, without constantly looking for a long-lost horizon. Once you have the right mindset – that your goal is to achieve what is before you – then you can develop a routine that will take you to that goal.

In addition, be adaptable. Everyone is different, and you should know yourself better than anyone. Don't fool yourself, but also listen to your internal voice. Magic never works like clockwork, and it ignores schedules. It ebbs and flows like a river, so learn to ebb and flow with its power. At times it is right to break your discipline, for inner or outer reasons, and other times you have to keep going with your practice even when you don't feel like it. The key is learning, by direct experience, how to have a constant relationship with magic and its practice.

Manage your time properly. Be pragmatic when you need to be. Remember, it is a long marathon, not a sprint. When you fail, pick yourself up, dust yourself off, and get walking the path again. Many failures on the way are inevitable, and you will learn as much from them as you will from your successes. The key to overall success is to enjoy the path, be challenged, learn, evolve, and grow; not to beat yourself up and sulk in the corner.

Set your study and practice schedules for a month and no longer; and sort out your meditation routine on a week-by-week basis. This allows for flexibility. Life sometimes throws curve balls at you, so being flexible will help.

Setting your meditation schedule for just a week at a time particularly allows you a lot of flexibility, as life is always changing. If you get locked in a routine that is too tight and too rigid, then either you will end up failing, or you will find yourself becoming dependant on your unchanging meditation schedule. Flexibility is always the key.

Also, for those of you who have problems with discipline generally or meditation specifically, setting a small, achievable goal for yourselves each week will greatly benefit you. Achievement makes you want to do more; failure can make you want to give up. So don't set yourself up for failure. And if you have a bad week and everything goes to shit, then simply write that week off and be fresh and ready for the following week.

2. Study approach

Do not approach the course as if you are cramming for exams. You are not. You are on an adventure. Let curiosity drive you, not ambition to be top of the class: there *is* no top of the class in Quareia. Each magician who becomes an adept through Quareia will be truly unique. Real, powerful magic creates individuals, which is why this is mostly a lone path. It does not create hierarchies, perfect students, or super groups: these are all things we wish for as a result of a subconscious search for power and status. That is not magic, that is misplaced ego.

Magical training is very much about having experiences that are subsequently informed by knowledge. Those experiences are then built on through repeated work, practice, and applying your new skills to the world around you. To flourish on such a path, take your time, enjoy the journey, and let the journey become your life.

One important point: follow the lessons exactly. Do not be tempted to change aspects of the work, as this will lock you out of the system. Everything in the lessons is there for a specific magical reason. I have come across students who want to change the directional pattern to suit their perspective, or to change the use of the tools, use a different tarot deck, or approach ritual or vision in a different way. This will set you up for failure, as you are working inside a coherent pattern. Change the pattern, and the whole structure will disengage.

In practical terms, there are some things that frequently trip up magical students in their study approach. Remember, this is not a degree course where simply doing lots of reading will get you where you want to go; it is a practical, skills-based course that is informed by reading.

Let us have a look at some of the things that can trip you up in your studies or cause you difficulties. Some of these have to do with how you approach your study, and others are dynamics that will trip you up if you are not careful. Because Quareia is not a theoretical course, a lot of the things that can derail you are not directly related to your study, but are practical dynamics to do with how you approach the magic, the material world, and yourself.

3. Confirmation bias

Confirmation bias can become a net that will easily entangle you due to the nature of magical study and the personal and psychological barriers we erect around us. It is something that in truth, you can never quite get away from. Magic uses our imagination, and our imaginations are informed by many things: our culture, experiences, likes, dislikes, and so forth. Survival mechanisms use patterns of recognition: we gravitate to what we recognise and we build upon that. As we build, we sort through our 'building materials' and take what we know fits, and we discard what doesn't.

This mechanism serves many purposes for us, but it can also hobble our learning and evolution: we can end up in an echo chamber of what we recognise, rejecting what does not fit. It is the same mechanism that discourages a child from trying new foods: they stay with familiarity unless there is peer pressure to try something different. The same mechanism also drives fundamentalism, and it can seriously warp our mental model of the world.

A lot of magical understanding comes from seeing, recognising, and working with patterns, whether these are patterns of behaviour, patterns of energy, patterns of mythos, or patterns of words. Normal magical development means seeing a pattern in something, *not noticing* the bits that do not fit, and coming to conclusions that form the magical action. This is a normal developmental process in one's personal magical evolution. The problems occur when the magician sees a pattern, *notices* parts that do not fit, and then *ignores them*. Any subsequent work that relies on that 'ignoring' will set up a path of devolution within the magician. This is the trap of the negative application of confirmation bias. It is also an important deep dynamic of mystical magic: not knowing, and acting from innocence is harmless. Knowing, and acting regardless of the 'knowing', by ignoring what you know, creates a power imbalance that quickly spins out of control.

4. Messiah trap

I speak a lot about this and repeat myself many times. This is not to annoy you, but because it is so important to be aware of it, as it is the biggest trap for all magicians at every level of competence. I spoke earlier in this book about this dynamic as a surface presentation, but the deadlier form is its deeper presentation, which works through the pattern recognition mechanisms of our consciousness.

When you read Classical, ancient, and mythic texts, on one level you are looking at the cultural and mythological aspects of a people. However, many of those texts also have a deeper layer that speaks to initiates of the Mysteries. Embedded within the texts are dynamics that tell of stages of mystical and magical development, and these layers appear in ancient Egyptian, Classical, and ancient Greek texts. They also appear in Jewish, Christian, and Islamic texts, with the dynamic attached to the prophets of these religions.

These dynamics also appear in magical visionary work, though for the most part they are not written about in magical texts. For the volumes of magical inner work in the Quareia course, a large percentage is left unsaid. These are the parts of magical work that must be found by the magician alone; when they are experienced, mentors and teachers know that their student is developing well and connecting with the deeper inner patterns of magic.

These deeper experiences come in dreams and visions, and occasionally in outer encounters in the world. The only way I can describe them is to say that they are inner narratives and experiences that any true magician on the path of development will experience in some form or another. Their presentation can vary from person to person, but their underlying patterns are the same.

When someone is thrust into one of these experiences, it can be intense and profoundly life changing. If the magician is grounded, is rooted in the pattern of their work, and has a good foundation under them, then the experience can show them the reality of the path they are walking, where it is going, or who they are at the deepest level: it is a pure revelation. It is something that has been recorded from ancient times: it is hidden in texts, and once you have experienced it then you will spot it lurking in the corner of an epic tale, or in a religious recitation. It is a shining light that truly awakens your spirit to your eternal self and to your communion with everything around you.

If someone is not properly prepared, through lack of training or through not adhering to it, or if they are not grounded and disciplined, and they still manage to trigger one of these experiences, then it can tip them over the edge into mental illness. Remember the quote at the top of this chapter about the cracked vessel? The messiah trap blows the cracked vessel wide open, spilling its contents, rather than healing the cracks.

In the Apprentice section, this can rear its head in the weakest way by tempting the student to become a pedestal stander, as is explained in the previous chapter.

If the student spots their ego trip and remedies the problem, then their vessel will be strengthened and prepared for the bigger exposure to that power later. A lot of magical training contains innate 'traps' in which weaknesses in the personality/ego are brought to the surface so that they can be recognised and dissolved. The work itself helps in that process: that is the layer of copper.

This is why it is so important to follow a classical training properly, and not jump about or dabble within it. The Apprentice and Initiate parts of the course are designed to close up your vessel's cracks gradually and strengthen it so that it is ready for such an experience.

So what happens when it all goes badly wrong? If the lessons in the Apprentice section are not learned or are ignored, then any creeping or deeply hidden wish to 'save the world' or be a 'prophet' will rapidly surface when the student has a powerful experience.

The student may have a strong visionary experience which can at times mirror the narrative of a Biblical or religious figure such as a prophet or messiah. This is because those narratives have their roots within the ancient Mysteries: these experiences are hallmarks of deep inner connection and soul evolution. Having one does not mean you are a messiah; it is simply you making a profound connection with Divinity and the Mysteries that transcends religion and culture.

When the student or magician is not fully grounded, having such an experience can trigger the feeling that the magician is a saviour, a Divine being of some sort, or a messiah (in Christian cultures). As soon as the magician takes that unbalanced narrative for the truth, they will begin to spin out of control. Obsession moves in, as does mental imbalance, and their resulting behaviour can mirror forms of fundamentalism.

This tends to happen in magicians with a mental health weakness or an imbalance of some sort – usually something minor or in remission. People with more serious mental health issues tend not to get far enough into magic for such experiences to trigger, though it does occasionally happen. When a person takes on contacted classical magical training and follows it properly, then the powers and contacts within it will slow the student down enough in their studies to make sure that their inner 'muscle' is slowly strengthened. Through this, they learn to work with any inherent issues to stabilise and build foundations. In such cases, any imbalance triggered by these experiences will be minor, and will be recovered from quickly enough.

But when that development process is circumvented, and the filters skipped over, then it can seriously unravel the student out of magic for that lifetime. They become vocal messiahs of a path, declaring or at least hinting at their own godhood, and the final result is a total mental breakdown from which they often never recover.

I have had to witness this many times with potentially brilliant magicians who felt that their natural ability excluded them from the need for long-term serious training. It is sad to see and so unnecessary: so please take heed of this warning.

As an aside, when you do read classical or ancient texts and you recognise some of your experiences within them, remember that the overall message to take from this is that you have had a powerful experience that shows you are treading in the footsteps of the many who have walked the path before you. You are not special; you are finally *awake*.

5. Narrowed attention

One of the common mistakes that people make in long, in-depth training is to let their perceptions and attention get narrow when they are studying. This is a normal mechanism that triggers with any specialised training, and in some subjects it can be useful: the more you focus on one aspect of a subject, the more you can get out of it – but the less you see peripheral details.

This enables, for example, a scientist to look in great detail at an aspect of their specialisation and spot things that an untrained person could never see. This is also important in magic, but here it is equally important not to miss the periphery, as often that is where magic leaves a trail of crumbs for you to follow.

It can be difficult to maintain adequate focus while also keeping enough of an eye out for information, contact, discovery, and development on the periphery. Magic flows through everything in life, and can speak to you out of many places. Because of this, the course is designed not only to teach you focus, but also to teach you to look outside of those areas which you perceive as magical. You will study many different things that are not directly related to magic, not only for the richness of experience and knowledge you can gain from them, but also to teach you how to find precious gems of magic in seemingly non-magical subjects.

If you stay aware of these two opposing dynamics of focus and peripheral attention, and keep a wide view of your surroundings while you focus carefully on the topic at hand, then you will do just fine. Magical focus on a specific thing will often trigger a response in a completely different area of your life: so pay attention, and you will harvest everything that you need to evolve and grow.

6. Not everything is magical

Many seemingly mundane things can happen as a result of magic, as it seeps throughout everything it touches and affects everything. However, it is easy to start thinking that everything that happens to you is magical: this is another trap. One of the skills a student magician must learn is how to discern what has been triggered by magic and what has not.

This becomes an issue when a student starts to believe that every time something negative happens it was caused by magic. Sometimes, shit happens. It can be that simple: it just is what it is. The skill of discernment is a mixture of practical experience, common sense, and divination when necessary. It is not easy, but it is an important skill to master. Thinking that everything is caused by magic means the student ends up not taking responsibility for themselves, and becomes a victim of life. But thinking that *nothing* is caused by magic stops the magician from developing, as often the magical kick-backs that affect your life can teach you a great deal.

It is about finding a healthy middle ground. I usually start by assuming that something has a mundane cause, but I will then look deeper just to check. Each experience you have can teach you something, so that you gradually build a vocabulary of 'effects' until eventually you learn to spot the hallmarks of magic. But even now I do not presume that an effect is magical: I always check, particularly when action may be needed.

7. Loss aversion

This can be a tough one, particularly in a consumer society. Magic triggers necessary change, and this is part of your growth and evolution as a magical student. Often the necessary change is to let go of something that you are clinging to.

In the Apprentice part of the course, there are exercises and actions that help trigger the skill of letting go. It really is a skill, and something that needs to be fostered and strengthened within you if you are to step forwards into adept magic. People cling to belongings, ideas, people, places, etc. When those things (or some of those things) no longer have a place or purpose in your life, they can act as bindings or traps that hold you back from evolving. One of the first things that can happen, when you first make inner contact, is that the contact may spot something you are clinging to that is detrimental to you, and will ask you to relinquish it. If you resist then the inner contact will withdraw, for if you cannot let go of something that is creating an imbalance within you, then you cannot handle power.

And that is the root of the dynamic: learning how to let go of things teaches you how to handle real power when it is necessary. If you are lent magical power for some necessary purpose and you then cling to that power, it will begin to unravel you – and ultimately it will destroy you.

This can be a difficult dynamic to understand when you are in a culture that judges you by your belongings and by how much you consume. That mentality seeps into relationships, creates obsessions, and locks people down into the trap of accumulation.

Learning to let go when asked, and when you realise that something is not necessary, it allows old, outworn patterns in your life to be shed. This makes room for what is necessary to come into your life. The key point, which many magicians do not understand, is that when you walk through life without clinging to things, people, or places, but instead walk a path of necessity, then when you lack what you need, it is given to you. Making sure that your path is clear of unnecessary clutter – physical clutter, emotional clutter, whatever – allows power triggered by inner contacts to flow through your life pattern so that you get whatever it is that you need.

It will flow through mundane channels: money, shoes, a car, a partner, an area to live in. Of course these things do not fall from the clouds and magically land at your feet; rather you are put in the right place at the right time to make sure that what you need flows to you through mundane channels. The deeper you go in magic and magical service, the stronger this dynamic becomes. But first the cupboards must be emptied and cleaned, and your attachments shed, before this dynamic can begin to trigger. Once you stop clinging and let go, then power can start to flow.

In the early Apprentice modules, this understanding and dynamic is triggered both by simple ritual – in which you learn to give/output before you take/input – and by some practical work in which you sort out your living space and belongings. It starts in the mundane world, and as you step deeper into the training different layers emerge, so that this process becomes ever more powerful and more profound. So if you have an ingrained aversion to loss, then you should start working on it now. Give away things that you like but do not need: pass them down the line to those who need them.

8. Mythic reading and psychologising

This is a major stumbling block for magicians when they look at ancient, classical, and mythological texts: they read them through a psychological filter. People are taught to think that ancient mythic texts were intended as stories to alter people's behaviour or to get them to search within themselves for answers to life's problems. Myths can indeed be used that way, and with a few of them that is indeed their main function. However, they are the minority: a large portion of mythic and ancient texts are really about *regional power dynamics*, and when read through a magical lens, their deeper layers of meaning surface.

They served, and still do serve, as guides: they tell you the inner power dynamics behind the presentation of something, and they often explain how to deal with specific regional magical issues and supply the correct keys for doing so. The issues they tackle are often those caused by clashes between humans and land beings or deities: the myths tell you what to do about them, and what *not* to do. If you are magically trained then you can spot the references to tools, methods, and actions. One of the skills of the magician is to read such texts, extract the necessary information, and put it into action.

Myths are a good example of how magic hides in plain sight. To the mundane reader, a myth is an exciting and interesting tale which often contains general advice for living. But beneath that layer hides magic for those with the keys to unlock it; this was a way of passing magical information down through the generations.

The habit of approaching myths through a psychological lens distances the student from real magical learning. It also belittles the knowledge and skill of those who wrote such texts. This is glaringly apparent when we look at ancient Egyptian texts. Such texts appear simplistic, but they are not – not by any stretch of the imagination. They contain layer after layer of magic and magical advice, and for the magician who has been trained to look at them properly, they are endless source of magical knowledge, wisdom, and instruction; and this is true for both the living and the dead.

This way of looking at myth is taught throughout the course. If you start by completely dropping the psychological approach to ancient and Classical mythic texts, then you will slowly begin to see all the other layers of communication hidden in them.

9. Discernment

The skills of sound judgement and discernment also need plenty of healthy development if you are going to become a magician. And discernment is one of the hardest skills to learn when you are confronted by a subject matter you know little or nothing about.

In the last few decades, magic has fairly burst into the public consciousness and into popular culture. More and more people have become interested in it, in various ways and for various reasons. Wherever there is an audience, there will be someone looking to sell product to them. Often the person doing selling the product has little real knowledge and is basically full of shit.

The result is students being overwhelmed by lots of different aspects of magic, some that have their roots in truth and some that have their roots in fantasy. The confusion has been compounded by movies and games: they become the narrative in the mind of the student, and this locks them out of real magic. The fake glamour takes precedence. Remember, not everything you see in a 'historical' movie is real, not every monster or demon on TV is real, and not everything you read on the internet is real.

A healthy bullshit detector is a good thing to develop, and that is done slowly and painfully by experience, study, and by staying objective. Sometimes it can be difficult to discern the truth from the make-believe, as real magic is often far weirder than fiction; but it is also rooted in common sense. One good general rule is that if someone is making huge sums of money from something 'magical,' then for the most part they will be selling bullshit with a few grains of truth mixed in.

10. Tides and timings

These catch out a lot of magicians, even adepts, so being aware of them from the beginning of your training will be helpful. Dealing with tides and timings is not something to obsess over or overthink; just be aware of them and keep them in the back of your mind.

We are surrounded by inner tides of energy and power all the time. They ebb and flow like the seasons, but often without the same predictability. These are inner tides of nature, and are usually creative or destructive: they are something you will learn a lot about in the course.

Magic has its own tides, as does your fate, your body energy, and so forth. We exist within a complex dance of powers and energies. When you engage in magical training, you become more aware of these tides, and that also magic has its own timing. As an apprentice you will likely not spot tides much, but you will slowly develop a feel for them and how they affect you.

As an apprentice, if you are flexible with your approach, you will notice that at times energy comes in and fills you, and at other times the tide goes out and you are left feeling tired and drained. There are lots of other reasons for such feelings, but you will slowly start to distinguish between these and when they come from some magical act or from an 'inner weather' tide. Once you engage with magical training, you develop more of a sensitivity to things, and you also become more visible to such tides: they affect a magician where they would not necessarily affect a mundane person.

This dynamic is too complex to go into here, and it is covered throughout the course in different ways. But some general good advice for you at this stage is *learn to bend with the wind so that you do not break in a storm*. Pace yourself, adapt when necessary, and rest when necessary. And go undercover – be mundane, do no magic, no readings, etc. – when you get the feeling that something threatening is looming.

Discernment is key here: are you just tired because you stayed up late or drank too much? Are you bored, grumpy, or coming down with a minor sickness? Or has a strange, unpleasant feeling, or a feeling of being drained, suddenly come upon you for no reason? If so, then it may be a tide affecting you. (There are other magical reasons for feeling like that, but they should not generally affect an apprentice.) This is where being truthful to yourself is important, and how you learn to discern between the different things that could be affecting you.

11. Emotions in magic

This is a major stumbling block for apprentices, for a variety of reasons. As you progress through the course and have various encounters and experiences, you will learn firsthand why emotions can be such a problem in magic. But as emotions can also affect your early studies, I will briefly address them here.

Quareia stretches in many directions of magic and looks at many different approaches to magic, so it is very likely that some students will trip up with the use of emotion at some point.

A new student with mystical leanings will likely bring into their practice Divine adoration, and/or the search for 'bliss.' This is purely the result of cultural and religious programming that has developed over thousands of years. Divine adoration and bliss are in fact deeply misunderstood terms, particularly in the West, and as we live in an emotive society, it is easy to bring a sort of emotive searching into our magical practice.

It is very important that you realise that when you are an apprentice, you have little experience with inner beings, and will be easily fooled. Certain types of beings are profoundly parasitical, and the food they seek is emotion, or the energy given off by emotions. These beings can manipulate your mind and practice to get you to have an emotional experience. You adore the being, the being says, 'thank you very much,' and it sucks up all your energy and leaves.

As a student develops into adepthood, they will begin to realise that there is a path in magic that opens an interface between themselves and the Divine, but no emotions are involved. The depth of the experience goes beyond the chemical emotions of the body, and reaches deep into their soul/spirit. It is a profound experience and changes you forever. But to get there, the magician needs to learn that deep connections that can be made that do not involve surface emotion.

At that point the magician usually realises that many of the emotions channelled towards the Divine really have to do with people looking for a substitute parent: they want someone to love, protect, and uphold them. An adept steps away from that parental grasping and works instead to connect with the consciousness that we call the Divine, and to connect in a way that is not so geared towards human needs, fears, and wants.

Learning how emotions can trip up the magician, and how unbalanced emotive connections can be abused and parasited, is very important, so there are many parts of the course that work with this dynamic. It is approached in many different ways, and with slow, steady exposure. Overriding a lifetime of emotive programming is not easy, but it is necessary. The adept magician must transcend as much cultural, emotive, religious, and social programming as possible if they are to step into power, and into direct communion with powerful beings.

The second use of emotion in magic that trips up the apprentice is 'results' magic. You have a desire, and you do some magical act to fulfil it. In its basest form, results magic tends to be pretty infantile: forcing someone to love you, smiting your enemies, getting a new car, and so forth.

Results magic uses emotion as fuel for the engine, which is an exhausting and scatter-gun approach, it also quickly becomes a feeding station for hungry parasites. It is also dangerous. A person who uses rage to magically attack an enemy has already lost: the magic is often poorly thought out, and thus bounces around causing all sorts of unforeseen calamities. It also exposes the weakness within the magician: if you are ruled by your emotions, then you can be ruled. Emotions catch us off-guard, and they make us act unwisely in many ways. And a soup made of unwise acts, emotion, parasites, and unthinking spontaneity with no long-term planning is a recipe for disaster. It is all about want, not necessity; and a being, inner contact, or *another magician* can spot this weaknesses in you easily and magically manipulate you to bring you down. This does not mean that magicians should not have emotion: that would be silly, and it would deny our humanity.

But the magician must learn early on that emotions often have no place in magic. Internal discipline, focus, and necessity drive powerful magic; not wants, emotions, or outbursts.

12. Reading and learning

Many people have asked me about whether they have to remember everything they read on the course, and how they will be tested. Many students are fearful at first that they will not retain everything. Not only is there a lot of information in the course itself, but there are also extensive reading tasks, where the student has to delve into classical and ancient writings as well as history, cultural geography, and so forth. So take notes as you go!

When a student reaches the Initiate level of their training and they wish to be mentored then their work will be tested and challenged: their notes will be looked at, and they will have some discussions with an adept. Many new students are fearful that they will not remember everything they have read, and will fail this process.

A lot of this fear comes from people who have been through the university system, or who have taken magical training where they were expected to cram for exams and written tests. Quareia does not work this way at all.

This course exposes you to a lot of different things that you have to take in, and you are introduced to some books that can be pretty dense and hard-going, particularly the Classical ones. These are not for you to revise, remember, and quote back to us; rather the intent is to expose you to something different, something that will change you at a deep level. You are often given only sections of books to read, and usually they are good books to have around for future reading. Read the indicated sections, take notes, and then, most importantly, think about what you have read in the context of magic.

The information will go in and percolate at a deep level, and when it mixes with your direct experiences then it will change you and deepen your understanding. It is your understanding that is challenged: you are not going to be tested on your texts like in college; rather a mentor speaks to you to see whether your understanding is dawning slowly, in layers.

If you are not being mentored, it is still about the change the studies create in you. Your studies are for *you*, for *your* alchemical evolution; you do not need to prove anything to anyone else. It is about the shifts and dawnings within you. Having to go through different texts yourself, rather than simply having bites of information fed to you, will teach you to spot peripheral information and knowledge. Of course you may get distracted down a side alley at times, but that too may lead you to an inspiration, which will further widen your view, internally and intellectually.

And you may get a layer of meaning that someone else will not. The Mysteries are not called Mysteries without good reason: they are woven layers of wisdom, experience, inspiration, and transformation; and they are always individual to each of us, even though together we form a collective. You will get what is necessary for you at each moment. When you return to a text a few years later, you will see other layers that you did not spot before.

13. THE HORIZON

There is no end to one's magical training. There is never a pinnacle that you can reach and think, you have got there, you can stop learning because you now know everything about magic. You *never* get there. You will always be a student, you will always be learning; and the more you learn, the more you will realise how much we just cannot comprehend. A magician has stood on an important stepping stone when he or she realises just how little we truly know.

I am constantly being asked, particularly by magicians in their earlier stages of development, how to 'get there,' as though there was some defined endpoint where someone has become an adept and has 'power.' The need for a horizon and a final destination, which is so inherent within us, has been a major influence on how magical lodges and groups have organised themselves and their paths of development.

Training groups, lodges, and organisations generally have clearly defined steps of training. Exams, hierarchies, and grades encourage a budding magician to study, strive, and achieve. The effect of such a path leads to magicians approaching magic like a college or university course. If they do the study, pass the exam, and get their certificate, then they will be a magical adept. It's an easily understood, predictable path to walk, and it gives the magician a sense of control: 'if I pay for a course and study, then I will get there.' Nothing could be further from the truth.

The reality is very different and unpredictable. Of course study is a major part of the magical path. But the study that is required is not just magical theory: you need a much wider net of knowledge that encompasses ancient history, medicine, biology, philosophy, religious texts, geometry, archaeology... the list is endless.

When someone starts along the more serious path of magical awakening, the climb up the mountain before them is steep indeed. And the mountain's summit is but a resting place for an adept before they launch into their next layer of learning. In truth, walking the Path of Hercules up the mountain is the achievement of the adept, not reaching its summit. Magic is constant death and renewal, an unpredictable force that flows like water, finding its own route, and it frequently changes its path according to land, weather, and creatures. It is a living force that cannot be contained or controlled.

> *"Hidden in a dark tree is a golden bough, golden in leaves and pliant stem,*
> *sacred to Persephone, the Underworld's Juno.*
> *All the groves shroud it, and shadows enclose the secret valleys.*
> *But only one who's taken a gold-leaved fruit from the tree is allowed to enter*
> *earth's hidden places."*
>
> — Virgil, *The Aeneid*, Book VI.

If a person truly wants to evolve within Magic and penetrate even a small fragment of Her Mysteries, then they must forge their magical path while they wander through the forest of life. There are no short cuts, no 'destination.' Magic is constantly all around you: the key is to pay attention.

Stillness, observation, and listening are the main skills a magician needs in their early stages. When someone wakes up to the path of magic, that awakening does not go unnoticed. Inner beings begin to draw close, to watch you, and to place things, people, and events in your path to help you take your next step forward. If you are too busy drawing out impressive sigils, scouring grimoires, or ironing your new robe that has magical script all along the hem, then you will miss the quiet voice that says 'hey, look at this: it's important' or 'go and make contact with that person: its important.'

Magical learning is a series of stepping stones that can often appear random and unconnected. And it can take you many years before you can look back on your path and see how your steps were in fact all well defined, necessary, and led you to points of major learning and/or training – and all without your realising it at the time.

Sometimes you will come across teachers – and not all teachers are obvious – who will come into your life for a while and teach you a great deal. Some of their lessons will be useful, and some will not. There will be teachers who you will not recognise as teachers: you will meet, shake hands, make eye contact, maybe have a single conversation, and then part ways. You will not recognise for a long time that your meeting marked a major turning point and that something, some knowledge, some connection, was transferred to you in that shared moment.

Perhaps you miss a train and end up waiting in a bookshop. A book catches your eye and you buy it. It sits on your shelf, maybe for years, before you pick it up. Then you pick it up at the right time and begin to read. What you learn, or what unfolds from that book, will lay down another stepping stone. Or perhaps you have a deep instinct to read a book, which you do, and it makes no sense to you but something within you tells you that it is important. Many years later the knowledge in that text suddenly unlocks for you, and understanding falls into place.

Occasionally the nudges from the inner beings can be insistent and if you do not get it, they will start shouting… Say an object comes your way, something strange or interesting. You have no idea about it other than you like it. It goes in a cupboard and you get on with your life. Then one day you start to see references to that type of object everywhere you turn. So you retrieve it from your cupboard and put it out, where you can see it. A few days or months later, you come across a text or teacher explaining what that object is, and how it works magically. Bingo! It was waiting patiently for you to join up the dots.

Once that door is open, the door of contact, whether you are aware of it or not, magic will begin seeping into your life. Your studies will help you and give you some foundation tools to work with, but beyond that it is about learning to listen, observe, explore, experiment, and practise. And above all, be truthful to yourself.

> *"A noble inner shrine waits for you too in our kingdom.*
> *There, gracious one, I will place your oracles, and mystic utterances spoken to my people, and consecrate picked men.*
> *Only do not write your verses on the leaves, lest they fly, disordered playthings of the rushing winds: chant them from your mouth."*
>
> — Virgil, *The Aeneid*, Book VI.

Appendix D
Meditation Issues

"To make no mistakes is not in the power of man; but from their errors and mistakes the wise and good learn wisdom for the future."

— Plutarch

The biggest stumbling block for a lot of people when starting their Quareia training is meditation, which is one of the main cornerstones of magic. Meditation teaches you two essential and necessary magical skills: focus and stillness. Focus is the ability to direct your thoughts and actions with absolute precision; stillness is the ability to stop what you are doing at any time and become silent and still within, quickly and efficiently.

These skills do not come overnight; they come with years of practice. Once you have gained some basic competency in them, the course then steers you towards other simple forms of meditation, such as meditation with your eyes open, meditation while you walk, and short but deeply silent meditation which lasts for a few minutes or less.

Meditation appears in Western culture in all sorts of ways, and is used for all sorts of reasons. The techniques taught in various schools of meditation can be complex or geared towards a specific goal. The approach in Quareia is different: the meditation in the course is one tool out of many, not a destination in itself. It is a tool that enables you to *do* something.

Most events that require an adept to work within a magical pattern come with little warning. Magic does not conveniently confine itself to Tuesday afternoons in your temple; it is part of your life. Sometimes danger approaches quickly and unseen. If you regularly work with stillness then you will feel its approach. If you regularly meditate in some form then you can fall silent within, focus quickly, and respond in an appropriate manner instead of being swept up with the approaching danger.

Being still allows you to bathe in the silence; and being in the silence within allows you to hear and feel subtle changes around you. Once you have touched truly deep silence, you will find that you can withdraw to it quickly while still functioning physically in everyday life. Getting to that point can take a long time for some, and not so long for others, but it is a natural state within you that, once touched and awakened in your conscious mind, will change you forever.

Stillness is doubly important in styles of magic which use visionary work. The mind and the imagination are the most powerful tools in magic, but for them to stay in good health, stillness needs to be part of the picture.

1. The stages of development

One of the big mistakes people make when they embark on meditation as part of their magical training is that they assume it is easy, as loads of people seem to be able to do it. But it is not easy; it is the hardest skill you will ever try to learn. It can quickly become a battle of wills if you are not careful. So here is a breakdown of the various stages people go through with meditation. Not everyone will go through each stage, and some people will have more difficulty with certain stages than others; but what follows should give you an idea of what can happen during your meditation, and how to develop and move forward.

And the word 'develop' should be imprinted upon your brain: a magician is a *Developing One*, and undertaking serious training means stepping off the treadmill of mundane life and stepping onto a path of constant development that does not end, not even when you die.

The movement and the noise

For a lot of people, once you sit down to be quiet and meditate, your body and mind seem to wake up. Your body wants to fidget, and your mind starts to chatter. Some people make the mistake of using music or guided meditation recordings to overcome this.

Remedies:

1. Set smaller goals if you are having too much difficulty: start at three or five minutes for each session, and build up from there.
2. Make your meditation exercise simply about shutting your eyes and sitting. Various aspect meditations are taught in the beginning of the course, which will give your mind something to think about. Training the mind is like training a feral toddler.
3. Try sitting and counting to ten (or whatever number you wish to work with). If your mind wanders by number five, then go back to number one and start again.
4. Passive meditation can help your meditation proper.

Passive meditation is where you do not sit down to meditate, but you do something that has only one focus, without any other distraction. It is a step towards meditation, and a good exercise for the mind in its own right. Passive meditation includes things like lying down and listening to a voice only (no music) meditation or self-hypnosis recording, or lying down and listening to calm music (with no voice) with eyes closed so that only your hearing sense is working. It can also be reading a book with no other distractions: no television, music, or other background noise (and your phone switched off).

Learning to focus your senses on one specific thing at a time is both helpful for meditation and calming to the mind in a world that is overloaded with sensory input.

The goal

Having goals is generally good for you, but in meditation it can have the opposite effect. It can set you up for failure, for struggle, and for reaching a 'destination' which runs counter to meditation being a journey, not an arrival. Simply take each day as it comes, and be aware of distractions around you in everyday life that you had become accustomed to. Being aware of the constant noise around you (televisions, phones, stereos, etc.) helps you realise how little peace and quiet your mind and body really get every day. The rest is a new journey each day.

The lapsing and wandering mind

Once you are able to sit down and meditate a little, your conscious mind often gets bored, and will try to amuse you by digging up memories or thinking about things in general. Focus on the meditation task in hand. It can also be helpful to develop a simple mantra or keyword that you think to yourself every time you find yourself wandering. The word 'silence' is a good one, as it is a reminder and also a command. If you use it every time you wander in your mind then it will become engrammed into your consciousness, so that when you are in a loud and busy place and you need to focus, simply saying the word 'silence' to yourself will start to trigger the process of becoming still even in the midst of chaos.

The illusions

This is a problem that often comes up for beginners: as you try to be still and silent, you start to imagine 'presences' or powers around you. As a beginner, you are not capable of differentiating between real contact and your mind simply amusing itself. Also, as a beginner, it is easy to follow a distraction and not have boundaries.

When you are meditating, that is all you are doing; nothing more. So anything that presents itself to you as a 'presence' or anything else is simply distracting you. Focus on the task in hand, and do not allow your mind to follow any form of distraction, even if it seems to be deep and meaningful. This is about discipline and focus, not about giving the dramas of your mind a platform to amuse your ego.

The arrogance

This issue can creep in at the beginning of any sort of training, and can be particularly damaging if it is allowed to emerge in magical training. Arrogance in meditation is where the student finds meditation somewhat easy, tries to go longer and longer with it, and feels superior because they can meditate for hours at a time.

Long meditation sessions are used in certain Eastern sects, but they are not valuable in magic, and can end up being counterproductive. Do not to try meditating in silence for as long as possible; aim for twenty minutes to an hour. This exercise is not about withdrawing into yourself and turning away from the world; it is about being able to be still *within* the world.

High achieving or particularly driven students can be tempted to push an exercise to its, and their own, limits. Then the act of meditation becomes a challenge of endurance. The student takes pride in the fact that they have meditated for hours, and begins to feel special. They forget that the point of the exercise is to learn how to become still and silent in a split second, and how to maintain that stillness and silence in their minds as they walk down a street.

Lengthy meditation sessions have their uses, but not ones that are valuable in magic. Going too deep or for too long on a regular basis will bring about changes that are likely to be detrimental to the magician. Sprinters and marathon runners must train differently, each according to their needs. The student magician needs to develop the ability to focus at speed, to touch the stillness quickly, and to maintain that stillness while they act. The 'inner muscle' necessary for doing that is different from the 'inner muscle' developed through lengthy meditation sessions. And the student needs to treat each exercise as a stepping stone, not as an end in itself or a badge of honour to be won.

Touching the stillness

This stage of development in meditation can come at any time. For some it can come quickly, and for others it can take longer. It is irrelevant how long it takes for this experience to emerge, and you cannot force it: it will open out when the time is right in your life. Meditating simply makes it easier to move closer to that state, and gives you the skill to maintain a presence in the stillness.

The key is that your first experience of it becomes a 'marker point' where you feel total silence, timelessness, and expanse. Once you experience it, you can recover the feeling within you simply by remembering it. And this is a key to achieving silence: you are not learning it, you are remembering it.

It does not always come from meditation, it can happen in other ways too; but once experienced it can become a state of mind that can be recalled. The more it is revisited, the stronger it becomes.

Refuge

Once a student becomes comfortable with meditation and can sit quietly in stillness, it can become a bit of a refuge from the crazy world outside. While this is not a problem in itself, it is important to remember that a magician, for the most part, works out in the world, not in a withdrawn state. If you can only be still and silent in refuge, then you will have problems with your magical work.

Because of this, the course includes meditation tasks, particularly later on, where you have to meditate around noise, people, and chaos. First you learn to meditate in silence; then you learn to meditate in noise. This teaches you to be still in a crisis, so that you can touch base with the silence and stillness while still functioning in an emergency.

If you find yourself seeking refuge in meditation, don't fight that; simply balance it with meditation in a busy chaotic place, and ensure that refuge is not something that you constantly seek.

Understanding necessity

One of the later stages of development in meditation is understanding necessity that is individual to you. There are many schools of thought about meditation, and they will all give you different advice about how to meditate, how long for, and so forth. This form of blanket advice may work for people in a religious, mystical, or health setting, but what works for magicians will vary according to the individual.

By the time you reach your adept training, you will have learned through experience, and also through divination, when is best for you to meditate, how long for, and which approach (short, long, silent, noisy, etc.) to use in which circumstances, as it becomes highly variable.

Sometimes it is not a good idea to meditate, for a variety of reasons. There are times, for your safety and invisibility, when you should not be still, but be as mundane as possible. There are times when you should withdraw into meditation. And there are times where you will need to use silence while out in the world to affect everything around you.

The use of meditation as a tool becomes very individual for each magician after certain skills have been achieved: flexibility, individuality, and common sense should then be your main guides.

2. Questions

What about Kundalini?

I have received endless questions about whether the Apprentice Module I meditations will 'raise' Kundalini energy. The short answer is no: these meditations are there as specific tools, and anything else is a distraction. In a world saturated with the concepts of 'abundance' and instant gratification, and stuffed full of wildly overstated 'products,' people can find it hard to accept a simple exercise as just that.

The subtlety of simplicity can get lost in people's minds in such a culture, which blocks them from deriving the real benefit and skill that can be drawn from such a simple exercise. The same applies to similar questions regarding the 'third eye.'

People have been programmed to think about the glittery, exciting aspects of meditation, and that its heights can be reached almost instantly. It can be quite a struggle for some magicians to pull away from the dangerous lure that is the glamour of power. The promise of instant enlightenment or 'bliss' is a subtle promise of power, and is the very first stumbling block of the student magician.

I already do meditation but I do it differently. Do I still have to do the apprentice meditation exercises?

The short answer is yes. The meditation exercises in your early Apprentice training are there for two reasons. The first and most obvious one is to get people used to regular meditation, to learn to sit down, shut up, and focus on stillness. The second and more pertinent answer to this question is that these specific meditations pave the way for other things to come. They are kindergarten exercises that prepare for work not directly linked to meditation; forerunner exercises that prepare the mind to work with power.

I am having trouble meditating for a long time because of my work and life commitments. And yet I want to progress through the course. What can I do?

This can be a tough one for many people, as today we often live in a hamster wheel society where we work long hours and then come home to more work with our children and family. In an ideal situation, you would have thirty to forty-five minutes a day to meditate.

We do not always live in that ideal situation, so you have to adjust. There are some key things to think about when you adjust your meditation time to fit with your life. The first key thing is *avoidance*: we often subconsciously rebel against meditation because of the changes it brings. It is a regular discipline, and all discipline is something we fight against in some way or another. If you are actually just trying to fool yourself into thinking that you do not have the time for meditation, then spot that and *make* time, regardless of how much some part of you wants not to do it.

If you really cannot dedicate a good slice of time to meditation each day, then break the task up across the day. I did this when my children were little: I meditated little and often, ten minutes or more in the morning with the flame before I got the kids up, five minutes as I sat on the bus to work, and five minutes before I went to sleep. You do not always have to sit before a candle in a quiet room, so long as you do at least one session a day before the flame. I took every opportunity I could to meditate, whether it was in a waiting room, at a street corner on a bench, or in a magical space. Use your common sense, and do not fool yourself. Your aim is to be able to sit in stillness and silence for around thirty minutes. Once you can do that, then how you maintain the skill is up to you. This is *your* training: you decide upon your own success or failure.

Do I have to use a candle flame, it is distracting?

Yes, you do. Working with fire and flame is a major part of magic, and being able to be still before a flame is a basic skill that you will need.

If the flame distracts you, then get over it: you are an adult, so act like one. If you are so easily distracted, then how on earth will you cope with holding a focused contact with an inner being? As an adept you will need to be able to go into stillness and then into vision in a busy street, while walking or talking to someone.

This basic meditation exercise is the very first practice of focus. Everything is in the course for a reason: you cannot cherry-pick aspects of serious training while thinking that you know better.

Do I have to meditate every day?

In the beginning, yes. Throughout your Apprentice training, having a regime of meditation that works with your life is very necessary. Things then shift in the Initiate section, and the method of meditation changes to teach you another level of focus. After the Apprentice section, how you manage your meditation routine is up to you, but it is highly recommended that you continue some form of daily meditation to keep your inner and outer balance. When such a discipline is kept up, when you miss a few days you will really feel the difference. But to get to that stage, you have to have laid a strong foundation of meditation that in turn brings about subtle but major shifts in how you handle power. Over the years I have approached it in different ways according to what was happening in my life. Again, use your common sense, and don't fool yourself.

3. Summary

Keep it simple. Don't be tempted to use gadgets, herbs (or other substances), sound recordings, bells, singing bowls, or anything else. There are no shortcuts, no distractions, and no product to buy. Just sit down in a quiet space, close your eyes, and gently, slowly, teach your mind that it is okay not to be chattering all the time.

> *"The end of the Work is unattainable.*
> *There is no Worker complete in his Radiance."*
>
> — *The Instruction of Ptahhotep*

Appendix E

Tarot

*"Happy the person who has learned the cause of things
and has put under his or her feet all fear, inexorable fate,
and the noisy strife of the hell of greed."*

— Virgil

1. Issues, problems and approaches

This chapter looks at issues, problems, and approaches to do with tarot, and some questions that have been posed on the subject by various students. I have also included various extracts from my blog in this chapter for those who have not found it, and also to have all the advice in one place for students.

Of all the core skills learned in Apprentice training, tarot divination is the one that it is advisable to *play* with. The more you do it, the more you will start to understand what you are working with, and how to draw meaning from it.

The one approach to tarot not used in Quareia, and that is currently popular in tarot circles, is the use of tarot for psychological counselling. While tarot readings can touch on or expose current psychological issues, this is a side alley of divination training that it is wise not to get stuck down as a magician. Tarot for a magician is used as a pair of eyes that can see into narrow aspects of the past, present, and future; it can also be used to converse with inner contacts, to check magical patterns for integrity, and to seek out what has been hidden. These skills develop slowly over the course of the training, and cannot truly be developed if tarot is approached as a psychological tool, which is not its true purpose.

The course's tarot training starts by looking at the inner energetic aspects of your surroundings, then slowly works outwards to other subject matter and approaches. Later the magician is trained to work with a specific magician's deck: *LXXXI The Quareia Magician's Deck*. They learn to work with its cards not only for divination, but also as windows for inner contacts and anchors for power points.

2. Working with a deck

At the beginning of the course, in Apprentice Module I: Core skills, the student is directed to get a Rider-Waite deck to work with. This deck is only used specifically in the Apprentice section of the course, but it is an important milestone deck for magical apprentices to work with in their early training. Don't be tempted to use a different deck at this stage, as the Rider-Waite is prescribed for particular reasons.

The Rider-Waite deck, on which many other tarot decks have been based, is not the perfect deck to work with, but it is a good foundation deck, as it draws from images and concepts deeply rooted in Western magic. It also passively teaches the student about the four elemental powers and energies, and how those elemental powers of Air, Fire, Water, and Earth are expressed in magic.

The symbolism in the Rider-Waite deck is also something that needs to be learned passively by using the deck. It is the language of the outer court of the Western Mysteries, and while the understanding of that symbolism has largely fallen by the wayside and been replaced by psychological interpretations, the deck's images still speak for themselves.

The cards themselves are not deep mystical powers; they are simply a vocabulary, an alphabet that the brain can use to decipher what your consciousness is reaching for. When you do a reading to look into the future, you are tapping into a pattern of energy. Without a vocabulary to decipher what you are looking at, the patterns are meaningless.

I can remember, at the tender age of fourteen or fifteen, laying out the major cards of the Rider-Waite in their numerical order. I 'knew' there were deeper meanings behind the images and the order in which they came; I 'knew' that if I could just penetrate that hidden variable then I would become 'wise.' It took me many years before I could lay out the cards in the same way and think, 'yeah, some interesting patterns, but the designers were limited in their thinking as far as magical development goes.' Now my opinion is, 'yeah, a bit useful, but... whatever.' It is an early developmental tool in magic – not the most powerful or profound thing you will ever work with, but a key component of the early stages of your training, nevertheless.

What a Rider-Waite tarot deck does is give shapes to the energies in the orbit of the Western Mysteries, so that you can translate them into meanings that you can grasp. Just as a farmer watches the behaviour of the birds, trees, and creatures to decide what weather is coming over the next couple of months, so the tarot reader lays out cards in a defined way to discern what patterns are currently in play and what their longer-term effect will be. More importantly, tarot also indicates what deeper powers are at play, using the visual vocabulary of the Western Mysteries. It is not the best magical vocabulary, which is why you only use it as an apprentice, but it is a foundational starting point for understanding.

The best way to learn that vocabulary is to get to know the cards. Lay them out, group the families together, look at their images and numbers, get to know their personalities. Look through whatever book comes with the deck and look at the pictures. Choose a key word or two for each card based on the information you have, and write that keyword on the card (or on a bit of tape stuck to it).

Just as a child learns to read by recognising single words at a time and may not get the whole sentence in one go, so a new tarot reader needs to learn their key words for each card. Don't dive into the mystical magical aspects of the card; just get to know its surface presentation to start with.

Do simple readings, lots of them, until you are familiar with the deck and with some layouts, and write down your results. Later, go back and reread your notes. Look at the readings you did, then compare them with what actually happened. This is how you truly begin to learn your vocabulary, as well as the deck.

3. Uses of tarot

Most people think of tarot as useful only for looking into the future and for psychological counselling. These are only two uses of this tool; there are many. Tarot can also be used to look at a present situation or a past situation, and as a shared vocabulary to speak to inner beings, spirits, and deities.

Why would you want to look at the here and now if you are already in it? Oh, many reasons. You could check on a missing child, look at the inner powers and hidden agendas behind a current situation, or investigate the suitability of a candidate. Tarot can used to throw light on a past event or person to help us better understand a past situation that is still unfolding in the present. Really there is no limit to what can be looked at; however, the accuracy and detail you can obtain from a reading depends on your ability to interpret objectively: you have to detach yourself from the situation.

4. The skill of interpretation

For people trying to learn tarot, the key is not just learning the deck's meanings, but also how to interpret readings. It is a skill that takes time and practice to develop, and for some it is easier than others. If you are used to viewing the world or taking in information in a 'black-or-white' way, then learning tarot will likely be a difficult task.

Interpretation uses the same mental skill as observing patterns. Just as a child learns to read the nuances of a human face and the emotions it expresses, so a reader has to learn the subtleties of each card and the patterns that they work within. It is not a skill that can be book-studied then applied in all its glory: like all aspects of magic, tarot truly is an art form that takes practice to develop properly.

All interpretation needs boundaries if it is not to devolve into flights of fancy. The boundaries that tarot operates within are context, specific questions, and time spans.

Let's have a look at a practical example. A person, let's call him Bill, buys a tarot deck, settles himself down, and decides to have a look at his future. So Bill shuffles like fury and asks the question, 'what does the future hold for me?' He lays out the cards, and the last card – the answer card – is Death. Immediately panic sets in, and Bill freaks out.

So what went wrong here? Well, nothing, really. Bill asked what the future holds for him, and death is the inevitable outcome for us all. His question was too far-reaching, too vague. Once he has calmed down, Bill decides to try another question.

'What job should I do?' Bill lays out the cards, but he is totally unable to make any sense out of the various cards that present themselves. He is still no wiser as to what the future holds for him or what direction should he go.

The cards do not have a sufficiently specific vocabulary to answer that sort of question: there is no card for 'you should be a welder,' or 'you should be an analyst.' You have to learn to pose questions that the cards can answer.

If Bill had asked something like 'Show me what major events will happen in my life over the next five years,' then he would have been shown the events in that timeframe that would have had the most impact on him. If he had asked the same question with a timeframe of twelve months, then he would have been shown the major and not-so-major events of that twelve-month period. The narrower the timeline for a reading, the more everyday, mundane situations will show. In a three-month reading, the Tower card can be anything from a serious catastrophe to merely *feeling* that the world is crashing down on you when it's not. A bad headache, bumping your car, or an upsetting argument – all these can show as the Tower in small time frames. With longer timeframes it is more likely saying, 'the destruction of something is ahead.' This could be the loss of a job, the break up of a relationship, or a storm that takes your roof off.

Having said this, an anomaly that can show in time defined readings is the showing of something big which is beyond the timeframe. When you limit the reading to a particular timeframe and nothing really is happening within it, but something much bigger, perhaps something life-changing, lies ahead beyond the timeframe, then it can sometimes show up.

The keys to narrowing things down and obtaining more specific answers are your choices of question and layout. When you see something major in a long-term reading, you can then use a layout of one card for each time unit – a month, a year – to narrow down when a particular event is likely to hit. So for example if you see something that looks pretty bad, and you need to know when it is likely to hit, then laying out a line of cards – twelve cards for the next twelve months, ten cards for the next ten years – will likely show you when the problem will occur. When you use a timeline of cards, make sure you are specific about when the timeline starts. For example, if you have seen a major incident in a long-term reading and you want to narrow down when it is likely to strike, and you wish to check the next ten years, then shuffle the cards while asking, 'which year will this event likely happen,' and also define in your mind that the first card you lay down is your current year, and each subsequent card is for each year that follows.

The further away in time a situation shows, the more likely it is that you can take evasive action now. Fate is like a series of intersecting roads: the further away something is, the more likely there are to be other paths that you can take. When something shows in a reading in the more distant future, the seeds of that event are already in your sphere – you are walking a path towards it already. By changing something in your present – plans, courses of action, behaviour – you can shift the path of your future.

This is a particularly important skill for magicians, as it also teaches you not to panic when you see bad things on the horizon. Put it in context. When you go to cross the road and you see a truck coming down the road quickly, you do not panic; you simply change your intention to cross the road at that point and you wait until it has passed. Life is full of good, bad, and mixed events, and they all have purposes to some extent. The difference between a magician and a mundane person is that the magician can see some things coming, and they can wait for them to pass, get out of the way, or change course. Some bad events cannot be avoided: those are often ones that you can draw a lot of learning from. Still, forewarned is forearmed, and you can make sure you are in a good position to weather the storm and draw as much learning as possible from it.

Treat tarot, and divination in general, like everything else in life: it can be terrifying and daunting at first, but once you begin to grasp the skill you start to learn from your experiences, and you learn that not all bad things are really bad. Treat learning divination as being like a child learning to play out on their own for the first time. It can be stressful and everything can be perceived as a threat to start with. But as you learn to interpret, you become more comfortable with the readings, and you can look, decipher, and act as though they were everyday things.

Choosing the right layout and the right question is always the key. A layout that is too detailed is often not helpful unless you need an absolute overview – which for a lot of things, you do not. If your layout is not detailed or specific enough, then you will only get vague information or an overview.

Shuffling is also important. People forget that how you shuffle is a major part of your success at reading cards. Some people will half-heartedly jumble the cards around as they chat or watch television! If you are not focused then your reading will not be properly focused. Close your eyes to shut out the world, think only of the question as you shuffle, and learn to feel the cards 'finding' their own places. When every card is where it needs to be, you will not shuffle any more: you will feel that they are done. They do not need 'cutting': you are not playing poker. Once they are all in place, simply put them down and start laying them out.

But what layout to use? Every layout has its strengths and weaknesses. And the layout needs to be relevant to the question: many experienced readers will have quite a few different layouts that they use to get specific answers. I use health layouts, layouts for magical questions, a specific layout for yes/no answers, a layout for energetic details, and a specific layout for when I need a lot of information.

Let's go back and revisit Bill, who is still struggling with his readings. He is at a job crossroads and wants to know what he should be doing in the future. Rather than asking the open-ended question that he originally attempted, Bill has now decided to think a bit more carefully. He has several career options open to him, so he writes them down as questions:

1. Should I stay with the company I am currently working for?
2. Should I go back to college and study nursing, which I have always wanted to do?
3. Should I take the job offer to work in the local store that I was offered?
4. Should I go self-employed?

These are four distinct questions, but he still has not really focused them properly. He has asked 'should I?' but what does 'should' really mean here? Is he concerned with his finances? Is he concerned with his satisfaction and happiness? First, Bill needs to think about what he wants from a job, and why is he looking for change. Bill decides that he is looking for satisfaction and happiness: he has a well-paid job at the moment, but he is deeply unhappy. He is willing to take a pay cut to be happy, if that is what it takes.

Bill decides to use the Tree of Life layout. With this layout, the last card is the answer, and the other cards are the details of how that answer happens. So he asks his first question. The last card is the Tower. It is a simple answer: no matter what other cards appear, the outcome is shit, so it is best not even to consider that option.

He asks question two, still using the Tree of Life layout. Here the answer is a bit broader. The cards that fall in their specific positions tell him that he will mentally enjoy the challenge (Three of Pentacles in the eighth position), that he will make friends and enjoy the experience (Four of Wands in the seventh position), and that he will struggle financially (Five of Pentacles in the ninth position); but for the outcome, he would be disappointed and most likely will have a bad time in his eventual job or may not even get one at all (Ten of Swords in the tenth position).

Bill asks about option three, the local store job, and again uses the same layout. In the ninth position is the Magician, and in the tenth position is the Ace of Cups. The fourth position, the new path forging ahead, has Five of Pentacles. The fifth position, 'withheld,' has the Ten of Swords, and the seventh position has the Three of Cups. In his store job, Bill would have a limited income – Five of Pentacles – but he would love the job and the hours – Three of Cups. He would learn a lot he didn't expect to learn – Magician in the ninth position – and he would be nourished by the job – Ace of Cups. The Tree of Life layout, which you learn in the course, gives straightforward answers. When you need more detail and more specifics, the Landscape layout (also in the course) gives you more information about specific aspects of the situation. When the question is mundane, the positions of the layout have simple meanings. When the question is magical, there are layers to each position. The skill of interpreting these layers comes from practice and experience.

5. Interpreting the cards

At first the vast array of meanings for each card can be confusing and overwhelming. To get basically proficient, it is best to narrow each card down to a key word or phrase, then look at the pictures. Using the Rider-Waite deck is good for this, as the card pictures are simple and straightforward. Someone has a bundle of sticks on their back – Nine of Wands – so they have a burden. What that burden *is* depends on the question and where it lands in a layout. If you are asking about a job and that card turns up in a relationship position, then it could mean that your relationship will have problems if you take that job, or that you will have burdens of difficulty with someone in the job itself. To narrow that down, you would then do a yes/no reading to ask how that job would affect your relationship with your partner. If it shows no particular problem, then you know the issue would be with someone at work. It is all about context, common sense, and simplicity.

For example, in a reading, the King of Pentacles can mean a man of wealth, finances, or property; or it can mean an ancestor or male elder within your family or community. If your question is about work or money, then it probably indicates a boss or financial advisor who is experienced. If you are asking a magical question then it could indicate an ancestor or older man an astrological earth sign. The real key is to make sure that your interpretation is relevant to the question. Don't interpret a card magically when you are asking about something mundane.

The more you work with simple word keys for each card, the more confident you will become. Your natural ability will slowly take over, and over time you will find that your own meanings develop for each card. With practice and time, you will become far more proficient at the subtleties of interpretation. You will also develop natural inner sight, which will further expand your ability to interpret the cards.

Remember when you first learned to drive and you were like an accident waiting to happen? But over time you developed your own driving style, and now you can drive without having to think about every action, every person on the road, every junction, sign, or other car. You work on autopilot and process lots of input at high speed: the same goes with tarot. Do lots of readings, write them down – then return to them after some time has passed. One of the greatest habits for effective learning is to make good use of hindsight. In the case of tarot, revisiting your old readings will often shed new light on what the cards were trying to tell you.

Tarot is a language, a vocabulary, and like all languages it has to be learned properly, then used frequently to build your fluency and sensitivity to its nuances. The attitude of 'oh, I don't need to bother learning it properly because I can just look up the meaning of each card,' makes about as much sense as expecting to be able to have deep and meaningful conversations in a language you do not speak because you have bought yourself a dictionary.

6. Looking at the present and the issue of privacy

When my kids were teens they were pretty good, and they would let me know if they were going to be home late so that I would not worry. One evening my daughter went to the local festival. She had agreed to be in by 10pm. It got to 10.30pm and there was still no sign of her. This was before the days when every living creature had a cellphone. I began to panic. By 11pm I was ready to call the police, as it was so unusual for her to be so late. But before I did that, I did a reading to see if she was okay. I used the Tree of Life and asked 'what is she doing at this moment in time.' Posing the question clearly is of the utmost importance.

The last card was the Chariot: she was in a car travelling somewhere. So I did a second reading and asked if she was in danger. The last card was the World: no, she was not in danger, she was busy enjoying the world. She finally came through the door twenty minutes later and was very apologetic. She had lost track of time as she was enjoying herself so much. I wanted to be angry with her, not because she had committed some terrible crime but because I had been out of my mind with worry. But we had a simple chat, and we worked out a strategy to avoid such a situation happening again. As a teen, she could not understand my panic, but she respected it. As an adult, I had to remember those heady moments of teenage joy when one forgets the mundane. I knew from her reading that she was being honest with me; and I, as a card-reading mother, had to be strict with myself about respecting her privacy.

Respecting people's privacy is important with tarot, especially with readings about the present. Be aware that it could very easily tip into spying or invading privacy and it should not be used to look at an individual without really good cause. When you develop in divination, you slowly start to realise what you can potentially do with it, and ethics of a true magical path must come into play. When it comes to your own family, then use your common sense: if it is a potential emergency, then use it. When it is not, do not spy on your family. And the same goes for readings about other people: divination can have all sorts of consequences both energetically, and in life dynamics, so tread ethically and sensibly.

When you need to practise you can use public figures: they, by nature of their job, have chosen to put their life out in the public eye. You can do readings about them, and in hindsight you will discover whether you were right about what the cards were telling you.

Many years ago I was teaching a tarot workshop in the USA at election time, and we looked at Bill Clinton. It showed him winning the election but not completing his term of office. The reading also seemed to show a hidden daughter coming to light and causing a scandal. Of course, in retrospect it turned out not to be a daughter, but a much younger woman and his hidden affair with her. This taught me that the pattern I had been interpreting as 'daughter' could simply mean a much younger woman where there was an emotional bond.

As you advance through with your training in Quareia, you will learn about weaving, connecting, and conversing with various energies. The deeper into the training you go, the more powerful your connections will become, and this will affect your divination. Your readings will become much more powerful, to the extent that sometimes you may unintentionally set up an energetic link with the situation or person you are reading about. The more empathic you are, the more easily this can happen without your realising.

When you read for a situation, a connection can be set up. Then, every time something major happens with that situation or person, it can tug on your energies. For years I would suddenly, and for no apparent reason, lose my vital force and collapse like a house of cards. Eventually I discovered that each of those times something important had happened to someone for whom I had read: my energy had been going into them to support them at a critical time. So choose carefully what you connect with, and how much you are willing to help.

Readings for the present can also be used to look at buildings (is someone in a building that should be empty?) or to locate something. When you need to locate something specific, like a child, pet, or object, then you have to define the cards you wish to work with in your interpretation. Let me give you an example.

You lose a pet and they are in danger: you need to find them quickly. Your first reading would ask, 'what direction should I look in to find X.' You would use a four-directional layout, and the first or last card for the centre (you define which), so five cards in total. You would ask that the card indicating the right direction be a 'success' type of card.

You must set in your mind what type of card you are looking for. If you do not do this, your answer may show a disaster card if the animal is in distress, or a 'doing' card if the animal is doing something. Can you see how much you are leaving to the tarot's interpretation, if you do not define *how* you wish the correct direction to be indicated? I would look for cards that denote success, like the Sun or Six of Wands (victory). The indicated direction then becomes the starting point: the next reading would ask, 'if I go and look in that direction, will I find them?' If the answer is no, then you need to look at whether they are trapped in a building (yes or no), are they injured, etc.

When one of my cats first came to live with me, he was a kitten, was partially blind, and had never been outdoors. Once he was introduced to the outside world through a cat flap, he went exploring. One day he vanished for several hours and I became worried. I did a directional reading which told me to look south of my house on a road with various cottages, fields, and farms. I asked whether if I looked there, I would find him. The answer was yes (Two of Pentacles, balance). I asked if he was injured. The answer was no, but that he was trapped (Eight of Swords, taken literally as a picture). So off I went, calling him loudly, checking and calling outside every garage and shed. After about twenty minutes I was a quarter of a mile south of my house, out by a farm and surrounded by fields. I heard a pitiful cry.

As I got closer, I found my cat stuck fast in a hedge. It was literally the Eight of Swords: he was surrounded and trapped by thorns. I hauled him out of the brambles, and he did not wander off again for a long time.

Another time it was a family member's cat that had vanished. A series of yes/no and directional readings showed that the cat was distressed, lost, and trapped somewhere. Having used a map to located the area where I thought the cat was, I asked what sort of building the cat was in. The answer was the Hierophant, which I read to be a church. I asked if the cat would eventually make it home, and the answer came back that it would take quite a while, but he would eventually return. (I used the Landscape layout: the immediate answer was Four of Pentacles, hunkering down and holding on, while the longer-term future card was the Sun: success). So I told the person that all they could do was wait and hope for the best. Nearly three weeks later, a rather thinner, sheepish, but relieved cat wandered home.

If you use these techniques to look for a missing child, then you must detach yourself from the emotions surrounding their disappearance, otherwise you will not get a clear reading. And if you are asked to do a reading for a missing child then you have to be willing and able to share any distressing answers: you must never, ever give false hope or try and make a person feel better. It is not your place to do that. I have worked on a couple of missing children cases in the past, and I found both of them distressing. Both times it was obvious in the readings that the children were already dead, and it was more a matter of recovering remains. Sometimes the truth is not pretty, and if you want to look through the veils, you have to be mature enough to accept what you see.

7. Energetic hygiene

Working with tarot can sometimes get messy in terms of energetic dirt: you are dipping into reflections of fate patterns, and at times parasited situations. All this collects on your hands and on your deck. If you are not careful, the energetic dirt can build up and start to affect your physical energy, leaving you vulnerable to parasites. Simple basic magical hygiene will avoid this.

If you work a lot with one deck, then it will get too grubby to use in the long term *even if* you periodically cleanse it. Decks are tools, and at times they will need replacing, so be aware that you will eventually need to buy a replacement deck. You will feel it when the deck has become too clogged to use: it will feel grubby and your hands will feel grubby after using it.

To avoid a build-up of energetic dirt, periodically place the cards in a large dish and pour a lot of dry, finely ground, ordinary salt over the cards so that they are covered. Leave them in the salt overnight, or for at least a few hours. Then take them out and give them a good shake.

Having a cloth that is only used to keep your cards in, and to read them on, is also a good idea. It does not need to be anything special: I have used a tea towel before.

You want a washable cloth to keep the cards wrapped in. When you do readings, spread it out and do the layout on it. Wash it monthly with soap and salt to keep it clean. I pop a few drops of frankincense oil on my cloth every so often, just to stop any build-up in the cloth. Don't let anyone touch or play with your cards: keep them only for your hands.

When you have finished your divination session, wash your hands immediately. Use dry salt and liquid soap to give your hands a good scrub. It is really important to make sure that any energetic residue does not stay in your hands.

In terms of keeping the 'inner air' clear while you are reading, light a candle and burn frankincense resin if you can. If you feel a bit of passive resistance in the space around you then play sacred music while you read. One of the best things I have found to play when I need clear readings is a CD recording of church bells. It has no music or other accompaniment: it's just bells, bells, bells. Sacred music will discourage any low-level parasite or local being from drawing closer and trying to interfere with your reading. This does not tend to happen a lot for apprentice-level magicians, but it can be an issue for more advanced practitioners. Beings can interfere with a reading to give you a false narrative if it is in their interests; or they may just wish to play around with you for their own amusement. Sound, smells, and a flame can discourage them.

In terms of energetic hygiene, I would caution against getting involved with public readings or 'tarot fairs' where a lot of people are doing a lot of readings: such events can quickly turn into parasite heaven. You generally leave them feeling exhausted, battered, and with a bad headache – a reaction to the inner grime that comes from a lot of mundane readings happening in a small space. Such events are not good for your long-term health, and they have no magical value at all.

A lot of tarot issues can be solved through common sense and recognising your weaknesses. Don't be tempted to continually read for the same thing. And don't use tarot as an income source: it can make you feel grubby, tired, and depressed. This is because such a practice is not only unnecessary, but it also often draws parasites and gets you linked to all sorts of things. Remember, tarot is a magical tool: treat it with respect and use it when it is necessary, or for your learning.

8. Some student questions

Do I have to use the Rider-Waite deck, as I don't like it?

Yes, you do. If you don't like it, suck it up, it is part of the training. Before you can move on to using other decks (particularly *The Quareia Magician's Deck*) you need to learn the common language of tarot, which is the Rider-Waite.

You do not need to study tarot in depth or dive into the ever-growing mountain of personal psychology tarot books. But you do need to be familiar with its images and their basic meanings, as they crop up in the weirdest places. The Rider-Waite is also not an easy deck to read with, which is *good*: it forces your inner senses to work a bit harder.

Do I still have to do the tarot lessons, as I am already a tarot reader?

Sort of. A tarot reader will have the skill of divination, but they may not be familiar with the layouts and methods that are particular to Quareia and the study of magic. If you are a tarot reader then read through the lessons, do the layout exercises so that you get familiar with them, and do any of the practical work that is unfamiliar or something you do not have a strong grasp of. The patterns that appear in the tarot lessons emerge later in the course as magical power patterns, so you will need to know them and be able to work with them. View this part of the course as adding to your skills as a reader rather than replacing them.

Can I just use my own layouts/spreads for the exercises?

No. You must work with the course's spreads, as they form a foundation for later magical work. By learning the layouts, you are also learning magical patterns. Of course you may use other spreads *as well*, but you must learn the pattern language of the specific layouts in the course, as they are far more than just layouts.

Can I make my own tarot deck?

If you wish. But you must make sure that the imagery on the cards is the same: there are certain keys in the Rider-Waite that will teach you a set magical vocabulary. And to be honest, by the time you have bought the blank card stock, pens, and paints, and have spent a month painting the images, you might as well have just bought a Rider-Waite deck. It is an inexpensive deck, as it is the most common deck still in use today (and really most tarot decks used today are variants of the Rider-Waite deck).

Can I skip the tarot sections, as I don't like divination?

You cannot skip any part of the course if you want to learn magic properly. Divination is a key skill, and its applications will develop and become more complex as you progress. The course itself is ungoverned, so what you do with it is your business; but if you truly want to develop into an adept – and particularly if you want any official recognition of your achievements by Quareia – then you will need to do every part of it. The tarot lessons in the course are not there for to look pretty or to pad the course out; they are a key element of your magical training. It is also character-building to do things that you do not particularly like. When you go to university you cannot opt out of parts of your course: it would leave gaping holes in your education.

Is using a card a day a good idea?

This has become a fashion in tarot circles over the last few decades: my question is, why would you do that? If you are using tarot to find out what your day will be like, then you will miss a great many major points about learning to walk the path of the magician. It is not harmful, it can be fun and interesting, and some people do use this technique to get a heads-up for their day. But it can also become a crutch and a distraction, and something that really serves no purpose of any depth.

> *"The lord whose is the oracle at Delphoi*
> *neither utters nor hides his meaning, but shows it by a sign.*
> *The Sibyl, with raving lips uttering things mirthless, unbedizened,*
> *and unperfumed, reaches over a thousand years with her voice,*
> *thanks to the god in her."*
>
> — Heraclitus

Appendix F
Visionary Work

1. Issues, techniques, and questions

> *"Glance at the sun. See the moon and stars. Gaze at the beauty of the green earth. Now think."*
>
> — Hildegard of Bingen

In the early stages of your training, in Apprentice Module I, you are given techniques that will prepare your mind for visionary work. In your early exercises, you are prompted to 'look in vision' around your home, your street, and so forth. This serves two main purposes: one is to prepare you for magical visionary work, and the other is to make sure that your mind works in the right way for vision work.

When we 'go into our heads,' the first layer of images, ideas, and sensations tend to come from our conscious and then our subconscious minds. A danger in the early stages of visionary training is to allow your subconscious mind to emerge and begin talking to you through imagery. While this may be useful in a psychological sense, to dig out what lurks in the dark corners of your mind, it is counterproductive in magical work.

If your subconscious is allowed or encouraged to 'play out' too much then it can become a loud voice that can be difficult get past. This can prevent the magician from casting their mind outwards into different realms.

To circumvent this problem, apprentice magicians learn the basics of using their mind for vision by casting outwards right from day one. Instead of turning inwards and allowing what wants to come up to the surface, you have to cast outwards and look at your familiar surroundings using your mind rather than your eyes. This can be difficult for some people in the early stages of their training, but it is worth the effort.

The more a student learns to cast their mind outwards, the more their 'inner muscle' grows which lets them operate first in their own familiar realm, and later, in realms beyond the physical world. By focusing their mind on imagery from their surroundings, and learning how to explore the physical world with their mind instead of their eyes, their subconscious slowly learns to stay in its place and do its job.

At first, the student will get a mix of what they have constructed from memory of their surroundings, along with bits from their subconscious, as it tries to assert imagery. But the more the mind casts outwards, the less the subconscious has a hold upon the imagery, which enables the student's deeper senses to pick up on beings, energies and constructs that have no physical form, but have a strong energetic presence.

As you progress, your inner vision will slowly start to develop until you have an experience which is clearly not being generated by your mind. This takes a lot of time, work, and effort, but it is a core skill in magic.

Some people do not see images with vision work, particularly early in their training; instead they get impressions, feelings, hunches, and so on. Some people never see any images at all, yet can function perfectly well as visionary adepts: those who do not have the faculty of seeing images in vision will find that other senses of theirs take over. As you develop in training, you will come to understand how your mind communicates information to you.

When a visionary contact is especially powerful, even the most image-strong visionary magicians may find that all imagery vanishes, to be replaced by a 'knowing.' They 'know' a being is there, what it is about, and what it is doing, but without any visual cues. This happens to me sometimes when imagery would get in the way of the contact: instead of receiving images, some deep and nameless inner sense provides all the information that is necessary for that particular working.

2. What is visionary magic?

Visionary magic is the use of the imagination as an interface and doorway between the physical world and the inner worlds. Our imagination makes use of 'templates' or constructs through which our consciousness can step: those templates are visions which have been worked with and built up over many generations. This is *not* psychological pathworking, though it uses similar techniques. With the psychological use of the imagination you explore yourself, and your subconscious talks to you. With visionary magic, you are exploring the non-physical worlds of which you are part.

So how does visionary magic work? Every outer manifestation of substance and power has an inner version, a version with energy and power but no physical form. Manifestation and inner pattern are always entwined, either by nature or by human design, and one drives the other. A temple, for instance, is built first in the imagination of its priests, who work to a series of magical parameters. Then the outer temple is built. One upholds the other, and allows power to flow from the inner worlds to the outer worlds. When the outer temple finally decays and falls apart, the inner pattern remains for a time before that too, begins to decay.

Working in vision, within prescribed magical patterns (templates) we can access the Inner Temples. These are structures and landscapes created by humans over long periods of time, often over many generations. We can also access the inner patterns of nature, of the land, and of consciousness. Just as the magician creates an 'inner structure' by using their mind, so Divinity creates an inner structure first, before the outer structure/life comes into being. We humans follow the same pathway of action that Divine creation uses.

The key is focus and working within the set boundaries, patterns, and structures that a particular magical or spiritual path lays down. Set keys that have been used for millennia become well-trodden paths that are safe and manageable to work with. If, on the other hand, you just play in your imagination until you manage to project yourself outwards, then you leave yourself exposed to all manner of unpleasant situations.

3. How do you know when it is real?

This is the age-old question asked of teachers. You will know when you have crossed over from your imagination when things start to happen that you were not expecting, and you are shown things or exposed to situations that you do not understand, or you see unusual things that other magicians are also seeing. You will see something or be told something that does not make sense, or that you do not already know about. Afterwards, sometimes quickly, sometimes months or even years later, you will then come across that 'something' in the manifest world. Perhaps you hear it described in some archaeological or scientific discovery; perhaps you come across some obscure text that describes what you saw. Or your inner contacts may make specific predictions that come true. Conformation of the inner worlds' reality can come in various ways, but however it comes, it comes when the time is right for you.

The key is to treat everything in the early stages of your work as if it were real. If you keep second-guessing and testing then you will fail, as your consciousness will be trying to control the situation. It will be clear when you eventually cross into the inner worlds: there is a massive difference between your imagination and true experience.

Magic is an art form, and like all art forms its treasures unfold slowly with time, work, and experience. You cannot speed up the process or cut corners. It is a craft that takes a long time to master. The Mysteries unfold themselves in their own time; they cannot be bought or dabbled with. That is why they are Mysteries.

4. The first step of visionary work

Visionary work can quickly be taken up by the mind as a browsing pastime, which must be avoided at all costs. This discipline has become much harder for young people who have been exposed to years of computer games: their minds expect to be playing and constantly changing focus. Meditation will train the mind away from these tendencies, and allow one's natural visionary skills to surface.

Before you begin to delve into magical structures, it is important to be aware of your inner surroundings: the inner manifestations of the land on which you live. The inner landscape of the land and the immediate realms surrounding that landscape are important foundations upon which any magical work must stand. It is pointless to reach for the moon before you know your own backyard. This is reflected in the early stages of training.

You must also be aware of the necessity for inner and outer boundaries. These boundaries do not have to be in place forever: indeed, the need for boundaries changes from generation to generation depending on each individual magician's consciousness and their collective culture. The course's early boundaries are there to safeguard your mind and spirit: natural visionary students can find themselves drawn to practising their visionary skills haphazardly to satisfy their curiosity or to push boundaries early on. This makes them vulnerable to parasites, feral beings, and latent imbalances within their personalities which can trigger mental illness. With visionary work comes great power, and as with wielding any great power one's mantras should be 'caution,' 'common sense,' and 'discipline.'

Once the boundaries are in place then you can begin to learn the inner highway code of conduct, the basics of 'stranger danger,' and how to tread the paths to various realms safely – or at least without too many mishaps. In times past, magical lodges put strict boundaries on where its members were permitted to travel in vision. In many of those lodges those boundaries are still in place today, but their original purpose seems to have been forgotten – as has the understanding of what magical visionary work is, and how it is done effectively.

Some lodges still use a slow and cumbersome ladder of inner contacts, as well as strict grades and top-heavy rituals. They also have an abundance of rules, regulations, and secrecy oaths. New contacts are rarely sought, and the health or balance of the current contacts is rarely challenged.

Instead, only the *information* given by the contacts is challenged – and this is usually conducted through trance mediumship with the occasional foray into vision. This way of working traps the flow of power in a small pot. The rigid reliance on a small group of recent human inner contacts, who can only be communed with inside of a tight hierarchy, eliminates the potential for deeper, older, and more profound contacts.

Some magical groups approach the visionary work as purely psychological constructs used to 'better' the student, and while that can have its uses, it is not magical visionary work, but something very different. This approach became a fashion with the rise in psychology in the early twentieth century, and although the experimentation of imaginary constructs within psychology has many uses, its cross over into magic effectively strangled both the use and understanding of magical vision.

Once you have worked for any length of time with magical visionary work, you will spot countless references to it when you read classical Greek philosophers, Ancient Egyptian texts, and early Christian writings, as well as the writings of thirteenth-century Sufi mystics like Ibn Al Arabi and eighteenth-century Jewish mystics like Israel ben Eliezer (Baal Shem Tov). Once you know the work and have practical experience of it, you will start to recognise when it is being spoken about. Magical visionary work is where magic and mysticism intersect; and throughout the course you will be introduced to various Classical, ancient, and medieval writers so that you can explore their work.

With that in mind, it is really important to understand from the start that visionary work is not psychological, and should not be used for psychological purposes. Later, when you have solid visionary skills as an adept, you will be able to use your mind and imagination in all sorts of different ways, including for psychological purposes. But first you must learn the skills properly, in context, and within the boundaries of your training.

5. What are boundaries?

In visionary magic, the 'boundaries' are the paradigm you work in. The landscape, the images, descriptions of places and how to get to them, the descriptions of the contacts, the method for opening the contact, the method for closing the contact – all these create a working magical format to operate within. This is called 'pattern making.' The boundaries are the maps, and the maps are visionary interfaces that have been passed down by magicians, mystics, and priests for millennia.

In Quareia training, you are eased slowly into vision work, first through exploring your surroundings, then through visions that connect you to inner contacts and structures that have been used for a very long time in magical and mystical history. Safely within these boundaries you can develop your unique visionary skills, strengthen your inner abilities, and learn to interact properly with different types of beings.

When a student has a strong imagination and their conscious and subconscious mind has a vast vocabulary derived from films and games, problems can occur. I have talked about this before in this guide, and I cannot stress how important it is to recognise when this internal vocabulary makes itself known. It is bound to happen to many people, particularly early in their training, and the best way to handle it is to see the influence affecting your imagination, be aware of it, and take note. Don't fight it, but do not feed it: simply recognise what is happening and move it to one side by ignoring it. How and where you put your focus in vision trains your mind what to treat as 'contamination' and to slowly filter it out. Also, do not be distracted by things happening or appearing in the periphery of your vision in the early and middle stages of your training. Don't allow your mind to overdress something, or fill in gaps with unnecessary detail.

6. I cannot see anything

When an apprentice student sees nothing, they can feel like a failure and be tempted to give up. There are a couple of reasons why this problem can happen. It could be that the person has what is termed 'aphantasia': they do not have a mind's eye, and therefore cannot imagine images. Or it could be that they do have a mind's eye, but it has not been used much.

One way of determining whether your issue is aphantasia is to close your eyes and imagine a tree. Can you construct a tree in your imagination and see some basic features like its trunk and leaves? Or does your mind create a feeling or 'knowing' of a tree? If you cannot create any mental image at all, but your mind is instead providing clues, feelings, or 'knowings' that you are thinking about a tree, then you likely have some sort of aphantasia. Of course, most of us fall somewhere on the spectrum between total aphantasia and a totally photorealistic imagination.

If you find that you may be aphantasic, then you need to learn how your mind works. Close your eyes and think about a person, place, or thing that you really care about, that you know well. What tells your mind that you are thinking about that subject? Are you drawing on what you already know about them? Does it come to you in a form of just 'knowing,' or are you using a list of attributes in your head? Spend time with this, and think about how you are recovering your memories and feelings of that subject.

Then take it a step further. Think about a place you know little about and have never visited. Close your eyes and think about that place. What sort of filters for information does your mind provide? How do you 'imagine' that place? Do you get a feeling or a sense of a place; or do you form an image of a city or place? Whatever way your brain uses to reference what you are trying to imagine is the filter through which your visionary work will flow.

So for example, if you are instructed in a lesson to go in vision to the Inner Library, then some people will see in their mind's eye a building with many books in it. Others will smell the books but not see anything, and though they will be aware that 'people' are in the Library, they could not tell you what they look like. And some people will get a narrative or list in their heads: 'a place of many books, there are people there, one of them wishes to talk to me, but I don't know what they look like.'

Most people have an element of that experience. I do. I see some things very strongly, and other times I get a feeling or knowing or I get a list. But for an aphantasic, there are no visuals at all. Learn to work with what you have: aphantasics can work just as well in vision as people with strong visual skills; they simply operate in a different way.

When it is not an issue of aphantasia, it is usually a matter of an imagination that has not been used much. This is a fairly modern phenomenon, and has emerged as a result of the exteriorisation of the imagination onto screens. With the advent of television, film, and computer games, a lot of imagination has become passive: you can see the characters on the screen, so you do not have imagine what they look like. This is quite an important topic for magic, so we will look at this a bit closer, not only for your own good, but also for your own deeper understanding for the future: some of you will become teachers and mentors to the next generations, so it pays to understand the issue. It is not really a problem so much as it is a shift in our human consciousness brought about by external change, and we need to adapt.

Until recently, a child growing up would be exposed to books, to inert toys that didn't speak or have screens, and to long hours of boredom. A child, particularly a lone child, would spend hours in imaginary play with their toys, outside in nature, and reading books while visualising the characters and the action in their heads. Boredom drives the mind to amuse itself and use its imagination to bring books and toys to life. That is why it is so important for children to experience boredom. Before there was free education for all, many children were illiterate and could not read; but in their communities storytelling was a major feature of their lives, not only for entertainment but also for the passing on of mythic histories and tribal identity. Children and adults alike would listen to storytellers, and their imaginations would form images of the characters and the action.

It is this same mechanism that comes into play when you read a novel, and then see the film: often the film is disappointing not because of the divergence from the storyline, but because the images on the film are not as good as the ones you formed in your head.

These days children in certain communities develop in a different way. They are placed before a screen/television from being babies, their toys are often computerised in action and voice, and they are constantly looking at screens all day – so many different aspects of their lives are projected outwards in computer games and movies, that the innate imaginary ability does not get as good a work out as it really needed. These are extremes, of course, but it is becoming more prevalent in developed countries, and that will bring with it a change in how children use their imaginations.

An adult who has grown up in such an environment will find it harder to use their imagination, but the brain is clever and can adapt, develop, and focus in the most amazing ways.

Some people have strong visualisation skills no matter what they did in childhood, and they will find visionary magic easy. However, if such a strong natural ability is combined with mental health conditions like schizophrenia, then magical visionary work will be impossible. Someone suffering from schizophrenia will have a strong imagination, but it is unfocused. Worst of all, the sufferer often cannot distinguish clearly between reality and fantasy.

The imagination is a complex mechanism that can do a great many different things, and can be used in many different ways. It is a good mechanism for memory: we remember things much better if we visualise them, and it is this use of the imagination that people used, via storytelling, to pass information on down through generations in communities that were illiterate.

The imagination can also be used to talk to deeper layers of ourselves, hence its use in psychology. And it is a mechanism that can be used to project our consciousness, our mind, beyond our body: we are not trapped in our skin. It can also allow other beings, non-physical (spirits, etc.) and physical (anything that is living), to talk with us.

A magician consciously learns and intentionally develops all these mechanisms as part of their foundational skills, and uses them extensively in magic. Where it can go badly wrong is when someone has an illness, disability, or condition that skews these mechanisms. Conditions like schizophrenia, psychosis, and hormone imbalance can affect these natural mechanisms, often to the point that the sufferer is not aware that there is a problem – though everyone else is.

With conditions like schizophrenia and psychosis, the person is often unable to distinguish what is their own voice, what voices in their heads are the result of their condition (i.e. their scrambled imagination), and what voices are from beings outside of them. Often it is a mixture of all three, and their imagination becomes like a constantly bleeding wound. It needs to 'output' all the time, to exteriorise itself constantly, and there is no focus, control, or discernment. The person cannot distinguish what is what or whom, and they become trapped in a nightmare of constant noise and stimuli.

From my own experience of helping and working with people with these mental health issues, I have found that a lot of the time, the output – voices, images, ideas, paranoias – are products of the imagination spiralling out of control. *But*, I have also come across sufferers where a few of the voices they hear are ones I can also hear, where I can perceive a being involved. I do not think the 'being' is the cause of the condition so much as part of the symptomatic picture: the sufferer has no inner boundaries to shut out such beings.

There is nothing you can do about this practically or magically: it is up to the medical profession to help them. However, I did find that when such people were told either to ignore the voices (or images) or to take control and tell them to shut up or go away, then they were more able to cope. Treating each voice as a 'real' entity enabled the sufferer to take control of the situation and make choices. John Forbes Nash Jr. took this approach successfully with his own mental health issues, and his writings on normality, schizophrenia, and evolutionary psychology are very interesting.

Basically, the brain has this wide-ranging mechanism of imagination that can be put to use for many things, magic included, and the key is understanding the various extremes that can present in people. With that understanding, you begin to see how wide ranging the spectrum can be for people in magic, and that as you move away from the centre point of 'absolute normal' in any direction, it comes with gifts and curses. The far extremes of these mechanisms, from one end of the spectrum of 'can't see, can't hear, can't do anything at all with the imagination, to the other end of the spectrum 'see, hear, and live everything all in a jumble', tend to exclude people from magic: if you cannot control and focus the mind and trigger the imagination, you are missing a major skill necessary in magic. But for the most part, magicians are somewhere on the spectrum away from the midpoint of total 'normality', and training, discipline, common sense, and discernment turn that quirk into a real high functioning skill.

The thing to take away from this as a student is that that 'absolute normal' is rarely found in magicians. It is not their quirks that make them magicians: those are more like raw ingredients. Rather it is their focus, training, and operating skills that the quirks can flow through that makes them magicians.

7. Advice

Here is some basic practical advice on how to approach visionary work.

1. Don't do visions lying down; it is too easy to drift off to sleep. Deeper into the course there are some visions that are done lying down intentionally, so that you will fall asleep and go into a deeper state of contact. In such cases, the vision becomes a stepping stone for your deeper self. The vision takes you to a place (and triggers the boundary protections), and if/when you need to commune with the contact at a very deep level, you will fall asleep. But this is a rare way of working that is only used in specific ways for very good reason.

2. Always follow the advice in the lesson. Never ignore or circumvent a prescribed action, like tuning and opening gates, lighting candles, or sitting in a particular way. Everything is there for a reason.

3. Always treat what you see in vision as real, unless you start to get things that you know are straight out of your mind, like cartoon characters, movie personalities, or internet game visuals. Treating all imaginative interactions as real, in the early stages of training, breaks down the barriers that our culture has erected in us. Overanalysing or questioning everything will quickly shut down the bridge of communion with the inner worlds. Once you have become used to working in vision, certain aspects of the vision will begin to solidify and you will start to recognise and feel what is real and what is just your imagination. Eventually you will learn to filter your imagination out naturally so that your interactions become clear and powerful.

4. Do not use the vision as entertainment, and do not veer from the intended visionary path and vanish into flights of fancy. Too many people follow their curiosity or flights of fancy and end up losing their contact as they play in a pool of their imagination. It takes great discipline and patience to develop the inner 'muscle' for true visionary magic. This is one of the places where the need for self-imposed discipline and boundaries comes in.

5. Keeping a diary of your visions and experiences is important so that you can go back and look at it in years to come. It also helps one to remember the vision, what happened, what contacts were made, and what your responses were. Later, when you come across something in your reading that you saw in vision, your notes will both help confirm this, and help you understand better what you are reading.

6. Finally, prepare properly for visionary work. When you are about to do work, lock doors, unplug or turn off phones, and if other people are in the house, ask them not to disturb you. Have no music playing, and no televisions on nearby.

> *"There is nothing constant in the universe.*
> *All ebb and flow, and every shape that's born,*
> *bears in its womb the seeds of change."*
>
> — Ovid

Appendix G
The Adversity Of Magical Training

*"For of all things good and fair,
the gods give nothing to man without toil and effort."*

— Prodicus, *The Education of Hercules*

Magic, real magic, is tough, hard work and a training that never ends. It is a vast, endless lake of learning, developing, evolving, and strengthening that brings with it the evolution of the personality, the soul, and the world around you. It turns you into an active participant with everything around you, rather than being a passive passenger at the mercy of the Fates. Sure you can buy a few grimoires and utter spells while holding a skull and waving a wand, but that is not the magic we are talking about.

There are many adversities on the path of magical training and magical living. Some are small, some are great; and as you develop you learn more and more coping skills to help you navigate past them. These coping strategies are both inner and outer, and they are also Divine. To balance these struggles, the magical path also gives great and wonderful gifts. It is with the balance of adversity that we can truly appreciate the gifts that come to us, instead of taking them for granted.

Once you are past the Apprentice section you will have a core of basic coping skills for building and strengthening as you progress through the rest of the course, and beyond. The tests never end: they are there to evolve and strengthen you, and to develop your wisdom. Most people who step onto the Apprentice path have little real skill for dealing with adversity, particularly when they come from a culture centred around making life comfortable and easy.

In this chapter we will look only at those adversities and problems that can crop up for an Apprentice, as the methods learned there will be the seeds that will grow into large and long-lived trees of wisdom. We will start with the simplest of adversities, and work our way through to the major hurdles of your training.

Some of what follows has already been covered a little in earlier chapters, but here we will look at things in more depth and breadth. Once you are past the Apprentice training, then what you will have achieved and learned, together with your developing wisdom and your mentor's assistance, will see you through the rest of your training.

First let us look at why certain adversities feature on the magical path, as cultures that have turned them into an enemy have trained people to fear them instead of embracing them as part of the process. We avoid what we fear; and what we avoid, we give up the chance to develop through.

1. The function of adversities

Adversities in magical or mystical training are dynamics that have been deeply understood for a long time, and yet recently the understanding of the necessity of adversity has become lost in a world where comfort and the fulfilling of wants is what drives the people. You cannot become a top-class athlete without pain, endurance, disappointment, challenge, and sacrifice. It is not that these adversities are sought after for themselves, i.e. someone who wants to be a top athlete does not purposely seek disappointment, rather it is simply part of the process that matures and strengthens the person.

And so it is with real magical training: you do not actively invite adversity, nor do you wallow in it or take pride in it, rather it is simply a byproduct of the training, but one that cannot be avoided as it is one of the main ingredients that forces the magician back upon themselves. This in turn makes them independent, strong, and mature. It is also through various adversities great and small that we truly come to learn balance not in theory, but in raw physical truth. Every adversity is specific to you, and what it is doing is showing you where imbalance lies, so that it can be rebalanced. You may fight against it, get angry, and at times feel defeated, but if you endure and develop, looking back you will see how each hurdle you overcame was very necessary, and in turn gave you great gifts.

Each person is different, and the adversities that will present are triggered by each magical step you take: whatever is imbalanced, wherever there is a weakness, wherever there is an immaturity, it will be brought to the surface for you to tackle. It can come in the form of outer mundane/practical issues, or in the form of situations/environment, or as inner personal struggles – usually it is all of these and more.

For some, their adversities start from their childhood. Some are born to walk a magical and mystical path, and life will pummel them from the earliest possible time to give them the necessary internal skills, strength, and coping mechanisms for attaining their greatest potential. However, if they do not step up to those experiences as adults and tackle them with as much courage as they can, then they will devolve into victimhood, and their potential path closes down. Many are called; many have potential, but only those who do not give up will get there.

And for those who do not give up, whatever you need will be placed in your path. Trust is a major aspect of mystical magic, as is paying attention. An old saying that my mother used to tell me helped me through much of the adversity of my childhood and young adulthood; and when I was walking the difficult years of my magical growth, it always turned out to be true: "When the door slams shut, turn and look for the window that has been opened for you: you will find it if you look." Anyone who seeks to develop and evolve on a magical or spiritual path, and is trying to walk that path while developing their balance, will never be allowed to fall. You may stumble many times, and you may have to scale high walls, rivers, and rocky roads – the adversities – but you will always be *upheld in necessity*: what you need will find a way to you, be it food, shelter, etc.

2. Simple adversities

The small adversities can present in a myriad of ways, and they present always for purpose: remember, any adversity or difficulty that you experience can teach you something, and also has a functional purpose: it may slow down your studies, or kick you into action. Most of all they are there to teach you the first skills you need in magic: ingenuity, and patience.

When people progress beyond Module I of their Apprentice training, they are exposed to ritual, ritual space, and ritual tools. The first thing that comes to mind for a lot of people is that they need a dedicated space, special altars, shiny tools, and lots of things to buy. Some people are lucky enough to have access to all of that, in which case one of the lessons they will have to learn is that such luxuries can become a trap that limits further development.

Most of us – me included – have no such dedicated space, or special altars or implements. For years I had five white cotton napkins for my altars, and wherever I was working I would lay them on furniture, stools, piles of books, even the cooker and the draining board. You work with what you have. I had little privacy, as I had a hostile husband and two small children. I would work either early in the morning before anyone got up, or wait for an hour alone in the house. At one point, I announced that I needed time to myself for half an hour or an hour, and did not want to be disturbed, and I would go into the bedroom and work. Other times I went outside when I lived near nature spots, and sometimes I had to do an outer ritual in my head, and walk around a space, seemingly just walking and pausing.

For tools I looked in thrift stores. I bought a plain bread knife for a sword, a mug for a vessel, and so forth. These days I have things scattered around my house so they look like ornaments: tools hidden in plain sight. To this day, when a visitor comes to my house, they may find it unusual looking, but they would not see any directional altars or tools, they will only see eccentric ornaments. Even when magicians visit, it often takes them an hour or two of being in the house – which is tiny, so nothing is hidden – before they suddenly smile and nod: they have spotted the pattern hidden in plain sight.

This ingenuity not only teaches you to flex and bend with life while staying within your training parameters, but it also teaches you what is important and what is not. A white tea towel on a cabinet or a pile of books is no different to a solid purpose-made altar with lots of fancy mystical carving. It is the focus, intent, and work that makes an object special, not the object itself. Each cloth I used as an altar I would mark with a tiny letter in the corner, to make sure that I always used it in the same direction:

they were the true magical directional altars. I never used them for anything else once they had been used as an altar: they became exclusive for the work.

It is a very important lesson in basic magic to understand that the trappings do not make the magic, you do. The trappings can become a trap, glamour that sucks you in, so that your magic becomes all about the look, the flourish, and the status, and not the actual work. That is the first trap of magic, and the biggest one that many never get beyond. Whole magical lodges are dedicated to trappings, and they are constantly stuck in the first stage of magic without even realising it.

An adept is one who can, with nothing other than the clothes they stand up in, do magic in its deepest and most powerful forms. An adept is not drawn into traps; he or she sees them and has no desire for them.

3. Loneliness

Loneliness is another little adversity that can present at the beginning of a person's magical path. This can either be because of their physical isolation, or because they are surrounded by people who think differently to them. This is something to be endured and recognised, before you step into connections that lift you up. Loneliness first teaches you how different you are from others. Then it teaches you how you may seek connection from outside of yourself, but first you must learn to be at peace with yourself. Such peace cannot be achieved through logic or psychology; it must be achieved by actually being alone. Through enforced isolation, you turn first to yourself, then to the Divine all around you.

Loneliness can appear at any time on your magical path, and it can return in different forms until you truly 'get it.' Its expression also depends on your fate path. You can be alone while surrounded by people, then alone with no day-to-day contact with others. However and whenever loneliness presents, do not despair and do not fight it. Simply be patient. First learn to endure, and then to settle into it. Later, you will learn to relish it. We do not voluntarily withdraw completely, as often the path of a magician is out in the world; rather we learn to accept isolation as sometimes necessary and functional.

Once we learn to accept and be comfortable with a state like loneliness, we have lost the 'want' and have accepted ourselves and the situation as necessary. Once the 'want' has passed and you understand it, then doors will start to open and connections will be made. The process of acquiring a magical family begins, and continues throughout your life. You will cross paths with magical people in the strangest of places, and directly through your training. At Quareia, we are always working hard to try and connect people through social media and gatherings where folks can meet, socialise, and make friends.

Understand that your need to connect with others is about your need to express yourself, or be taken care of, or to have an audience, or to be comforted. Whatever the basis of your want, once you understand it, see it, and recognise it, then it can no longer rule you, your decisions, or your magic. You have spotted part of yourself that could be a weakness, and that awareness will serve you in your development. The endurance will give you strength and patience, and you will never again feel threatened by the prospect of being alone. And as many other serious magicians will tell you, once lessons are learned and you are ready to step forward on your path, you will never feel really alone again.

4. Cultural persecution

This can be a serious issue for magicians in some parts of the world, even today. For the most part, your magic is hidden behind closed doors; but sometimes you have to go outside and work in nature or out in the community. This is where a person living in a society hostile to magic has to be careful.

For a student, there are ways around things for most of the tasks in the course. Using a kitchen knife as your sword is not ideal, but it will work. Wandering around looking like a tourist, pretending that you are doing a science experiment, or doing something to help your child with a science experiment, can often be effective disguises.

When even such adaptations will not work, then look carefully at the task you have been set. What is the reason behind it? Is there any way to adapt it to do some of the work physically? If not, then it must be all done in your mind. This is much harder, but it can still trigger what is necessary. Working a ritual completely in vision is not impossible, but it does require mental focus. Sometimes a task may just simply be impossible: in such a case, write down why you cannot do it, and leave the door open for that lesson in case an opportunity arises for you to complete it.

The basic premise is to do whatever you can, no matter how hard it is, and accept the things you cannot do. If you are totally honest with yourself and not just being lazy, then the pattern will work around you. The magical pattern of the course is built around balance and necessity, and what is truly necessary for your training will be made available to you in some way or another. And what is truly not necessary, you will not do. It is individual to the person, and you will find that the powers will work with and around you if you are brutally honest with yourself. I have worked rituals where the sword needed to be buried briefly, then cast in water. I had to work in a strict Islamic community, and being found doing magic could have meant violence directed at me – or worse. I bought a pendant that was a sword, aligned it with my sword at home – you learn about this in the course – and when it came time to do the work, I sat beside a river, took off my pendant, and quietly stuck it in the ground by my side. After waiting a while, I took out a handkerchief, pulled out the pendant, and slipped it into the cloth. I then pretended to dampen the cloth in the river to wipe my forehead. All the recitations and actions were done in my head or whispered, and once I had finished, I put the pendant back on my chain and slipped it back under my clothing. I did this in full view of others, and simply appeared to sit but the river looking out over the landscape, and at one point dampened a cloth to cool myself.

The problems for someone in a culturally repressive society are not like those faced by someone who simply lives in a big city, where getting to nature is a bit of a struggle. Struggle is good; oppression is not. Never risk getting yourself arrested, and never avoid doing something simply because it is hard work or inconvenient. And learn to think sideways. Many homes have a decorative, cultural, or antique sword or dagger hanging on a wall: there is your magical blade, hiding in plain sight.

If you have to be out in nature for a task and you truly cannot get there, then work in a garden, a friend's garden, a public park, or anywhere with a bit of grass. Figuring out how to do something is all part of the process. Nothing is ever easy in magic, and the difficulty teaches you skills you didn't know you were capable of mastering.

5. Lack of money

We covered things like resources in a previous chapter, and how Quareia will help when absolutely necessary; but there is also a dynamic here that can defeat you if you are not aware of it. Most Quareia work can be done without spending much (or any) money, but sometimes you will need to acquire something, and the task cannot be adapted or skipped.

If you truly do not have the resources, and what you need is absolutely necessary, then open the gates and tell the contacts this. By the time you come to need something, you will know how to do this. Also get in contact and ask Quareia.

But in general, people who think they have no resources are in fact pretty well resourced: it is about choice. No inner contact – or Quareia – will help you if you simply choose not to use a resource you have. If you eat out, buy coffees while going to work, can choose not to work, or pay to get your nails done, then you have resources. It is amazing how many people think they are broke who are not, particularly in first world countries. You need to look carefully at yourself, weigh your life against necessity, and decide how important the magical path is to you. When you are truly without, the universe will step up and help you, if you are true to yourself and your path.

> *"Adversity has the effect of eliciting talents, which in prosperous circumstances would have lain dormant."*
>
> — Horace (65 BC–8 BC)

6. Complex adversities

The two most prominent powers that run through the Apprentice section are what I call the Grindstone and the Unraveller. These powers are thoroughly discussed in the course, but let us look here at how they actually manifest in the life of a student. This will give you far more understanding of what is happening to you as you train.

The effects of these powers – and they are indeed *conscious* powers – start from the moment you begin training, and they will stay with you for the rest of your life. In the early days of your training, they will be tough taskmasters, but as you evolve and develop they will become your greatest 'wingmen' in magic and in your life. They are life's greatest trainers.

Think about an Olympic athlete or a military Marine. When they first start training, their trainers are tough, uncompromising, and completely focused on pushing the recruit to their limits. Later, these trainers become guides, upholders, and advisors who help the athlete or soldier attain their best, while holding them within the network of support. So it is with magical training.

But why does it have to be so difficult? True magical training will only be as difficult as it needs to be for each individual. The more baggage we carry, the more has to be seen, understood, and shed before we can truly move forward; and the weaker our muscles, the more training is needed to strengthen them. Humans are pretty lazy: if we are not pushed then we will often just float around happily until something upsets our stasis. This is not true only of humans: need drives action in every creature, and in every cell in our bodies.

Stepping onto the path of magical training means undergoing a series of little deaths until everything useless has been taken away and composted. We are left stripped, exposed, and battered, but lightened of many loads and ready to start the process of rebuilding.

So what are these loads that need stripping? It varies from person to person, and they are presented and taken off layer by layer. One of the first major layers presented for removal is abundance. This can be easy for some and difficult for others. In the USA, for example, some religions and spiritual paths seek to convince people that abundance is good, that you deserve it, and that it is a sign that God loves you. This is a marketing ploy which plays to our evolutionary 'squirrel' mechanism discussed earlier. Behind such marketing ploys are products, mega-churches, and con men.

But in the west, and particularly the USA, the population has been trained to think that more is better. On a magical path, such thinking becomes a problem, as magic must be driven by necessity if it is to be balanced and successful. So one the first steps in magical training is to learn to look around you and what you have. You are encouraged to clear out your cupboards and wardrobes, take out whatever you do not use, and give them away. Suddenly that coat that has hung there for three years without use is taken out of stasis and put where it is necessary: you give it to a shelter, charity, a homeless person on the street, or someone you know who needs a coat. This changes the energy dynamics around you: you become part of the pattern of *necessity*. How you can you possibly expect a being or spirit to help you when you sit on unused resources while others go without?

This action triggers the Unraveller power: the hoarding mechanism is slowly unravelled from you until you start to realise that everything you do (and *are*) in life is affected by magic, and that life *is* magical. You let go of what you do not need so that it can go to those who do need it. What you need will then start to make its way to you. If you are doing what you should be doing, then what you need will find its way to you. This simple dynamic becomes powerful indeed on the magical path, and the first step is to let go of excess. Do you really need your watch to be a Rolex whose price could feed a family for a year? Or do you just need to watch to keep time?

For some, the changes brought by the training will be massive; for others they will be small and simple. It all depends on what state your life is in.

As the power flow is Ma'at, the other side of the coin can also happen: if you are without and struggling, then what you need in true necessity will be put in your path. If you are in a bad place, location, or situation and are trying to get free, and it is necessary for your fate to be free of it, then the power will open doors for you to move forward. All this depends on your willingness to walk the path in truth and integrity. And it is a long process: it doesn't happen all at once, but unfolds as and when it is necessary, at a pace you can truly cope with – though this is often not a pace you would prefer!

There is a saying in the Qur'an, 'God does not burden any human being with more than he is well able to bear. Allah, the Most High, Speaks the truth.' (Surah 2:285–6.) This saying has a lot of magical knowledge within it. When you walk on the mystical and magical path, you are never given a burden you cannot truly cope with. And when you truly reach your limit and utter it, then you have then found your limitation. Knowing the limits of what you can cope with is important, and once you reach your limit in some situation and understand it, then the pressure backs off and necessity flows to you.

That does not mean you are never given burdens; in fact the reverse is true. The deeper in a mystical magical path you go, the harder your work and life gets; yet greater also are the necessary gifts placed in your path. The problem, most of the time, is that we do not realise how strong we really can be, how much grit we actually have, and how our perseverance can make us strong, stable, and balanced people. This strengthening process, as I have said before in this guide, is the 'gym for the soul.' To work with real power in magic, you have to be as strong and as balanced as possible.

It is also wise to understand that a great deal of our adversities – not all of them – come from our own actions and choices. This is why in the Apprentice section you learn a lot about cause and effect in magic and in life, a subject that has truly fallen by the wayside in modern magical training.

> *"To accuse others for one's own misfortunes is a sign of want of education. To accuse oneself shows that one's education has begun. To accuse neither oneself nor others shows that one's education is complete."*
>
> — Epictetus (AD 55–135)

Once you have examined the surface layers of 'abundance' in your life, then your training starts to dig deeper. What is out of balance in your body? If how you tend to your body is out of balance, or your body itself has become toxic, weak, or imbalanced, then your health will be next on the agenda. It is pretty common in one's early classical magical training to have illnesses crop up or come to light, and they can be harsh ones that bash you. This is not a punishment or a test of endurance; rather it is to force you to look at how you care for your body, to be aware of your toxic eating habits, or of toxic behaviour that will ultimately poison you if it continues. Once magic is triggered in your body, then your body will start to respond by showing you where it is struggling.

This also changes your relationship with your body, and also changes your understanding of your own body. You will begin to learn its unique strengths and weaknesses, and what you can really cope with, and what you cannot. Some people have a tough time with this; for others it is not such a big deal. It all depends on what state your body is in, what your attitude is towards it, and whether that attitude is right or not. Some people merely have to change their diet: through magic, they start to react to certain foods which start to make them feel ill or toxic. But for me it was a tough road.

When I wrote the Apprentice section, I was also doing the work, not only to revisit it, but also to observe it from a different angle to evolve and 'better' that work. So I went through every single process in the course, in the short time of three years. That was truly the toughest thing I have ever done in my life – and I have done some pretty tough things. I was also going through an accelerated menopause as I wrote the course, and the way I had learned to look after my body was now no longer applicable. I had to find another way, and I was bashed until I learned.

Lastly, some of the adversities which will undoubtedly trigger are mythic ones. This is why you were encouraged to read mythic tales and mystical legends. They are key adversities that will mark your progress on the path, and will bring about magical change within you. The mythic patterns that trigger will vary from person to person: it will depend, among other things, on your history, ancestral bloodlines, and culture.

For example, there is a lot of Egyptian mythology and mystical magic in this course, and one myth in particular triggered for me intensely when I came to writing that part of the course. There were two physical manifestations in rapid succession. The first was an attack of shingles in my left eye, which caused great pain, a fixed pupil, and loss of sight. I kept writing regardless. All it did was slow me down a little, and at first I did not get the magical message. Then, shortly after, I was working in the garden cutting things back, and a thorn flew into my left eye and embedded itself in my eyeball.

I visited the hospital again to get my eye checked, and once again, I experienced a loss of sight, pain, and a slow recovery. Only in that second recovery did I realise that I was manifesting the injured Eye of Horus – the left eye – which is explored briefly in the course and which I was working on at the time.

So I went back and explored the myth and the magical dynamics of the Eye of Horus, and realised that I was manifesting the magical dynamic. My sight and the 'casting of my glance' with the left eye was being changed. And change it did. My physical sight in my left eye is now changed permanently, but the inner magical aspect of the left eye dynamic was also changed, for the good. Through knowing the mythic pattern of the Eye of Horus, I came to understand why those incidents happened, and I learned how to work with the magical gift I had been given. That is how magical adversity works.

7. A challenge to preconceptions

Another dynamic that kicks in is having your preconceptions and prejudices challenged. One thing to remember in all this is that magic transforms you to help you *evolve*. If your magical training is focused on yourself, on improving yourself, then it will not happen, and in fact the reverse is likely to happen. (Some magical training systems really do not understand this dynamic.) The change *within* comes from your work casting *outwards*, in service. I have talked about this a lot before, as it is so important.

As you work outwards, first in connection, then in service, you start to change within. As each layer surfaces, it challenges you with exterior and interior events. The layer of us that houses our prejudices, preconceptions, and thoughtlessness starts to make itself known once the more superficial challenges have been met.

We all have preconceived ideas about things. Usually they are incorrect and fed by our prejudice. Prejudice is a defence and survival mechanism deeply embedded in our psyche. Its aim is to bond a small community together so that it stays safe. But in the world we now live in, this mechanism serves only to devolve us and cut us off from each other.

Prejudice comes from not knowing, not understanding, and from deeply fearing *the other*. It is fed by a lack of wider education, by a lack of opportunity to mix, and by a lack of ability to step into the shoes of others. Base human dynamics like this have no place in magic, and particularly not in Quareia magic. To step into the deeper magical Mysteries, we have to leave such base instincts behind, and step into a way of thinking rooted in Ma'at and necessity.

It is vitally important in magic to know why things happen; why beings, people, and creatures behave a certain way; and to distinguish between rejecting a person or community because of their colour, culture, religion, appearance, or sexuality, and rejecting them because they are unbalanced, violent, or inherently degenerate. Every community in the world has a group it defines as *the other*, some minority within it that it believes must be 'kept down.' Often the *other* group is poorly educated and/or poorly resourced, and various differences will keep it apart from the surrounding community. And yet within that group there will be good and bad, bright and stupid, healthy and diseased, nasty and nice. We are all human, and every group, *without exception*, has its good and bad members.

If you turn your back on a whole group of people, then that is an imbalanced and unjust action, as you are also turning your back on the good people, the honest people, the bright people: this breaks the laws of Ma'at. It is up to the magician, as they develop, to look beyond their base instincts and to judge each individual on their own merits. There are killers, extremists, and rapists in 'rich' and 'good' communities just as there are in 'bad' communities.

Excluding people who are unjust, violent, or very racist can be a balanced exclusion, but it depends on what your role is in life. If you are a doctor, a lawyer, a mediator – someone duty-bound to help others regardless of their beliefs and behaviours – then such an exclusion is unbalanced and unjust. If, however, you are trying to build, evolve, and create in your work, then whom you exclude should be decided individual by individual, based on the person's long-term inherent behaviour towards others. You should not be excluding people simply because they are members of some group such as a race, religion, or sexuality. Exposure to different people with different ideas brings growth. Even if you do not agree with them, they will expose you to different viewpoints, which will expand your awareness and knowledge.

It is vitally important in magical development not to beat yourself up if you find, on self-examination, that you do harbour some prejudice. Rather it is a matter of learning to step back from your old beliefs and examine them in the cold light of day. What is their root? Where did those ideas come from? Do they have real merit? How do they affect your development? What behaviour in others triggers your prejudice? Where do those behaviours come from – what causes them? This will start you on a journey not only of self-discovery, but also of learning about other people, what makes them tick, and why they are as they are.

This in turn teaches you how to analyse, which is a major skill in magic: through visionary and contacted work, you will come across many different types of inner beings, and through being able to analyse their behaviour/presentation, you will learn how to communicate properly, how to assess the value of your work, and most importantly, how to not let preconceived ideas steer your work. Magic is true exploration, and learning how to step forward with common sense and logic as opposed to emotive reactions will put you in a strong position upon your magical path.

Let's just spend some time looking at the root causes of 'difference' and those behaviours that can trigger prejudice. For some, particularly those students who have travelled a lot or have been exposed to many different cultures from childhood, the following comments will be obvious. But for others, particularly those who have not travelled much outside their own country other than for holidays, the following comments may trigger deeper thought, analysis, and understanding.

8. Crime and disease

Many minority groups in different countries have fled war, poverty, disease, and oppression. Some have ended up in a foreign country through slavery, and the deep history of their oppression continues to define their present day community. Such minority communities are often plagued by high crime, poverty, and disease. Poverty and oppression are fuel to the fire of crime, and where there is a lot of poverty, there will also be crime.

It is easy to say, "oh, this minority community are a bunch of thieves and thugs," but when you are in long-term poverty and cannot feed or clothe your children properly, theft can be part of your existence. I have lived in minority communities that had serious poverty, and I realised that while high ideals are great when you have a full stomach, when you have nothing, you fight to survive.

It is also easy, as a well-fed and housed person, to cast judgement and talk about choices, and to imagine what in such a situation you would do to make it better. *Never judge until you, too, have lived for a good length of time in such conditions.* Poverty, disempowerment, and oppression destroy the depths of a person, and you cannot stand in judgement until you have walked in their shoes.

Lack of education

In minority and poor communities, the chance of getting a decent education is often nonexistent. Without a good solid education, rising out of poverty can be difficult, if not impossible. Not everyone is bright and able to pull themselves out of a poverty cycle without help. And a lack of education in a poor and/or minority community can be a breeding ground for extremism, whatever their religion or culture. It is the root of poverty, oppression, and violence. When you are oppressed and have no education, then you have no way to express or understand why that oppression is happening: your only way to fight back is through violence and aggression. When you have an education, you have a voice and you know how to use it.

This is one of the reasons that governments with authoritarian leanings tend to advocate policies that strip schools and universities of funding: it takes them out of the reach of the poor. If the bottom layer of society cannot voice its discontent, then it cannot overthrow the regime. It will simply become a violent layer of society, which can then be used as an excuse for more oppressive policies.

Appearing different

Minority cultures that appear different because of their clothing are often attacked, maligned, and feared. Usually this is due to a lack of understanding, and the inherent human drive to favour conformity. Currently in the west, Muslim women wearing the hijab is a major driver of racist and violent attacks on the streets. So let us use the hijab as an example.

Different cultures develop different ways of dressing, at first due to climate, health, and environmental necessity. Ever tried wandering around in the desert in full sun, or avoiding head lice without a head covering? These dress codes of necessity become status symbols: if you work in the fields as a peasant, you cannot be wearing layers of fabric that are going to get in your way. So a woman wearing layers of silk is stating that she does not have to work in the fields, therefore she is from a wealthy family. Her skin will be fairer as it will be exposed less to the sun. Thus her light skin and her veil are status symbols of wealth and privilege. The veil as a female status symbol is first mentioned in history in the Assyrian sumptuary laws (Middle Assyrian 1114–1076 BC) though there are carvings of veiled women dating from around 2500 BC. So the veil has deep and ancient roots in the cultures of the Near and Middle East.

Later, the pecking order of society asserts itself further through religion. If the woman is covered, then not only is she from a wealthy family, but she is also from a 'good and modest' family. The veils start to become not only symbols of wealth and status, but also of religious and moral standing. The politics of Islam and the West have further intensified in the last twenty years, and in many countries the hijab has become a political football as a result.

But a woman who walks down the street in the West wearing the hijab is dressing in a way that has been normal in her culture for thousands of years. Who has the right to tell her to stop? Why should a person be feared or reviled simply because they are dressing normally for their own family, culture, and religion? People in the West may say, "when in the West, do as we do." This is the age-old instinct that associates conformity with security: recognise it for what it is. Understand where the hijab comes from and what it means to the wearer, then examine the negative reactions to it without emotion.

So how does prejudice become a magical adversity in training? Magic is about connections, conversations, bridging, mediating, opening, and closing. To operate in any real depth a true adept, you need to work these dynamics on a deep level, and any imbalance or baggage of yours will affect that work. You cannot in truth get rid of all your baggage and imbalances, but you can get them right down to the minimum, and govern them with logic and necessity. That way, your emotional and instinctive patterns of behaviour – your prejudices – can be transformed into an early warning system as opposed to a blockage.

By examining and challenging your preconceived ideas, and exploring the background, root, and reasoning behind different behaviours, you learn to apply logic and understanding. This starts to change you, first on the surface, then deeper at an inner level. It prepares you for all the different sorts of inner contact that you will have, and to respond to those contacts on their own merits rather than by your preconceived notions or prejudices. This is particularly important for magicians who have grown up as Jews, Christians, or Muslims, as the polarised view of good and evil in the three Abrahamic religions will be a filter through which you view inner contacts. Inner contact and inner beings are not grouped into nice identifiable bundles of 'angels' and 'demons,' so it is important, and especially so when you become Adept, to be prepared to see into the depths of a situation or contact, and use logic to assess its merits. Your subconscious, then your inner self, will start to shift from its tribal affiliation with what is familiar to what is necessary for balance.

Being prejudiced is as unbalanced and unhealthy as being 'all accepting,' which is the other end of the scale. The more you work on your preconceived ideas and dig for their reasoning and logic, the more you will develop as a bridge that allows communication with any 'being' that is necessary, and that blocks whatever is unbalanced and unnecessary. So you begin to see how important it is to move away from your cultural programming and towards logical thought, so that you mind can start to learn flexibility. (As an aside, it also teaches you to look beyond the surface appearance of a thing, which is extremely important in magic.)

> *"Adversity is the first path to truth."*
>
> — **Lord Byron** (AD 1788–1824)

9. Gender and identity

Gender and sexuality can be a major issue for people going into magic, as a lot of magic, particularly western magic, is seemingly geared towards the white straight male. The overall structure of many western magical schools is one that was put in place during the late 19th century where the world and people were viewed through a very polarised lens: white and not white, male and female, good and bad. A gay man was considered an abomination, and a woman doing anything other than producing babies and running households was scandalous. If you were not white Anglo Saxon then you were considered inferior.

To give the magical schools at the time some credit, they tried hard to step away from such closed mentalities, but the aroma of discrimination still lingered. A lot of that fixed mentality still exists in the world of magical training, and it is important for students to be aware of it so they can look out for each other. They must know that such attitudes are not okay, and are not a part of magic.

In terms of gender identity, if a student is fluid with their gender identity, then they should approach their magical work with the same fluidity. However, in general you should not be approaching your magic in terms of your sexual identity, but in terms of what each of your individual magical workings *needs*. Magic is always rooted in necessity, and each magical act should be approached as an individual unit of action. What does *this* pattern need to function? How do I fit within it?

A lot of magic works from you as an individual, so it really does not matter what gender you are or how you identify. You just plug in and get to work. Issues can arise, however, when a magical pattern, usually in ritual, involves polarity power dynamics.

It is important for all magicians to learn how to work with polarised power, even if you as an individual are anything but polarised.

The key is to approach each such working individually and decide for yourself where you fit in the pattern and polarity of that particular working. If you are gender fluid, or have a complex gender identity, then you are far luckier than most: you will be flexible enough to fit anywhere on the pattern according to its needs and the intention of the magic. Just remember that each magical working is different, even if it appears superficially the same as a previous one. Don't take anything for granted, and be flexible with how you approach the work.

Gender fluidity has not been much explored in Western magic, so if you are a Quareia student and your gender or sexual identity is complex or not polarised, then take notes. Keep records of your workings, their effects, and so forth. Your experiences and development will help the next generation, and if you make it through the Adept training and become a mentor then you will be invaluable to the next generation not only as a mentor those going through the same identity development, but also in educating those who have no knowledge, understanding, or experience of such issues.

Women and gender is still, sadly a major issue in magic. We women in magic still have to work twice as hard to get any sort of respect, and in some areas of magic we are still relegated to a pseudo-sexual role, for instance as a 'Scarlet Woman,' which is nothing more than a male sexual fantasy.

In Quareia there are no gender defined roles, as in classical magic there are no such things. Polarity workings form a small part of the more advanced work, but they are not as gender defined as they appear, and their purpose is to force the magician to think beyond the stereotypes and to work out, in each particular working, whether they are outputting or receiving energy. This can change from working to working depending on how the person and their body are functioning at the time, and what the flow of energy is: what it is doing and where it is going. The advice I would give to women is this: do not allow anyone to sideline your work simply because you are a woman, and do not allow any magical group, lodge, or school to keep you down or relegate you to a role simply because of your gender. Ability and hard work is everything in magic, not gender; and I can say that as a postmenopausal woman who has excelled in her field of magic.

When a woman hits menopause (as I did, at high speed) her power does change. It goes through a flux for a few short years, but if you understand not to try and hold on to what you were before menopause, but step forward into a new and often quite different pattern of working, then you will do just fine. Your power and skill set shifts, and it is important not to fight to stay as you were, but to step forward with the understanding that you are morphing into something far more profound. The changes menopause brings to your magic are wonderful: your magic becomes deeper and far more mystical, and once you are over the two or three years of feeling like a madwoman – swinging hormones can do that to you – then you will find a level of stillness that you did not have before. As a female magician I can say that now, on the other side of menopause, is the best time of my magical life.

10. The Challenge of the Gods

Once you have divested yourself of things holding you back, the way adversity comes at you changes. It can often present when something is wrong: you may have taken a wrong turn in your life or magical work, or you may need to change but are clinging to a mentality of 'keep on the same path of action, don't keep changing.' Such a mentality comes from the need for security, which is often drilled into people from a young age. But magic is all about change, constant change, and development.

When my energy levels suddenly dip right down, or everything I try to do is blocked or unworkable, I step back and look at what I am doing in every aspect of my life, why I am doing it, and where it could potentially lead. Once I have done as much thinking as I can muster, I will then use divination to see if the blockage, loss of energy, or adversity is there to hold me back for my own good, or whether something I am doing is blocking off my future path.

Often our present actions – or lack of action – can close down future fate patterns. That closing down will drag on your energy or cause everything around you to become unworkable. Often the culprit of the energy drain is a simple little thing, akin to a grain of sand grinding away in your shoe, eventually giving you blisters. Use divination to see what you are doing, or not doing, that is affecting your future fate pattern. When you go off course in a way that affects your future, your energy will really start to drag on you, to force you to step back into the stream of fate and time that will lead you to your greatest potential.

Now you will begin to see why divination is such an important tool in magic, as it helps you navigate these challenges and bring in necessary change. These adversities are there as warnings, so once you are past the first half of your Apprentice training and you suspect that one of these warning adversities has activated, use divination to figure out what is happening. First get an overview of where your path is taking you with the Landscape layout; then use a simple Tree of Life layout to ask if you are indeed on the right path in everything that you do. If you are not, then it will show in the last card.

You then have to look at where the adversity is striking. Is it your health or energy? Or is it your work? Your family? Something else? Finding the root cause of the adversity is not easy and can take some time, but often inspiration will come from the readings, or dreams will highlight the problem for you if it is getting important enough. Pay attention, dodge the bullets, and make the necessary changes. Never get to thinking that you must not make changes: magic itself triggers change.

Make changes when they are necessary, and hold your course steady in a storm when that is necessary.

To summarise, we all approach adversity in different ways, and it is important for you to find your own coping mechanisms, and to meet each challenge with a brave heart and a clear mind. My method is to expect and plan for plague, then celebrate when it is simply a cold. Your approach may be different. Find out what works for you. As you are challenged more and more, your coping mechanisms will develop and mature if you do not run away from difficulties, but step up to them and treat each one as a chance for development and learning.

When you fail to overcome an obstacle in your path, pick yourself up, dust yourself off, learn whatever you need to from the experience, and be truthful with yourself. Then step out again with more determination. The more you engage with obstacles that block your path and solve the problems or dodge around them, the stronger and wiser you will get. If you run away or give in, the same obstacle will keep coming back in different guises until you get the message.

The more you learn from adversities, the less harsh and more subtle the adversities will eventually become. You will increasingly pay attention to what may lie ahead (divination is a good tool) and find the path at each crossroads which bears the best fruit for you. The magical pattern will increasingly fit itself more perfectly to you, ensuring that you have exactly what you need, and removing what you do not.

A real adept has generally been through many adversities and learned many lessons, and has extracted knowledge and wisdom from each one. When they stand before you their adepthood is revealed in their eyes and their actions, not by a certificate on their wall or a fancy badge on their lapel. Life is one of the major trainers in magic, so engage with it in all its dysfunctional glory!

> *"March on. Do not tarry. To go forward is to move toward perfection. March on, and fear not the thorns, or the sharp stones on life's path."*
>
> — Kahlil Gibran (AD 1883–1931)

Appendix H
Religions

> *"Beware of confining yourself to a particular belief and denying all else, for much good would elude you – indeed, the knowledge of reality would elude you. Be in yourself a matter for all forms of belief, for God is too vast and tremendous to be restricted to one belief rather than another."*
>
> — Shayhk Myhyi al-Din Ibn al-Arabi

Since writing the course I have been getting a lot of questions about religion, and especially about what religion a magician should be, and whether you can still do the course while practising certain ones. Because religion can so strongly influence both individuals and cultures, I think it would be useful for people to have a better overview of how religions can intersect with magic, and in particular with Quareia's magic. If you have no religion, or have left behind a religious family, then this chapter will give you insight into various workings within the course, why they are there, and how to approach them.

The foundation and basis of Quareia training is that it covers knowledge, skills and techniques that are not specific to any particular system, but are often found in many different magical systems: it gets to the core of magic without being hobbled by one specific religious pattern. Most magical systems today have one religion at its core – it is usually because that system grew out of a group of people who were all from one religion, which in turn was the overarching religion of that country/culture. But why does religion appear in magic at all?

To answer that question, you have to step back from the religious mindset – which is harder than it sounds – and look from the outside in. What actually *is* a religion? A religion is a cultural framework that provides a method for communicating and connecting with the Divine. Its dogmas and rules are often rooted in the culture it grew from, and they generally include whatever civil traditions are necessary for a harmonious community.

Before the twentieth century, most countries generally had one overarching religion dominating their culture, though they may also have had some minority religions brought in by immigration. Even in secular countries today there is generally one especially prominent religion that has a defined influence on how the culture works, what laws are enacted, and what the social norms are.

In magic the same happens, even today. There is often an overarching religious pattern at the bedrock of a magical system (though parts of other religions may also be included to add spice). This limits the scope of the system's magic and its inner contact, and it can entrench in the system any latent suppressions or imbalances that run through the religion or the system's magicians.

However, in any magic that reaches beyond petty spells and role playing, there is a strong presence of the Divine. In magic you are working with the powers of the universe, the consciousness of creation. As such, you bump up against the Divine pretty early on. The key is to understand that the Divine – God, Allah, the Unknowable One – is not religious: the Divine and religion are two different things. Religion is man-made, and as such has all the flaws and weaknesses of humans. Divine consciousness, on the other hand, is all around us and within us, regardless of our religion and regardless of humanity. When we eventually become extinct as a species, the Divine will continue, but our religions will not.

1. Why does a magician need to learn about religions?

This is the most common question I get from Quareia students, and though this is discussed briefly in the course, people tend to glaze over it or miss it. So an in-depth answer here would probably be useful.

As a magician, you do not work in isolation. You are surrounded by people and communities, and a lot of your magic, both as a student and as an adept, will be about service and helping. You cannot help someone or something (a landmass, for example), if you do not understand the deeper workings behind a religion that is prominent in a culture, or understand where and why things go wrong within a religion, and how that affects everything around them. When a person goes to see a doctor, the doctor will ask about their symptoms, but he will also ask (depending on the issue) about their diet, their job, and so forth. Getting a wider perspective gives the doctor clues about what could be causing their patient's problem, and also what could limit their recovery.

As a magician, you will cross paths with people from all different sorts of religions and cultures who will ask for your help. If you understand their deeper religious mindsets or childhood religious influences, then you will get a wider picture of their story, and also of the method to resolve their problem.

The other, and I feel more important, reason for a serious magician to learn about different religions, is that it shows them the magical commonalities and mystical similarities between various religions, and how those mystical and magical concepts eventually became religious dogmas. The course looks at this in many different ways, sometimes directly, and sometimes with a focus that crosses paths with religious thought.

Once you are able to step back and look at different religions and how they developed – and if you can look without prejudice – then you notice how many times an ancient religious or magical practice is co-opted by a newer religion. Magic was an integral part of ancient religions: the separation between religion and magic only really began with the rise of monotheism.

2. Understanding the evolution of religion

To understand magic as it exists in religions, you have to understand how the function of religion has changed over the millennia. In ancient cultures, magical practices were part of the religious duties of the priesthoods (male and female). Ancient religions were greatly concerned with subduing certain powers, keeping other powers happy, and talking to the Divine on behalf of the people. The unwashed masses were not allowed anywhere near the inner parts of the temples, and religious rituals were generally conducted for the deities, and done behind closed doors.

The deities were considered the children of the creator: different expressions of the Divine. They were looked after day and night. A lot of ancient ritual had to do with keeping all the plates spinning to achieve balance and subdue chaos. In the Ancient Egyptian religion, the monarch and elite priesthood were expected to adhere to a code of balance and justice themselves, so that they would be part of the balance and not a cause of chaos.

This created a social order that flowed from the religious structure, which in turn, became a defining feature of the culture. Everything was enmeshed, and when it all went wrong, the finger of blame would be pointed at the Monarch, then the priesthood, and finally the people.

As with all human organisations, in every religion that develops, a power grab eventually happens. Temples would fight each other for supremacy over wealth and resources, and the whole thing would begin to rot and fall apart. Power grabs happen in different ways in different religions, but it happens in all of them, without fail. Power grabs often appear as factionalism at first, with one group accusing another of heresy. But lurking behind this is simply the wish to be on top.

In the Christian church, the Mass, or Eucharist, was originally a ritual performed for God and humanity as a whole, not for the local people. The priest would face the altar with his back to the people, and often there was even a rood screen to block their view, so they could only hear what was happening. Later, some Christian factions did away with most of their rituals and turned churchgoing into a weekly social lecture and prayer session. Finally, in the twentieth century, even the Catholic church turned their priests around, got rid of the altar rails and rood screens, and made Mass much more of an interactive social event.

Of course I am generalising here, and skipping across the surface of a complex story about how human interaction with the Divine has evolved, but an in-depth lecture is not necessary here. The point is that all religions have a lot in common when it comes to how they were structured, how they evolved, and what their purpose was. Knowing that, and stepping away from any degenerate, ingrained belief in 'one true way' can help a magician enormously, as it allows them to see through a religion's dogma to the inherent patterns that underpin it. This allows the magician to spot the religion's magical aspects (they all have them) and especially any magical patterns taken from earlier systems that have been inserted into the newer religion with a few changes to make them fit.

It is those magical patterns that you learn in Quareia, through study and comparison, and through practice. You cannot fully understand any magical or mystical pattern before you have actually worked within an aspect of it. Studying alone will not allow the Deeper Mysteries of a pattern to surface in your mind. So let us look at how that is approached.

3. Working with different religious patterns in Quareia

In your Quareia training you will come across workings that connect you to the Divine without a religion dressing, where there is a simple communion between yourself and the Universal Divine. Later you will work with exercises anchored in a specific religion, so that you get the 'inner' aspect learning of what can flow through that religion, for good and bad. Often these are exercises that you have to repeat, so that you can learn how connections develop over time, what they bring to you for good and bad, and where their magical roots lie.

You are also given exercises that can trigger some of the issues that can flow through a religious pattern, so that you can experience them firsthand. You are not warned about what could happen: personal experience is always the best teacher. And of course everyone is different, and will have different experiences.

In the Adept section, you work with an ancient state religion's pattern that has magic closely enmeshed within it, so that you can have certain extremely direct evolutionary experiences. Here the pattern is used as a vehicle for the adept transformational Justification process.

You will also study a lot of different religious texts, exploring their magical and mystical aspects while looking at where their ideas came from, and how they have evolved over time.

Though only a few religious patterns are worked with directly, the workings themselves will teach you how to approach any religious pattern to learn from it, so that you can, if you wish to, explore other religions using the same methods.

I use the rule of absolutes to get you used to the 'operate from within' method: you are placed within a mystical, magical, or spiritual mindset and structure, and trained to operate an aspect of magic from within that mindset. Sometimes you are not told why, or how long you will be in that structure, or indeed if you will ever be pulled back from it. This enables you to focus your consciousness fully in the pattern.

When you are finally pulled out of a religious or magical pattern and introduced to the next one, you will have gained a much deeper experience of it by working within it, and you will understand better its pitfalls, benefits, beings, issues, and patterns.

When we study magic, we tend to think of that magic within our own cultural and social mindset. That affects how we project that magic outward in our work, service, and action. However, we live in an ever-shrinking world, and we are constantly bumping up against different cultures, religions, and systems. We therefore must be able to confront our biases towards or against many different religions. A true adept not only understands all these different systems, but they can also operate briefly and respectfully from within them as and when necessary in order to achieve something. Healing, exorcism, construction… all these tasks, and many others, require you to understand fully any religious, magical, or cultural systems that may be in play.

To this end, the Quareia student has to be immersed in different religions and magical systems, not to become part of them, but to be informed and to understand them. The working knowledge you gain as a result makes you useful, and it also, as a byproduct, helps you gain a deeper understanding of the sort of issues that can arise within a system or religion. It also helps you spot the many areas of degeneration, imbalance, and sometimes just sheer madness that often develop within such systems during certain periods of history.

So while the actual mechanics of magic that you learn in Quareia are free of any religious or magical systems, you still have to dip into them as a focus or subject matter, and sometimes briefly immerse yourself in them, while also maintaining detached observation, in order to become a knowledgeable, well-rounded adept. This in turn will also, by the time you get to adept level study, lead you to question what is divinity, what is religion, what is magic, what does it mean to you, and how do you either develop your own unique interface with these various energetic structures, or how do you tear such concepts apart and find new evolved expressions.

I also put initiates and adepts in situations where they step over the line from magical work with deities into a more religious, priestly role of tending to a deity. Approaching a deity as a magician is very different from approaching a deity as a devotee; yet often people do not realise there is a difference, or why there is a difference. Rather than just explain it, which is how the apprentices are exposed to this difference, an initiate and adept crosses that line for a while, then steps back. Over the course of a few months, they learn their lessons by direct, practical experience. After that, they can choose from a place of gnosis whether they wish to be a priest or devotee of some aspect of Divinity as well as a magician, and they will *know* the difference between the two roles.

4. Dogmas and dangers

Although we tend to associate dogmas with religion, they also crop up in magic, and you will find as you get deeper into the course, that there are many parallels between religion and magic (as they grew up together), and understanding one helps you understand the other.

The dictionary definition of dogma is 'a principle or set of principles laid down by an authority as incontrovertibly true.' Dogmas are created and used to lay down norms of behaviour and to pin down modes of belief that cannot be questioned (unless you are a heretic). Dogmas can be insidious, and can shift the mindset of a large number of people in a particular direction that is accepted as 'the way things are.'

Dogmas are rarely constructed in completion; usually dogmas build slowly, with each layer being added by different 'voices of authority' to tighten the belief structure. We see this in the beginnings of Christianity, from the development of Jesus from 'Christ the Messiah' or prophet, to 'Christ the God'. When we study the gospels, you can see the development between the first gospel (Mark, approx. AD 70), and the final gospel of John (approx. AD 100) which was not part of the synoptic tradition, where there is the first mention of the divinity of Jesus. It is also worth mentioning here that at that time, it was not unknown for a very special leader to also be called a god – the Roman Emperor being a good example.

Fast forward two hundred years, and Christianity is no longer a Jewish sect closed to Gentiles, but a whole new religion complete with a hierarchy of priesthoods. At the First Council of Nicaea (AD 325), the Church's religious leaders met to debate and draw up the specifics of their dogma. Later councils added to this 'creed' of belief, until there was a fully-functioning dogmatic structure that could not be questioned.

If you are interested in teaching or forming a new magical school or pattern in the future, then it is important to understand, while you are a student, how these dogmatic constructs are formed, as they can also occur in magical structures, and to a lesser extent in cultural ones.

Dogmas in magical lines tend to appear when the initial power of formation of the magical line is fading, and that fading tends to happen when people start to bring their agendas to the line. A dogma is about control of thought, the suppressing of questions, and the blocking of individual paths. When a student is in the 'learning phase', often absolutes are used as boundaries so that learning can happen and evolve within a set of parameters. But beyond that learning phase once the absolutes have been dispensed with, the individual's relationship with the Divine and with magic, is unique to that person based upon their experiences. So it is important to fully understand the differences between training absolutes which flex, change and then vanish as the student develops, and magical dogma which is unchanging and cannot be challenged.

But when a trained magician develops their own personal understanding through direct experience, two things can sometimes go wrong: their lodge seeks to reassert its control to contain and 'own' them, or the magician decides that their personal experience is 'the way' for all others. They then seek to enforce their dogma on the rest of the line to ensure uniformity of thought, which is an act of power and control. This is why so much time is spent in the course looking at the complexities of power and control.

For this reason, when a mentored Quareia student completes their Adept training and is accepted as a Fellow of Quareia, they are not expected to conform to any set of rules, modes of behaviour, or trains of thought. They are accepted as they are; and they are also expected to accept every other Quareia adept, regardless of any differences of opinion. This sidesteps the issue of dogma creeping into a magical line, and allows plenty of room for evolution. Quareia adepts in Far Eastern countries, for example, will be different from Quareia adepts in the USA or Europe, as the cultural and social modes of thinking are so different, at least on the surface.

Religions, and particularly the Abrahamic religions, all have factions and splinter groups that each adhere to a different set of dogmas. Because a dogma is like an unbreachable brick wall, each faction believes that they are the 'true way,' and all the others are heretics and failures. Again, this is all about power and control. This pattern of behaviour can also be observed in some magical lines, particularly the Golden Dawn line of magic. Many factions in that line battle over who is the 'one true line,' and whose myths and dogmas are correct.

This happens when students and adepts (or followers, in a religion) are not fully immersed in the direct experience of contact, and access to any such contact is restricted to a select few. This sets up a hierarchy of control and power, which ultimately locks people out and away from the direct experience of deep magic.

As you go through your training, you will learn the dynamics of cause and effect in magic, as well as certain rules and set behaviours that are rooted in cause and effect. These are not the same as dogmas: they are mutable, and as each magical generation develops and matures, the cause and effect dynamic of magic shifts. It constantly evolves, just as the people who come into a magical line also constantly evolve and change as generations develop and change. The way you learn Quareia magic, and the way someone in a hundred years will learn Quareia magic, will be different. Dogma would stop this development and change, which is why it is really important to understand the dynamics of dogma, and the allure of a set of immovable absolutes which give a sense of continuation and predictability. Don't fall into the dogma trap as an adept, and understand fully the uniqueness of your own development and understanding.

5. What if you are an adherent of a specific religion?

Magic is about two things: learning about yourself in great depth, and learning about how the universe around you works, from an inner magical perspective. Through learning about those two things, you learn how to become a player in the production instead of a passive recipient. Really this is the difference between a magician and a non-magician: a magician is about action and intent.

When a magician is young or immature, they stride out to use action and intent to change their world for themselves. If they are successful, they may become curious about how and why their success happened. That brings them face to face with consciousness and beings that are not human like themselves. The experience is a bit like coming face to face with your first elephant as it crashes out of the jungle.

The elephant and you look at each other, the elephant thinks, "oh shit, not again," and you think, "woah, that is one big dude... what the hell is that?"

Having made that connection, a slow series of steps takes the magician in ever-widening circles, like ripples on a pond, until they start to bump up against the power of Divinity – the power and presence of God within everything. At first the magician does not know how to connect with that power, or even what it is. But in time their encounters become more and more powerful and meaningful until, one day, the magician realises they are connecting with Divinity in their own unique way, not through any religious pattern. That is when the magician flowers as a mystic, and the mystic flowers as a magician. Neither religion nor belief comes into it at all: it is simply a real, powerful, practical experience that they will never, ever forget.

Once the magician has experienced Divinity in their unique one-to-one way, they begin to see fragments of what they experienced in the religious and mystical writings of others: mystics, priests, priestesses, poets, artists, hermits...It is irrelevant what religion they are, as the baseline of the experience is the same. But in order to recognise it, to truly recognise it in the writings of others, you have to experience it for yourself. You cannot theorise or read about it and think you 'know.' You don't.

The experience comes from the slow unpeeling of the magician that results from their gradual steps through the cold waters of magic. Any type of magic, just like any religion, can bring a person to this point, if the potential is within them. But if the potential is not there, then no amount of studying magical systems or immersion in religion will trigger it. It is a latent 'something' that is either already there, or not. It is in most people drawn to magic by some strange compulsion, a memory, some voice, or through dreams. Usually magic calls such people in their childhood, then waits for them to catch up.

Some magical leaders have claimed that a magician must have a religion, because the most important magical path is to develop a relationship with Divinity and work with it. This is the other stumbling block that magicians may be tripping over when they feel that religion is a must for magic. A *deity* is a *god*, like Amun, Durga, Isis, Christ, or Thor. A *deity* is not *Divinity*; Divinity flows through deities. Deities are aspects and substations of creation, all of which are expressions of Divinity. Understanding the difference between having a relationship with the Divine, and being part of a religion, is paramount in magic: one does not necessarily include the other.

For a magician, a religion is viewed specifically as an operating system that functions between the magician and Divinity, an operating system that can be worked with when necessary. It is important that magicians know how a religion works from an inner as well as outer perspective, and understands the construction, energetic expression and collective consciousness of that religion. Through that knowledge, the magician can operate from within that religion if it is necessary, and can then back out afterwards – and remember, they are backing away from the structure, the man-made religion, not from Divinity itself. That is only possible if the magician fully understands that religions are simply constructs, and to gain that understanding, they need to be exposed to more than one religion, more than one operating system in their training. Through such exposure, and working from the inside of that system and then backing out, the magician can begin to understand the layers of complexity within construction, and apply that knowledge in their own work.

Divinity existed before religion and will exist after humanity has ceased to be. Divinity can flow into religions, and can reach out through deities and humans alike. Divinity is the consciousness behind creation, and the consciousness that flows through all creation. Most religions have a special designation for Divinity, above and beyond their deities. Often Divinity is expressed as the 'unseen,' or 'unknowable' one. In magic, Divine power is present in everything we do, and in everything around us, waiting until we stumble blindly into its presence, which opens our awareness. As a power it is neither good nor bad: it is simply *necessary*.

If you are an adherent to a specific religion, and wish to develop in depth in magic, then you will have to divorce yourself from the belief that your way is right and all other ways and religions are wrong. You will also have to put your religious identity to one side on occasions and immerse yourself in, and learn from, other religions without thinking that you are betraying yours. Nor must you succumb to the dogmatic idea that doing this would be acting contrary to the 'laws of God.'

God, Divinity, is everywhere and in everything. Religion is simply a man-made mechanism for communion between us and God. Once you move that mechanism of communion aside, then you will see how all the dogma is simply control, social structure, and boundaries to provide a group identity. Learn to wear your religion lightly, while deepening your relationship with the Divine through both your religion and your magical work. If everything about your religion – identity, outfits, bells, rituals, dogmas – is important to you, then it is not God you are looking for, but a *home* that you can identify with. Understand that for yourself by learning to *know yourself*, because without knowing yourself, you cannot know the Divine.

> *"The swimmer in the Nu is one with the darkness and silence.*
> *The swimmer does not know he is a swimmer: he is and is within the Nu.*
> *The golden rays of Re fall upon the swimmer,*
> *lighting up that which was in darkness.*
> *The swimmer reflects the light of Re,*
> *and is thus no longer one with the Nu."*
>
> — Josephine McCarthy

Summary

Here is a list of basic things to remember and answers to simple, technical questions.

- Remember to always take notes.

- Save all your essays and research as Word documents, so that it can all be submitted to Quareia should you wish to be mentored or included in Quareia community groups. And make sure you regularly back up your files. (If you cannot afford to buy Word then you can use a free, open source alternative like Libreoffice that can produce Word files.)

- Be adaptable, and use your common sense. If you cannot stand in ritual then sit in a chair. Whenever you need to adapt something out of real necessity, look carefully at the action that needs adapting and make sure that your modification will still be functional for its magical purpose. If elements are being used – fire, water, earth – then make sure you still use those elements. And electricity is neither fire nor flame!

- When you get stuck, self-question and search for an answer yourself. Make your own decisions: do not expect others to decide things for you. You are bound to make some mistakes – that is normal. Just learn from them.

- There is no race, but there is rhythm. Work at a pace that works around your life, but do keep working. Slow and steady is better than cramming, then doing nothing for months.

- Don't expect to understand everything fully, particularly in the Apprentice section. It is okay not to understand things: understanding dawns in its own time. The Mysteries can be complicated, and they unfold according to their own schedule. Realise that a lot of the territory you will cover will be entirely new for you, and just keep moving forward.

- Don't be tempted to change the ritual patterns or visions to suit yourself. Everything is as it is for a good reason. If you change the structure – for example, changing the directions or tools used, or bits of the visions – then it will lock you out of the system.

- In light of the two above comments, keep an open mind.

- Remember, simply reading a lesson is not doing it! If you skip any practical work, then you will not have gained the experience, understanding, and inner transformation that you need to develop and progress. The Mysteries are learned by doing, not by studying. Studying is for filling the gaps in your surface knowledge; the Magical Mysteries are triggered by actual work.

- Enjoy it. Don't treat the course as some terrible thing that must be overcome as quickly as possible. It is a long and winding path, so enjoy the views and the companions that you will discover on the way.

- *The Quareia Magician's Deck* is not used formally until the Initiate section, but if you wish to explore it while you are still an apprentice, then it will not harm your training. Just try not to terrify yourself with it!
- *The Book of Gates* is not required reading, but it is suggested. It would be most helpful for people at the Adept level of training. But if it interests you before you get there, then nothing is stopping you from studying it.
- With ritual baths, if you do not have access to a bath then use a bucket of water. Wash your face, each foot, and all of your body that you can reach. Pay attention to the back of your neck, then pour water over your head and back. Be careful to make sure every part of you has been cleansed.
- If you are not a native English speaker and have problems understanding some of the course's terminology, then take note of what you do not understand, research the word or phrase if you can, or come back to it later. You may find as you progress that your understanding of the term begins to develop. If you are reading a translation of Quareia in a different language, then be aware that it may not be a good or accurate translation. There are many subtle undertones used in the language of this course, so bear that in mind.
- When you truly do not understand something, or there is a particular working that you truly cannot do at the present time, then move forward with the intent of going back and revisiting it in the near future.
- Don't overthink or overanalyse something, or obsess over a simple action. It can be tempting to overthink something and end up tied in knots over a simple detail, like the exact direction of a door, or which Rider-Waite deck to use (they are all the same – who cares?!). Learn to be mutable, and try not to control every little detail.
- Keep a sense of humour. It is one of the most valuable things in magic.

> "*I do nothing but go about persuading you all, old and young alike, not to take thought for your persons or your properties, but and chiefly to care about the greatest improvement of the soul.*
> *I tell you that virtue is not given by money, but that from virtue comes money and every other good of man, public as well as private.*
> *This is my teaching, and if this is the doctrine which corrupts the youth, I am a mischievous person.*"
>
> — Plato, *Apologia* (29d), recounting the words of Socrates at his trial.

Quareia

A New, Free School of Magic
for the 21st Century

*Advancing education in Mystical Magic
and the Western Esoteric Mysteries.*

www.quareia.com

Quareia is a practical magical training course written in its entirety by adept Josephine McCarthy, and presented freely through an online school, Quareia, founded by Josephine and Frater Acher.

It is a complete and freely available course designed to develop a student from a complete beginner into an adept. There are no barriers to entry: the course is accessible regardless of income, race, gender, religion, or spiritual beliefs.

Quareia is aligned to no particular school or specific religious, mystical, or magical system; rather it looks at and works with various magical, religious, and mystical practices that have influenced magical thinking in the Near Eastern and Western world from the early Bronze Age to the present day.

The entire course is free and openly available without any registration on the Quareia website.

www.ingramcontent.com/pod-product-compliance
Lightning Source LLC
Chambersburg PA
CBHW042320090526
44584CB00030BA/4139